Music and Society

The imagined village

Georgina Boyes

The imagined village

Culture, ideology and the English Folk Revival

Manchester University Press
Manchester and New York
Distributed exclusively in the USA and Canada by St. Martin's Press

Copyright © Georgina Boyes 1993

Published by Manchester University Press
Oxford Road, Manchester M13 9PL, UK
and Room 400, 175 Fifth Avenue,
New York, NY 10010, USA

Distributed exclusively in the USA and Canada
by St. Martin's Press, Inc.,
175 Fifth Avenue, New York, NY 10010, USA

British Library cataloguing in publication data

A catalogue record for this book is available from the British Library

Library of Congress cataloging in publication data
Boyes, Georgina.
  The imagined village: culture, ideology, and the English folk revival /
Georgina Boyes.
    p.   cm.
  Includes bibliographical references and index.
  ISBN 0-7190-2914-7
  1. Folklore--England--History--20th century. 2. England--Social
life and customs--20th century. I. Title.
  GR141.B63 1993
  307.72'0941--dc20   92-40257

ISBN 0 7190 2914 7 *hardback*

Printed and bound in Great Britain by
Bookcraft (Bath) Limited

Contents

Series editor's preface

Modernism, writes John Carey, was above all a strategy by which literary intellectuals sought to distance themselves from the newly literate masses, to protect and preserve their status as a cultural elite. It is a forceful argument, especially now that modernity is increasingly regarded as an era which has drawn to a close rather than as the central characteristic of culture in industrial societies. It is also an argument which might usefully serve to guide studies of the links between music and society in such societies, illuminating the ways in which stylistic developments in music were influenced by the social circumstances in which they occurred. Already there is research which shows how the fading aristocrats of late eighteenth-century Vienna supported Beethoven's new music as a means of preserving their special status, how the emerging bourgeoisie of the United States subscribed to art-music concerts in the nineteenth century in order to consolidate their dominant social position (and in doing so encouraged the separation of 'serious' and 'popular' music), and of how radical young black musicians in the New York of the 1940s developed modern jazz as part of the process of putting some distance between themselves and the conventions of white society. In each of these cases, in different times and places, the development of certain sorts of musical work – and not others – was facilitated by the social context of their production: it follows that an understanding of the works requires more than an interrogation of the texts. What work gets produced, the form it takes and the reception it receives all depend on the outcome of co-operation, conflict, negociation, competition and so on among a range of individuals and groups, all with different interests and – crucially – different resources with which to pursue them.

In short, an understanding of the creation and reception of music involves a consideration of the social processes through which it is produced and the situations in which it may be heard; all the books in this series, in their various ways, are arguments for this propositon. More specifically, in each of the examples above, developments in musical styles may be seen in terms of what some sociologists, following Max Weber, have called 'exclusionary strategies': activities undertaken in order to maintain or defend the special status of a group against perceived threats from outsiders. There could be few better examples than Carey's analysis of modernism as a reaction of intellectuals against what they saw, and fear, as an encroaching mass, and there is widespread agreement that the historical period in which the modernist movements developed was one for which the much-abused term 'crisis' is, for once, probably justified. In the years leading up to the Great War the certainties and confidence of British society in the Victorian era seemed to be evaporating fast. The very engine of progress, industrial production, had itself generated a vast, brutalised and threatening proletariat, or so it seemed to many in what had been regarded, until then, as the governing classes. Capitalist economic relations – the cash nexus, as Marx had put it – were rapidly eroding the decencies and social obligations of a gentler age. Sprawling and menacing urban slums had replaced the villages and hedgerows. And to compound these anxieties, the rapid rise of the German nation-state – imperialistic, militarily strong and industrially powerful – seemed to challenge the very basis of Britain's dominant position in the world.

Yet modernism was not the only response to the cultural crisis of confidence which ensued. The alternative, ideologically speaking, was to seek the restoration or regeneration of that traditional culture which, it was held, had been all but obliterated by the relentless march of capitalist industrialisation. So there was, as Georgina Boyes recounts in this fascinating study of the English 'folk' revival, as a real sense of urgency about the mission on which Cecil Sharp and his collaborators embarked in the early years of the century. The songs and dances of the 'folk' were, it was believed, in a literal sense the voice of the people, a distillation of that authentic English culture which was on the verge of extinction; the revitalisation of the nation could only come about through the rescue of this musical heritage and its systematic dissemination through the schools.

The task of the revivalists, then, was the restoration of the 'organic community' which was thought to have been lost, and the retrieval of its traditions. Yet it turns out that, like so many other allegedly venerable activities and conventions, the music of the people was in large measure what Eric Hobsbawm and other historians have called an invented tradition. The extent to which Cecil Sharp's presumptions and presuppositions, and his overbearing nature, led to a highly selective reconstruction of the song and dance of the 'folk' has long been recognised; here Georgina Boyes places his activities and their effects in the context of the folk revival as a social movement which displayed many of the political and ideological concerns of its time. Like Martin Wiener, she emphasises the way in which Englishness was defined not in terms of the urban industrial reality but as a fantasised rural community, an imagined village of sturdy, simple – and suitably deferential – country folk. Moreover, once the theme is developed, the remarkably pervasive effects of this myth are revealed and its echoes may be heard in the words of leading politicians, the policies of educational authorities, the works of 'serious' composers and across the whole spectrum of intellectual movements. There would have been no Bunyan or Shakespeare, wrote F.R. Leavis, without the 'rich traditional culture' from which they sprang and which has been all but obliterated by the vulgar outpourings of commercialised entertainment and the mass media.

The achievement of this study , therefore, is that it goes far beyond a domonstration of the gulf between the image of Merrie England and the altogether harsher historical reality; Georgina Boyes has documented the ways in which images of the 'folk' and their music served as powerful ideological weapons in debates about political direction, cultural values and national identity. Clearly one of the reasons for the wide appeal of such symbols was their ambiguity: the songs and dances of the 'folk' could be appropriated, in their different ways, by socialist reformers and arch-conservatives alike. What they shared, despite evident doctrinal differences, was a will to take control of a culture perceived to be in a state of disintegration; there are abundant ironies here in the spectacle of these earnest elites trying to save the people from themselves. But there is more than mere irony in all this, just as there is more than innocent fun in the sight of children prancing round the maypole in 'peasant' costumes of uncertain pedigree. For the idea, and the ideal, of the 'folk' can, and did, shade into the notion of the 'race', and a concern with its superiority or purity is clearly apparent in the 1930s, when fascist and anti-semitic views were openly promulgated.

In this, of course, the revivalist movement was once more reflecting the ideological currents of the times. The same might be said, perhaps with greater emphasis, about the patriarchal assumptions and values which were engrained in the revival's beliefs and practices. Indeed, Sharp seems to have personally assumed the role of patriarch early on, and the rise and development of the movement might well be seen, using Weber's terms once again, as a process in which Sharp's charismatic authority was gradually 'routinised' into rigid dogma. Along the way, the crushing of the challenge from Mary Neal and her 'Espérance' movement was of immense significance, both practically and symbolically: the assertive woman subordinated, her contribution and perspective marginalised. It is evident, as Georgina Boyes demonstrates, that despite their immense contribution to all aspects of the revivalist project, women's status in it was constantly problematic, and remains so. Even in recent times, she writes, those who have sought to banish the bucolic fantasies of Merrie England and the imaginary village have usually tried to replace them with eulogies to 'male struggles in heavy industry....somehow, the industries worth researching or writing about were never catering or nursing, hairdressing or office work, and only the heroic was celebrated'.

In its misogyny, its flirtation with fascism and its elitism, then, the traditionalist response to the threat of mass culture displays similarities – uncomfortably close, perhaps – with John Carey's view of the modernists. Moreover, just as the 'masses' were always portrayed as an anonymous aggregate, so the 'folk' were always someone else – never us, rarely even real people. The elderly rural worthies from whom Sharp and his collaborators 'collected' (if that is the right word) their little hoard of 'folk songs and dances' were almost invariably consigned to historical oblivion, whereas the collectors received lasting recognition in the movement. (Needless to say, royalties on publications were payable to the latter rather than the former, an arrangement which suggests much about the social relationships of those involved, and emphasises the specifically ideological nature of the concept of 'folk'.)

Of course there were real, rather than imagined, villages, though the evidence is that they were rather less pleasant than the imagery suggests, and there was always singing and dancing, though these, too, tended to be rather less innocent than the genteel members of the English Folk Song Society seemed to believe. Yet the fact is that there never was a 'folk', in the sense of a harmonious organic community, nor did 'folk' music spring spontaneously from its heart, expressing the spirit and the soul of the people. It follows that the folk music tradition must be understood as an invented one, constructed by real people in specific times and places, for particular purposes – just like the songs themselves. But here we are back to Max Weber once again, and to his image of societies, not as integrated organic communities, but as arenas of conflict and struggle where individuals and groups pursue their interests as best they can. From such a perspective, cultural forms may be understood as outcomes of an essentially political process – of conflict, challenge and appropriation, in which the various involved parties seek to defend or improve their situation.

In illuminating this process, Georgina Boyes has done much to explain how and why 'folk music' in England came to take the cultural forms that it did and, incidentally but significantly, to suggest what – from a purely musicological point of view – might have been done but was not. In their making and remaking of the folksong tradition, the proselytisers of the movement, no less than the literary modernists, revealed more about their own concerns and commitments than about the music they were determined to rescue.

                                                            Pete Martin

Foreword

The Folk Revival has succeeded. English folksongs, music and folk dances of every type are now widely practised and accessible to anyone who wishes to see, hear or perform them. We are all Post-Revivalists. But from its inception, the English Folk Revival involved more than a generalised intention to increase the availability or public awareness of the products of folk culture. It was conceived as a movement to promote specific changes – and this inevitably raises a number of questions. Why and how did it start? Who was involved? What were their aims and motives? How and where did it spread? And perhaps most fundamentally – what was the Revival? Can it be regarded as a single entity? What were the common assumptions, values and ideology reproduced in this complex of activities, involving a multiplicity of groups and individuals, throughout the country?

The English Folk Revival has been a significant part of the experience of many thousands of people over the past ninety years. From the conscious attempts to reform culture initiated by Cecil Sharp and Mary Neal at the beginning of the century, the institutions fostering the performance of folk dances and songs involved around twenty-one thousand people by 1935. An equally spectacular growth in folk clubs – from nine in 1959 to approximately seventeen hundred by 1979 – brought contact with the Revival to countless thousands of the post-war generations. The Revival is therefore, one of the few contemporary movements which a large number of individuals not only perceive discretely but regard themselves as having played a historical role in developing. In describing their activities as singers or dancers, members or organisers of folk clubs, researchers in folksong or folk musicians,

Revivalists frequently express a sharp and direct sense of their
contribution to the growth of the movement and the formation of
its social and institutional bases. But being a founder member of
a folk club or having attended a particular festival over a number
of years is not only a matter of personal satisfaction, it is also
widely perceived as effective in national and ideological terms –
'making music, listening to each other's music, and being supportive of the whole movement to ensure that music which is not
commercially controlled remains alive.'[1]

As well as accounts of personal and localised activities, Revivalists also share a larger perception of the movement – a 'received
history' of the Revival. In a role akin to myth, the received history
supports a 'factual' and symbolic definition of the structure and
purpose of the movement which is continuously reinforced
through the Revival's formal and informal institutions. As an
account of the Revival's development over the past eighty years,
the received history has serious limitations. It is largely metropolitan, though the Revival is clearly a national phenomenon with
strong regional structures and influences. Apart from the reduction
in the scale of activity during the two world wars, the movement
has continued in an unbroken form, incorporating apparently
contrary external influences with comparatively little change in its
definitions and values.[2] No suggestion of this is present in the
received history's set of isolated tableaux such as Cecil Sharp
overhearing John England singing at his work and 'whipping out
his notebook' to record his first folksong or Ewan MacColl and
Alan Lomax's 1951 decision to make 'a theoretical British folk-
music revival ... become a reality.'

Underlying these discontinuities, however, are numerous complexes of unstated process. The Folk Revival is, and has been, a
large-scale movement, but the experiences and contributions of a
few individuals have been privileged and given centrality. There is
no major attempt in the received history to account for the Revival's existence as a social movement, developing through the
enthusiasm, enjoyment and creativity of thousands. Where some
indication of the contribution of the membership of the movement
is presented, however, a still greater absence becomes apparent.
The role of women is almost entirely unrepresented – as individuals and as a constituent part of the Revival, women are at best
marginalised, at worst trivialised or ignored. But most obviously,

the ideologies which generated the movement and are reproduced
in its sub-culture are absent, or presented so transparently as to
require no analysis. These omissions might, perhaps, be explained
as natural simplifications in the case of oral forms of the received
history. Written studies have, however, proved equally silent. Fred
Woods's *Folk Revival: The Rediscovery of a National Music*,[4]
merely notes that there was a period of folksong collection arising
from the 'unusually inquiring turn of mind' of a number of
individuals at the turn of the century. This, he proposes, was then
followed by the Folk Revival which developed in several stages
following the recommencement of the collection of songs after the
Second World War and their subsequent dissemination through
mass communications. A. L. Lloyd's *Folksong in England* is
scarcely more illuminating. Lloyd divides the Revival into two
parts. The first one:

occurred sometime at the beginning of the present century and inspired,
and was inspired by, the great collectors such as Cecil Sharp, Vaughan
Williams, Percy Grainger. It came about when educated people, mostly
of liberal outlook, stumbled on the riches of poetry and music preserved
by working people in the countryside, and began to make some of those
treasures more widely available.[5]

This process was not, Lloyd suggests, entirely successful:

Fruitful as that revival was, many young people of the time resisted it,
suspecting that a 'tradition' was being imposed on them for their own
good and against their inclinations. However, within the last twenty
years or so a new interest in folk song has arisen, nourished by the
former revival, but coming from below now, not imposed from above,
affecting a broader section of society, employing a wider repertory and
involving a greater variety of uses and usages than were ever imagined
in Sharp's time.[6]

The absence of any discussion of the socio-cultural background of
the 'urban folk song revival' or the motives and ideology of the
individuals and groups involved is striking. The impression Lloyd
gives is one of disinterested chance investigations and publications
leading to the discovery and re-introduction of a valuable, but
somewhat unexpected national treasure.

Detailed consideration of the rationale of the Revival and the
assumptions, values and rewards for those involved in its development remain therefore, generally unrepresented. Indeed, the Revi-

val's innocence of ideology is frequently used as an argument
against attempts to raise its cultural politics in theoretical discussion or through performance. But from attempts to use folk
music to create a national consensus at the turn of the century to
plans to remotivate folk performance and build a new social order
in the 1930s, and in its reproduction of Englishness from its
inception to the present day, the Folk Revival has been used to
serve a range of ideological purposes. Implicit within these is a
justification for undertaking a major cultural transfer – having
created the category of the near-defunct and unconscious 'Folk',
their replacement with a responsible, caring and knowledgeable
body of performers and adapters could be presented as a vital and
continuing cultural duty.

Notes

1 Roger Watson, 'Letter to Editor,' *Shire Folk*, XLIII (Sept.-Dec.
1991), 3.
2 For examples and brief discussion of this see Ruth Finnegan, *The
Hidden Musicians: Music-Making in an English Town* (Cambridge:
Cambridge University Press, 1989), pp. 66–8.
3 Ewan MacColl, *Journeyman: An Autobiography* (London: Sidgwick and Jackson Ltd, 1990), p. 272.
4 Poole, Dorset: Blandford Press, 1979.
5 London: Panther Books, 1969, pp. 395–6.
6 *Ibid.*, p. 5.

Acknowledgements

The generosity, kindness and enthusiasm of the numerous participants in the Folk Revival who have provided the background information for this book have been a constant source of encouragement. As well as the individuals who contributed specific material acknowledged in the footnotes to various chapters, I would also like to thank Heather Bradley who set it all off, Malcolm and Jenny Fox, John and Sally Tams, Mike and Lal Waterson and George Knight, Danny Thompson, Roger Glover, Judy Moody, Malcolm Storey, Dave Wood, Ray Fisher, Bob Davenport, Dick Gaughan, Roy Bailey, Chris Wade, Chris Sugden, Rob Shaw, Alan Bearman, Steve Heap, Ian Anderson, Dave Burland, Pat Shaw, Fi Fraser, Barry Coope, Val Carman, Lester Simpson, Nic and Alison Broomhead, Maddy Prior, Rick Kemp, Mick Peat, Allan Taylor, Taffy Thomas, Robin Stonebridge, John Clough, Sean McGhee, Colin Davies, David Suff, John Barrow, David Corser, Dave Sheasby, Owen Jones, Piet Chielens and my colleagues, Natascha Würzbach, David Buchan, Peter Narváez, David Lowenthal, Tony Green, John Erickson and Cyril Pearce. I am also particularly grateful to Pete Martin, John Banks and Anita Roy of Manchester University Press for patience beyond the call of duty, the Library Staff at Bretton Hall College of Leeds University for their unfailing good humour and professionalism, and the Staff at the Centre for English Cultural Tradition and Language at the University of Sheffield for their helpfulness with the Russell Wortley and Harker Collections. There can be no adequate acknowledgement here for the unstinting support of Mary and George Hallam, Sam and Claire McDonnell-Smith, Robin and Alanna Greene-Smith, Toby, Ivan and William Boyes and above all, Jim Boyes.

To Jim
'It takes a while to settle to the task'

Chapter I

A name for our ignorance:
the invention of the Folk

The needs and expectations channelling interest towards traditions have from the very beginning, and even in recent times, almost without exception originated outside the communities maintaining the tradition. In speaking of interpretations of folklore it must be remembered that they are seldom the interpretations of the people actually producing and using this tradition. The discovery of tradition is usually followed by its transfer to some other use, archives, publication, as an instrument of cultural policy.... The administrative or cultural elite setting the collection of tradition in motion also bears the responsibility for the new use of the tradition in an environment quite unlike that in which it existed before its discovery. [1]

The existence of a Folk Revival in England is presented as a direct and urgent response to a cultural crisis. The pressures of industrialisation and urbanisation had produced a context in which folksongs and dances were ceasing to be performed. Already found only at the social and geographical margins, they were known by a few elderly people in remote villages. Under these circumstances, as entirely oral traditions, hundreds of years of artistic development would be irretrievably lost within a generation. To seek out, record and thus preserve such musically unique, beautiful and historical cultural products was therefore a matter of immediate and transparent need. That folksongs and dances should then, through re-performance, be reinstated in their rightful place at the forefront of English culture seemed so obvious a corollary that it hardly required further justification.

The compelling necessity of such a rescue mission tends to overwhelm any consideration of its other functions or the premises on which it was based. The job of salvaging a heritage needed to be done first – and when completed, it seems churlish to question the motives of those who dedicated themselves to doing so. Without their efforts English cultural life would be incalculably poorer. Major attention should rather be focused on the rich materials revivers' work has reclaimed, not how or why the task was undertaken.

It is, however, of considerable importance that the values and ideological complexes associated with the Folk Revival should be examined. The emergence of the movement to foster the conscious performance of first 'folksongs' and later 'folk dances' at the beginning of the twentieth century represented a fundamental change in the treatment of popular culture which has had wide-ranging effects. Through the institutions of the Revival, new concepts of folksong, custom and most critically, of the social groups by whom they were performed, have been formulated and reproduced. These have since become accepted as accurate representations of working-class culture within and outside the Revival. To reach any conclusion about the validity of such representations, an understanding of the processes involved in their creation and maintenance is necessary.

The centrality of the Folk Revival in developing and reproducing perceptions of rural and urban working-class culture has given it an influence which is at odds with its relatively short history and overtones of the quaintly twee. A number of exceptionally gifted publicists and communicators such as Cecil Sharp, Ralph Vaughan Williams and A. L. Lloyd have been involved in formulating and promoting the Revival's concepts of traditional expressive culture. Their theoretical propositions have also had the benefit of rapid dissemination and reinforcement through institutions of the Revival movement. The English Folk Dance and Song Society, the Morris Ring, the Folklore Society and a variety of *ad hoc* groupings like folk clubs, dance clubs and mummers' teams all propagandised and applied the conceptual formulae of the Revival in public performance. Subsequently, the growth of a 'folkies' subculture has comprehended not merely reperformance but the embodiment of attitudes, values and concepts associated with the Revival in a lifestyle.

Outside the movement, however, the assimilation and continuing acceptability of its premises argues for mechanisms beyond a defined community with efficient and persuasive internal com-

munications. The broad attractions of their arcadian connotations
have assured the Revival's signifiers a place in high and mass
culture. Morris dancers, maypoles on the village green and orchestrated folksongs have been used to represent – and sell – 'Englishness' throughout the world.

The implications of the history of culture propounded by the
Revival have also profoundly affected commentary in the arts. The
view that a pure and spontaneous stream of artistic expression
derives from 'folklife' or 'country traditions' or 'organic communities' provides the sub-text for almost all discussion of the
condition of historical and contemporary artistic production.
More specifically, groups as diverse as the Leavises and their
followers and the Workers' Music Association have based their
entire approach to the aesthetics of popular culture on ideas of
working-class creativity developed within the Folk Revival. What
is the source of such broad and consistent acceptability?

To some extent, the range of appeal of the Folk Revival movement lies within the Janus-faced concept of revival itself. A revival
is inherently both revolutionary and conservative. It simultaneously comprehends a demand for a change in an existing situation and a requirement of reversion to an older form. In the case
of the English Folk Revival, however, to this structural possibility
was added a further dimension of counter-interpretation. Within
the concepts of the Folk and their society which the Folk Revival
propagated, a variety of apparently contradictory ideological
premisses could be supported. These revolved around the issue of
the nature of culture in industrialised society. Given the evidence
of aesthetic creativity inherent in the Revival's definition of folk-
song, for example, how were past and present cultural manifesta-
tions to be interpreted? On one hand, urban popular culture, its
context and consumers, could be demonstrated to be inferior,
because folk culture had such high aesthetic, academic and historical connotations. Old, lost, rural 'organic communities', rather
than newly developed, urban existence could therefore, be held up
as the only valid source of an alternative, uncultivated art. Conversely, however, as a form of working-class expressive culture,
folksong could also be presented as evidence of the artistic creativity of the proletariat. The continued existence of folk traditions,
their use and adaptation in working-class life, offered a line of
cultural development traceable from pre-history to post-industrial-

ism. Moreover, in the harder edged form of 'Industrial Song', the art of folksong still lived to prove that the inhabitants of the urban present had not been disinherited of the greatness of their ancestors' rural past. And for all shades of political opinion, both folksong and Industrial Song could be represented as a source of genuinely popular performance uncontaminated by mass culture, capitalism and commercialism.

It is, however, in its ability to offer a concrete existence to its conceptual dimension that the Folk Revival's most significant potential lies. From its inception to the present, what differentiates the movement from earlier publication of songs and dances collected from the people is its directly interventionist intent. Folk songs and dances are not to be transcribed for archival purposes or popular entertainment but used as an instrument to effect a cultural change. Inherent in the Revival of folksong and dance is the intention that the values and characteristics of the past are not merely being re-asserted but are actually capable of attainment again through their 'return' to and re-incorporation in contemporary living culture. The prospect the Revival offers is not simply a world as it had been but a world as it could be again.

Singing the songs and dancing the dances handed down by the Folk were the acts of Revival. The material for performing these – texts, tunes and descriptions – were minutely noted, studied, analysed and revised. But what were the concepts of the Folk themselves, the sources of the culture on which so much theorising has since been developed? From their first comprehensive definition in the latter part of the nineteenth century, they have remained remarkably constant:

in every society there are people who do not progress either in religion or in polity with the foremost of the nation. They are left stranded amidst the progress. They live in out-of-the-way villages, or in places where the general culture does not penetrate easily; they keep to old ways, practices, and ideas, following with religious awe all that their parents had held to be necessary in their lives. These people are living depositories of ancient history – a history that has not been written down, but which has come down by tradition. [2]

The cultural background of such irreplaceable human storehouses was equally well defined. They were the last survivors of 'the period of history when English social life was represented by a net-work of independent self-acting village communities'[3] – an organic culture which 'built its own church, hanged its own rogues, made its own boots, shirts and wedding rings, and chanted its own tunes'.[4]

These concepts derived from authoritative and experienced academic sources. Leading theorists in Folklore and Anthropology – Sir Laurence and Lady Gomme, Andrew Lang, Dr R. R. Marrett, Charlotte Burne and Cecil Sharp – set out this view of the Folk and their expressive culture in a wide variety of popular and specialist publications. More importantly for the long term, however, similar definitions were also the basis of institutional approaches, as in the various editions of *The Handbook of Folklore* – a guide to collecting and recording folklore for 'travellers or residents among backward folk at home and abroad',[5] and influential publications such as Cecil Sharp's *English Folk-Song: Some Conclusions*,[6] and A. L. Lloyd's *Folk Song in England*.[7]

The use of the past that such proposals represent can, however, be traced in earlier intellectual developments. The study of Folklore grew out of the older interest in Popular Antiquities – a pursuit which had concentrated on the historicity and consequent legitimation of aspects of contemporary culture:

With the sixteenth century, we come into a new world of learning in which antiquarian studies as such take a place from the start. They took this place, not as a disinterested intellectual activity, but as part of the contemporary search for authority in all branches of life and thought, and above all in the quest for respectable antecedents. Scholars, churchmen, and statesmen in Tudor England were concerned with establishing their new world on newly defined foundations, but these foundations had themselves to be recognisably a part of the ancient world of classical or biblical antiquity.[8]

Over the next two hundred years, this possibility for providing a foundation for existing practice in the records of the past became an overt justification for antiquarian research. Francis Grose (1731–91), the founding editor of *The Antiquarian Repertory* for example, introduced his first issue with a comprehensive rebuttal of the view that Popular Antiquities was a dilettante pursuit. Studying ancient charters, records of ecclesiastical ceremonies and medieval castles would, as he explained in detail, provide the member of the House of Lords, cleric, and modern general with the means of understanding more clearly, and thus carrying out more authoritatively, the duties they undertook in the present. Even the study of historical costume had its place in maintaining the status quo by preserving the 'man of leisure' from the embarrassment of appearing at a masquerade in anachronistic attire.[9]

All aspects of contemporary social organisation and activity were considered in the light of their putative historical origins. Within such pre-industrial Antiquarian studies, the 'common people' – 'those *little ones*, who occupy the lowest place in the political arrangement of human beings' – were represented as a conservative force. In some instances the classical parallels discovered for the 'rites and traditions of the vulgar' were valued as evidence of a line of greatness running from the glories of ancient Greece and Rome to contemporary England. But particularly where beliefs and customs were found to derive from that fountain of all superstition the Church of Rome, the common people were derided for their irrationality, and suppression or reformation of their customs proposed to preserve the integrity of the Established Church and the moral fibre of the nation:

I would not be thought a reviver of old rites and ceremonies to the burdening of the people, nor an abolisher of innocent customs, which are their pleasures and recreations: I aim at nothing, but a regulation of those which are in being amongst them, which they themselves are far from thinking burdensome, and abolishing such only as are sinful and wicked.

Some of the customs they hold, have been originally good, though at present they retain little of their primitive purity; the true meaning and design of them being either lost, or very much in the dark through folly and superstition. To wipe off therefore the dust they have contracted, to clear them of superstition, and make known their end and design, may turn to some account, and be of advantage; whereas observing them in the present way, is not only of no advantage, but of very great detriment.

Others they hold, are really sinful, notwithstanding in outward appearance they seem very harmless, being a scandal to religion, and an encouraging of wickedness. And therefore to aim at abolishing these, will I hope be no crime, though they be the diversions of the people.

As to the opinions they hold, they are almost all superstitious, being generally either the produce of heathenism, or the inventions of indolent Monks, who having nothing else to do, were the forgers of many silly and wicked opinions, to keep the world in awe and ignorance. And indeed the ignorant part of the world is so still awed, that they follow the idle traditions of the one, more than the Word of GOD; and have more dependance [sic] upon the lucky omens of the other than his providence, more dread of their unlucky ones, than his wrath and punishment. The regulating therefore of these opinions and customs, is what I proposed....[10]

The eighteenth-century 'discovery' of the existence and contribution of rural labour in contemporary life was, however, partially instrumental in bringing about an alteration in the approach of Antiquarian researches. Developing with and into Romanticism, it produced an intellectual climate in which the countryside and its workers were presented as a locus of spiritual values in a rapidly industrialising, urban age. The common people were increasingly divided into 'the mob of the streets, who never sing or compose but shriek and mutilate' and the simple, untainted, country-dwelling peasants – 'the Folk'.[11] Much of the English Folk Revival's emotional appeal echoes the characteristic themes of Romanticism. The cultural and spiritual superiority of rural as opposed to town life, the peasant as opposed to the factory worker, the spontaneous simplicity of the folksong as opposed to the sophistication of art music, occur as recurrent motifs in writings associated with the Revival. Although the influences of the Romantic movement are ever present in perceptions of folk culture, however, Romanticism in isolation, did not provide the essential paradigmatic shift from which the Revival eventually developed.

The essence of the differentiation between the concept of the Folk inherent in Romanticism and that presented by the Revival lies in the development of the social sciences in the mid nineteenth century. The Revival's major theoretical premises grew out of the application of Darwin's theories of biological evolution to the emerging discipline of Anthropology. From his work on 'primitive' societies in this field, E. B. Tylor (1832–1917) put forward the theory that all cultures evolve in unilinear sequence through stages of savagery and barbarism to civilisation. This rise to civilisation was not, however, seen as taking place in discrete steps. Tylor proposed that residual expressive culture from early stages of the progression 'survived' into the civilised era in the form of traditional songs, games, narratives and customs. Traditional performances and beliefs found in contemporary or historical Britain could, therefore, be equated with formally similar activities taking place in any other geographical area or temporal period:

Surveyed in a broad view, the character and habit of mankind at once display that similarity and consistency of phenomena which led the Italian proverb-maker to declare that 'all the world is one country'. To general likeness in human nature on the one hand, and to general likeness in the circumstances of life on the other, this similarity and consistency may no doubt be traced, and they may be studied with especial fitness in comparing races near the same grade of civilization. Little respect need be had in such comparisons for date in history or for place on the map; the ancient Swiss lake-dweller may be set beside the mediaeval Aztec, and the Ojibwa of North America beside the Zulu of South Africa.... Even when it comes to comparing barbarous hordes with civilized nations, the consideration thrusts itself upon our minds, how far item after item of the life of the lower races passes into analogous proceedings of the higher, in forms not too far changed to be recognized, and sometimes hardly changed at all. Look at the modern European peasant using his hatchet and his hoe, see his food boiling or roasting over the log-fire, observe the exact place which beer holds in his calculation of happiness, hear his tale of the ghost in the nearest haunted house, and of the farmer's niece who was bewitched with knots in her inside till she fell into fits and died. If we choose out in this way things which have altered little in a long course of centuries, we may draw a picture where there shall be scarce a hand's breadth difference between an English ploughman and a negro of Central Africa.[12]

On the publication of *Primitive Culture*, a small group of middle-class men and women whose interests included both Anthropological and Antiquarian research combined to create the discipline of 'Folk-lore'.[13] This new academic field became increasingly distinct from Popular Antiquities in methodology and theory. The emergence of a unified theory of development, encompassing cultural expression from the remotest past to the present day, made the older study's concentration on providing piecemeal historical verification of any form of expressive culture associated with all social classes seem diffuse and unsystematic. Antiquarian scholarship had largely rested on the existence of physical records from literate Western societies, whilst Folklore's area of study and method were defined by processes of 'traditionality' and 'orality' evidenced by field collection throughout the world. In keeping with the ever-widening scope of nineteenth-century communications, folklorists were liberated to build cultural hypotheses unconstrained by temporal, geographical or physical limitations. And from this point, the Folk – at first a rather insubstantially defined body of 'country people', who knew 'old fashioned' songs, tales or beliefs, became the central source of research material, their culture available for analysis by the most up-to-date of scientific principles. By the 1890s, therefore, Folklore came to prominence as 'the expression of the psychology of early man, whether in the fields of philosophy, religion, science and medicine, in social organization and ceremonial, or in the more strictly intellectual regions of history, poetry and other literature'.[14] Albeit unknowingly, the Folk – now clearly conceptualised – were found to offer the key to understanding the development of culture – the means for elucidating the 'unwritten history of the past'.

The need for an 'unwritten history' to 'explain' the present had several strands, but one principal aim:

The study of traditional lore began with the observation that among the less cultured inhabitants of all the countries of modern Europe there exists a vast body of curious beliefs, customs, and stories, orally handed down from generation to generation, and essentially the property of the unlearned and backward portion of the community.
It was then noted that similar, and even identical beliefs, customs, and stories, are current among savage and barbaric nations.... The similarity may reasonably be accounted for by the hypothesis that such ideas and practices among civilized peoples must be derived, by inheritance or otherwise, from a savage or barbaric state of society. They have accordingly received the technical name of 'survivals;' and the establishment of the existence of 'survivals in culture' as an observable phenomenon may be taken as the first-fruits of the scientific study of Folklore.
But the matter does not end there.... Eventually we may hope to adjust the balance between circumstance and character, and to arrive at the causes which retain some races in a state of arrested progress while others develop a highly-organized civilization.[15]

The social and political implications of this new definition were manifold. The superiority of white Aryan races, the inferiority of women and the evolutionary inevitability of patriarchy were all 'proved' on the basis of cultural data gathered throughout the world.[16] Through the study of folklore, in particular, imperialism and the existence of class stratification could be shown to be justified on the basis of detailed research and empirical evidence. The two cases were indeed usefully inter-related – the beliefs and

customs of the 'primitive' natives abroad providing a more comprehensive cultural context from which the 'fragmented' practices
of 'backward folk' in England could be 'scientifically' recon-
structed.[17] Critically, however, they were also interdependent
propositions and this intellectual strategy was paradoxically their
most attractive yet weakest feature.

Cultural survivals theory proposed that persisting activities –
traditions – originated directly in the formalising of primitive belief
systems in ritual actions. Morris dances were, for example, hypothesised as survivals of 'pagan observances prevalent amongst
primitive communities, and associated in some occult way with the
fertilization of all living things, animal and vegetable' in ceremonies which involved the slaughter of a sacred animal synonymous with the clan deity and thus the clan itself.[18] The children's
game of 'Here we go round the Mulberry Bush' was a survival of
primitive marriage customs and 'Tag' was regarded as deriving
from the choice of an individual to be a scapegoat or more
temporary victim of taboo.[19] Uninferred evidence of animism or
tribal taboo in late nineteenth- century England, however, proved
rather hard to come by. One or two misogynistic comments about
women dancing were available to be represented as surviving,
vestigial memories of a male ritual priesthood. But aside from this,
when questioned by fieldworkers about their motives, most participants in 'survivals of primitive rituals' referred to aesthetics and
socio-economic factors, to the status or cash profits deriving from
their activities – none of which had found a place in Tylor's
minutely argued volumes.[20] Without missionaries' and colonial
administrators' reports of primitive beliefs, there were no data to
support the universality of the evolutionary hypothesis. A Folk
which had no real conception of what it was doing was therefore
a necessity in 'proving' the survivals in culture theory.

Collective amnesia in terms of the significance of their performances had, however, to be allied with monumental consistency
of action. The mummers' play, for example, could only be defined
as:

a traditional revitalisation ceremony whose purpose had long been
forgotten by performers and audience alike, but which was deep-rooted
because it survived from primitive times, resilient enough to adapt itself
to growing sophistication as the centuries passed, and tenacious enough
to have persisted into modern times unchanged in action though altered

by being given a stereotyped text.[21]

The circularity of such an argument is, however, only one symptom of the shortcomings of this aspect of survivals theory. The comparative method, on which the survivals in culture thesis was based, posited that uniquely among cultural phenomena, customs such as morris and sword dances and mummers' plays were static in form and transmitted in linear fashion at a relatively constant geographic location. Ignorance or forgetfulness on the part of the Folk might of course, lead to the 'fragmentation' of customs, but where this was detected, 'reconstruction' of ceremonies using 'full versions' available from peasant or savage societies elsewhere would show what the true, original form had been. That recent diffusion, amalgamation or outright invention might account for the form and occurrence of a performance tradition was rarely mooted – still less investigated. Even as late as 1968, therefore, it was possible for a leading American folksong theorist to contend that 'Folk society and folk art do not accept, reflect, or value change'.[22]

Where researchers' observations could not bear out the lack of alteration required by survivals theory, consistency with the proposition was achieved by presenting all non-fragmentary modifications in the forms of expressive culture as 'degenerate later accretions'. Any recognisable alterations – particularly those which affected the purity of a custom's supposed ritual character, such as the change from male to young female dancers in the northwestern morris, or which could be attributed to the influence of popular culture, rendered a tradition 'untraditional', and thus unacceptable for study. Equally, material which showed evidence of recent development was either not recorded by collectors or omitted from their published accounts. A version of the morris dance 'Bean Setting' collected from a Northamptonshire man in 1910 was publicly denounced as non-folkloric because it had been 'invented ... some three years ago'. Its creator was moreover, defined as 'not a 'traditional dancer'' though he had previously been a member of morris teams in Lancashire.[23] But even acceptedly valid bearers of genuine traditions could become 'non-Folk' when they failed to observe the behaviours defined as appropriate for them. If individuals manifested any signs of creativity in the reproduction of folk culture, for example, their initiatives were not collected on the grounds that they were 'uncharacteristic'. 'Having a chantyman's gift for verse-making,' the song collector Anne Gilchrist (1864–1954) wrote of the singer William Bolton, he had himself supplied words for a hiatus between verses one and two in the shanty 'Rounding Cape Horn'. 'But as his own verses were less artless than the remainder of this genuine if doggerel production of some sailor bard, I have', declared Gilchrist, a prominent member of the Folk-Song Society, 'omitted them, in order to maintain its character'.[24]

The cardinal premiss in survivals theory was, therefore, a definition of the Folk as manifesting a comprehensive absence of creativity. This lack of aesthetic ability and appreciation represented a grave cultural problem. Whilst the dangers of 'fragmentation' in customs could be overcome by the use of comparative data, the Folk's manifest insensibility was seen as posing a serious threat to more artistic genres within their own culture. An early corollary of the premiss led to the development of the concept of *zersingen* (literally 'singing to pieces')[25] to describe the fate which 'original full versions' of texts suffered at the hands of the boorish, illiterate Folk. At best, as one expert noted in his study of the influence of transmission on English ballads, 'The ballad-singers are unable to create anything equal to the songs which they have received'.[26] Clearly, in their current existence, the Folk were a source of potential destruction to the very culture they preserved.

The paradoxes, contradictions and circularities of the survivals thesis itself were not its only limitations. Positing a primitive origin for traditional expressive culture also leaves a number of practical questions open. Tradition is, by definition, a function not of origin but of continuance. Folklorists operating within 'survivals' premisses directed their researches to the origin of customary performance, 'rather than its latter end'. Individual performers and the social groups who were known to maintain songs, dances and customs were therefore, rarely investigated. Why whole communities would continue to perform actions which had ceased to be meaningful hundreds – perhaps thousands – of years before was simply not touched on. Violet Alford's late proposal of 'pagan folk memory' persisting for over a thousand years offers no discussion of the psychological and sociological dynamics of such retention, let alone any demonstration of its widespread existence.[27]

Issues of visibility and record also remain outstanding. Where traditions did continue, why did no one notice them? Survivals theory does not engage the questions raised by the absence of documentary evidence for the presumed lengthy existence of many forms of performance. Whilst it might be argued that the individual or domestic practices of the poor, such as singing or storytelling within the family, might not have been accessible or important enough for the literate to comment on, public exhibitions such as the mummers' play are less easily overlooked. How widely performed, spectacular dramas involving song, dance, combat, death and miraculous bringing to life again escaped notice until the mid eighteenth century is not explained.[28] To meet therequirements of the theory, mummers' plays had to have existed in England in relatively consonant form since prehistoric times, unnoted by medieval chroniclers, Renaissance poets, censorious Reformation churchmen, or even the merely curious.

To complete the survivals in culture theory, forms of social organisation and belief systems within groups taking part in formally similar activities in all places and at all times had to be assumed to be identical. The Folk at any stage of evolution in any place at any time would manifest like cultural features. Even in total isolation, cultures at the same stage would produce the same beliefs and expressive forms. Thus Francis Barton Gummere based his influential theory of the development of the European ballad on reports of the songs of one tribe of Amazonian Indians and a single, unsupported and textless description of a performance by Faroese fishermen.[29] More recently, 'a racial mythology and psychology that extends unbroken from pre-Christian times' to 'people in the West of England in the present century' was presented as evidence of a Celtic ritual origin for a number of local songs and ballads.[30] Linkages between similarly eclectic sources – Dionysiac worship in classical Greece, early twentieth-century Thracian calendar customs and traditional performances in different parts of England in the eighteenth, nineteenth and twentieth centuries – are also given in support of the most recent ritual origin theory for other forms of 'folk' performance such as mummers' plays and sword dances.[31] This use of anthropological and historical data to provide a universal, 'scientific' explanation for the existence of all aspects of folk culture had a number of vital implications for the development of the Folk Revival in England. A history without record, it produced a perception of traditions

which moved the derivation of their significance and meaning
from the socio-cultural context of their contemporary performance
to an undocumented area of the past, accessible only to specialists
through the application of Folkloristic theory.

In terms of folksong, this altered focus of scholarship privileged
hypothesised 'historical forms' over the actuality of contemporary
performances. Ballads, with their ascribed origin in primitive communal composition, art literature and historical associations, were
presented separately from other songs and their collection was the
subject of intense competition among fieldworkers. Similarly,
songs with tunes in the 'ancient church modes' were privileged and
treated as representative rather than unusual forms. Songs of
obviously recent date or known authorship, no matter by whom,
how or where they were performed were rejected and set outside
the definition. More fundamentally, however, by constructing the
concept of a rural, uneducated, uncreative Folk as the cultural
source of their definition, the proponents of the survivals thesis
obviated the need for close examination of the role and individual
contribution of performers of all folk traditions. Their unequal
status and ignorance of the 'real' significance of what they 'un-
thinkingly' inherited from their ancestors placed the Folk outside
the need for consultation or lengthy consideration. As mere temporary custodians of a common culture, they had no individual
rights of ownership in what was clearly a heritage of the nation
as a whole.

Even at the time of their expression at the turn of the century,
these concepts of the Folk and folk culture were inherently problematic when applied to practical fieldwork in folksong. S. O. Addy
(1848–1933) was a longstanding and active member of the Folk-
Lore Society who also worked closely with many of the founders
of the Folk-Song Society. But he apparently saw no anomaly in
collecting ballads and lore from families such as the Johnstons,
enthusiastic advocates of tourism, genteel musical evenings and
picturesque customs, who opened the first golf club in north
Derbyshire. Similarly, in the same period in Scotland, the Reverend
James Duncan, M.A. (1848–1917) chose to record over three
hundred and fifty songs from his sister, Mrs Gillespie – who could
hardly be represented as a person who had 'never been brought
into close enough contact with educated people to be influenced
by them'. Both Addy and Duncan were outside the metropolitan

clique which came to dominate the folksong and folklore institutions.[32] Their approach was, moreover, based on direct contact
with performers through fieldwork, rather than distant analyses of
'the Folk' drawn from written reports. Experience in the field was,
however, no guarantee against misrepresentation – what we know
of Cecil Sharp's collecting in rural Somerset hardly supports his
published contentions. The information available on the life his-
tories of the residents of market towns who sang to the Revival's
leading theoretician bears no relation to the unlettered and se-
cluded archetype of his definition – applying it to the miners and
steelworkers from whom he collected sword dances in the Sheffield
area in 1913 cannot be justified at all.[34] The proposal that folk-
songs were sung by 'remnants of the peasantry', following with
unquestioning awe the traditions of their forebears in total isolation from contact with formal education and any other aspect of
contemporary life, is simply not borne out by the work of contemporary collectors. In fact, as early as 1893, Joseph Jacobs described the Folk as 'a fraud, a delusion, a myth' and 'simply a
name for our ignorance':

During the discussions which took place some years ago in the Folk-lore
Society as to the nature of folk-lore, there was one curious omission.
Much was said about what the Folk believed, what the Folk did, and
how these sayings and doing of the Folk should be arranged and
classified. But very little indeed was said as to what the Folk was that
said and did these things, and nothing at all was said as to how they
said and did them and especially as to how they began to say and do
them. In short, in dealing with Folk-lore, much was said of the Lore,
almost nothing was said of the Folk ...

'Little masterpieces', like *Cinderella, Puss in Boots* and *Rumpel-
stiltskin*, Jacobs insisted, emanated from 'an artist, who had the
grin of conscious creation on his face as he told [the story] for the
first time in the world's history':

Let us try to realise in imagination what must have happened when, for
the first time, the saying was uttered that was afterwards to become a
proverb or a tale that was destined to be a folk- or fairy-tale was first
told. Was it the Folk that said the one or told the other? Did the
collective Folk assembled in the folk-moot simultaneously shout 'When
the wine's in, the wit's out' or 'Penny wise, pound foolish?' No, it was
some bucolic wit, already the chartered libertine of his social circle, who
first raised hearty guffaws by these homely pieces of wisdom.

Most fundamentally, Jacobs rejected the concept of a separate, historical, non-literate and anonymous Folk:

For, after all, we are the Folk as well as the rustic, though their lore may be other than ours, as ours will be different from that of those that follow us.... Survivals are folk-lore, but folk-lore need not be all survivals. We ought to learn valuable hints as to the spread of folk-lore by studying the Folk of to-day. The music-hall, from this point of view, will have its charm for the folk-lorist, who will there find the *Volkslieder* of to-day.[34]

Despite such clearly expressed contemporary scepticism and the existence of a fundamental disjunction between idea of the Folk and the people from whom folk dances and songs were – and are – recorded, the definition of the Folk and folksong have remained effectively unchanged for a century. Today, 'The Foggy Dew', as arranged by Benjamin Britten and sung by highly trained professionals to an audience of thousands at the Festival Hall, is still basically defined as 'folksong', whilst a mother, sitting alone and lulling her child to sleep by singing 'Brahms's Lullaby' is operating outside the scope of 'folk' performance. The contradictions and anomalies of a definition which privileges source and item, rather than activity and context, are highlighted by cases such as the lullaby. Relatively few examples of 'folk' lullabies have been collected in England and this has led to the suggestion that the genre is rare in this country. Fieldwork, however, rapidly establishes the fact that English babies are frequently sung to sleep, but that the songs used are not 'folksongs' – items produced by 'the Folk'. In general, the songs functioning as lullabies in England are popular. For at least the past seventy years, the traditional activity of lulling babies to sleep has been accompanied by any comparatively current song with a gentle but regular rhythm. Specifically composed lullabies (such as Brahms's) and songs with textual references to night and sleep appear to be widespread initial choices – though rhythmic songs of any kind seem to be used subsequently if the activity of lulling is performed over a long period. So in spite of the occurrence of a manifestly traditional function (singing a baby to sleep), and an informal context of performance (no tickets, auditorium, rehearsals or conductor), the absence of a song produced by the Folk negates all other factors in the performance. Such anomalies are removed if singing – the activity, rather than song – the transient item, is considered.[35]

But although, over the 1980s, folksong theory in England has reportedly taken a 'new direction' into studies emphasising context and process, today most research associated with the Revival employs only a slightly broader approach to the source of songs than the movement's founders. While the overwhelming majority of instances of informal performance are left unrecorded, marginal groups such as gypsies, the musical culture of rural areas in Britain and North America and, increasingly, historical records, are chosen for examination. And as the possible areas for work with acceptably 'folk' material decline with the spread of cities and education, many regions and performers are researched and re-researched time and time again. Even as careful an observer of popular culture as E. P. Thompson has suggested as late as 1978:

any British collector... might consider himself [sic] lucky if in the course of one year's collecting he found *one* original folk-song, as well as a few corrupt variants of songs already known.
So what we have to do, in England, is to re-examine old, long-collected material, asking new questions of it, and seeking to recover lost customs and the beliefs which informed them.[36]

The cumulative effect of the appearance of yet another study of East Anglian pub singers, Scottish travellers or a manuscript collection made in 1904 thus serves to confirm the 'survivals' paradigm within and outside the Revival. A thesis offering scientific support to a range of racial, sexual, class and culturally dominant positions had been created, but at the cost of omitting the source of the evidence on which it was based. The Folk, at least in their reality as the creators and performers of contemporary cultural traditions, could not be present as witnesses to their own activities. Who they were, and what they did, could not substantiate the thesis. The persistence of the Folk as a concept, however, suggests that despite the intellectual duplicity it required, such costs could be borne.

Underlying and supporting the specific needs of the survivals in culture thesis, however, are the possibilities the Folk offer for the construction of cultural alternatives. Their existence as a source of 'otherness', of a better and more natural state, offers a powerfully attractive rationale for their acceptance as fact. The way of life inherent in the concepts of the Folk and folk culture presented by

the Revival did not exist in the English countryside of the late
nineteenth or twentieth centuries. For a variety of ideological
purposes, however, their fragile, threatened presence was a structural necessity. Theirs was the culture which had to be revived
through reperformance. And without the notional existence of the
rapidly disappearing Folk, there would be no rationale for a Folk
Revival.

Notes

1 Lauri Honko, 'The Kaleval and Myths,' *Nordic Institute of Folklore Newsletter*, XII:4 (1984–5), 2–3.

2 Sir Laurence and Lady Gomme, *British Folk-Lore, Folk-Songs, and
Singing-Games* National Home-Reading Union Pamphlets Literature
Series, no. 4 (London: National Home-Reading Union, ND [1916]), p.
10.

3 George Laurence Gomme, FSA, *Folk-Lore Relics of Early Village
Life* (London: Elliot Stock, 1883), pp. vii-viii.

4 C. J. Sharp and C. L. Marson, *Folk Songs from Somerset: Vol. I*
(Taunton: The Wessex Press, 1904), p. xv.

5 Charlotte Sophia Burne, ed. *The Handbook of Folklore*, rev. edn
(London: The Folklore Society, 1957), p. 6. This edition 'in no way
alters the original definition of folklore' contained in the *Handbook* of
1914 and the original form published in 1890, edited by G. L. Gomme.

6 Taunton: Barnicott and Pearce, 1907.

7 London: Panther Books, 1969.

8 Stuart Piggott, *Ruins in a Landscape: Essays in Antiquarianism*
(Edinburgh: Edinburgh University Press, 1976), p. 65.

9 Francis Grose, 'Introduction,' *The Antiquarian Repertory*, I (London, 1775), pp. iii-viii reproduced in R. M. Dorson, ed., *Peasant
Customs and Savage Myths: Selections from the British Folklorists* (2
vols; London: Routledge and Kegan Paul, 1968), I, pp. 2–6.

10 Henry Bourne, 'Preface', *Antiquitates Vulgares; or, the Antiquities
of the Common people; Giving An Account of several of their Opinions
and Ceremonies with Proper Reflections upon each of them; shewing
which may be retain'd, and which ought to be laid aside* (Newcastle:
For the author, 1725) – a classic (and virulent) example of the ideological uses of Antiquarian study.

11 Peter Burke, *Popular Culture in Early Modern Europe* (London:
Temple Smith, 1978), pp. 3–22, the same author's 'The 'Discovery' of
Popular Culture' in Raphael Samuel, ed., *Peoples' History and Socialist
Theory* (London: Routledge & Kegan Paul Ltd, 1981), pp. 216–26 and

Raymond Williams, *The Country and the City* (St Albans, Herts: Paladin, 1975), pp. 87–98 offer further discussion of these developments.

12 Edward B. Tylor, *Primitive Culture: Researches into the Development of Mythology, Philosphy, Religion, Language, Art, and Custom* (2 vols; London: John Murray, 1871), I, pp. 6–7.

13 See Georgina Boyes [Smith], 'Literary Sources and Folklore Studies in the Nineteenth Century: A re-assessment of Armchair Scholarship,' *Lore and Language*, II:9 (1978), 26–42 for a more extensive discussion of the background to development of Folkloristics in England.

14 Burne, *Handbook of Folklore*, pp. 1–2.

15 *Ibid.*, pp. 2–3.

16 See Elizabeth Fee, 'The Sexual Politics of Victorian Social Anthropology,' in Mary Hartman and Lois Banner, ed., *Clio's Consciousness Raised: New Perspectives on the History of Women* (New York: Harper & Row, 1974), pp. 86–102.

17 See for example, the direct correlation between 'Little Englanders' and non-anthropological approaches to Folkloristics in R. R. Maretts's Presidential Address to the Folklore Society, 'Folklore and Psychology,' *Folk-Lore*, XXVII:1 (1914), 13. Marett also suggested that collecting folklore from English 'peasants' represented a useful source for practising the skills needed to elicit similar types of data from less developed cultures in the colonies.

18 Cecil Sharp and Herbert C. MacIlwaine, *The Morris Book*, 2nd rev. edn (London: Novello & Co. Ltd, 1912), I, p. 11.

19 See Alice Bertha Gomme, *The Traditional Games of England, Scotland and Ireland* (2 vols; New York: Dover Publications Inc., 1964) [first published 1894–8], for an extensive body of examples of survivals theory applied to children's games.

20 See for example the comments on costs and collection in Cecil Sharp, 'Some Notes on the Morris Dance,' *EFDS Journal,* I:1 (1914), 7 and 'Sheffield 'Mummers': Twenty Minutes of Old English Comedy,' *Sheffield Telegraph*, 10 Jan. 1920, p. 6.

21 Alex Helm, *The Chapbook Mummers' Plays: A Study of the Printed Versions of the North-West of England* (Ibstock, Leics: Guizer Press, 1969), pp. 5–6.

22 Roger D. Abrahams and George Foss, *Anglo-American Folksong Style* (Englewood Cliffs, New Jersey: Prentice-Hall Inc., 1968), p. 11.

23 This and other examples appear in Cecil Sharp, 'English Folk-Dances,' *The Morning Post*, 10 May 1910, p. 6.

24 Gilchrist quoted in Mike Yates, "The Best Bar in the Capstan': William Bolton Sailor and Chantyman,' *Traditional Music*, VII (mid-

1977), 10. Bolton's 'chantyman's gift' for writing also ran to producing a series of autobiographical articles for his local paper and poems ('he was particularly fond of the acrostic form') which appeared in local and national publications. See Frank Sellors, 'William Bolton,' *English Dance and Song*, XLVIII:1 (spring 1986), 30–1.

25 This term was coined by Hans Naumann in *Grundzuge der deutschen Volkskunde* (Leipzig: 1922), but had been current as a concept since at least the mid-nineteenth century.

26 J. R. Moore, 'The Influence of Transmission on the English Ballads,' *Modern Language Review*, II (Oct. 1916), 389.

27 *Sword Dance and Drama* (London: Merlin Press, 1962), pp. 22–3.

28 For a discussion of this dating, see Georgina Boyes [Smith], 'Chapbooks and Traditional Plays: Communication and Performance,' *Folklore*, XCII:2 (1981), 209–10.

29 A brief but illuminating discussion of the constant re-use of the same examples drawn from 'tribes of whom anthropologists know nothing' and inferences from absent records appears in D. K. Wilgus, *Anglo-American Folksong Scholarship Since 1898* (New Brunswick, New Jersey: Rutgers University Press, 1959), pp. 23–4 .

30 Bob Stewart, *Where is Saint George: Pagan Imagery in English Folksong* (Bradford-on-Avon, Wilts: Moonraker Press, 1977).

31 Margaret Dean-Smith, 'The Life-Cycle Play or Folk Play: Some Conclusions Following the Examination of the Ordish Papers and Other Sources,' *Folklore*, LXIX (1958), 237–53.

32 The common membership on committees of the Folk-Song Society, English Folk Dance Society (and later English Folk Dance and Song Society), Folklore Society, the International Folk Music Council and various anthropological, archaeological and antiquarian societies at different periods makes an interesting study in itself.

33 See Lloyd, *Folk Song in England*, pp. 15–17 for general discussion of the problematic areas of Sharp's proposals. A more extensive critique and detailed analysis of the socio-cultural background of Sharp's Somerset informants is contained in David Harker, 'Cecil Sharp in Somerset: Some Conclusions,' *Folk Music Journal*, II:3 (1972), 225–36 and *Fakesong: The Manufacture of British 'Folksong' 1700 to the Present Day* (Milton Keynes: Open University Press, 1985), pp. 187–94. Cindy Sughrue, 'Continuity, Conflict and Change: A Contextual and Comparative Study of Three South Yorkshire Longsword Dance Teams' (unpublished PhD dissertation, University of Sheffield, 1989), pp. 23–4 also provides considerable evidence of the Gatty family's direct involvement with the Grenoside Sword Dance team from the mid-nineteenth century until the

1950s. The Gattys, well connected literati and friends of Vaughan
Williams, who wrote and researched extensively on folklore, were locally recognised 'for keeping the folk dance and its traditions alive to
this day. Were it not for the Gattys, the Grenoside dance probably
would have been lost in obscurity.... They provided the dress of the
dancers at times, kept the oral tradition alive and the words by commit-
ting them to manuscripts; and as Mr. Cecil Sharp ... told me, they
introduced him to the almost forgotten dance.' J. T. Higgins, 'The Folk
Dance Revival: Grenoside and Gatty Traditions,' *Sheffield Daily Independent*, 31 Dec. 1925, p. 9 quoted in Sughrue. In this case at least, it
seems Sharp can hardly have been unaware of the possibility that the
folk had been 'brought into close enough contact with educated people
to be influenced by them'.

34 Joseph Jacobs, 'The Folk,' *Folk-Lore*, V (1893), 233–8. The whole
article, which accurately suggests the form Folkloristic theory eventually
developed in the 1960s, is of considerable interest. Jacobs, like Addy,
left the Folklore Society not long after the turn of the century.

35 For extended discussion of this point, see my 'Performance and
Context: an Examination of the Effects of the English Folksong Revival
on Song Repertoire and Style,' in Georgina Boyes, ed., *The Ballad
Today: History, Performance and Revival* (Addiscombe, Surrey: January
Books, 1985), pp. 43–52 and 'New Directions – Old Destinations: A
Consideration of the Role of the Tradition-Bearer in Folksong Re-
search,' in Ian Russell ed., *Singer, Song and Scholar* (Sheffield: Sheffield
Academic Press, 1886), p. 9. A similar conclusion is also reached by
Reimund Kvideland, see particularly 'Tradition: Objectivations or Social
Behaviour,' in Rita Pedersen and Flemming G. Andersen, ed., *The
Concept of Tradition in Ballad Research: A Symposium* (Odense:
Odense University Press, 1985), p. 12 and 'Folk Ballad and Folk Song,'
Studia Fennica, XXVII (1983), 177–83.

36 'Folklore, Anthropology and Social History,' *Indian Historical
Review*, III: 2 (1978), 250–1.

Chapter 2

The Folk and why they were replaced: the background to a cultural transfer

there are enthusiastic people now living who spend all their energy, and bestow all their time and lavish all their love upon the revival of traditional dances, traditional songs, and traditional children's games.... There is a Guild which exists for no other reason than to rehabilitate and hand down that pastoral and only true medium for rejoicing which the fever of industrialism nearly killed forever. If you are of a strangely hopeful disposition and are one of those who manage to sit tight somehow when learned people of high foreheads and overhanging brows talk of the decay of the race, the ultimate annihilation of Europe, and things like that – it is probable that you take a hand yourself in the work of this Guild.[1]

The existence of the Folk in turn-of-the-century England was taken as fact. Somewhere, remote and isolated, there still lived survivors of the old, lost national culture. The instrumentality of such a concept – with its potential for support of both dominant and alternative ideologies – offers much to explain its widespread acceptance. What are less easily determined, though, are the processes which promoted the Folk's extension from structurally effective, but abstract, theory to source of interventionist action. Why, when 'popular' songs and dances had been gathered by antiquarians, folklorists and musical entrepreneurs from at least the mid seventeenth century, did their conscious reperformance become the explicit rationale of collection in the late nineteenth and early twentieth centuries? What were the cultural, ideological and social triggers of the proposition that the Folk didn't merely exist but that their culture should be comprehensively 'revived'? And what promoted the conclusion that the Folk's role in culture should henceforward be fulfilled by new, self-appointed replacements?

Any attempt to describe – let alone allocate causality – within a cultural shift is problematic. Culture is transitional and protean. The assumptions of any individual or group, even those co-existing within time and space, are transactional and offer an infinite variety of possibilities. When the additional dimensions of interpreting over time and a range of social groupings are also involved, the task takes on herculean proportions. In trying to determine how the complex of socio-cultural factors influencing late nineteenth- and early twentieth-century attitudes were modified, negotiated and reproduced into the idea of a Folk Revival, therefore, it is inevitable that simplifications and omissions will occur. However, the existence of a significant change argues for at least making the attempt to assess what may have been the principal sources of the emergence of the concept. Equally, the ideologies and institutions which then promoted the concept's relative consonance over ninety years of considerable socio-cultural turbulence must themselves warrant closer examination.

From the viewpoint of the founders of the Revival at the turn of the century, a concatenation of developments threatened England as an imperial nation, undermining its pre-eminence as a political and cultural power. Externally, German manufacturing, expansionism, military strength, intellectual and cultural influences were seen as posing increasing dangers. From within, the inter-relation of industrialisation, urbanisation and mass production were widely felt to have produced a cultural crisis in which refined aesthetics were being overwhelmed by a tide of vulgarity.

Underlying these threats, however, lurked a still more ominous possibility. It was not merely art which was at risk but its living producers and consumers. A biological time bomb in the shape of the degenerating inhabitants of the towns was widely believed to form the next step in the inexorable march of evolution. Ideologically, the acceptance of Darwinism in belief systems created a vacuum which left ample room for doubt about the continuance of divinely ordained social systems. Subsequent discoveries in the science of genetics then compounded anxieties with results that suggested social and cultural traits were also capable of biological transmission. The removal of the questionable prospect of the meek inheriting the earth was, to many contemporary observers, of little comfort if it could only be replaced by a vision of the ultimate dominance of the degenerate working class.

These perceived menaces intersected and reinforced each other.[2] Empire, class and gender dominance were based on interdependent concepts of racial and cultural superiority. A threat to one brought all into peril. The prevalence of German music in the concert hall was as insidious a symptom of national decline as the reported refusal of middle-class women to undertake their allotted role in the maintenance of empire by producing large families. The working classes – a group whose political and economic power was already demonstrably growing – bred prolifically. City life had, however, brought them to physical deterioration and cultural decadence. An apocalyptic, but scientifically supported, process was held to be already in train; the sheer weight of working-class numbers, combined with their inherited physical and moral weaknesses would inexorably lead to the political and cultural obliteration of the race, the nation, the empire and the social structures which supported them. 'The feeble, ailing and unfit' would drag society down 'to that bottomless pit of decaying life'.[3]

In the face of a catastrophe of this magnitude, a ferment of actions and writings ensued. Pressure groups were formed and proffered solutions. Proposals for strict eugenic control, enforced drill for schoolboys and garden cities with allotments to provide the poor with home-grown vegetables were all presented as means of dealing with the physical implications of the crisis. Although as early as 1887 the *Lancet* suggested that the improvement in mortality rates in towns after the 1840s indicated that the presumptions of decadence were 'more visionary than real' and military recruitment officials pointed to the imposition of higher standards as the source of increased rejections of recruits, public opinion was not swayed.[4] Even the fact that moralists had – to little observable effect – regularly prophesied the total destruction of society from at least the sixteenth century offered nothing to counter widespread fears.[5] All that constituted the British way of life was believed to be in imminent danger. And undoubtedly, those with most invested in society's current form also had most to lose.

In this climate, it is perhaps not surprising that a 'seasonable enterprise' aimed at remedying the cultural effects of the 'science of heredity' was inaugurated in the early summer of 1898. The Folk-Song Society was founded.[6] Although it was constituted with

the primary object of 'the collection and preservation of Folk
Songs, Ballads, and Tunes, etc. and the publication of such of these
as may be deemed advisable',[7] Sir Hubert Parry's inaugural address
clearly articulated the nature and scale of menace which underlay
the stated rationale for the Society's formation:

If one thinks of the outer circumference of our terribly overgrown
towns, where the jerry-builder holds sway; where one sees all around
the tawdriness of sham jewellery and shoddy clothes, pawnshops and
flaming gin-palaces; where stale fish and miserable piles of Covent
Garden refuse which pass for vegetables are offered for food – all such
things suggest to one's mind the boundless regions of sham. It is for the
people who live in these unhealthy regions – people who, for the most
part, have false ideals, or none at all – who are always struggling for
existence, who think that the commonest rowdyism is the highest expression of human emotion; it is for them that the modern popular
music is made, and it is made with a commercial intention out of
snippets of musical slang. And this product it is which will drive out
folk-music if we do not save it .... old folk-music is among the purest
products of the human mind. It grew in the hearts of the people before
they devoted themselves so assiduously to the making of quick returns
....
[English folk tunes] are characteristic of the race, of the quiet reticence
of our country folk, courageous and content, ready to meet what chance
shall bring with a cheery heart. All the things that make the folk-music
of the race also betoken the qualities of the race, and, as a faithful
reflection of ourselves, we needs must cherish it.... [Folk-song] outlasts
the greatest works of art, and becomes an heritage to generations. And
in that heritage may lie the ultimate solution to the problem of characteristic national art.
I think also we may legitimately reflect that in these late days when we
are beginning to realize how little happiness money profits can bring,
and how much joy there lies in the simple beauty of primitive thought,
and the emotions which are common to all men alike, even to the
sophisticated, it is a hopeful sign that a society like ours should be
founded: to save something primitive and genuine from extinction; to
put on record what lovable qualities there are in unsophisticated humanity; and to comfort ourselves by the hope that at bottom, our
puzzling friend, Democracy, has permanent qualities hidden away somewhere, which may yet bring it out of the slough which the scramble
after false ideals, the strife between the heads that organise and the
workmen who execute, and the sordid vulgarity of our great city-popu-
lations, seem in our pessimistic moments to indicate as its inevitable

destiny.[8]

Even over a distance of ninety years, the fear and contempt embodied in Parry's evocation of urban working-class life are striking. Cultural and physical squalor, political and economic threat breed in the towns and spread ever outwards to menace him and all who share his values. His language reeks and festers. Amid the stench of rotting fish, the glare of gin palaces and the meretricious catchiness of music hall tunes, he sees false new ideals coming to pervade and emasculate. Politically empowered by democracy, 'workmen who execute' are no longer 'content' and 'cheery', but have set up in financial and artistic competition against 'heads that organise'. 'Sordid vulgarity' seems an almost 'inevitable destiny'.

But Parry was an optimist. It was, he suggested, remotely possible that such a fate could be avoided. Culture could be rescued at the last minute. Like the other Vice-Presidents invited to join the emergent Folk-Song Society,[9] Sir Hubert Parry (1848–1918) was a member of the high culture establishment. As the Director of the Royal College of Music and a Professor of Music at Oxford, it is perhaps unsurprising that he should offer a well-tried artistic strategy to deal with a cultural problem. The need for 'a characteristic national art' could, as had already been successfully demonstrated in other countries, be met by looking to folk music for models. Carl Engel's proposition – all the worse for coming from a Hanovarian – that the English 'unlike the German and other Continental nations' had hardly any national music could at last be shown to be groundless. Thanks to the work of folksong collectors, England had now been proved to be a land *with* music. Not only German works but German influence on English compositions could be obviated by use of the country's artistic 'heritage' of folk music. The concert hall could be saved for the race.

Parry's address however, proposed a solution which went beyond exclusively musical concerns. He suggested that through the work of the Folk-Song Society, more comprehensive needs could be met. It was not merely the forms but the values embodied in folksong which he invoked. In 'true' folksong, there was 'no sham, no got up glitter, and no vulgarity', nothing 'common or unclean'. In a unique encapsulation, the qualities distinguishing English folk music 'also betoken the qualities of the race'. There was a common cultural standard which could be drawn upon to reverse the process of degeneration, and restore the old social balance. A source of culture uncontaminated by contemporary decline was still in existence. In Sir Hubert Parry's view, artistic, social and political salvation lay in the pure, quintessentially English culture of the rural Folk.

This proposition transcends an appeal to Romanticism and the complex of images and concepts associated with historicism, anti-industrialism and the innate superiority of the primitive. It is not the peasantry, or rural life in the abstract, which Parry offered as a means of restoration, but folk culture in its specific expression. By collecting and making available the forms of folk music, their inherent values would also be propagated – values which, moreover, were common to each member of the race. Folk music had been collectively created by all the English, it embodied their deepest feelings, characteristics and aspirations. 'A faithful reflection of ourselves', it represented a fundamental racial expression, transcending later developments such as status and class. From recognition of this national core, a new socio-cultural consensus could develop to restore the status quo.

Parry's call for a resumption of shared racial expression offers a significant development in establishment approaches to popular culture. Although explicit attempts to build a national consensus had formed part of earlier 'solutions' to the perceived cultural and political crisis of the period, they had been of circumscribed type. Aiming to associate the working classes in 'a common national goal which would inspire them to turn their minds to a higher purpose, and to elevate them from the drudgery of their own hardships',[10] appeals had largely been based around nationalism, the crown and imperialism.[11] In citing an aspect of lower-class culture – albeit a highly specialised one – as a means of national consolidation, Parry articulated the ultimate consequence of a development which was already in train. His suggestion formalised the conflation of two major contemporary cultural processes – the invention of national traditions and the rehabilitation of popular traditions. Implicit within this synthesis was a strand of consensus which linked the new rituals and practices of the crown, empire, national anthem and flag with older, historically-grounded phenomena.

The attitudes of various institutions within the establishment to

popular traditions had undergone several changes in the course of
the nineteenth century. Following the upheavals centring on popular culture in the seventeenth century,[12] for most of the eighteenth
century it had generally been considered 'of the highest political
utility to encourage innocent sports and games' amongst 'the
common people'. The celebrations marking and ameliorating the
operation of the agricultural year were beneficial to the maintenance of social relations in pre-industrial communities. Although
the performance of many customs continued during and after the
emergence of industrialisation, from around the turn of the nineteenth century traditional popular culture increasingly became a
focus of middle- and upper-class intervention. Communal customs
such as wakes, rushbearings and morris dancing, which were
almost invariably associated with drunken licence, and on occasion, provided symbolic and formal structures for political protest,
were early targets of official discouragement and suppression. At
the same time, the development of evangelical pressure groups and
subsequent legislation on the treatment of animals affected other
forms of popular custom. Seasonal sports such as bull running and
'cock-squailing' (throwing loaded sticks at tethered cockerels) were
banned and driven underground. Changing attitudes to the respectability of public performance – particularly in customs involving drinking – also led to the suppression or curtailing of other
pastimes in the interests of promoting 'decency and decorum'.
Women were especially vulnerable to such social pressure, and
from the 1820s and 1830s, their public participation in customary
activities was greatly reduced. They came to 'service' customs by
making food, drink and costumes, rather than actively performing
in them. Overall, intervention on moral, religious, rational and
educational grounds by a variety of authorities was effective in
presenting customary performances as dangerous anachronisms.[13]
By the 1860s, therefore, many customs which had relied on the
middle, upper and 'respectable' working classes for material support ceased entirely or were reduced in scale, as reciprocality came
to be regarded as begging.

Traditional customs had existed through and for the social
structures of earlier, reciprocal forms of community. The new
social relations of nation, industrialism and class, however, had
relatively little outlet for public expression. If the values and norms
associated with the new order were to be embodied and asserted,

then new traditions would have to evolve or – more deterministically – be actively created. By the last quarter of the nineteenth century, the expressive vacuum proceeding from 'change, crisis and dislocation' brought about the invention of traditions to provide symbols of national unity and permanence. Ceremonials associated with the royal family and state – coronations, weddings, jubilees, the opening of Parliament – all became highly formalised. New and well established civic and religious institutions developed equally ritualised observances to mark their existence and operation. The forms and components of such performances were, moreover, rapidly and widely disseminated through increasingly complex transport and printed communications systems. In a comparatively short space of time, processional grandeur, flags, military display and national music came both to provide the images for, and to symbolise, the structures of contemporary society.

Although newly developed, invented traditions were not distinctively neoteric or innovatory in form. An important factor in the process of legitimising such rituals was implicit or overt evocation of historical tradition as a source of apparent continuity with the past.[14] From the choice of Gothic styles of architecture for the new buildings which provided their setting to the modification of archaic dress for participants, the appearance and connotations of antiquity were fostered in all aspects of the performance of invented traditions.

'Tradition' is, however, relatively indivisible. Considered in isolation, invented traditions appear as sporadic, staged events, presented by an elite to an uninvolved populace. But within the combination of history, consistency and semi-dramatic performance embodied in invented traditions was an implicit resonance of earlier customary observances – particularly those involving public display. Whilst not necessarily deployed on the same occasions, the symbolic power of contemporary national pageantry was effectively reinforced by the prior existence of communal exhibition customs such as morris and sword dancing, well dressings and wakes processions.

Within this interaction, a complex of dynamics involving antiquarian, scientific and informal constructions of customary performance came into play. The socio-cultural and political developments which fostered the invention of traditions were also influential in supporting a rise in popular historical studies. Anti-

quarian articles and 'Notes and Queries' columns came to form a
regular section of most newspapers in the rapidly growing local
press. There was also a contemporary increase in the number of
books and periodicals devoted to antiquarian subjects.[15] A combination of public interest and accessible information therefore ensured that morris dancing and mumming evoked the splendour of
medieval monarchy, court masques, the world of Shakespeare and
the Elizabethan Renaissance. Equally, 'fancy dress history' and a
more serious taste for concrete, accurate representation, which was
'purposefully historical, an interest in the past and the recreation
of history in painting, poetry, the novel, the theatre, and scholarship', was a growing force in culture as the century progressed.[16]
In the Church of England, antiquarian researches which demonstrated the centrality of the parish church in many customary
performances and publicised the forms of earlier church music
provided the background to 'Ritualism' and 'the archaeological
element in the Oxford movement'. Architectural changes arising
from 'the desire to restore the parish churches of England to what
was supposed to be more or less their original state had the effect
of making people want to adorn churches as they had been
adorned in the Middle Ages and to use them for the rites and
ceremonies for which they had been designed'.[17] From the 1870s,
the fashionable new sciences of Folklore and Anthropology directly linked almost all customary exhibitions with the rituals of
kingship in their most ancient, racial forms. Race and nation,
crown and imperial destiny could now be given academically
sound and popularly familiar roots in traditional expressive culture.

The national 'audience' for invented traditions moreover,
brought personal as well as more broadly cultural perceptions to
their performance. The formal elements of invented traditions –
processions, specialised costume and ritualised action – had also
marked out the communal traditions of the past. Equally, their
focal characters were frequently denominated 'King', 'Queen',
'Lady' or 'Captain'. The appearance of real Kings and Queens
surrounded by a train of costumed followers and accompanied by
bands, bunting and a general sense of holiday liminality was
therefore not completely innocent of social and cultural resonance.
There were possibilities for ample association in personal or familial memory of earlier forms to fill in the vacuum between sup-

pressed or unfashionable old traditions and burgeoning invented
ones. Indeed, the speed with which new traditions gained acceptance may have reflected their use of psychologically familiar elements. The ethos which fostered the invention of national
traditions drew support from, and was supportive of, less exalted,
but historically well attested forms of popular ceremony.

Increasingly, through the latter third of the nineteenth century,
therefore, attitudes to traditional performance underwent revision.
A strategy of carefully policed reform came to be preferred to the
suppression of old traditions.[18] At the instigation of local enthusiasts for the antiquarian and quaint, defunct customs were revived
and existing traditions refurbished, with what their middle- class
supporters conceived to be their appropriate historical trappings.
Drunkenness and licence were reduced by establishment supervision of events, and material support reappeared as a positive
reinforcement to decorous behaviour and the maintenance of links
with the past.[19]

Beyond antiquarian involvement, however, concerned middle-
class attention to traditional customs and beliefs was encouraged
for its 'practical bearing on the affairs of human life'. The analogy
between the civilising mission of the English in the colonies and
the role of those 'placed in a position of authority over uneducated
folk' in Britain was made by at least one leading folklorist: 'the
cardinal fact that widely separated stages of progress may coexist
in the same country at the same time', Charlotte S. Burne proposed, ensured that there were 'barbarians nearer home than in
India or New Zealand'. But, she suggested, 'When people understand the prejudices of uneducated folk they must know better
how to deal with them, and how to set about trying to reconcile
them with the principles of modern culture and civilization.' [20]
Taking up the white man's burden could, therefore, be a domestic
as well as an imperial duty.

As the acceptance of invented traditions developed and scholarship brought about a change in perceptions of historical popular
culture, a community's possession of an historical custom often
became a subject for public celebration. The civic institutions in
emerging boroughs were quick to manifest – and exploit – local
pride in displays and processions at their own 'Olde Englishe
ceremonies'. In some cases, the addition of elements associated
with national rituals meant that the formal content of older cus-

toms became virtually indistinguishable from invented ones. Church services or blessings by local clergy were incorporated into traditional performances, and attendance by civic dignitaries and other members of the local establishment became an expected feature of events. Uniformed silver or brass bands replaced *ad hoc* groups of musicians. Paralleling the use of historical styles of dress in invented traditions, the costumes of performers in traditional customs were renewed or 'reinterpreted' in the light of the custom's presumed historical origin. With the rosy glow of hindsight, the raucous and potentially violent were transformed into a source of contact with the robustness of a less prim and sophisticated age. What had previously been perceived as grotesquely anachronistic became an honoured survival of 'Merrie England'. As *Jackson's Oxford Journal* commented on the reformed Whitsun pastimes of 'The Valentia' club at Bletchington:

It was a pleasing sight to see nearly a hundred young, fine, clean, and well-dressed labourers follow their banner ... to the quiet old church – it was convincing proof of what unanimity and good feeling can affect.... This was a meeting in strong contrast to those of years gone by, when riot and drunkeness *[sic]* was the result ... [21]

Historically, traditional customs had been hierarchical but socially comprehensive. In some cases, the local elite had taken part in performances – at Castleton in Derbyshire, the administrator of the leadminers' court and his brother danced with the village morris dancers in the mid nineteenth century, while at Kirtlington, in the early part of the nineteenth century, although labourers formed the basis on the morris side, farmers' sons 'did not decline joining the dancers, but rather prided themselves on being selected as one of them'. Elsewhere, customs were organised jointly by 'gentlemen amateurs' and local publicans – each, however, keeping to 'separate spheres' of sociability and 'business'. Perhaps the most telling description of this earlier form of 'communal' participation is Mary Russell Mitford's comments on the May festival in Three Mile Cross in Hampshire: 'the band struck up in the May-house, and the dance, after a little demur, was fairly set afloat – an honest English country dance ... with ladies and gentlemen at the top, and country lads and lasses at the bottom; a happy mixture of cordial kindness on the one hand, and pleased respect on the other.'[22]

This earlier approach to public festivals had much to offer later nineteenth-century advocates of consensus. In many places, the new attitudes to historical custom brought back the local establishment's association with their performance. The nature of such involvement in traditions was recast, however, as participation came to reflect less reciprocal forms of relationship. Aside from exerting influence to ensure the continuance of customs, members of the middle class took up a number of different roles. Local schoolteachers, 'progressive' clergymen and antiquarian squires became innovators, introducing and organising the performance of suitably decorous and 'historical' activities such as maypole dancing or May Queen ceremonies into their areas. In the majority of customs, however, the middle classes limited their activities to supervisory roles. They did not perform themselves, but as their social inferiors provided refined re-creations of 'Olde Englishe' pastimes, they encouraged middle-class behavioural norms and the inclusion of elements of national culture by their observing presence and material support.

Reformed or re-invented customs represented only one element in a wide range of vernacular performances which could be instrumental in serving the aims of developing consensus. The symbols of national unity and the message of ideological convergence were also presented in a variety of other performances outside the compass of state occasions. These popular presentations acted to reinforce the wider existence of consensus and its symbols, whilst linking them with specifically local phenomena. Increasingly accustomed to forming the audience for actualisations of historical events in the graphic arts and at the theatre, in many of these newer types of performance the middle and upper classes took the final step towards acceptance and involvement by participating directly.

One particularly influential genre, enjoying wide middle- and upper-class support, was the historical pageant. Imaginative re-enactments of 'important' events in local history grew in popularity over the latter third of the nineteenth and early decades of the twentieth centuries. They combined processions, community drama, 'romance' and education – particularly 'the education of a community in its own past'.[23] The form of such history and the nature of the education presented were summed up by Louis N. Parker, a proponent of spectacular theatre and fashionable pageant organiser: 'It reminds the old of the history of their home, and shows the young what treasures are in their keeping. It is the great incentive to the right kind of patriotism: love of hearth; love of town; love of country; love of England.'[24]

Given the formal interaction between all types of public ritual during this period, it is unsurprising that traditional performances were also frequently incorporated in pageants. D'Arcy Ferris,[25] the chief reviver of the pageant genre in the nineteenth century, brought the Kirkby Malzeard sword dancers to perform in the complex of civic, church, educational and theatrical events comprising the Ripon Millenary Festival in 1886. The semiotics of the scene which included their dance were typically eclectic. Watched by visitors from 'cottage and mansion, village and town', the Mayoress of Ripon (representing the Genius of the City), accompanied by Loyalty and Charity (draped in 'spotless white silk') and trainbearers in Grecian dress (pea green and coral silk), arrived in a specially made civic carriage of 'classical design'. The three Graces ('in elegant drapery') and 'young ladies representing the four seasons' also drew up in their carriage, to be surrounded by flower girls, maypole dancers, civic banner bearers, Union Jack carriers, the Kirkby Malzeard sword dancers, shepherds and shepherdesses (with live lambs) and 'a horse with pillion, representing a Georgian farmer with his wife'. Mayday in Merrie England was then enthusiastically celebrated.[26]

Historical pageants did not merely incorporate customs as resonant cultural features. Pageants themselves manifested a number of social and formal characteristics of customary performance in a way which was particularly supportive of conjoint performance. Pageants and customs alike were 'community drama', performed in and for particular social and physical environments. Performers in both types of activity were usually known to their audience and came from the area in which they appeared. Like older traditional customs, pageants involved members of a range of social groups, from squire to farm labourer, mill hand to local manufacturer. Although relatively comprehensive, however, both types of performance reflected the hierarchical structure of local society. The Hampshire May Day dance with 'ladies and gentlemen at the top, and country lads and lasses at the bottom' was mirrored in the pageant's assignment of romantic starring roles as King Richard the Lionheart or Queen Henrietta Maria to local notables and crowd parts as Roundhead soldiery to the respectable working classes. Through the historical pageant, therefore, aspects of public performance previously associated with traditional custom emerged, yet again, to form part of middle-class participatory experience.

The historical pageant's potential as a means of consolidating a consensus which did not affect the basis of class relations was recognised by its proponents. Following the Ripon Millenary Pageant of 1886, in which they had taken an active though subordinate part, 'Robin Hood's foresters' were addressed in precisely such terms by the 'Master of the Revels', D'Arcy Ferris:

> Mr Ferris then went on to describe the festival as a moral, social and artistic triumph.... It was a social triumph in that it had brought all classes of society together, by which means a spirit of goodwill and friendship had been increased. In his early life he had spent some time in Yorkshire where he had gained experience of the working classes, with whom he had great sympathy; and in that celebration he had a object in view, viz., the breaking down of class prejudice. (Hear, hear). The distinctions of class of course could not be disturbed, but class prejudices could be broken down, and those gatherings that had been held during the past week were eminently calculated to do that.[27]

Ferris's pragmatic outline of the effects and function of the Ripon pageant draws together the key social dynamics which linked vernacular 'community drama', popular, artistic and invented traditions. His comments encapsulate an approach to public ritual which had a number of significant socio-cultural implications. In this context, many traditional customs were not just rehabilitated as social behaviour but enjoyed an enlarged status as significant cultural forms. For their working-class performers, this could entail vindication of their pre-existing views or at least, the possibility of a new confidence in what they did. Royal and noble participation in public ritual and 'historical re-enactments', and genteel experience of traditional and vernacular performances, implied a new respectability and moral obligation in which duty and fashion coincided.[28] Common to the experience of participation in all was the creation of an effective *communitas*, 'giving recognition to an essential and generic human bond, without which there could be *no* society'.[29] Following from this was the affirmation that a range of ritualised public actions were acceptable and effective means of symbolic communication on a national and supra-national scale.

Parry's suggestion that folk culture offered the sophisticated and vulgar a means of salvation was an appeal to *communitas*. In the face of the all-embracing crisis which threatened to overwhelm social and cultural life in England, the sense that performance as a public activity was of positive symbolic and practical value offered a possible means of avoiding annihilation. The culture of the Folk was a heritage common to all – it was the product of the race, not of the working class. In a society threatened internally by division through inequality, folk culture represented an uncontaminated and non-aligned source from which all later, less innocent forms developed. By preserving and propagating this original culture, the future of culture itself might be assured. As folk culture's possessors were themselves failing, however, what activity would be more positive than reproducing it in their place? A conscious choice to replace the Folk by a new, knowledgeable, aware group of performers could be made.

Notes

1 Philip Macer-Wright, 'England-to-Be: The Espérance Guild of National Joy,' *Westminster Gazette*, reprinted in Mary Neal, *The Espérance Morris Book: Part II* (London: J. Curwen & Sons Ltd, 1912), pp. xiv-xv.

2 The literature in this area is itself now imperial in scale. Of particular value for the purposes of this study however, are Gareth Stedman Jones, *Outcast London: A Study in the Relationship Between Classes in Victorian Society* (Oxford: Oxford University Press, 1971); Anna Davin, 'Imperialism and Motherhood,' *History Workshop Journal*, V (spring 1977), 9–65; Richard Solway, 'Counting the Degenerates: The Statistics of Race Degeneration in Edwardian England,' *Journal of Contemporary History*, XVII (1982), 137–64 and the range of papers in Paul Kennedy and Anthony Nicholls, ed., *Nationalist and Racialist Movements in Britain and Germany Before 1914* St Antony's/Macmillan Series; (Oxford & London: Macmillan & St Antony's College, 1981). Specifically musical dimensions are discussed in Frank Howes, *The English Musical Renaissance* (London: Martin Secker & Warburg Ltd, 1966) and E. D. Mackerness, *A Social History of English Music* (London: Routledge & Kegan Paul, 1964), pp. 214–29.

3 Arnold White and Beatrice Potter quoted in Stedman Jones, *Outcast London*, pp. 287 and 284.

4 *Lancet*, II (1887), 342, 768 and other sources quoted in Solway, 'Counting the Degenerates,' p. 141.

5 For a succinct account of this particular cultural tradition, see Graham Pearson, 'Falling Standards: A Short Sharp History of Moral Decline,' in Martin Barker, ed., *The Video Nasties: Freedom & Censorship in the Media* (London: Pluto Press, 1984), pp. 88–103.

6 As a result of 'a conversation' between Charles Graves (1856–1944), his brother Alfred Perceval Graves, the Hon. Secretary of the Irish Literary Society (1846–1931) and Henry Plunkett Greene (1865–1936). The initial meeting, chaired by J. A. Fuller-Maitland (1856–1936), was held in the rooms of the Irish Literary Society in Adelphi Terrace, London. See Alfred Perceval Graves, 'Ireland's Share in Folk Song Revival,' *Journal of the Irish Folk Song Society*, XIV (April 1914), 19–21.

7 Folk Song Society Minute Book (1898–1901), Minute of Meeting of 16 May 1898, quoted in Ian A. Olson, 'The Influence of the Folk Song Society on the Greig-Duncan Folk Song Collection: Methodology,' *Folk Music Journal*, V:2 (1986), 180.

8 Nendeln, Liechtenstein: Kraus Reprint, 1975, p. 1.

9 The other Vice-Presidents were Sir Charles Villiers Stanford (1852–1924), Chief Professor of Composition at the Royal College of Music and Professor of Music at Cambridge; Sir John Stainer (1840–1901), Inspector to the National Board of Education and Professor of Music at Oxford and Sir Alexander Mackenzie (1847–1935), Principal of the Royal Academy of Music. According to Alfred Graves, they were intended to represent the interests of the 'sister nations' of Britain – Parry, Wales; Stanford, Ireland and Mackenzie, Scotland. Lord Tennyson, the President, represented England. See Graves, 'Ireland's Share in Folk Song Revival,' p. 20 and *Irish Literary and Musical Studies* (London: Elkin Mathews, 1913), p. 176. I am most grateful to Tom Munnelly for bringing these sources to my attention.

10 Annie E. S Coombes, "For God and for England': Contributions to an Image of Africa in the First Decade of the Twentieth Century,' *Art History*, VIII:4 (Dec. 1985), 455.

11 For a comprehensive discussion of this ideological cluster see John M. MacKenzie, *Propaganda and Empire: The Manipulation of British Public Opinion 1880–1960* (Manchester: Manchester University Press, 1984).

12 See David Underdown, *Revel, Riot and Rebellion: Popular Politics and Culture in England 1603–1660* (Oxford: Oxford University Press, 1985), particularly pp. 44–72 for a valuable study of differing attitudes to popular traditions in the sixteenth and seventeenth centuries.

13 For supporting material see John K. Walton and Robert Poole, 'The Lancashire Wakes in the Nineteenth Century,' in Robert D. Storch,

ed., *Popular Culture and Custom in Nineteenth-Century England* (London & Canberra: Croom Helm, 1982), pp. 102–3, P. Joyce, *Work, Society and Politics: The Factory North of England 1860–1890* (Brighton: Harvester Press Ltd, 1980) and Keith Chandler, 'Morris Dancing at Spelsbury: An Analytical Essay,' *Oxfordshire Local History*, I:7 (1983), 2–13.

14 See Eric Hobsbawm, 'Introduction: Inventing Traditions,' in Eric Hobsbawm and Terence Ranger, ed., *The Invention of Tradition* Past & Present Publications; (Cambridge: Cambridge University Press, 1983), for a valuable and stimulating discussion of this area – though in Folkloristic terms, his distinction between 'tradition' and 'custom' is too exclusive to be a fully effective source of analysis.

15 More detailed consideration of the interaction between forms of publication and the rise of Folklore Studies in England is contained in Georgina Boyes [Smith], 'Literary Sources and Folklore Studies in the Nineteenth Century: A Re-assessment of Armchair Scholarship,' *Lore & Language,* II:9 (1978), 26–42.

16 See Michael R. Booth, *Victorian Spectacular Theatre 1850–1910* (London: Routledge & Kegan Paul Ltd, 1981), p. 17. The reader is, however, referred to the volume as a whole for a stimulating discussion of the development of an audience for the actualisation of historical and contemporary experience in Victorian expressive culture. Specific examples are also detailed in Roy Judge, 'May Day and Merrie England,' *Folklore*, CII:2 (1991), 131–48.

17 Alec R. Vidler, *The Church in an Age of Revolution: 1789 to the Present Day* (Harmondsworth, Middx: Penguin Books, 1980), p. 159.

18 Alun Howkins, *Whitsun in 19th Century Oxfordshire*, History Workshop Pamphlets No. 8 (Oxford: History Workshop Pamphlets, 1973) provides a useful survey of the form and effects of these developments.

19 See Georgina Boyes [Smith], 'Winster Morris Dance: The Sources of an Oikotype,' in T. Buckland, ed., *Traditional Dance: Vol. I* (Crewe: Crewe & Alsager College of Higher Education, 1982), pp. 93–108 for an extended discussion of the role of intervention in the performance of a single custom.

20 Charlotte S. Burne, 'Some Simple Methods of Promoting the Study of Folk-Lore, and the Extension of the Folk-Lore Society,' *Folk-Lore*, V (1887–8), 64–5 quoted in Robert Ackerman, *J. G. Frazer: His Life and Work* (Cambridge: Cambridge University Press, 1987), p. 101.

21 *Jackson's Oxford Journal*, 21 June 1862, p. 8. See also Roy Judge, 'Tradition and the Plaited Maypole Dance', in Theresa Buckland, ed., *Traditional Dance: Vol. II – Historical Perspectives* (Crewe: Crewe &

Alsager College of Higher Education, 1983), pp. 1–21 for a wide variety
of other examples of similar forms of supervised order and gentility.

22 Mary R. Mitford, *Sketches of English Life & Character* (Edinburgh & London: T. N. Foulis, 1909), p. 197; the original vignettes of
'Our Village' were first published in *The Lady* from 1819, increasing its
sales from 250 to 2000. Mary Russell Mitford's collected writings on
Three Mile Cross were published in five volumes between 1824 and
1832 and were widely reprinted and anthologised thereafter. Her approach and style created a genre and has directly influenced cultural
attitudes to village life. Further discussion of 'commingling within specific morris sides between men from several levels of the social hierarchy' appears in Keith Chandler, 'Morris Dancing in the South
Midlands: The Socio-Cultural Background to 1914,' in Buckland, *Traditional Dance: Vol. II – Historical Perspectives*, pp. 58–90.

23 See Robert Withington, *English Pageantry: An Historical Outline*
2 vols, (Cambridge: Harvard University Press, 1918), pp. xv-xx for a
general description of the form.

24 Quotation taken from Louis N. Parker's autobiography, *Several
of My Lives* and reprinted in his grandson, Anthony Parker's, *Pageants:
Their Presentation and Production* (London: Bodley Head, 1954), p. 14.
Louis Napoleon Parker worked on town pageants from 1906 and the
historical section of the Lord Mayor of London's Shows in 1907 and
1908. He also collaborated with the actor-manager Herbert Beerbohm
Tree (1853–1917) on a number of spectacular theatrical productions,
writing the pageant plays *Drake* (1912) and *Joseph and his Brethren*
(1913) for him and acting as his assistant producer for the staging of
Shakespeare's *King Henry VIII* at His Majesty's Theatre in 1910. See
Booth, *Victorian Spectacular Theatre 1850–1910,* pp. 127–60 for additional details.

25 Later 'D'Arcy de Ferrars', perhaps the most influential advocate
of the inclusion of traditional dance in pageant performances. For fuller
details of his career, see E. C. Cawte, *Ritual Animal Disguise: A
Historical and Geographical Study of Animal Disguise in the British
Isles* (London: Folklore Society, 1978), pp. 181–5 and Roy Judge,
'Tradition and the Plaited Maypole Dance,' in Buckland, *Traditional
Dance: Historical Perspectives*, pp.16–17.

26 W. Harrison, *Ripon Millenary: A Record of the Festival Also a
History of the City arranged under its Wakemen and Mayors from the
Year 1400* (Ripon: W. Harrison, 1892), pp. 89–92. It should also be
noted that, although included in a 're-creation' of May Day, the Kirkby
Malzeard sword dance was usually performed between Christmas and
New Year.

27 *Ibid.*, p. 149.

28 As in the vogue for tournaments detailed in Mark Girouard, *The Return to Camelot: Chivalry and the English Gentleman* (New Haven & London: Yale University Press, 1981).

29 Victor W. Turner, *The Ritual Process: Structure and Anti-Structure* (Harmondsworth, Middx: Penguin Books, 1969), p. 83. On such occasions, work and everyday routine were largely set aside, the effects of social systems were to some extent reduced, and for a defined period, *anyone* could see the Queen, the Lord Mayor or Bishop. Festive behaviour was the norm and the physical context of the performance was often changed by the use of street decorations, Sunday best dress or special costume.

Chapter 3

The source is open to all: collecting and its uses in the Revival

For CJS

You found our songs and dances all but spent
Lingering in ancient memories, voices frail
Limbs weak with years, and with long labours bent.
Had you not been, that age-old beauty's tale
Of movement and sweet music, perfected
Through countless generations, father, son,
And grandson, all that richness must have sped
Forgotten, lost, inanimate, unknown.
You seized that treasure from Time's thieving hand,
You played for youth the part age could not play,
Summed in yourself tradition's faltering power
And from the dying past made every hour
Of future time with living music gay.
While England dances, proud your name shall stand.[1]

The potential of folk culture as a source of replacement for an ailing and perverted national culture proved widely acceptable. But it was also equally well established that folk culture was itself in danger. If the tradition on which so much depended were not to become 'entirely forgotten', a programme of rescue by collection and propagation by publication had to be set in train with utmost urgency. But proposing to fellow members of the Folk-Song Society, in agreeable West End surroundings, that the only way to avoid racial catastrophe was to collect folksongs was one thing. Actually journeying to rural areas to knock on unknown cottage doors with a request that the inhabitants sing to you, proved to hold fewer attractions. Despite the strength of the case, theory and practice in the salvaging of folk culture were not easily reconciled

with the demands of social convention. And even where the difficulties of establishing the roles of collector and informant were
overcome, the more fundamental issues of what was to be collected and how it should be returned to culture remained to be
answered. Initially, however, the aims and structure of the Folk-
Song Society were, paradoxically, the major obstacles to the development of a Folk Revival.

Although leading composers such as Elgar, Dvořák and Grieg
joined the Folk-Song Society's ranks by invitation, and a number
of active folksong collectors were drawn into membership after its
foundation, ultimately the early Folk-Song Society was a genteel
talking-shop, whose proceedings Vaughan Williams later characterised as of 'a dilettante and 'tea-party' order'.[2] There were two
classes of membership, those paying half a guinea to receive the
Society's *Journal* and attend its meetings alone, and those paying
one guinea, who could additionally bring three friends with them
to 'all meetings and *conversaziones*'. The ranking of aims among
the Society's fourteen rules is also significantly social. 'The collection and preservation of Folk Songs, Ballads, and Tunes, etc. and
the publication of such of these as may be deemed advisable' is
indeed set forth as its primary object, but this is followed by
allocation to the Committee of 'power to elect a limited number
of Honorary Members from among distinguished foreign authorities on the subject of Folk Music' and instructions to hold
meetings 'from time to time ... at which vocal and instrumental
illustrations of Folk Songs, Ballads and Tunes shall be given'.
Scholarship, in the form of papers written on the subject being
read and discussed, follows this, but no concrete proposals for
bringing the results of such work to the adherents of 'common
popular song' are offered.[3] As Iolo Williams concluded, 'The ...
Folk-Song Society, for all but a fraction of its career, was little
more than a publishing society'.[4] Moreover, the Society's *Journal*,
which was its main vehicle for presenting both folksongs themselves and the aims of their associated scholarship, was available
only to members.

Despite the need for material on which to base scholarly or
potential revivalist approaches, experience in folksong collection
was not among the early Society's strengths. Its membership consisted, Ralph Vaughan Williams later reported, largely of 'professional singers, musical journalists and the official heads of the

profession, most of them not distinguished for their knowledge of folk song, however eminent they might be as performers and composers'.[5] And although the Committee of Management circulated a leaflet of *Hints to the Collectors of Folk Music*, as Frederick Keel pointed out, 'it must be remembered that the Folk Song Society were *amateurs*, in the strict sense of the word. They could only learn their chosen work by doing it, and there were few among them so experienced in it that they could 'teach' to others.'[6]

The results for the new Society of such an absence of practical experience, knowledge and commitment among its recruits could, perhaps, have been predicted. Shortly after its inauguration, the Folk-Song Society ran out of impetus, publishable material, members and money. At its first General Meeting in Mayfair on 2 February 1899, there were 73 members and the Society had a balance of £24 in its accounts. This rose in 1901 to £78. By 1903, however, there had been 'a serious drop in revenue' to £4 14s 6d, no issue of the *Journal* had been published and, in part because of indecision in replacing the Honorary Secretary during a protracted illness, the Society had become 'inactive'.

Vaughan Williams, Iolo Williams and Keel are writing history as victors in the struggle for control which ultimately brought the Folk-Song Society into the ambit of Revival performance through its amalgamation with the English Folk Dance Society. None of them was a founder member with direct experience of the Folk-Song Society at its inception. But, as Sir Hubert Parry himself had acknowledged in his inaugural lecture, field collection is not a simple matter and the difficulties facing the Society's 'amateur' membership were not entirely the product of triumphant hindsight. Other contemporary groups of well-intentioned neophytes in folklore collection were similarly dogged by 'inactivity' – as Mrs Waller R. Bullock's naively candid exposition of the difficulties of the Baltimore Folk-Lore Society indicates:

The Baltimore Folk-Lore Society has for its chief *raison d'etre* the collecting of superstitions and tales still to be found existing in Maryland. This is an unexplored region, offering many inducements to seek for its scattered treasures; especially for those vestiges of a savage race and a distant land found among the superstitions of the colored people. This object of collecting has always been kept before our members. Lists of suggestive topics were distributed at the close of our first year, in the spring of 1895. The next year, large tabulated papers were prepared for

use in collecting tales; others were arranged for customs and sayings. We separated hopefully at the close of the season's work, expecting a good harvesting in the fall. But summer ease and folk-lore labors did not bring the anticipated results.
The next move was the usual recourse of a perplexed assembly, the appointment of a committee. This committee, composed of five, including the president, the secretary and the treasurer, met frequently in council, feeling that something was expected of them. But who would offer himself for this difficult work? Every one of us was occupied with professional duties or binding claims of society and home. Who would go out single-handed, to gather from the lips of the uninstructed folk the darling faiths and practices of their daily lives: and to do so by long, patient effort, helped by skilful address and pains to charm the secret from its jealous depths?[7]

In 1903 the Folk-Song Society appeared to be as moribund as its Baltimore counterpart. By 1904, however, it had members whose 'active work as collectors brought the society into considerable prominence with the general public' and in 1905 was bringing 'the idiom of the people' to pupils in schools throughout the country. The catalyst responsible for initiating this dramatic change in both the fortunes and emphasis in the Folk-Song Society's work was Cecil James Sharp (1859–1924), a fashionable musician and newly recruited folksong collector. Although Sharp never succeeded in turning the Folk-Song Society into a major force for aesthetic revival and eventually left to found the English Folk Dance Society, his role in stimulating collection and formulating the academic premises about the Folk into a full-blown ideology for revival was crucial. As Maud Karpeles, the most devoted of his many 'disciples', later recorded, his perception of folk culture was unique. It was not merely data for historical study or a source for other cultural developments but could itself be revitalised through performance:

Cecil Sharp did a great work in preserving and accurately recording so many songs and dances which would otherwise have become extinct, but his real greatness lies in what a friend has called his power of recognition. He perceived immediately that these songs and dances which had lingered on in the memories of old people were something more than a relic of the past – the mere shell of beliefs that had been outgrown and forgotten. He saw that they contained the germs of life, and that as a living expression of those unchanging human emotions which we share with our ancestors they belonged as much to this generation as to the past. This fundamental quality of the dances was well expressed by a traditional Morris dancer, who said of them: 'Our dances are now what they were and what they always will be.'[8]

Sharp rapidly developed a clear programme for initiating aesthetic change and promoting consensus through the re-introduction of the performance of folksongs. A process of internalisation begun in childhood was to be the source of both a specifically English high musical culture and 'an improvement in the musical taste of the people' intended 'to refine and strengthen the national character'. A 'National School of English music' could, he proposed, emerge only when 'every English child is, as a matter of course, made acquainted with the folk songs of his own country, then, from whatever class the musician of the future may spring, he will speak in the national musical idiom'.[9]

It is not enough to 'play with local colour'. Brahms did not write Hungarian music when he borrowed Hungarian themes. Nor did Beethoven write Russian quartets when he made use of Russian folk song. Both Brahms and Beethoven wrote German music always, because they were Germans and had been brought up on the traditions of German music. Similarly, the English musician will not necessarily write English music simply by going to English folk music for his themes. It is highly desirable that he should do so; what effect it has upon him will be all in the right direction, and it will, at least, aid in popularizing English folk song. But an English school of music is not going to be founded in that way. For that we must wait until the younger generations have been familiarized with folk song. We must leave it to them to restore English music to its rightful position – to do for our country what Glinka and his followers did for theirs.[10]

The education system was to be the key to promoting such a generation:

The ideal school song should satisfy two conditions. It should, of course, be music of the highest and purest quality. But this is not enough. It must also be attractive to children and be easily assimilated by them. Many, perhaps most, of the songs that are now sung in our elementary schools satisfy one or other of these requirements; few satisfy both. Good music is often dull to children, difficult to sing, and difficult to understand; while the music which is immediately attractive to them is often little better than rubbish. These considerations point to the folk song as the ideal musical food for very young children. Folk songs most certainly belong to the category of good music; they are natural, pure and simple. They are, moreover, attractive to children, easily comprehended, and easily learned by them.... Above all, they must be of the same nationality as that of the children: English folk songs for English children, not German, French, or even Scottish or Irish....

If some such scheme as this which we have been considering were adopted in the State schools throughout the country, and in the preparatory schools of the upper and middle classes as well, not only would the musical taste of the nation be materially raised, but a beneficent and enduring effect would be produced upon the national character. For good music purifies, just as bad music vulgarizes; indeed, the effect of music upon the minds of children is so subtle and so far-reaching that it is impossible to exaggerate the harmful influence upon character which the singing of coarse and vulgar tunes may have. Up till now, the street song has had an open field; the music taught in the schools has been hopelessly beaten in the fight for supremacy. But the mind that has been fed upon the pure melody of the folk will instinctively detect the poverty-stricken tones of the music-hall, and refuse to be captivated and deluded by their superficial attractiveness.[11]

Sharp's proposals were made in 1907, just over four years after his accidental first collection of a folksong in a Somerset garden. His subsequent experiences apparently bore out contemporary views that degeneration was not merely affecting urban life but was spreading outwards to contaminate rural culture. Even in 1892, Lucy Broadwood suggested, few country people were interested in listening to folksongs: 'when once started, the greater number of the singers find a good deal of difficulty in leaving off, for they are not unnaturally pleased to see their old songs appreciated by anybody in these degenerate days'.[12]

By 1907, Sharp could conclude that the visits of the middle-class fieldworker were welcomed with excited anticipation as offering the only audience for the elderly inheritors of folk culture:

Imagine, then, their joy when the collector calls upon them and tells them of his love for the old ditties. He has only to convince them of his sincerity to have them at his mercy. They will sing to him in their old quavering voices until they can sing no more; and, when he is gone, they will ransack their memories that they may give him of their best, should he, perchance, call again, as he promised.[13]

A Folk Revival was therefore held up as performing a dual service to national culture and contemporary society. The enticing prospect Sharp offered to potential revivalists was the existence of a grateful and welcoming peasantry eagerly awaiting the collector of folksongs who, by re-introducing their music into culture through the education system, could then ensure that, re-unified, 'the English people enter once again into the full possession of their musical heritage'.

Today, this 'rescue' of England's folksongs and dances is no longer presented with quite such uncritical triumphalism. Cecil Sharp's role and motives in advocating a Folk Revival are in question, and increasingly, the processes through which the Revival developed have come to be discussed in terms of mediation and expropriation. Through the Revival, it is now suggested, cultural products of the rural working class were taken from them and daintily and selectively re-worked for school and drawing room performance by a coterie of upper-middle-class collectors who profited financially and in status as a result.[14]

Contemporary sources offer much to support such positions. Publications of the time voluminously demonstrate that Cecil Sharp's assumption of a leading role and undermining of possible rivals to hegemonic control of the Revival were the subject of private and public controversy among fellow collectors and would-be revivalists. 'He puffed and boomed and shoved and ousted, and used the Press to advertise himself' was the epitaph of one bruised former colleague.[15] And despite claims of editorial transparency, the representation of folk culture appears to have fared little better. Setting aside the already well documented issue of bowdlerisation, discrepancies between field notes and published material indicate that rewriting of texts and privileging of findings supportive of current theory were widely practised by Revival collectors. Conversely, research which challenged established assumptions and practices was dismissed as not conforming to 'the general experience of collectors' and subsequently ignored.[16] Under such circumstances, how far what was presented as 'folksong and dance' represents the actual repertoires and performances of the turn of the century rural working class becomes highly problematic.

A more critical evaluation of the processes of collection than is offered by the image of an engaging eccentric on a bicycle offering to swap songs for pints can also be sustained. For all collectors' protestations, the peasantry did not necessarily overflow with joy at the arrival of a stranger bent on notating their songs and dances. 'Our old village people have a wonderful knack of turning the conversation onto the subject of their own ailments as soon as one begins to try and elicit any information', sighed Margaret Lee of her unsuccessful 'efforts to find out something that might be of use'. Another correspondent, asked to 'seek out songs' for the collector Lucy Broadwood, frankly admitted defeat: 'I had no idea that our old men were so stupid. No sooner do they see my paper and pencil than they become dumb: in fact, not only dumb, but sulky: so I have abandoned the pursuit.'[17] Among more determined collectors, means of achieving co-operation were not always well judged. The strain put on relationships within close communities by Cecil Sharp's 'buying' the Bampton morris dances from William Wells [18] and the Winster tune from 'Dodger' Boam[19] was, even recently, considered worthy of comment among local people. The process the collector presented as 'Friendliness, combined with judicious *backsheesh*, in the way of snuff, tobacco, tea, and ale' as the means of 'unloosening tongues' and 'reviving memories'[20] was often perceived very differently by fellow villagers, intimately aware of the network of occupational and familial obligations inherent in social life. Contemporary descriptions of collection do not address the moral implications of paying individuals to obtain details of what was clearly a matter of group knowledge, still less the issue of possible loss of marginal earnings by traditional performers when publication rendered their dances and plays generally available for revival re-creation.[21]

Persistence or cunning in obtaining traditions against the odds – usually consisting of the wishes of the Folk themselves – was presented as a necessary constituent of collection. Sharp's 'persuasion' of the Kirkby Malzeard sword team that they should undertake the laborious process of dancing for his notation, although it was nine o'clock at night and they were just returning from a day's work in the fields, is most clearly representative of this aspect of contemporary collector-source relationships.[22] Kate Lee's 'enterprise' in taking a job as a waitress 'to get hold of some folk songs which she knew were reserved for the ears of the frequenters of a country inn in the Broads' was construed as a 'desperate' but laudable action, saving 'precious folk songs ... for the benefit of society'.[23] Even within this context, however, Percy Grainger's tricking an elderly woman into singing songs he had earlier been refused, by hiding under her bed and recording the results of a request for them from her grand-daughter, cannot easily be characterised as anything but ruthless expropriation.[24]

Where singers were willing participants in the collection process, their permitted role was highly restricted. As E. V. Lucas noted in his lightly fictionalised account of Cecil Sharp's working practices, 'extraneous' activity was generally discouraged:

I took all the opportunities I could of getting Uncle Jonah, the voiceless shepherd in the smock, to talk of old times; but always with the fear of the Director [Sharp] very lively in me. For anecdotage is nothing to him. His purpose in life is to fill blank bars with little magical dots; for this and this only does he scour the coloured counties. All conversation is therefore an interruption, if not a misdemeanour.[25]

As observed by Lucas, the other side of this relationship was equally closely drawn. Collectors might perceive 'something rather pretty about the willingness of the poor to sing hunting-songs – to praise a sport which exists wholly for their masters and in which they cannot participate'. They might note that after a long day's work in the fields and the rain, 'the English peasant' was paid 'insufficient shillings to add meat to the family table' , but their role was limited to 'merely recording the fact'. Or in Sharp's description of his own work, 'he is merely a collector and preserver of the best old English songs that he has the fortune to hear'.[26]

Once attained, possession of the materials of folk culture was put to a variety of purposes. In the early struggle between Cecil Sharp and Mary Neal for supremacy within the Revival, the amount of traditional material accrued and access to its performers was offered as a crucial indicator of suitability for leadership. Mary Neal juxtaposed her 'quite long list of people and places as yet unvisited which may yield dances yet unrecorded' with the comment that 'Mr Cecil Sharp has announced many dances and variants collected but not published'.[27] Indeed, J. A. Fuller-Maitland's description of the folksong movement arising out of the need of collectors to 'gather together their *trophies* [my italics] in a permanent record'[28] seems particularly apposite at a time when the drive for acquisition was such that, in one case at least, two fieldworkers representing the rival groups were in daily competition to be first to reach a local workhouse and record the inhabitants.[29] In more exalted cultural circles, 'the unexpected treasure

trove of English folk song' provided proponents of the Revival like
Ralph Vaughan Williams, Gustav Holst, Percy Grainger and
George Butterworth with the materials to 'found themselves' and
assume significant roles in the renaissance of English orchestral
music.[30] The nature of the relationship between such uses of
folksongs and songs as they existed in performers' repertoires is,
however, problematic. In what ways, for example, does Vaughan
Williams's smooth, rhapsodic treatment of 'Lovely Joan' relate to
the uneasy sexual politics of collected texts, or his creation of a
triumphal march meet the parable of material inequities, good, evil
and their eternal consequences in 'Dives and Lazarus'? The aesthetic possibilities of a combination of notes and intervals, rather
than the fusion of text, music and personal identification inherent
in singers' performances, appears to have characterised any composition that was not simply 'a folksong setting'. By expropriating
only a few elements of complex performances, classical musicians
elided 'treasure trove' and travesty.

What financial returns collectors acquired from copyrighting
folk music, producing songbooks, instructional manuals for dancing, arrangements of folksongs or the supervision of teaching
courses has never been fully investigated. The royalties from his
six arrangements of the morris dance tune 'Country Gardens' were
significant enough for Percy Grainger to be able, in 1924, to offer
'a proportion' to Sharp for assistance with his work. In 1910,
Sharp's income from full-time promotion of the Revival was
£5136 – £373 of which was from royalties and £161 from lecturing. By 1922, he was earning enough from his publications and
lecturing to consider it appropriate to relinquish his Civil List
Pension. But a clash of interest in the need to recommend his own
works – which arose following his appointment as Occasional
Inspector of Training Colleges in Folk-Song and Dancing by H. A.
L. Fisher, Vaughan Williams's brother in law, was left unresolved
after Sharp declined the suggestion that he 'should get rid of his
rights in the books' and continued in the job.

Detail of the amounts of royalty and other payments is difficult
to establish. Even in correspondence among literary collaborators,
actual figures rarely seem to be mentioned. During the lengthy
wrangle over *Singing Games*, a series edited by Lady Gomme and
Cecil Sharp and published by Novello, Alfred Nutt, the publisher
of earlier volumes edited by Lady Gomme under an identical title,

addressed her very clearly on the issues, though not the sums, involved:

I am more than ever convinced that the projected publication of Mr Sharp would effectually destroy the sale of our Singing Games. I must again point out that profit could only accrue from the Singing Games provided the sales of the latter were to be continued in the same proportion [approximately 250 copies per year] as during the last two years. If the two books [published by Nutt] are kept on sale and your interest in them is continued there would be immediately (as you would have a royalty) profit for you and ultimately there would be profit for me.

It is this certain profit derivable from the Singing Games which I maintain you are throwing away for an interest in Mr Sharp's book. Doubtless however you consider that *you* will be amply compensated, but you must yourself see that I should be absolutely sacrificed for honestly I cannot believe that Mr Sharp is serious in believing that his book would be a help to the sale of Singing Games.

Under these circumstances I can only consent to the matter in which I claim a copyright being used in the compilation of another book, upon the terms of my receiving a royalty on the copies sold. You have not stated upon what terms it is proposed that Novellos should bring out the book but these can surely be modified so as to admit me to such a share as would compensate me for the loss the publication would otherwise entail upon me.

Gomme and Sharp stuck to their guns, and the Novello *Singing Games* were published. The problem of paying royalties to Nutt for singing games collected by Alice Gomme was evaded by using near-identical variants which had been collected by Cecil Sharp. The Novello booklets are still in print and the descendants of Lady Gomme ceased receiving royalties from them only in 1988.[32] Within the English Folk Dance and Song Society, breaking the monopoly which allowed the Sharp Trustees and Novello to control the form, price and returns from performance of the folksongs and dances the Society used led to prolonged and acrimonious debate, and ultimately the resignation of the most vocal of Sharp's Trustees, Maud Karpeles, and other longstanding members, from its Executive Committee in 1937/8. Although the immediate controversy arose from Novello's decision to join the Performing Rights Society in 1936 – perhaps to ensure full returns from the use of published versions of folksongs in programmes of Community Singing – the issue of copyright clearly raised larger, ethical questions for the Revival. How, in the first instance, had Sharp come to set up a national organisation solely devoted to the performance of his own copyright works? The answer, the Chairman of the English Folk Dance and Song Society reported not altogether convincingly, lay in timing – Sharp 'had not lived long enough to regularise the position'.[33] On Sharp's death, therefore, 'the inheritance which he left to his children' consisted of a fifteen per cent royalty from all his publications and 'artistic control' of their use – effectively exercised by Maud Karpeles. After two years of vituperation, the Society's Executive Committee took the matter out of the hands of the Sharp Trustees by making its own arrangements of the 'country, morris and sword dance airs' Sharp had collected, and doing a deal with Novello's which allocated ten per cent of royalties to the Sharp Trust and five per cent to the Society itself. This move also 'liberated' the price of publications – the cost of the *Country Dance Books*, for example, was reduced from four shillings to sixpence within a year. But in the longer term, what Frank Howes, the Chairman of the Society's National Executive, identified as the structural paradox remained unresolved – 'the difficulty of reconciling the view that it is fantastic that the dances and tunes which three or four hundred years ago belonged to the people of England should now be private property with the other view that the collector who has spent time, trouble and money upon the work of collection has a legal right to a financial reward'.[34]

Whether the moneys deriving from their roles as collectors, arrangers or administrators were substantial or negligible however, there was no legal necessity for collectors to offer payment to the material's original performers. The ruling that 'the 'report' or 'version' of the words and tune of a song, or the melody of a tune is the property of the person who has noted it' is contemporary with the rise of the Folk Revival.[35] As a legal adviser from Novello, the major folksong publishers, pointed out:

The source is open to all, and any one is at liberty to make use of that source, and provided his matter is derived directly from the source and not from someone else's work, he has the copyright of the matter which his enquiries have produced. The copyright of the matter which you have collected is therefore yours so long as you can show that you have obtained it direct from the source and not from [another collector's] work.[36]

Revival collectors' actions must, of course, be considered in light of contemporary, rather than late twentieth-century, attitudes. In such a highly stratified society, was what appears to us today as widespread exploitation – or at least patronisation of – performers necessarily felt to be so at the time? Were singers and dancers in fact, generally flattered by middle-class attention or gratified that their activities were considered worthy of publication? So little evidence of performers' reactions exists that we have no means of judging. Genuine regard seems to pervade the letters from Cecil Sharp's informants published in his biography and some of them certainly maintained an exchange of correspondence – and gifts – with him over a period of years.[37] But for all their lengthy and close association, letters from William Kimber were addressed respectfully to 'Mr Sharp', whereas Sharp replied with the more familiar 'Kimber'. And, if only for the sake of balance, it would be useful to have some idea of how the men of the Ilminster morris team – whom Sharp described as being 'very uncouth' referred to him. The disjunction between what the theory of the Folk prescribed and the reality of the living singers and dancers encountered in fieldwork in rural England admitted little publishable interchange. And despite innovative approaches, such as Percy Grainger's detailed consideration of the interaction between named singers' background, temperament and approach to performance, during the early period of the Revival the evidence on relations between the majority of collectors and the individual men and women who constituted 'the source' seems to consist of vague generalities about the 'hard working, jovial and respectfully independent' salt of the earth on the one part, and silence on the other.[38]

The Folk were not, in any case, the central concern of turn-of-the-century Revival collection. By definition, they represented only a scattered and dwindling handful of individuals, who had 'but little idea' of the importance of the culture they possessed. A more significant dynamic in collection was their culture's 'rescue' by those who *had* a clear idea of its worth. Even at the time, a certain unease was felt at the moral implications of this process. Sharp noted his 'embarrassment' when a singer's neighbours asked him whether he was 'going to make a deal o' money out o' this, sir ?' He was 'relieved' when the singer explained to them that it was only his hobby.[39] Agricultural labourers' wages at the turn of the century were often less than a pound per week. Although there is no suggestion that collectors made a fortune from their activities, whatever their earnings from folksong, they can hardly have been unaware that they were considerably more wealthy than the villagers whose songs they profited from. Moreover, because folksongs were presumed to be nearly extinct, it was often from the old and infirm, the inhabitants of workhouses, that material was sought. In these, or indeed in other circumstances, there is no evidence that a choice between peppermints, a one-off payment or an income from copyright was ever offered.

The implications of expropriation are not, however, simplistically financial. Sharp commented that in buying songs from a singer, he didn't 'rob them as I should if I bought their old tables and chairs'.[40] And, from the contemporary singer's point of view, some aspects of the transformation involved were relatively unproblematic in kind. Performers had sold broadsides and chapbooks at fairs and public gatherings until the recent past, and the sale of sheet music was a major commercial enterprise. Some singers had a semi-professional role within their own communities, and were rewarded with money, drink and status for performances in pubs, at weddings or harvest homes. Equally, public performance of traditional dances and plays had long had commodity value. A money-for-singing exchange was not, therefore, unfamiliar.

Although it contained some of the elements of a communal performance, however, the transaction between a collector and singer was different in its implications and results. The distinction between Grainger's acquisition of material by deceit and Henry Burstow, the Sussex bellringer and singer, exploiting a fellow bellringer's competitiveness to obtain a performance of a song he had earlier refused to let Burstow hear, lies in the purpose to which that acquisition was put.[41] A collector's purchase of songs involved not an individual singer's or a community's response to performance, but the extraction of an item of culture for an extrinsic purpose. What had been a social activity, with a range of personally and locally determined symbolic and material rewards, was objectified. As a result of the process of collection, singing became a number of folksongs, dancing a fashionable form of exercise or a professional requirement for the school curriculum – each was isolated in a new, constructed setting.

Where comments from singers and dancers involved in this process have been recorded, the sense of loss of control and specific association with their culture assumes at least as great importance as questions of money. Publishing instructions for performance removed a cardinal function and privilege of morris or sword team membership – the power of choosing who could dance their dance. In many instances, such considerations formed only a part of much larger issues associated with the perception of particular customary performances within communities. However apocryphal the events, the status of being a member of a morris team which had reputedly danced before the Prince of Wales or on carpets of gold sovereigns was effective and genuine for performers and home audience. A village custom which was 'the only one of its kind' gave distinction to the whole community. Opening up the personnel and locations in which a performance could take place reduced the perceived uniqueness supporting a team's or village's identity.

Within communities, particular songs were also frequently associated with individual singers and, although known to others, were sung only by that one singer. Recent research has suggested that in such cases, the identification of the material and performer can be total:

At one point, then, Janet perceives that this song *is* her mother, and at another she thinks the song is *me*. The song is so familiar that it has gained the power of a symbol, an expressive form which somehow expresses, represents and even defines the essence of two people. Just as for Tibby the song had associations with her grandfather and her childhood, so for Janet to hear 'The Magdalen Green' was to be 'put in contact' with the aura of her past, and if anything, this association has gained power since the death of her mother. Her mother is gone, but the song that *was* her, remains.[42]

However skilled and considerate the intervention of a collector in these circumstance, difficulties can be felt:

For Janet to sing one of her mother's songs without her approval was somehow tantamount to theft in Tibby's view, and similarly, Janet expressed a feeling of guilt or disloyalty after having only talked about Tibby's songs to a Scottish folklorist. To her, this was akin to exposing something very personal to strangers.[43]

This existence of songs as highly condensed and powerful symbols of personal identity creates questions about the interpretation of the experiences recorded by early collectors. Lucy Broadwood noted that a singer might be 'reserved' about singing a song which was 'most truly a *part of himself*' (my italics), but saw an elderly woman as putting on 'all the airs of a capricious operatic favourite' when, on the occasion the collectors arrived to visit her, the singer felt her voice was not capable of doing her songs justice.[44] Equally, Frank Kidson noted the congruence of personal feeling and choice of song among the singers he collected from. But we can only surmise what memories and concepts of self are unrecorded in his conclusion that it is 'from stupidity' that 'an old fellow ... will only give voice to some bygone favourite comic song of fifty years ago that was the joy of his boyhood days'.[45] An awareness of the identification of a singer and a song which developed over time among perceptive collectors was not necessarily outweighed by their drive to obtain the song for culture – and their personal collections.

In whatever ways Revival collection was – or is – interpreted, therefore, one incontrovertible outcome remains. Outside all but a small number of specialist publications, it is not the names of singers like Louie Hooper, Lucy White, Joseph Taylor and Dean Robinson which are linked with English folk music at the turn of the century but those of Cecil Sharp, Sabine Baring-Gould, Ralph Vaughan Williams and Percy Grainger. As Kidson, himself a notable collector, proposed: 'Soon their fathers' and grandfathers' songs will be entirely forgotten, and we must thank those people who have rescued so many beautiful folk-songs from oblivion, and given them a permanent place in their admirable collections.'[46]

Concentrating exclusively on the relations between collectors and the expressive culture collected, however, offers relatively little to illuminate the processes of the Folk Revival as a mass movement. In terms of the Revival as a whole, issues such as the establishment of a hegemonic position and profiting from the development of a popular market in folk culture are dynamic effects rather than directly causal factors in the change from archival collection to collection for conscious re-performance. Though their significance as mechanisms for continuance should not be underestimated, the possibilities for deriving status and cash through the creation of a Folk Revival applied only to a limited number of individuals. In the drive to replace the Folk, the *duty* of salvaging culture was taken on by large numbers of people. It is not simply the implications of instituting and actively directing a Revival which can be engaged but also the ideology and socio-cultural context of those involved in the mass movement. To understand the development of a nationwide society, it is necessary to attempt to assess why numbers of middle- and some working-class people found it necessary and appealing to take on the role of 'the peasantry'.

Notes

1 A. L. P., 'For C.J.S.,' *English Dance and Song*, XIII:5 (Sept. 1949), 76. Sections of this chapter were first presented as a paper at the Kommission für Volksdichtung at the Deutsches Volksliedarchiv in Freiburg in May 1989 and were then published in the volume of conference proceedings – see Tom Cheesman, ed., *Recent Ballad Research*, vol. 2, Folklore Society Library Publications no. 5 (London: Folklore Society Library, 1990), pp. 75–90.

2 Ralph Vaughan Williams, 'Lucy Broadwood 1858–1929,' *Journal of the English Folk Dance and Song Society*, V:3 (1948), 137. Having begun collecting folksong in 1903, Vaughan Williams (1872–1958) became a member of the Folk-Song Society's Committee in 1904 as a result of a move, largely initiated by Cecil Sharp, to revive it from its 'moribund' state. He was a consistent supporter of Sharp's position in the latter's many battles over the revival of folksong and dance. As a member of the Executive and Board of Artistic Control of the English Folk Dance Society and the English Folk Dance and Song Society, Vaughan Williams maintained a lifelong and active association with the movement Sharp founded.

3 Frederick Keel, 'The Folk Song Society 1898–1948,' *ibid.*, 111. Keel trained as a singer at the Royal Academy of Music, where he later taught. He was elected to the Committee of the Folk-Song Society in 1905, consolidating the 'infusion' of a 'new spirit' begun the previous year. With him came the musicians Percy Grainger and Roger Quilter and the collector Anne G. Gilchrist. Keel was to play a major role in organising the amalgamation of the Folk-Song Society and the English Folk Dance Society in 1932. See his obituary in *English Dance and Song*, XIX:2 (Oct.- Nov. 1954), 69–70 for further details of his career and associations with the folksong movement.

4 Iolo A. Williams *English Folk-Song and Dance* (London: Longmans, Green & Co., 1935), p. 190.

5 Vaughan Williams, 'Lucy Broadwood 1858–1929,' p. 137.

6 Keel, 'The Folk Song Society 1898–1948,' pp. 112–13. Lucy Broadwood, Frank Kidson, Alice Gomme and Kate Lee were probably the only members with any experience as collectors on this committee of fourteen. With the exception of Kidson, even among this small number, experience of field collecting was of limited type. More typical was A. P. Graves, who suggested the founding of the Folk-Song Society, the Welsh Folk Song Society and the Irish Folk Song Society. Graves apparently only ever collected one folk tune – as a result of hearing a street musician playing outside his study window. See Alfred Perceval Graves, *Irish Literary and Musical Studies* (London: Elkin Mathews, 1913), p. 178. I am most grateful to Tom Munnelly for drawing this article to my attention.

7 Mrs Waller R. Bullock, 'The Collection of Maryland Folk-Lore,' *Journal of American Folklore*, XI (1898), 7–16.

8 Maud Karpeles, 'English Folk Dances, their Survival and Revival,' *Folk-Lore*, XLIII (1932), 139. Karpeles's partiality, however, exaggerates Sharp's foresight in terms of folk dance.

9 Cecil Sharp, *English Folk-Song: Some Conclusions*, ed. Maud Karpeles (Wakefield: E.P. Publishing Ltd, 1972), pp. 169 and 173. [Originally published in 1907 in Taunton by Barnicott and Pearce.]

10 *Ibid.*, pp. 169–70.

11 *Ibid.*, pp. 171–3 [passim]

12. Lucy E. Broadwood and J. A. Fuller Maitland, *English County Songs* (London: J. B. Cramer & Son Ltd, ND [1892]), p. iv.

13 Sharp, *Some Conclusions*, p. 133.

14 See for example, James Reeves, *The Idiom of the People: English Traditional Verse Edited with an Introduction and Notes from the Manuscripts of Cecil Sharp* (London: William Heinemann Ltd, 1958) and *The Everlasting Circle: English Traditional Verse from the Mss of S. Baring-Gould, H. E. D. Hammond and George B. Gardiner* (London: William Heinemann Ltd, 1960); A. L. Lloyd, *Folksong in England* (London: Lawrence & Wishart, 1967) on bowdlerisation and mediation and Vic Gammon, 'Folk Song Collecting in Sussex and Surrey, 1843–1914,' *History Workshop Journal*, X (autumn 1980), 61–89; Michael Pickering, *Village Song and Culture: A Study Based on the Blunt Collection of Song from Adderbury North Oxfordshire* (London: Croom Helm, 1982) and Dave Harker, *Fakesong: The Manufacture of British 'Folksong' 1700 to the Present Day* (Milton Keynes: Open University Press, 1985) for lengthy discussions of aspects of mediation and expropriation. A succinct overview of 'the assemblage of an English folk song tradition' is also presented in Michael Pickering and Tony Green's 'Towards a Cartography of the Vernacular Milieu,' in Michael

Pickering and Tony Green, ed., *Everyday Culture: Popular Song and the Vernacular Milieu* (Milton Keynes: Open University, 1987), pp. 1–37.

15 Letter from Lucy Broadwood (sometime Hon. Secretary of the Folk-Song Society and Editor of its *Journal*) to her sister Bertha, 22 July 1924 held in Papers of Lucy Etheldred Broadwood, Surrey Record Office, 2297/3/. See also Frank Kidson's less than enthusiastic review of *English Folk-Song: Some Conclusions* in *The Musical Times*, 1 Jan. 1908, 23–4. Kidson's suggestion that Sharp's 'assured conviction' cannot have 'been hastily arrived at' seems a deliberate irony in view of the comments of his friend and colleague, Broadwood, on the same subject. Writing to fellow collector, the Rev. James Duncan, Broadwood said, 'I wish rather that Mr Sharp had been an older folk-songist before bringing out this book – generalisations, exaggerations, loose statements, hastily written, self contradictory' (Letter dated 28 Nov. 1907 in Aberdeen University Library Archives MSS 988/16/28 quoted in Ian A. Olson 'The Influence of the Folk Song Society on the Greig-Duncan Folk Song Collection: Methodology,' *Folk Music Journal*, V:2 (1986), 176–201). Mary Neal, whose work on a national revival of folk dance predated that of Sharp, was equally forthright in public: see for example her description of Sharp's actions in the section on 'The Present-Day Revival of the Folk-Dance' in Frank Kidson and Mary Neal, *English Folk-Song & Dance* (Cambridge: Cambridge University Press, 1915), pp. 158–73.

16 See the Editorial Committee's comment (p. 159) on Percy Grainger's 'Collecting with the Phonograph,' *Journal of the Folk-Song Society*, III:3 (May 1908), 147–242.

17 Letter from Margaret L. Lee to Alice Gomme, 18 Sept. 1891, Gomme Collection, Folklore Society Archive, University College London and anonymous correspondent quoted in Broadwood and Maitland, *English County Songs*, p. iv.

18 'Sharp invited Wells over to Stow in August 1909 and got him to teach the [Bampton] dances to a side of family, servants and friends for which he was paid. This money never found its way back to the team and Wells was accused of selling the morris.' Roy Dommett, 'The Cotswold Morris in the Twentieth Century,' in T. Buckland, ed., *Traditional Dance: Vol. I* (Crewe: Crewe & Alsager College of Education, 1982), p. 70.

19 'He [Cecil Sharp] sat behind a wall. The music hadn't been set down – and me dad said he got if off for a pint of beer.' Lewis Boam [no relation to 'Dodger'], private communication, 4 March, 1986.

20 Alfred Perceval Graves, *Irish Literary and Musical Studies*, p. 180.

21 As Sharp himself recorded ('Folk Dance Notes,' vol. 1, folio 200), the practice of charging for teaching dances to new members was well

established in morris teams. The comments of Joseph Druce, reported in Sharp's 'Some Notes on the Morris Dance,' *EFDS Journal*, I:1 (1914), 7, should be seen as much in this light as in Sharp's representation of it as an expression of scorn for the Espérance Revival. For more comprehensive discussion of the role of charges to novice dancers (and examples of its occurrence in longsword teams) see Cindy Sughrue, 'Continuity, Conflict and Change: A Contextual and Comparative Study of Three South Yorkshire Longsword Dance Teams' (unpublished PhD thesis, University of Sheffield, 1989), pp. 20–1. I am most grateful to Ms Sughrue for providing me with copies of relevant sections of her exemplary and enjoyable thesis.

22 Montague Rendall, 'Personal Memories of Cecil Sharp,' *EFDS News*, II:16 (Feb. 1928), 79.

23 Graves, *Irish Literary and Musical Studies*, p. 179

24 John Bird, *Percy Grainger* (London: Elek Books Ltd, 1976), p. 105. Cecil Sharp also reportedly notated the tune of the first folksong he ever collected 'unbeknownst to John England' (the singer): see Maud Karpeles, 'New Members' Page: Talk Broadcast by Maud Karpeles,' *English Dance and Song*, XVIII:4 (Feb.-Mar. 1954), 113.

25 E. V. Lucas, *London Lavender* (London: Methuen & Co. Ltd, 1912), p. 141.

26 *Ibid.*, pp. 139–46.

27 Kidson and Neal, *English Folk-Song & Dance*, p. 130

28 J.A. Fuller-Maitland, 'The Beginning of the Folk-Song Society,' *Journal of the Folk-Song Society*, VIII:7 (1927), 46–70.

29 Michael Barlow, 'George Butterworth and the Folksong Revival,' *English Dance and Song*, XLVII:3 (autumn-winter 1985), 10.

30 The role of folk music in the careers of these and associated composers is outside the scope of this study, but see for example comments on the subject in Bird, *Percy Grainger*; Imogen Holst, *Gustav Holst: A Biography* (London: Oxford University Press, 1969); Michael Kennedy, *The Works of Ralph Vaughan Williams* (London: Oxford University Press, 1964) and Percy M. Young, *Vaughan Williams* (London: Dennis Dobson Ltd, 1953) for an indication of its significance.

31 Letter from Alfred Nutt to Lady Gomme, 29 June 1909. Copy held in Sharp Correspondence, Vaughan Williams Memorial Library, Cecil Sharp House, London.

32 Tony Gomme, private communication, Nov. 1988.

33 English Folk Dance and Song Society, *The English Folk Dance and Song Society Report September 1st, 1936, to August 31st, 1937* (London: The English Folk Dance and Song Society, 1937), pp. 15–16; *The English Folk Dance and Song Society Report September 1st, 1937,*

to *August 31st, 1938*, pp. 13–14; and *The English Folk Dance and Song Society Report September 1st, 1938, to August 31st, 1939*, pp. 17–20, 23 and 27 provide an outline of the controversy and its implications.

34 *English Folk Dance and Song Society Report September 1st, 1938, to August 31st, 1939*, pp. 18–19.

35 The rules of the Folk-Song Society, accepted by its first general meeting on 2 Feb. 1899, included the provision that 'All contributions of Members or others, whether literary or musical, accepted by the Society, shall be considered, as far as any other publication than in the Society's *Journal* is concerned, the property of the contributor, and the Society shall not reprint such contribution without his or her consent.' This rule was later supported by Counsel's Opinion (obtained around 1907), and subsequently recognised in the Copyright Act of 1911, which confirmed that the 'report' or 'version' of a Folk song is the property of the person collecting such a version or report. Keel, 'The Folk Song Society 1898–1948,' pp. 111–12.

36 Letter from Novello & Co. to Cecil Sharp, 15 Feb. 1909 held in Sharp Correspondence, Vaughan Williams Memorial Library, Cecil Sharp House, London.

37 A. H. Fox Strangways, *Cecil Sharp* (Oxford: Oxford University Press, 1933), pp. 45–6.

38 Description of team of 'Tipteers' (Sussex 'mummers') by R. J. Sharp, held in typscript in the Tyler Collection at the Centre for English Cultural Tradition and Language at the University of Sheffield. For 'The Impress of Personality in Traditional Singing,' see Grainger, 'Collecting with the Phonograph,' pp. 163–6.

39 Fox Strangways, *Cecil Sharp*, p. 36

40 *Ibid.*, p. 43.

41 'He [Henry Burstow] once set his heart upon learning a very long ballad 'off' a fellow bell-ringer, a ploughman in a neighbouring village. The ploughman declined to sing it .... So Mr. Burstow plotted. He induced a friend to lure the ploughman into the front parlour of a tavern, himself hiding in the back room. After a time Mr. Burstow's accomplice challenged the ploughman to sing as long a 'ballet' as himself. A duel of songs arose; the ballads grew and grew in length. At last the ploughman, filled with desire to 'go one verse better' than his opponent, burst out into the very song for which the bell-ringer was patiently waiting. He learned it then and there!' Lucy E. Broadwood, 'On the Collecting of English Folk-Songs,' *Proceedings of the Royal Musical Association*, (1904–5), 14 Mar. 1905, p. 99.

42 Edward Kerr Miller, 'An Ethnography of Singing: The Use and Meaning of Song Within a Scottish Family' (unpublished PhD disserta-

tion, University of Texas at Austin, 1981), p. 211. I am also most grateful to Dr Sheila Douglas for additional comments on the Weatherston family's view of their roles as singers.

43 Miller, 'An Ethnography of Singing,' p. 207.

44 Lucy E. Broadwood, 'On the Collecting of English Folk-Songs,' p. 94.

45 Kidson, *A Garland of English Folk-Songs* (London: Ascherberg, Hopwood & Crew Ltd, ND [1926]), p. v.

Chapter 4

'Merrie England once more': the battle to be the Folk

A door has been opened into a new country, which is yet as old as Merrie England.[1]

By the beginning of the twentieth century, the need for a radical reform of all manifestations of popular culture was accepted as an urgent priority across the ideological spectrum. Commercial popular culture – particularly that associated with the working classes – had implications which were as unacceptable to the political, arts and educational establishments as to Utopian socialists and Fabians. Uneasily accommodated within the processes re-creating dominant ideology, popular music was variously perceived as a challenge to the class system, a threat to morality and a perverter of art. The construction of folk culture as a national art with 'no sham, no got-up glitter and no vulgarity', produced by the race before the emergence of capitalism and class, offered both a welcome counterbalance and an obvious and necessary source of replacement.

But this potential fount of national salvation had itself fallen into unreliable hands. The Folk, it was authoritatively maintained, had imperilled the existence of their own culture. When they moved into towns during the Industrial Revolution, they abandoned their priceless heritage of folk traditions – songs, dances, customs, and stories all ceased to be performed.[2] Moreover, the case against the Folk proceeds, the heritage wasn't just endangered by changed physical surroundings. Folk culture hadn't simply proved incapable of transference into a new urban context, an irreplaceable loss had almost occurred because the Folk had been wilfully derelict in their duty towards their culture. By the mid nineteenth century, 'the modern spirit' had 'infected' all the natural inheritors of folk tradition, and 'the raucous, unlovely and vulgarising music hall song' held sway. Even in rural areas, folksongs had actually been 'rejected' by country people, 'who forty or fifty years ago had scornfully refused to accept these ... songs from their parents'.[3] The common people had proved unsuitable heirs of the national culture.

Such a failing was not, however, entirely unexpected. It had long been understood that the Folk had lost any creative ability. This, coupled with their forgetfulness and lack of sensibility, was actively damaging what traditions they did unwittingly retain. Steps to replace this dwindling, elderly, anachronistic body with new, aware and active inheritors would therefore be not merely logical but just. A national movement was called for so that all that was deepest, most characteristic and best in English culture would once again be in the hands of the race, where its true value would be fully appreciated.

But despite this general agreement about the nature of the crises underlying the need for a Folk Revival, in almost every other respect unanimity among its proponents was rare. In the attempts to create the basis of a nationwide movement between 1904 and 1911, the main cultural form chosen for revival was switched from folksong to dance. Characteristically, this shift was not the result of considered analysis of the genre best suited to propagation but arose from profound disagreement within the membership of the Folk-Song Society Committee. Following the subsequent moves to popularise dance, an intense struggle was joined over the style, means of dissemination and purpose of revival. Every aspect of performance, from the type of dress required to the social groups taking part, were the subject of controversy in an increasingly acrimonious public campaign.

The nature and influence of such differences should not be underestimated. What was involved was more than petulance among a coterie of enthusiasts for tripping it featly over the greensward. The conflicts, and their results, had significant long-term implications. Taking the decision to turn performance for interest and entertainment in a single place into a movement to revivify traditional forms of performance nationally posed a variety of question about the nature and purposes of such a revival. To a great extent, action and reaction to the multiplicity of trivial

and major issues raised during this period have influenced the
form and ideology of the movement to the present day. In some
extreme cases, what was a hastily concocted response to a rival's
letter to the press later assumed the significance of carefully formulated doctrine.

But at the time of the Revival's inception, these internal matters
were subsumed within an even greater issue – the potential of a
Folk Revival as a source of hegemony in national culture. For all
its contrived rusticity, the Revival's existence as the expression of
the perceived culture and social cohesiveness of the pre-industrial
village had a power beyond the fashionable and quaint. Folk
dances and songs and the processes of their regeneration offered
the content and means for the actualising 'Merrie England' – a
potent symbol for a range of contemporary ideological positions.
Culture had developed in ways which were widely perceived as
'unnatural'. Commercialism, progress, irreligion, science, capitalism or greed were variously proposed as fuelling a perverted
descent into industrialisation, mass culture and urbanisation.
'Natural' forms of social expression – particularly the rural, com-
munity-based, 'native arts' cohering around 'Merrie England' –
were therefore found a role in considerably differing ideological
formulations. To conservatives, the concept implied a reversion to
the historical balance of contented class relations, a pastorale,
where the middle as well as the labouring classes happily accepted
their allotted places. Removal of the consequences of capitalism
also characterised the just and joyous, de-industrialised common-
wealth represented by the 'Merrie England' of socialists like William Morris and Robert Blatchford.[4] All that might be projected
into 'Englishness' – the emergent form of national consciousness
which was 'the preoccupation not only of the political culture, but
also of what we might now call the institutions and practices of a
cultural politics' – was at stake.[5] To gain control of the Revival
was, therefore, of major cultural and political significance. Before
this could be achieved, however, opposing intellectual, class, gender, commercial and political interests would have to be confronted. The proposed culture and identity of the new Folk were
thus bitterly contested.

Ostensibly, early battles were based on rather esoteric grounds
of definition. Personality, hegemonic control within the Revival
and the influence of the musical and educational establishments

were, however, more significant determinants of the conflict and its outcome. Cecil Sharp came to folksong scholarship later than a number of existing committee members of the Folk-Song Society and his experience was of a highly specific type. His field collecting had taken place over a short and recent period and had been based entirely in the rural areas of the south-west of England. More seriously for his standing in a group whose approach to scholarship was essentially antiquarian, Sharp's knowledge of songs in earlier printed sources – especially in broadside and other popular literature was not extensive. His theorising on folksong was none the less confident, wide-ranging and dogmatic; folksongs were racial products which had been spontaneously created by continuity, variation and selection among the common people. Almost all existing forms of scholarship were misconceived. 'To search for the originals of folk songs amongst the printed music of olden days is mere waste of time', he asserted, since folksongs were entirely oral in origin and transmission. The corollary of his proposals was inescapable; the only musical source of cultural improvement was pure folksong, and the only accurate, logical and acceptable definition of such folksong was that developed by Cecil Sharp. Although Sharp and his admirers brought coherence and direction to the Folk-Song Society, his abrasive, highly public advocacy of his own views did little to foster the support of a majority of committee members.

Underlying resentment within the Folk-Song Society Committee soon found a focus in a controversy over the role of 'national songs' in education.[6] Seventeenth- and eighteenth-century British songs of known authorship had formed a significant part of school repertoire since 1871, when provision was first made for the inclusion of music in the curriculum. With the rise of interest in folksong at the turn of the century, however, there was increasing support for its introduction into schools. In 1905, this epidemic of 'Folksongitis' resulted in the Board of Education recommending in their *Suggestions for the Consideration of Teachers* that 'national or folk songs' should provide the basis of music teaching. Although he had, only three years earlier, himself compiled *A Book of British Song for Home and School* which included both national and 'country songs' drawn from the works of Folk-Song Society members,[7] Sharp publicly repudiated the validity of this conjoint formula. National and folksongs should not be confused and were certainly not of equal educational value, he insisted. National songs were 'obviously lacking in those especial qualities that characterize ... folksongs'. Folksongs alone were 'the ideal musical food for very young children' and 'above all', they must be English – 'English folk songs for English children, ... German, French, or even Scottish or Irish' would not do.

Fired by such a 'reckless and unjustifiable attack upon the list of songs issued by the Board of Education', Sir Charles Stanford, the Vice-President of the Folk-Song Society, opened an equally public campaign against Sharp. Supported by notables such as Arthur Somervell, the Chief Music Inspector, and W. G. McNaught, the editor of both Curwen's *School Music Series* and the *School Music Review*, the Folk-Song Society Committee reinforced their alignment with the Board of Education. With Somervell's encouragement and the agreement of the majority of the Committee, Stanford first attacked Sharp's thesis in the press and then went on in 1906 to produce an extremely successful *National Song Book*. Sharp countered with a book of *Folk-Songs for Schools*, advertised as a collection 'made to meet the requirements of the Board of Education' and dedicated 'by permission' to his former pupils 'their Royal Highnesses Prince Edward and Prince Albert of Wales'. This shrewd piece of marketing allowed him to maintain his position in the educational field. But his extended theoretical riposte, hastily-written, contradictory and wearisomely overburdened with justification of his position in the national songs controversy, was *English Folk-Song: Some Conclusions*.[8] Although later presented as a 'towering beacon' which expressed his 'considered opinion' on English folksong, *Some Conclusions'* chief contemporary effect was to exacerbate Sharp's isolation and compound the rift with the folksong establishment. From 1907, it became virtually inevitable that the 'popularization' Sharp envisaged could occur only outside the Folk-Song Society.

Sharp's autocratic temperament and uncompromising approach to the specialist field were not the only sources of dissatisfaction with his views. In the main, his theoretical writings on folksong, dance and custom were based on combinations of proposals put forward by other scholars, rather than original premises deriving from his own research.[9] The contradictions this synthesised approach could entail on occasion forced him 'to change very materially [his] views'. As, however, each successive position was presented with equal conviction, initially, these shifts undercut Sharp's pretensions to 'expert' status, and this, combined with his lack of knowledge of historical material, reduced the intellectual credibility of his writings.[10] Professional antagonism was not necessarily the only reason for the omission of his name from the article on folksong in the 1910 edition of Grove's *Dictionary of Music*. 'The truth is', his pupil Arnold Bax later concluded, 'Sharp often talked a great deal of nonsense.'[11]

A number of commentators outside folksong scholarship were also straightforwardly unimpressed with the grandiosity of his claims for 'rural effusions'. A body of unadorned four-line melodies and their naive texts were, they suggested, an unlikely foundation for the national musical renaissance Sharp depicted. And what was to be made of the fact that Sir Edward Elgar, the nation's leading and 'quintessentially English' composer, specifically rejected the influence of folk music in his work?

Suppose a composer never to have heard a folk-song in his life, how much worse off would he be? The enthusiasts who assert that there is some peculiar efficacy in the folk-song should be able to tell us precisely how its virtues act. Would the music of 'Gerontius' have been any the better if Elgar had known all the folk-songs of England, or any the worse if he had never known one of them? What light upon the problem of Gerontius's soul, dazed and shaken at the thought of death, can be thrown by 'Tarry Trowsers' or 'I'm seventeen come Sunday,' or 'Mowing the Barley'? [12]

Sharp suggested that 'as Wagner had found a similar prescription beneficial', Elgar might discover experimentation with folk music equally worthwhile. Sharp's adherents – pointedly discounting Elgar's work altogether – insisted that the absence of folksong as a basis for 'a really national school of music' meant that 'We have had no composer of first rank since Purcell'.[13] Neither position, however, provided the detailed exposition of the meaning of 'a national musical idiom' which sceptics sought. Educationalists opposed Sharp's proposals on a number of fronts – 'The pages of *School Music Review* of the time were full of criticism. For example, L. C. Venables, a disciple of John Curwen, objected not only to the bacchanalian or amorous nature of many folk songs, but also regarded the associated encouragement of singing by ear and in unison, as a retrograde step.' Concerns about the use of rote learning by less able teachers and the possibility that 'too exclusive use of national melodies and unison singing ... would limit the development of musical taste, lower the standard of our note work, diminish the need for careful vocal culture and afford fewer opportunities for refined vocal utterance' were also voiced.[14] On a less exalted level, though perhaps with greater practical intent, Sydney Nicholson pondered the specific mechanisms by which singing 'The Spotted Cow' would bring about the promised moral regeneration of naughty schoolboys.[15]

But lack of precision in these instances tended to be overwhelmed by doubts surrounding Sharp's central thesis. However frequently he cited the socio-cultural abstract of 'the race' as the ultimate producer of folksong, the low status of its contemporary performers remained to challenge established ideas about art and its creators. Sharp's sweeping assertions and contradictions raised legitimate questions about the culture he described. They also provided ample ammunition for the class prejudices of some of his readers. Earlier discussions of the history of folksong offered a relatively unproblematic process of a *gesunkenes Kulturgut* of music – originating with the upper classes and their professional musicians, descending through the social strata and coming to rest in ragged and simplified form among the stolidly conservative Folk. Sharp agreed that the practice of singing folksongs had 'fallen into abeyance amongst all classes, save only the peasantry', but also claimed that the music produced by selection and variation among the 'unlettered' was distinctive and often of a very beautiful quality. To agree with this, the music critic Ernest Newman argued, you had 'to suppose that the random shots of a lot of unmusical peasants are more likely to lead to perfection of feeling and of form than the similar shots of the same number of townspeople to-day'. He for one was unable to defer to 'the judgement of any rural Tom, Dick or Harry'.[16]

For every questioner, cynic, professional interest group and downright elitist who rejected his theories, however, a growing number found Sharp's vision convincing. The publicity deriving from his newspaper battles with the Folk-Song Society and the publication of *English Folk-Song: Some Conclusions* in 1907 brought his views to a national audience – and in this wider context they proved to have considerable appeal. In political terms, a thesis that upheld patriotism, reinforced consensus, of-

fered a source of cultural improvement with many possible appli-
cations and provided a positive interpretation of a form of lower-
class culture could draw support from virtually the whole
ideological spectrum. For the cultural strand which defined metro-
politanism as 'un-English' and produced the 'flight to the rural',
the Revival offered additional expressive forms – a music that was
of the countryside, a source to inspire the settings for Georgian
poetry; songs and dances which could aptly be performed in rooms
decorated with Arts and Crafts products, or against a backdrop of
vernacular architecture.

Turn-of-the-century historicism was also supportive of the
emerging movement's interests. The culture of the newly fashionable Tudor period could be directly linked with the Revival
through the performance of recently discovered folk dances as part
of Shakespearean plays in London and at the Stratford-upon-Avon
Shakespeare Festival. Indirectly, the association in the Folk Revival
of prominent figures such as Ralph Vaughan Williams, R. R.
Terry, J. A. Fuller-Maitland and Frederick Keel, in the revival of
music of the Tudor period and Lady Gomme, Harley Granville
Barker and Sharp in pioneering 'authentic' stagings of Shakespearean plays, also offered productive reinforcement of the relationship.[17] Indeed, the identification of Tudor England with
'Merrie England' and 'Merrie England' with 'laughter in the air',
'maypoles, hock-carts, wassails, wakes' and a social order of
'comradeship' in which 'The ploughman salutes the lord of the
manor as he rides by' [18] informed responses to the Revival at all
levels and in areas ranging from literature and fashion to politics.
As formal structures to embody the aims and values of the Revival
were developed, the movement interacted with and drew its membership from a society already receptive to the idea of re-estab-
lishing a universal culture, happily free of the taint of present
social and political ills.

For individuals, however, this combination of dynamics was
initially overlaid with a more immediate and overwhelming reaction – a sense of discovery. Something of great value had –
apparently – been lost and was now here to be found again.
Concerts of newly collected folksongs and dances were greeted
with a sort of recognition – 'a pageant of white voices and woven
gestures conjured out of the half-forgotten past – only half-forgotten, because none of us has altogether lost the ancestral memory

of 'merrie England' and the ancestral hopefulness that goes with it'.[19] Existing preconceptions and novelty combined to reinforce an impression of familiarity that was compounded with excitement at encountering something different and other.

it was not only the music; it was the idea too. It was the thought of this lost England of ours – the exquisite freshness of the early days – the old simplicities and candours. I do not suppose that human nature has changed very much, but there must, all the same, have been a very different spirit abroad when these were the people's songs than inspires us to-day. What do we hear sung in the village to-day? Last year's music hall successes. It was the thought of the loss of that spirit that perhaps formed part of my emotion. I do not know that the words had much to do with it; one did not hear them all, except the refrains. But the idea of a sweet and simple England was intensely vivid ... [20]

Clearly more than the enjoyment of a number of new musical pieces was involved. First-hand accounts are vibrant with anticipation of a rehabilitated nation, a united and happy England-to-be. All the values projected on to rural life – simplicity, purity, directness, unaffected beauty – were suddenly given a focus and made available in the concrete forms of song and dance. A lyrical summation of the national character appeared in place of vulgar jingoism. At a stroke, the possibility appeared that the urban working class could be re-made in unthreatening form and provided with a role in a culture for all:

they have the most to teach you, for only they can demonstrate the ease and grace with which they are able to clothe themselves in the mode abandoned years ago at the shrill call of the factory and during the hurried exodus from the countryside....
It is impossible to keep your foot still as to keep your head still. You feel as though you too were dancing. There is nothing languid or sensuous about it, nor is there on the other hand, any fierce beating up of emotional excitement. It is English. The kindliness of English scenery, the equitability of English climate, the pleasant healthy sentiment of the English countryside inspired these dances.[21]

The first opportunities for the general public to see this exciting embodiment of England past and future arose as a result of earlier socio-cultural intervention. One response to the panic engendered by the fears of physical and cultural degeneration in the later nineteenth century was the development of the Settlement movement. These 'experiments in religious and social action, conducted by people who accepted a responsibility as Christians and gentlemen to live for a time among the urban working classes', were based upon the belief 'that clergymen alone would never succeed in the slums without the partnership of squires'.[22] From the 1880s, this missionary duty to act as resident urban gentry spread and diversified as middle-class members of secular and political groups involved themselves in the 'worthy (and perhaps fashionable) cause' of bringing education and civilisation to the working classes. One such initiative was the Espérance Club, which met at 50 Cumberland Market in St Pancras with the aim of 'making life more interesting socially' for working girls 'who for the most part follow sedentary occupations'.[23] In place of the programme of school cantatas (which were acquired with limited enthusiasm by their charges), Herbert MacIlwaine, the Musical Director, suggested to Mary Neal, the co-founder and Honorary Secretary of the Espérance Club, that 'old English folk-songs collected in country districts by Mr Cecil Sharp' would be 'the very thing for her Club'. In the autumn of 1905, Mary Neal contacted Sharp and the result was most gratifying:

'The teaching of these songs to the girls,' said Miss Neal, 'had the effect of magic. They were always singing them at home and at work. Then I thought we would have them instead of a cantata for our Christmas party. I brought from Oxfordshire one of the men whom Mr. Sharp had seen dance, and in two evenings he taught the girls six dances that had been in the family for five generations. I never saw such charming dances, and I have had a good deal of experience. Those who attended our party said the entertainment was the prettiest thing on the London boards. So we are going to repeat it at the Queen's Hall....

'I think,' said Miss Neal enthusiastically, 'that I have struck a really good thing. I want to get specimen dances from all over England, and have them taught to Londoners in social work.'[24]

With characteristic vigour, Mary Neal set about 'in all sincerity and good faith' organising the 'well-being of some hundred girls and boys' by introducing them to folksong, dance and traditional children's games. The success of the Queen's Hall concert and subsequent performances in front of philanthropically minded audiences by these 'regular London working girls' was rapid. Tours were arranged and additional groups started, illustrated lectures given, an instructional book on morris dancing published, further traditional dances were researched and a staff of two full-time and eight part-time dance teachers provided classes from the Espérance Club. Within three years of its own first concert, Neal informed *The Daily Telegraph*, three hundred clubs, villages and schools had been taught folk dances and songs. Impetus and a potential structure were developing – could this burgeoning organisation involving the urban working class form the nucleus of a unified cultural resurgence based on traditional materials – a Folk Revival? 'The beauty of spirit of this spontaneous, unregenerate, and truly national music are becoming known amongst the elect. And with that knowledge has arisen a question of practical character – whether the indigenous melody thus discovered does not open up new lines of popular culture amongst the class to which its origin must be credited.'[25]

Enthusiasm for a nationally based movement among 'the elect' began to take concrete form. On 14 November 1907, following a well-orchestrated campaign of support in the press, Neal called 'an informal conference' at the Goupil Gallery in London, aimed at 'reviving active interest' in English folk music. Mr Neville Lytton took the chair, Lady Constance Lytton, Mrs Gomme, Mrs Pethick Lawrence, Cecil Sharp and other educational and socially concerned personalities were in attendance. It was resolved that a Society 'for the further development of the popular practice of English folk-music in Dance and Song' be formed, 'to hand on the music to the people of the day' and that a Provisional Committee be appointed to draw up rules. On the following day, The *Morning Post* reported on the 'scores of letters ... from country people interested in village life, Poor Law instructors, drill teachers', girls' school mistresses, club leaders, etc., asking where and how the songs and dances can be had'. An institutionalised reformation of culture, drawing together all social classes, seemed to be an immediate and uncontroversial prospect.

But were the young working-class men and women who had become involved through Espérance's work harbouring an equally active interest in regenerating a consensus culture based on a new growth from 'common' national roots? As in the case of the rural singers from whom the songs and dances had originally been collected, the views of working-class teachers and performers from the Club were not sought and records of their independent activity are limited. What they thought of the material they performed is only available indirectly. They had, Neal reported, 'gone mad' over folksong and been 'perfectly intoxicated with the beauty of the music'. Audiences commented upon the 'manifest enjoyment' of the dancers during their concert performances and young members of the Club were seen teaching non-members the dances informally in a local park. But equally, the material officially acceptable for Espérance performance was carefully restricted. Contemporary popular music, particularly the new forms originating in America, was not permitted – as Miss Neal crisply indicated, she 'never would have a cake-walk in the Club, for I don't think we ought to depend for our songs and dances upon niggers'.[26] For all that working-class 'instructresses', like Florence Warren and May Start, proved 'as quick to teach as to learn' and, 'showing an amazing facility and power of organisation', provided classes for the gentry and groups of primary school teachers, their role was to carry out rather than initiate policy.[27] Although it 'contained an element of spontaneous joy most refreshing compared to the oppressive straight-jackets of national or private philanthropists',[28] middle-class supervision and guidance were the keynotes of the introduction of folk culture in the Espérance Club and provided the basis of approaches to working-class performance at its many offshoots.

Given these circumstances, the voice of 'the elect', in the columns of The Times, evinced no doubt about the cultural – and political – value of introducing Londoners to 'Merrie England' through folk dance and song. Reviving folk culture offered pleasing prospects of a comprehensive remedy for vulgarity and a distraction from social agitation:

Young men, maidens, and children, from twenty years old to four, they are Cockneys, born and bred. You expect, therefore, to see and hear in them the rough but sheepish noisiness of the young Cockney, the hideous vulgarity of the Cockney twang. But you find you are mistaken. You will sometimes come across these undesirable London products on the variety stage, but never amongst the girls and boys of the Espérance Guild. And the conclusion is irresistible that it is the folk-spirit which makes the difference in joyousness, and accent, and general unselfconscious refinement. It is the real folk-spirit that has set these eight young mechanics and artisans who were one of the charms of the performance at the Kensington Town Hall last night dancing and singing as young England should, instead of loafing at street corners, or, still more hideous thought, spouting at political clubs. [29]

The potential of a Folk Revival as a means of social control was also openly canvassed by members of the educational establishment. Describing events in 'Utopia', his vision of an ideal school, Edgar Holmes, a former Chief Inspector for Elementary Schools, wrote in 1911:

> I was once present when the Utopian children were going through a programme of Folk Songs and Morris Dances in the village hall. A lady who was looking on remarked to me: 'this is all very fine but if this sort of thing goes on where are we going to find our servants?' The selfishness of this remark is obvious. What is less obvious but more significant is its purblindness. In point of fact the Utopian girls make excellent domestic servants and are well content to 'go into service'.

A 'Utopian' boy taking on low-paid, repetitive, 'dull and tiresome' work, Holmes also opined, would go about his tasks 'with cheery goodwill' since while undertaking them 'he sang his Folksongs with all the spontaneous happiness of a soaring lark'.[30]

This view of the purpose and future of the movement was not shared by all the Espérance Club's supporters. Rather than interpreting the Folk Revival as a restraining or refining influence, some observers identified the 'ease and grace' of the Espérance members as the re-emergence of existing traits which had 'remained intact through all the vicissitudes of slumland and the London streets'. Indeed, the urban background of the group offered positive benefits, 'giving to the rustic dance a new element sprung from cockney alertness, assurance, and humour'. Inherent within the Folk Revival movement, Philip Macer-Wright contended, was the promise of an England which would be 'less stiff and less self-conscious'. Renewed national culture would embody a fulfilling affirmation of humanity, with the working class as its core. In 'Utopian England', 'the accumulated folk-lore of her ancient sons and daughters', he foresaw, would provide 'the expression of national joy'. Espérance's 'common children, from mean streets' were 'small prophets' of 'England-to-Be'.[31]

Differing interpretations of the function of the Revival were not, however, confined to observers and supporters. Significant divisions began to emerge between Mary Neal, 'the founder of the movement', and Cecil Sharp, the 'expert on tradition'.[32] From the beginning of the Espérance Club's work of revival, Sharp had been heavily involved in a range of disputes with his employers at

Hampstead Conservatoire, the Folk-Song Society and the full
weight of the musical and educational establishments at their
highest levels. Engrossed in lecturing, collecting and campaigning,
between 1906 and 1907 he had also produced *English Folk-Song:
Some Conclusions*. Throughout this time, his major concerns had
been aesthetic, and focused on creating a national school of art
music by educating rising generations into a shared culture of
folksong. He welcomed the removal from the streets and concert
halls of 'alien sounds, or sounds fugitive and flashy, or pretty and
insincere, or ugly and downright harmful' which he felt would
result from folk music's introduction. But otherwise, the main
social outcome he embraced was the development of a patriotic
consensus. From this standpoint, the 'philanthropic' use of a handful of songs and dances by one of the many settlements in working-class areas of London may have appeared to have little of
distinction to contribute.

As the work of the Espérance Club gained 'reach and strength'
through the 'powers of help and organisation' of Mary Neal,[33]
however, Sharp became more involved with their work. Although
extensively committed to other concerns, in 1906 he provided
technical assistance in the notation of tunes (though not the dances)
for the first part of *The Morris Book* and used Club performers
to illustrate his lectures. As in his theoretical writing, Sharp seems
to have adopted – without detailed consideration – many of Neal's
existing ideas about the rationale of a Folk Revival.[34] The comprehensive break with the musical establishment resulting from his
actions during the national songs controversy, however, restricted
his fields of operation. Propagandising through dance teaching had
not formed part of his original agenda. He had notated only the
tunes of the morris he had seen in 1899 – it took Neal's 1904
request for material 'in harmony' with his songs to provide a use
for it. But dance now emerged as the only area of activity open to
him if he were to have a real impact on the public and the issue
of revival through performance came to the centre of his attention.
What he saw did not meet with his approval. During 1908 Sharp
concluded that the Espérance approach could not be accommodated
with his view of the processes of Revival, and despite Neal's attempts
over the following two years to arrange compromises which kept
both of them within a single movement, he consistently acted to
distance himself from the organisation and its ideology.

As in the earlier split with the Folk-Song Society, Sharp's auto-cratic personality was a significant factor in promoting dissention. He was himself convinced – and proved effective in convincing others – that the knowledge of tradition he had acquired through his fieldwork gave him unique insight into folk performances of all types. He 'knew the habits of our people'. His alone was the sensibility that could determine which traditions were 'trust-worthy' and which were not. Only he possessed the authority to decide how particular dances should be performed. His 'higher artistic ideals' were to identify the aims and provide the direction for the movement. The precise form and means of disseminating traditional dances had to meet his requirements and be entirely within his control. Acolytes, rather than co-workers, were to assist him in popularising the Revival, which would thus become a movement of 'recognised authority' suitable to 'command con-fidence'. As his new Folk, therefore, Sharp brought forward the trainee teachers from Chelsea Physical Training College and a group of genteel admirers who formed the Folk Dance Club. That no one appears to have questioned the ability of a man who only started dancing in his fifties to give practical classes says much for the strenght of his personality and the pliancy of his chosen students.

Although he now intended taking over the direction of the movement, Sharp's view of a performance-based Revival was limited and his plan for its achievement mechanistic. Politically, philosophically and in personal terms, Sharp disliked change. As he conceived it, the process of popularisation had to be based in developing the means of systematising identical cultural forms. Replication rather than dynamic re-creation was his aim. Sharp therefore put forward formal teaching, graded examinations and the incorporation of folksong and dance in the education system as a means of both establishing national standards of performance and ensuring their consistent reproduction. Songs in schools were to be learned by rote – 'All the teacher need do is to sing the air with the words line by line, and make the children sing after him, until the whole song is learned'. And any individuality in perfor-mance was to be avoided – 'Sing it as simply and straightforwardly as possible and ... forbear ... from actively and deliberately at-tempting to improve it by the introduction of frequent changes of time, crescendo, diminuendo etc.'[35] Mindful of the earlier cultural

treachery of the peasantry, Sharp did not trust the new Folk as
creative inheritors of tradition.

The aims, means and values embodied in this approach ran
directly counter to Mary Neal's vision of the Revival. Although
begun philanthropically, as means of promoting the greater happiness of the members of her Club 'with no consciousness then
that there was more in this folk music than just that', as her work
developed (and Sharp put forward his alternatives), she came to
see the Revival in much broader terms:

I know to-day that our work, our aims, that all we most care for has
in truth been set to music ... life harmonious and more abundant has
filled out the form of social work. A door has been opened away out
into a new country, which is yet as old as England itself, and we have
learned something of that realm of imagination and beauty, of fear and
of a sheltering power which is all around us in our childhood, and which
comes again to us from the childhood of the world in the simple folk
who may still be found remote from town and city life, dwelling by deep
and silent waters, by swiftly running rivers, deep in the woods and in
sheltered valleys among the hills.
... This revival of the practice and use of our English folk music is, as
many helpers have told me, part of a great national revival, a going back
from town to country, a reaction against all that is demoralising in city
life. It is a re-awakening of that part of our national consciousness
which makes for wholeness, saneness, and healthy merriment.
We can never, as a nation, go back to the days when country life
sufficed for everything. The town has come too near to the country for
that. But an interchange between town and country is what we must
look for in the future. The musician will go into the country and will
set down for us dance and game and song from the old folks in whose
memory the music still lives. The town folk will learn them and add
something to them of their own life and generation, something of the
charm and vivacity of the city, and they in their turn will teach the
young folk of the village.
... One has always felt that the national treasure was not all in gold and
silver and merchandise, nor with the great and learned, but that somewhere, somehow, it was in the people themselves. It has seemed to us
that in this music we have made a great discovery of a hidden treasure,
and that having discovered it we have become a medium through which
others may discover it too.[36]

Neal's proposals for the processes of Revival were equally at odds
with Sharp's system of assessment and enforced standards. 'For

the first time,' she wrote in 'Set to Music', 'we have something in our possession for which others are glad to ask, and which we are glad to share.' Experience of performances by the 'original country dancers' was to be the key to handing on not merely the form but the 'spirit' of traditional dance. To Sharp's publicly expressed displeasure, she opined that since traditional dancers were themselves untrained, to refer to an 'expert' in Morris dances 'seems as unreasonable to talk about' as 'an expert in making people happy'.[37] Although she recognised the importance of giving 'teachers the opportunity of seeing the traditional dancers at work, so that they may be equipped to hand on the dances to the school children', the inclusion of morris dance in the Board of Education's Syllabus of Physical Exercises for public elementary schools, which Sharp had used all his influence to bring about, did not recommend itself to her:

It was held by some that discipline, strictness, absolute uniformity were a necessary part of the teaching, but she did not believe in making poor children more miserable than they were already. What the little boys and girls of the humbler classes needed was not so much discipline as joy and freedom; and the sense of co-operation felt in the acquirement of these songs and dances was discipline enough....[38]

But for all Sharp's 'intensity of purpose' and insistence on total control, the increasingly bitter conflict overtaking the Revival did not emerge simply from a clash of personality between him and Neal. The divisions within the Revival which significantly altered the developing character of the movement reflected and formed part of wider attempts to affect national hegemonic control. Between 1906 and 1911, challenges to all that constituted established class and gender relations became increasingly overt. The Tory government lost the General Election of 1906, and the incoming Liberal administration soon began a lengthy battle to curb the power of the House of Lords. Equally ominously for establishment concerns, existing political alignments began to break up, as the alliance between socialists and the Trades Unions produced the election of twenty-nine official Labour members of Parliament. For the first time a Labour Party was a reality in the House of Commons. 'Those who are now grouped under the standard of party'. Parliament was warned in March 1910, 'will re-form themselves under the standard of class. When the party system is

shattered the class line must be the line of demarcation.'[39] More
directly, a Tory politician's wife anxiously confided to a friend
abroad, 'It made me feel, that the French Revolution had come
upon us again.' [40]

Separating the personal sphere from conflicts in national life is,
however, particularly difficult in the case of the Revival at this
time. The group associated with the Espérance Club were not
involved in pursuing cultural change alone, nor were they merely
passive observers of national struggles for greater democracy.
From 1906, as agitation for women's enfranchisement became an
increasingly contentious public issue, leading members of Espérance joined the campaign to gain the vote for women. In February
1906, Keir Hardie, the leader of the Independent Labour Party,
asked Emmeline Pankhurst to contact Emmeline Pethick-Lawrence, the co-founder of the Espérance Club. He suggested she
would be the best person to organise the London work of the new,
direct action organisation, the Women's Suffrage and Political
Union.[41] As a result of this approach, with her husband, Frederick
Pethick-Lawrence, and Mrs Pankhurst she formed the directorate
which headed the suffragette movement. Mary Neal also became
a founder and committee member of the WSPU, writing articles
for its periodical, Votes for Women, and providing Espérance
dance teams for its public events.[42] Charlotte Lytton, who joined
the suffragettes in 1908 as a result of meeting leading WSPU
members at Espérance's Littlehampton holiday house, shortly became a cause célèbre following her ill-treatment on hunger-strike.
Like the Pethick-Lawrences, she served highly publicised prison
terms on a number of occasions as a result of militant activities.[43]
The artist and writer Neville Lytton (Charlotte's younger brother)
was also a vocal advocate of the cause, becoming Chairman of the
Conciliation Committee for Woman Suffrage. Less prominently,
Lady Gomme was an active supporter of non-violent agitation for
the vote. [44] Five of the twelve individuals forming the Provisional
Committee of the Society for the Revival and Practice of Folk-
Music meeting in November 1907 became involved in the 'revolutionary movement for women's suffrage'. Few were untouched
by it – including Herbert MacIlwaine, who resigned from the
Espérance Club as a result of his objections to suffragette activity,
and Sharp, 'opposed for a long time to Women's Suffrage by
prejudice', whose sister Evelyn was also jailed and went on hunger

strike.[45] By May of 1910, as Sharp's differences with Neal descended into acrimonious personal attacks in the press, their confrontation offered a microcosm of growing national turmoil:

The King [Edward VII] died on 6 May 1910, with the country in a combative mood. George V succeeded in the middle of a constitutional crisis, having to face the Liberal demand for the creation of enough peers to swamp the recalcitrant diehards who proposed to fight a last-ditch for the power of the Lords. The trade unions were gripped by a mood of militancy unmatched since the struggle of the early Nineties, and great strikes were looming. The suffragette movement, drifting towards direct action, converted the sexual repressions of the Victorian age into political rebellion. The Irish question was lurching towards another confrontation between Unionists and Home Rulers. Public life had become a melee of wills in which all values were subordinated to conflicting ambitions and ideals.[46]

Battle lines for the Revival were drawn around the concept of 'Merrie England'. It was, Neal recalled, the publication of Bernard Partridge's *Punch* cartoon of Espérance dancers, titled 'Merrie England Once More', on 13 November 1907 which produced the first signs of division between herself and Sharp.[47] As the differences between their two positions became defined and entrenched, 'Merrie England' – not the reactionary, mock-Tudor quaintness of conservative formulations but the socialist vision of practical equality and improved living conditions put forward by Robert Blatchford – encapsulated their ideological breach. For Neal and the group associated with Espérance, the Revival was to be instrumental in initiating a revolution, transforming the whole of English culture and establishing a new basis for class relations. As she now saw it, the role of 'those of us to whom has been entrusted the guidance and the helping of this movement' was to be superseded. The working class were to be the new Folk and provide the performance vanguard of the Revival. The form of folk dance was to be left to them to develop at will.

Such a radical agenda was particularly unacceptable to Sharp who, although he had suggested the creation of 'a Merry England of the present' at the Goupil Gallery, now dismissed it as 'the sentimental view'. Personally, he was in favour of the maintenance of the status quo. Despite his powerful advocacy of his own position in the controversies surrounding state education, 'he accepted certain conditions as insuperable barriers. For instance, although he lectured on song and dance (with illustrations) in nearly every boys' public school in England, he made no serious endeavour to get the dances generally taught in the schools, knowing that the curriculum would not allow it'.[48] Social change did not enter into his plans for the Revival. 'Given the right environment,' he wrote early in his collecting career, country singers 'would not be making shirts at 2d a dozen or clearing out pigstyes', but 'would be singing in public-halls and ministering to the joys and needs of thousands of their fellow-creatures'. [49] But neither then nor at any later juncture did he put forward proposals for the means by which this socio-cultural transformation might be achieved. Characteristically, his biographer noted, 'in words ... he appeared to be an enlightened socialist, but in deeds he could be an autocrat.' [50]

Ideologically, therefore, it is perhaps unsurprising that Sharp aligned himself with the section of the Fabian Society associated with Sidney and Beatrice Webb. The Webbs' 'conception of collectivism designed to serve the whole nation rather than merely to improve the lot of the working classes' chimed with his own views. His programme for achieving and maintaining a Folk Revival also echoed the Webbs' Fabian approach, particularly its espousal of 'strong leadership', 'intolerant of the cumbersome and apparently wasteful processes of democracy'. Social improvement, the Webbs believed, depended upon education and 'the training of the superior manpower needed to carry out the schemes of reform'.[51]

By 1912, differing ideologies, personalities, chance and the dynamics of confrontation itself had resulted in the formulation of diametrically opposed concepts of a revived Folk.[52] Two rival organisations offered mirror-images of a proposed Revival, completely divergent in personnel, method and ideology. Neal was the organiser of the Espérance Guild of Morris Dancers, its invitation to membership from 'All men and women of goodwill who wish to see a fairer and a happier life for the people of England' and choice of name highlighting its socialist approach. From 6 December 1911, Sharp headed the English Folk Dance Society, its title and stated objectives reflecting the language of control, authority and nationalism which characterised his philosophy of revival performance. Attempts to provide a unified framework in which both Sharp and Neal could work as directors of a new National Board of Folk-Song and Dance withered in the face of Sharp's intransigence.[53] A Folk Revival was not to be side-tracked into use for any overt social purpose – 'art' as a national expression was to be the only criterion for its existence. There remained no possible area for mediation or compromise – a public gladiatorial contest ensued, outweighed in ferocity only by the guerrilla warfare of private exchanges and attempts by both sides to gain the confidence of the influential. Accusation and counter-claim, denunciations of false forms of tradition and vulgarity of dress, all, eventually, reached summation in Neal's development of a single pointed question:

Which interpretation of the peasant dance we prefer, whether that given by the working folk themselves or that given by those trained in physical culture and dancing technique, depends on what we believe this revival of folk dances will ultimately stand for. Is it to be a real expression of the life of the people, a setting free of the best aspirations and ideals of those who toil for daily bread? Is it to bring back to them some dignity, the self-possession, and the joy which is their birthright, and, above all, is it to be possible to say to any boy or girl, as they leave their work, 'Come and learn dances and songs, for which you need as training only your youth and love of life?' Or is this movement to be only an accomplishment for those who can afford to spend years in the attainment of physical culture? Is it to be a subject for lectures merely? Is it to become so technical that only the learned and the leisured will dare to take part in it? On the answers to these question it depends whether this revival of folk dancing remains a permanent part of our national life, or whether it passes away, never, perhaps, to be revived again.[54]

Sharp won the battle. By 1914, a series of decisive events had left him sole leader of the only widely accepted form of the Folk Revival movement. Initially, as Douglas Kennedy, his successor as Director of the English Folk Dance Society, later recounted, he 'was *chosen* by Sir Archibald Flower in the summer of 1911 to adjudicate the country dancing and singing at Stratford-upon-Avon in preference to Mary Neal who had done the job probably in a rather slap-dash manner in the summer of 1910'.[55] The Vacation School of Folk-Song and Dance at Stratford-upon-Avon was a prestigious Revival showpiece organised by the governors of the Shakespeare Memorial Theatre. That during Neal's absence in America Sharp persuaded the governors to give him the School directorship in place of Mary Neal is incontrovertible. The reasons for their about-face are, however, far less easily discerned than

Kennedy's partiality suggests or Sharp's description of an inspired personal interview implies. Sharp's arguments for replacing Neal were supported by letters he had solicited from knowledgeable and influential figures such as Lady Gomme. In 1911 – as today – the fact that Neal was a woman would not have counted in her favour where positions of responsibility were in question. Equally her association with left-wing political groups and 'extremists' in the women's movement might also have affected the choice. Neal herself felt the governors had not 'played the game' and would 'find it difficult to justify' their actions 'to anyone but to Mr Sharp'. What is not borne out by any contemporary source, however, is the suggestion that Neal's organising ability was a factor – Sharp himself noted that the governors had in fact proposed to give him 'technical direction' while leaving all the organising in Neal's hands. [56]

The scope and depth of Sharp's dance collection was also advanced in support of his claims to leadership. Throughout their power struggle, both Neal and Sharp used their experience of fieldwork to symbolise the superiority of their respective insights into the life of 'the Folk'. Neither appears, however, fully to have comprehended the dynamic nature of customary performance, and at the outset of their contest both were equally inexperienced in dance collection.[57] As the rivalry between them reached its crucial stage, Neal attempted to use the differing versions of morris dances in Headington to discredit Sharp's attribution of 'true traditional form' to the variant he had collected from William Kimber. Meanwhile, Sharp hastened round the country, collecting as quickly as possible, then rushing precipitately from collection to print. This resulted in confusion of detail in a number of the dances he obtained and failure to gather the full material available to him,[58] causing considerable difficulty when his strictures on absolute accuracy to the printed form were applied in practice. More seriously, in the case of the Ampleforth Sword Play, the exigencies of bolstering his position seems to have resulted in his using dubious methods to produce an oikotypical version of this 'significant' tradition.[59] In terms of the battle for control, his attack on Neal's use of 'untraditional' dances such as that of Ilmington sits ill with his presentation of the Winster morris dance as 'genuine' and the result of 'continuous tradition'. It had, in fact, lapsed at least twice, being revived with additional trappings by a local antiquarian in 1873 and most recently, as he was well aware, as a result of publicity deriving from his own work.[60] Both Neal and Sharp used the press, publicity and influential connections in attempts to gain advantage, but overall throughout the period of the struggle for hegemony within the Revival, Sharp's statements and behaviour were frequently inconsistent, hypocritical and un-principled. All that can be offered in defence of his actions was his conviction that his view was the correct one. The end, he clearly felt, justified any means.

As the loser in the contest, Neal's concept of the Revival was rapidly rendered invisible.[61] In general, the fact that Sharp was not the initiator of a performance-based Revival is omitted from dis-cussions of the phenomenon. Where the issue is commented on, Neal's contribution and the differing character of the Espérance philosophy are almost invariably misrepresented.[62] The clearly stated political objectives underlying Espérance's later stance are passed off as social work or philanthropy, Neal's ideology and abilities to direct and inspire reduced to 'do-gooding':

Looking back on my own early 'appreciation' (in the military sense) of the rival leaders I should say that Mary Neal was essentially a 'do-gooder', more concerned with giving enjoyment than with the idea of rescuing a threatened species. Mary Neal certainly had the support of the 'social' workers. Both she and Sharp were politically of the Left but Sharp had the backing of the 'Establishment' in terms of Education and the Academics; Hal Fisher at the Board [of Education] and later the Hon. Edward Wood (later Lord Halifax our Foreign Secretary in Cham-berlain's 1939 Government).[63]

Espérance's urban working-class dancers, their 'vulgarised' cos-tumes taking a displaced condemnation which opponents were too mealy-mouthed to apply publicly to seamstresses as people, were removed from the cultural, social and political consideration of the Revival. In later years, the names of Cecil Sharp's first all-male demonstration team of morris dancers were repeatedly listed, the deaths of four of its six members in the First World War con-stantly set forth as a symbol of the lost promise of a generation and a more glorious Revival that might have been. [64] The names and fates of the Espérance teams, 'some hundred' female and male dancers, the earliest originators of the Revival, are, however, almost entirely unknown.[65] As losers in the battle to be the Folk, they, and the approach to Folk Revival their participation embodied, failed to form a permanent part of national life. 'Merrie England' was not achieved.

Notes

1 Anon., *Morning Post*, 15 Nov 1907 reprinted in Mary Neal, *The Espérance Morris Book: Part I A Manual of Morris Dances, Folk-Songs and Singing Games,* 3rd edn (London: J. Curwen & Sons Ltd, 1910), p. 61.

2 See for example, Douglas Kennedy, *England's Dances: Folk Dancing Today and Yesterday* (London: G. Bell & Sons Ltd, 1949), p. 13; E. C. Cawte, Alex Helm and N. Peacock, *English Ritual Drama: A Geographical Index* (London: Folklore Society, 1967), p. 29; A. L. Lloyd, *Folk Song in England* (London: Panther, 1969), p. 317; Fred Woods, *Folk Revival: The Rediscovery of a National Music* (Poole, Dorset: Blandford Press Ltd, 1979), p. 14 and *The Observer's Book of Folk Song in Britain,* Observers Pocket Series (London: Frederick Warne (Publishers) Ltd, 1980), p. 21.

3 Cecil Sharp, *English Folk-Song: Some Conclusions*, ed. Maud Karpeles (Wakefield: E. P. Publishing Ltd, 1972), pp. 151–2.

4 See particularly William Morris, 'How We Live and How We Might Live' and 'The Hopes of Civilization,' in A. L. Morton, ed., *Political Writings of William Morris* (London: Lawrence & Wishart Ltd, 1984), pp. 134–81 and Robert Blatchford, *Merrie England* (London: Clarion Press, 1894; reprinted 1908). See also Martin J. Wiener, *English Culture and the Decline of the Industrial Spirit 1850–1980* (Cambridge: Cambridge University Press, 1981), pp. 98–126 for an excellent discussion of this and related approaches across the political spectrum.

5. Philip Dodd, 'Englishness and the National Culture,' in Robert Colls and Philip Dodd, ed., *Englishness: Politics and Culture 1880–1920* (London: Croom Helm, 1986), p. 1.

6 Discussion of this controversy is based on material drawn from A. H. Fox Strangways, *Cecil Sharp* (Oxford: Oxford University Press, 1933), p. 58–67; Reginald Nettel, *Sing a Song of England: A Social History of Traditional Song* (London: Phoenix House, ND [1954]), pp. 241–5; Dave Harker, *Fakesong: The Manufacture of British 'Folksong' 1700 to the Present Day,* Popular Music in Britain (Milton Keynes: Open University Press, 1985), pp. 181–4; Dave Russell, *Popular Music in England 1840–1914: A Social History,* Music and Society (Manchester: Manchester University Press, 1987), pp. 45–6 and Gordon Cox, 'The Legacy of Folk Song: The Influence of Cecil Sharp on Music

Education,' *British Journal of Music Education,* VII:2 (1990), 89–97. As indicated below, Cecil Sharp's, *English Folk-Song: Some Conclusions* also offers ample evidence on the nature and form of the debate – particularly the later chapters, pp. 131–80.

7 London: John Murray, 1902.

8 Originally published in 1907 by Barnicott and Pearce of Taunton.

9 Discussion of the sources of Sharp's theories is contained in Theresa Buckland, 'English Folk Dance Scholarship: A Review,' in Theresa Buckland, ed., *Traditional Dance: Proceedings of the Traditional Dance Conference Vol. I* (Crewe: Crewe & Alsager College of Higher Education, 1982), 3–18; John Forrest, *Morris and Matachin: A Study in Comparative Choreography;* CECTAL Publication no. 4 (Sheffield: Centre for English Cultural Tradition & Language, 1984), pp. 5–14, passim; Harker, *Fakesong,* pp. 186–189; Frank Howes, *The English Musical Renaissance* (London: Martin Secker & Warburg Ltd, 1966), pp. 74–5 and Nettel, *Sing a Song of England,* p. 243. See also Sharp, *English Folk-Song: Some Conclusions,* pp. 6–20 for examples of the methodology and E. Phillips Barker, 'Cecil James Sharp,' *EFDS News,* I:8 (Nov. 1924), 209 for contemporary comment.

10 See for example, Frank Kidson, 'English Folk-Song,' *The Musical Times,* 1 Jan. 1908, pp. 23–5 and the reported comments in Anon., 'Folk-Songs and their Singers: Mr. Ernest Newman on their Universality,' undated [1906] cutting in Gomme Collection, Folklore Society Archives, University College London. For instances of Sharp's theoretical revisions, see Cecil J. Sharp and Herbert C. MacIlwaine, *The Morris Book: Part I,* rev. edn (London: Novello & Co. Ltd, 1912), pp. 7–11. In her 1972 edition of *English Folk Song: Some Conclusions,* Maud Karpeles also took the opportunity to add corrections of statements which 'may give a false impression of what were, in fact, Sharp's views' (p. 153), were 'perhaps too dogmatic' (p. 89), modify his sweeping condemnation of broadsides (p. 126) and re-write 'in the light of Cecil Sharp's later views' the chapter on modes (pp. 47–67). Additionally, a later change of view provides the basis for a complete reversal of Sharp's statements on the origin of country dance in Karpeles's revised edition of Cecil J. Sharp, *The Country Dance Book: Part I* (London: Novello & Co. Ltd, 1934) (first published 1909), pp. 7 and 11.

11 Arnold Bax, *Farewell, My Youth* (London: Longmans, Green & Co., 1943), p. 16.

12 Ernest Newman, 'The Folk-Song Fallacy,' *English Review,* V (1912), 267–8. See also Jeremy Crump, 'The Identity of English Music: The Reception of Elgar 1898–1935,' in Colls and Dodd, *Englishness,* pp. 164–90 for a discussion of the processes by which the identity of

Elgar as a pre-eminently 'English' composer developed.

13 See Cecil Sharp, "The Folk-Song Fallacy': A Reply,' *English Review*, V (1912), 548. Comments on the absence of 'racial character' in English music appear in Anon., *Morning Post*, 15 Nov. 1907 reprinted in Neal, *Espérance Morris Book: Part I*, p. 61 and E. V. Lucas, 'Introduction', *ibid.*, p. viii [originally published in *The County Gentleman*].

14 A. L. Cowley, Music Instructor to the London School Board, *School Music Review*, Jan. 1904. This and the quotation relating to Venables and other educationalists appears in Cox's succinctly illuminating 'The Legacy of Folk Song', p. 93.

15 Nicholson's splendidly ironic review is quoted in Russell, *Popular Music in England 1840–1914*, p. 46.

16 Newman, 'The Folk-Song Fallacy,' pp. 260–1.

17 The Gomme family and Harley Granville Barker (1877–1946) worked with and supported William Poel's (1852–1934) attempts to establish 'authentic' stagings of Shakespearian plays through the London Shakespeare League and the Elizabethan Stage Society. Additionally, Sharp was 'given an early opportunity to produce a programme of folk dances at the Savoy Theatre by his friend, Granville Barker, who had a season of Shakespeare plays running there'. Douglas Kennedy, 'A Jubilee Symposium: 2. Folk Dance Revival,' *Folk Music Journal*, II:2 (1971), 85–6. See Howes, *The English Musical Renaissance*, pp. 84–110 for a discussion of inter-relationships in the musical field.

18 The quotations, taken from F. L. Stevens, *Through Merrie England* (London: Frederick Warne & Co. Ltd, 1928, pp. 1–3, are typical of the romantically reactionary interpretation of 'Merrie England' informing reactions of the Folk Revival. See also Roy Judge's characteristically detailed and enjoyable 'May Day and Merrie England,' *Folklore*, CII:2 (1991), 131–48.

19 Anon., *The Morning Post*, 16 Nov. 1907 reprinted in Neal, *Espérance Morris Book: Part I*, p. 61.

20 E. V. Lucas, 'Introduction,' *ibid.*, p. vii.

21 Philip Macer-Wright, 'England-to-Be: The Espérance Guild of National Joy,' first published in the *Westminster Gazette* and reprinted in Mary Neal, *The Espérance Morris Book: Part II Morris Dances, Country Dances, Sword Dances and Sea Shanties* (London: J. Curwen & Sons Ltd, 1912), p. xv.

22 K. S. Inglis, *Churches and the Working Classes in Victorian England*, Studies in Social History (London: Routledge & Kegan Paul, 1963), p. 143. Popular contemporary views are revealingly detailed in Walter Besant, *The Alabaster Box* (London: Thomas Burleigh, 1900).

23 Anon., *Daily News*, 23 Mar. 1906 quoted in Neal, *Espérance Morris Book: Part I*, p. 59. For additional examples of middle-class intervention in the concerns of working-class women contemporary with the Espérance Club, see Anna Davin, 'Imperialism and Motherhood,' *History Workshop Journal*, V (spring 1977), 38–9 and 41–2. Specific discussion of music in the Settlement movement appears in E. D. Mackerness, *A Social History of English Music* (London: Routledge & Kegan Paul Ltd, 1964), pp. 199–201.

24 *Espérance Morris Book: Part I*, p. 59.

25 Anon., *Pall Mall*, 27 Mar. 1906, reprinted in Neal, *ibid.*, p. 59.

26 Anon., *Daily News*, 23 Mar. 1906, reprinted in Neal, *ibid.*, p. 59.

27 Constance Lytton, *Prisons and Prisoners* quoted in Neville Lytton, *The English Country Gentleman* (London: Hurst & Blackett Ltd, ND), p. 267. An indication of Florence Warren's approach and thoughtful observation can be gained from comments in her letter to Sharp on the form of Headington dances, reprinted in full in A. D. Townsend, 'Cecil James Sharp as Collector and Editor of Traditional Dance,' in Theresa Buckland, ed., *Traditional Dance: Proceedings of the Traditional Dance Conference Vols. V & VI* (Crewe: Crewe & Alsager College of Higher Education, 1988), p. 64.

28 Lytton, *Prisons and Prisoners* quoted in Neville Lytton, *The English Country Gentleman*, p. 265. This moreover records that members of the Espérance Club came to teach in Charlotte Lytton's home village at her invitation. See also Jonathan T. Barter, 'The Oldest Folk Dance Club,' *English Dance and Song*, XXXVII:1 (spring 1975), 29 for details of the Lincoln Folk Dance Club, founded in 1902 'by a Mrs. E. Giles, the wife of a local millionaire', which 'at first consisted of Mrs. Giles, a few friends, and her employees' and the contacts between Miriam Noel and Mary Neal which led to the introduction of folk dancing in Thaxted, in Reg Groves, *Conrad Noel and the Thaxted Movement: An Adventure in Christian Socialism* (New York: Augustus M. Kelley, 1968), pp. 68–74. Similar examples of middle-class invitation appear in Neal, 'Appendix I: Some Opinions of the Dances,' *Espérance Morris Book: Part I*, pp. 57–8.

29 Anon., *The Times*, reprinted in Neal, *Espérance Morris Book: Part II*, p. 50.

30 Edgar Holmes, *What Is and What Might Be: A Study of Education in General and Elementary Education in Particular* (London: Constable, 1911), pp. 228 and 193 respectively, quoted in Cox, 'The Legacy of Folk Song,' p. 95.

31 Macer-Wright, reprinted in Neal, *Espérance Morris Book: Part*

II, pp. xiv-xv.

32 Details of Mary Neal's association with the Folk Revival and the circumstances of the Sharp-Neal controversy appear in Roy Judge's excellent 'Mary Neal and the Espérance Morris,' *Folk Music Journal*, V:5 (1989), 545–91.

33 Cecil J. Sharp and Herbert C. MacIlwaine, 'Dedication', *The Morris Book: A History of Morris Dancing with a Description of Eleven Dances as Performed by the Morris-Men of England* (London: Novello & Co. Ltd, 1907), p. 10; see Judge, 'Mary Neal and the Espérance Morris,' pp. 552–3 for comments on the authorship of the passage.

34 See his comments at the Goupil Gallery Conference in Anon., 'English Folk-Music in Dance and Song: Report on Conference held at The Goupil Gallery, 5 Regent Street, Thursday, November 14th, 1907 – 8.30 p.m.' (unpublished verbatim transcription of Conference proceedings), pp. 3–4. I am most grateful to Keith Chandler for letting me see this uniquely informative document.

35 C. J. Sharp, *Folk-Singing in Schools* (London: The English Folk Dance Society, 1912), pp. 17–18, quoted in Cox, 'The Legacy of Folk Song', pp. 92–3.

36 Neal, 'Set to Music', *Espérance Morris Book: Part I*, pp. 1–2.

37 Sharp's response to Neal's comments in the *Morning Post*, 5 May 1910, p. 5 appears in his letter to the same newspaper on 10 May 1910, p. 6.

38 Anon., *T.P.'s Weekly*, reprinted in Neal, *Espérance Morris Book: Part II*, p. 51.

39 Anon., 'Parliamentary Report,' *The Morning Post*, 1 April 1910.

40 Norman and Jeanne MacKenzie, *The First Fabians* (London: Quartet Books, 1979), p. 379.

41 See Midge Mackenzie, *Shoulder to Shoulder: A Documentary* (Harmondsworth, Middx: Penguin Books Ltd, 1975), p. 35.

42 See Judge, 'Mary Neal and the Espérance Morris,' p. 558 and associated footnotes for additional details.

43 See Lytton, *The English Country Gentleman*, pp. 265–83 and Mackenzie, *Shoulder to Shoulder*, pp. 46–193, passim.

44 Anon., 'Lady Gomme Here on First American Visit: Ex-Suffragist Worker, 83, Founder of Folk Lore Society, Admires New York,' cutting from unnamed American newspaper held in Gomme Collection, Folklore Society Archive, University College London. I am most grateful to Steve Roud, the Hon. Librarian of the Folklore Society, for bringing this to my attention. Lilah McCarthy, the wife of Harley Granville Barker (Alice Gomme and Sharp's longtime theatrical associate), was also a leading member of the Actresses' Franchise League.

45 Evelyn Sharp (1870–1955) was a militant suffragette, a friend and assistant to the 'Nealite' Pethick-Lawrences. She emerged from serving her first sentence in Holloway (for breaking a window at the War Office) a few days before her elder brother founded the English Folk Dance Society. Douglas Kennedy refers to her as 'another do-gooder [who] was on Mary Neal's side while Cecil was alive ...' ('Cecil Sharp and Mary Neal,' *English Dance and Song*, L:1 (April-May 1988), 5). In her autobiography, Evelyn Sharp makes no reference to her stance on the Revival, other than noting that she first came into folk dancing at an English Folk Dance Society Vacation School in Cheltenham in 1923. See *Unfinished Adventure: Selected Reminiscences from an Englishwoman's Life* (London: Bodley Head Ltd, 1933), p. 293 for details of this and her earlier life. Later, she also lectured and wrote on folk dance and was an active member of the English Folk Dance (and Song) Society, serving on its Executive Committee and National Advisory Council. For Sharp's opposition to women's suffrage, see Fox Strangways, *Cecil Sharp*, p. 202 and Mary Neal, 'The Broken Law,' *The Adelphi*, XVI (Jan. 1940), 149.

46 MacKenzie, *The First Fabians*, pp. 373–4.

47 See Judge, 'Mary Neal and the Espérance Morris,' p. 553.

48 Fox Strangways, *Cecil Sharp*, p. 111.

49 Sharp Collection, *Somerset County Gazette*, 21 May 1904.

50 A. H. Fox Strangways, 'Cecil Sharp: Obituary,' *The London Mercury*, reprinted in *EFDS News*, I:8 (Nov. 1924), 233.

51 All quotes from MacKenzie, *The First Fabians*, pp. 290–1. Sharp described himself as a 'Conservative Socialist'. A longtime acquaintance of George Bernard Shaw, he joined the Fabian Society in December 1900 after the departure of most of its London Independent Labour Party membership over the Fabians' support for imperialism (Sharp was also a member of the expansionist and militaristic Navy League). He resigned from the Fabians in May 1913 when the Society aligned itself with the Labour Party, but apparently 'withdrew his resignation at the request of Mrs. Sidney Webb, who thus justified the Society's action: 'It was felt that we had to take some part in the organization of a Labour Party, as perhaps the most important instrument for permeating working-class opinion. I admit all the deficiencies of the Labour Party. But incidentally its establishment has had the effect of bringing about a forward movement both in Trade Unionism and in co-operation. Moreover the very fact of its existence means that the Liberal Party is more anxious to take up collectivist measures.' Quoted in Maud Karpeles's highly selective and partial *Cecil Sharp: His Life and Work* (London: Routledge & Kegan Paul Ltd, 1967), p. 19n.

52 The Goupil Gallery Conference transcript of 1907 indicates at least two areas of common ground at that time, Sharp's clear acceptance of a role for 'Merry England' and Neal's comments on the need 'to guard the purity of Folk Music' by using only certificated teachers. See 'English Folk Music in Dance and Song', pp. 2–4. (Given that the proceedings were recorded verbatim, the orthographic basis of the use of both 'Merrie England' and 'Merry England' in transcriptions of Sharp's contributions is questionable.)

53 As late as December 1912, Neal responded to offers of a representative committee by proposing that Sharp should have the position of Director, with herself acting as Secretary. She also suggested putting Espérance teachers in for the EFDS Certificate. Sharp, however, maintained privately that 'she wouldn't cooperate on any terms, rejecting every kind of olive branch offered. This is perhaps as well for I am left with a free hand.' See Judge, 'Mary Neal and the Espérance Morris,' pp. 572 and 567.

54 Mary Neal, 'The National Revival of the Folk Dance: no. III - Present Day Interpreters of the Folk Dance,' *The Observer*, 3 Dec. 1911, p. 20.

55 Kennedy, 'Cecil Sharp and Mary Neal,' p. 5.

56 See Judge, 'Mary Neal and the Espérance Morris,' p. 567. For Sharp's use of influential supporters in his attempts to gain the directorship at Stratford, see final paragraph of letter from Cecil Sharp to Lady Gomme, 26 Mar. 1911 held in Sharp Correspondence, Vaughan Williams Memorial Library, Cecil Sharp House.

57 See Townsend, 'Cecil James Sharp as Collector and Editor of Traditional Dance,' pp. 60–6.

58 See, for example, comments on confusion and omission in F. B. Hamer, 'The Hinton and Brackley Morris,' and E. D. Mackerness, 'The Yardley Gobion Morris,' *Journal of the English Folk Dance & Song Society*, VII:4 (Dec. 1955), 205–16 and 216–17 and differences between the version of the Kirkby Malzeard Sword Dance published by Sharp and that actually performed by the local team in D. N. Kennedy, 'The Director Writes: Traditional Form,' *English Dance and Song*, XVII:3 (Dec. 1952–Jan. 1953), 76.

59 The circumstances surrounding the production of the published version of this text are detailed in my 'Excellent Examples: The Influence of Exemplar Texts on Traditional Drama Scholarship,' in Paul Smith and J. D. A. Widdowson, ed., *Traditional Drama Studies: Volume I* (Sheffield: Centre for English Cultural Tradition and Language & Traditional Drama Research Group, 1985), pp. 24–7.

60 Details of the history of the Winster dance in the nineteenth

century appear in my, 'Winster Morris Dance: The Sources of an Oikotype,' in Buckland, *Traditional Dance: Vol. I*, pp. 93–108. The particular significance in Sharp's campaign of asserting Winster's traditionality is indicated in Townsend, 'Cecil James Sharp as Collector and Editor of Traditional Dance,' p. 67.

61 See Judge, 'Mary Neal and the Espérance Morris,' pp. 573–4 for comments on lack of national publicity concerning Espérance by 1914.

62 For example Anon., *The Story of the English Folk Dance and Song Society*, Leaflet no. 12, rev. edn (London: EFDSS, 1974), p. 3 held in Wortley Collection, Centre for English Cultural Tradition & Language, University of Sheffield and Francis Toye, *For What We Have Received: An Autobiography* (London: William Heinemann Ltd, 1950), p. 98: 'in the end Sharp triumphed, and now his memory is revered by all musical folk-lorists, whereas of Mary Neal the very name is forgotten. Nevertheless in the beginning the movement owed a great deal to her disinterested enthusiasm.' See also 'Cecil Sharp,' *EFDS News*, I:8 (Nov. 1924), 201 and 204 and Rolf Gardiner, *The English Folk Dance Tradition: An Essay* (Hellerau: Neue Schule Hellerau, 1923), p. 28 for statements on Sharp as the sole collector and source of the revival of folk dance.

63 Kennedy, 'Cecil Sharp and Mary Neal', p. 5.

64 For examples see Mrs Kennedy, 'Early Days,' *EFDS News*, I:7 (May 1924), 174 and 'Early Days (cont),' *ibid.*, I:9 [ND], 278–81; Fox Strangways, *Cecil Sharp*, pp. 112–15, 140 and 186; Percy M. Young, *Vaughan Williams* (London: Dennis Dobson Ltd, 1953), p. 24; Kennedy, 'Folk Dance Revival,' pp. 82–3; Doc Rowe, '*With a Crash and a Din Comes the Morris Dancer in: A Celebration of Fifty Years of The Morris Ring 1934–1984* (NP: The Morris Ring, 1984), p. 9.

65 Aside from Florence Warren and May Start, who appear in the Espérance instruction books, only Rosina Mallet – 'an East London club girl, looking about fourteen, almost a slum girl, probably a gypsy, a brown-eyed goblin with feet trained by London barrel organs,' and Vic Ghiradi are named in published works. See Roy Judge, 'A Branch of May,' *Folk Music Journal*, II:2 (1971), 91 and Judge, 'Mary Neal and the Espérance Morris,' p. 577 respectively.

Chapter 5

'Teaching people how to be jolly': Sharp's legacy and the new Folk

We were ever so keen on Folk-dancing in our village of Turnsingle. Mrs. Dose, the doctor's wife dotes on it. The young newly-married couple at Kozy Kot are quite dabs at it, and it is thought likely that people who are building the new large garage and small bungalow may be interested, as well as the wealthy stockbroker, single, who is having the old 'Gorgonzola Cheese' converted into an old-world country cottage replete with oak beams and modern conveniences. When our Lady President can spare an evening from the exacting demands of a London season, she is always so sporting, and is the life and soul of the evening.... What we are short of, to make the thing really hum, is the Folk. Need I explain that we are doing this thing entirely on behalf of the Folk? We are trying to restore to them their lost heritage of dance and song. It is so difficult, however, to make them see how much they would enjoy it if they tried it.[1]

At the Stratford-upon-Avon Summer School in August 1913, Cecil Sharp was presented with the original of a cartoon which had appeared in *Punch* the previous December. Just as 'Merrie England Once More', the 1907 *Punch* cartoon given to Mary Neal, had encapsulated the cultural politics generating the Espérance Folk Revival, this later work embodied much of the ideology and practices of Sharp's new English Folk Dance Society. Entitled 'The Midgley-Tomlinsons, in order to be in the movement, hurriedly decide among their house-party to introduce morris-dances at a ball at their little place in the country', it consists of four vignettes showing characters in evening dress attempting various morris and country dances and performing a long sword dance with walking canes and umbrellas.[2] The impression created is at odds with the demands for 'faultless accuracy' and 'true traditional form' associated with the founding of the English Folk Dance Society. It does, however, support the accounts of genteel and inexpert enthusiasm provided by early recruits such as Helen and Douglas Kennedy.[3] Folk dance classes, more social than instructional, Douglas Kennedy recalled, were held at Lady Mary Trevelyan's town house in Smith Square, Westminster. As might be expected of the friends of such a 'brilliant young hostess and wife of one of the rising political figures of the time', the classes 'suffered frequent interruptions from calls for individual young men, who had hurriedly to abandon their young lady partners on a summons from Winston or Charles or even the P.M.'.[4] St Pancras and the formative role of the underclass had been firmly left behind. The leading representatives of the new folk were members of the fashion-conscious upper middle class.

Powered by such glittering associations, the years between the setting up of the English Folk Dance Society's organisation in 1912–13 and Cecil Sharp's death in 1924 saw the apogee of his approach to folk culture. Almost immediately, his decision to use the well-bred young as his dancers and men who could afford to do 'something honorary and useful' as his associates gave his work a status which Neal's combination of seamstresses and suffragettes could not hope to emulate. Already in decline by the summer of 1914, the Espérance Guild did not re-form in 1918. Control of the Folk Revival now lay entirely in Sharp's hands. The 'golden days of London as a musical centre' before the First World War, and the production of major symphonic works by Vaughan Williams and Holst in the mid-1920s, were also closely tied to the influence of Sharp's concept of folk music on a generation of composers. Attitudes within the musical establishment underwent a concomitant change, as old opponents like Ernest Newman and Sir Arthur Somervell became warm advocates of his position. For all its contradictions, Sharp's theory of folksong became international orthodoxy. His appointment as Occasional Inspector of Training Colleges in Folk-Song and Dancing in 1919, and increasing support for folk culture in schools under successive Presidents of the Board of Education in the 1920s, reflected views of Sharp as 'one of the greatest educational influences of the time'. And while calling for censorship of the 'frivolous and the vicious' in films and the theatre, the 1924 Report on Leisure by the Christian Politics, Economics and Citizenship movement founded by Archbishop

William Temple commended folk dancing as a most suitable pas-time for the working classes.[5] The English Folk Dance Society burgeoned. In 1924, London classes attracted an average weekly attendance of one thousand dancers. For the remainder of England (and Edinburgh), a county organisation was devised to provide a framework for the near-doubling of branch numbers – from twenty-three to forty-three – between 1918 and 1924. Vacation schools, conferences, festivals, competitions and displays 'carried the name of the Society into all parts of the country'. By 1928, the place of Sharp's concept of folk music in national culture was sufficiently established for a governor of the BBC to assure Society members, 'when our programme-makers are sometimes worried for lack of matter, they always gladly take refuge in folk music'. Speaking for the board of governors as a whole, he guaranteed to do 'all in our power to advance what we believe to be not only a great, but a national cause'.[6]

Virtually all that is now comprehended in the term Folk Revival came into being during this period. The ideology, institutions and public perceptions of folk culture and the processes by which it should be re-established were developed and reproduced. Cecil Sharp, as leader, arbiter and theorist, dominated these manifesta-tions. His construction of the Revival secured continuing hege-monic control for himself in his lifetime, and left little scope for anything other than total replication by his followers after his death.[7] Although much of what was inherent in his theory, institu-tions and practices was simply a negative image of the Espérance Revival, the combination of his dogmatism and the safe political alternative his approach offered ensured the acceptability of Sharp's version of the movement as a coherent and independent entity over which he reigned unchallenged.

Sharp's influence as a cultural leader was not limited to direction of the Folk Revival. His work also introduced a significant dimen-sion to contemporary perceptions of national culture. From the early 1850s, the majority of the English population lived in towns, their culture technically advanced, mass produced and 'popular'. As it came to be formulated in the first two decades of the twentieth century, however, national identity contained none of the elements of this preponderant daily experience. 'Englishness' resided in the 'land of the hedgerow and the village spire', its consummate inhabitant, the 'immemorial peasant', a literary fiction whom 'all countrymen of all conditions and periods, are merged into a singular legendary figure'.[8] The similarity between this archetype and the 'scientific' definition of the Folk is striking – but unsurprising. For all their apparent differences in source and methodology, the reproduction of Folkloristic theories and broader neo-pastoralist concepts involved identical assumptions about high and national culture. Specific inter-relationships were also furthered through the work of individuals who were equally active in both areas. E. V. Lucas, who became Sharp's assistant in the English Folk Dance Society for example, was a popular writer of travel books on England and also the author of the archetypal poetic evocation of Englishness, 'The Old Country'. But concepts of the unchanging, unindividuated Folk who were the sources of national culture, and literary depictions of the 'timeless inventor' of national culture 'who is more readily seen than any actual people', did not simply interact in middle-class observation to manifest like features in a range of Georgian writing. Especially after Sharp's collecting 'English' folksongs in remote settlements in the Appalachian Mountains of the United States had 'proved' his theory of the causal relationship between folksong and organic culture, neither the mythic literary archetype nor the academically instrumental Folk could be dismissed as mere constructs.[9] Sharp's undeviating advocacy of folksong as 'the faithful expression in musical idiom of the qualities and characteristics of the nation' introduced a mutually reinforcing dimension of objectivity to their reproduction. In the folksongs of Cecil Sharp, the immemorial peasant, the 'sweetest and most insidious' symbol of nation culture, became possessed of, and was authenticated by, a referential reality in expressive culture. Empirically grounded in Sharp's 'wide research', the musical idiom which characterised the nation emerged as the product of a pre-industrial idyll, devoid of politics, urbanism, social disquiet and any contemporaneity.

A neatly insulated symbiosis thus came into being. Sharp, his work and status benefited from, and became part of, the wider hegemonic reproduction of Englishness. In figures such as Edward Thomas's Lob, the shadowy mechanism that was the Folk were given a realised yet distanced personification – 'rural labour and rural revolt, foreign wars and internal dynastic wars, history, legend and literature ... indiscriminately enfolded into a single emotional gesture'.[10] Englishness was strengthened by tangential reference to England. But unlike Morris's or Blatchford's concepts of 'Merrie England', Englishness was unthreatening in its absence of any direct engagement with contemporary society. Socially untidy and politically awkward questions arising from the exist-ence of living singers and dancers in the external, industrial world of the England-outside-Englishness could be justifiably obviated. As revealed by field research, surviving examples of folk culture were rural and offered no stage of conflict larger than the familial, no national issue more immediate than the Napoleonic Wars. Thanks to folksong collectors' preconceptions and judicious selec-tivity, artwork and life were found to be identical. The ideological innocence which was the essence of the immemorial peasant was also a 'natural' characteristic of the Folk and their song. 'Merrie England' in its revolutionary, anti-capitalist formulation could thus be dismissed as 'un-English', just as 'the political unrest which followed the passing of the Reform Bill and the repeal of the corn laws' was presented as a specific cause of the decay of folk culture. Political consciousness and the root source of English culture were clearly inimical. Nationality was encapsulated in 'The Secret People', who spoke quiescently through middle-class poets and sang of meadows and primroses and a tapestry of lords and ladies in the carefully mediated folksongs of Cecil Sharp.

Resonances of these mutually supportive dynamics in art culture also acted in the reproduction of Englishness in popular culture. Here, however, it was the image of the landscape which predomi-nated: a summation of every depiction of country cottages, rolling farmland and the village set-piece of parish church, green, inn and duckpond. Like Sharp's construction of the Folk and folksong, the land of Englishness could be verified in regional landscapes and architecture in southern England. Equally, however, even this 'real' countryside existed in an intersubjectivity which condensed time and space and was thus independent of them. The lens of culture ensured that any thatched cottage was seen as an index of Eng-lishness first, and only secondly (if at all) as a form of housing. Specificity, and the requirement of confronting a particular village, the state of its buildings, its water supply and sanitation could be overlooked. A timeless landscape, dotted with villages which were 'typically English' rather than named locations, it was also peopled by representations of national character. Popular historicism elided sturdy Saxon freemen, honest Georgian yeomen and the dimpled milkmaids of Tudor England and set them disporting on a summer morning, on the green of a conceptual village in 'the country south of the Thames and Severn and East of Exmoor'. Authenticated in numberless chocolate box tops and picture postcards, evoked in railway poster and political speeches, given a form and rationale in the echo structuring of *Puck of Pook's Hill*, whose characters – from Roman legionary to modern child – simultaneously inhabit the same space, the 'South Country' was constantly identified as not just the image but a reality which was the embodiment of Englishness.

Acting within this formulation, folk performance was also recreated as an index of Englishness. By 1914, those villagers who hadn't left the countryside in search of better wages and working conditions might well spend their evenings at a film show, in dance halls or singing 'Alexander's Ragtime Band'. But in 'the South Country', the peasantry were irremovably 'Gathering Peascods' with 'Lovely Joan' on 'The Banks of Green Willow'. The village green of Englishness existed to be folk-danced on, its inn to be a setting for bucolic singing, innocent of the influence of 'vulgar' mass culture and 'negroid' jazz. Through Folk Revival performances, this refuge, untouched by war, unrest and modernity was made available to be experienced. The Revival offered a nationalistic, respectable and fashionable entertainment to its supporters. Each performance – and perhaps more especially those associated with displays and pageants – provided the possibility of realising the village in the mind which was the essence of national culture. Equally insulated from reality and change, Englishness and the Folk Revival interacted to create self-reflexive images of national history and popular culture which still exert considerable potency.

Throughout the period of Cecil Sharp's ascendancy, the English Folk Dance Society was the sole instrument of revival. Created by Sharp, it not only embodied his theories of folk performance but through its structure and practices reproduced his concept of the processes of revival. A virtual monopoly, and the form and type of performance permissible under its auspices were strictly regulated. Dances notated by collectors outside Sharp's circle were discouraged – 'You will never', Lavender Jones was warned before appearing at the Society's All England Festival at the Albert Hall in 1927, 'be allowed to perform anything *not* collected by Cecil Sharp.' [11] Indeed, the very existence of other collectors was disavowed – 'I am quite aware that a few people had discovered a few folk-songs before Sharp came into the field', Vaughan Williams wrote, abrogating the work of Sharp's contemporaries in the Folk-Song Society, nevertheless, 'it remains absolutely true' that 'Cecil Sharp discovered our national heritage of song and dance'. [12] To learn and exactly replicate the songs and dances collected by Cecil Sharp, in precisely the forms published by Cecil Sharp, following minutely the styles decreed by Cecil Sharp, became the essence of the English Folk Dance Society's activity.

Limitations were not only set on songs and dances from other researchers; Sharp also applied considerable selectivity to his own material. His rationale for re-introducing folk music to culture had been very clearly stated – neither nationalism, historical interest nor sentiment were sufficient in themselves, a case could be made entirely on aesthetic grounds. English folksong was, Sharp concluded, 'music of the very highest quality, that alone is sufficient justification for advocating its revival'. [13] Yet from the corpus of around 4500 songs which he collected, he put forward only a tiny proportion for widespread use, reprinting material from his earliest work in Somerset time and again in different publications. Equally restrictive criteria guided the belief that untrained singers should not be overtaxed by 'difficult' pieces. A handful of songs – 'Waly, Waly', 'Lord Randal', 'The Keeper' and 'Spanish Ladies' – therefore appeared with wearisome regularity on English Folk Dance Society programmes. To initial mediation on theoretical grounds during the process of collection, and subsequent bowdlerisation and collation of texts to ensure 'singability' for publication, were added still more opaque, unstated editorial judgements determining which were 'the best' or 'most suitable' songs to be returned to culture. Thus, despite his claims for folk music's universal aesthetic superiority, and the much vaunted scale of his field collection, Sharp's final word on the subject of his life's work, the two-volume *English Folk Songs: Selected Edition*, consisted of one hundred songs, only ten of which had not appeared elsewhere. [14] With the vast bulk of his collection remaining in manuscript, the musical heritage Sharp offered to revive for the nation in his publications was slight, unrepresentative and constrained.

Available forms of dance were also very selectively treated. Step dancing – a free, non-repeating combination of three or four basic movements, performed by men or women, usually as a solo, was,

Sharp reported in 1911, 'the most popular folk dance' among villagers. This perception is supported by regional studies indicating that 'in the first quarter of this century step dancers and musicians could be found in almost every family' in north Norfolk, with step dancing regularly taking place in pubs, at parties and at socials organised in village institutes. Despite its acknowledged vigour and wide distribution, however, Sharp never attempted to incorporate English step dancing in the Society's performances or examination system. It might be argued that Sharp recognised that the tradition was active and therefore felt it was not in need of revival. If this were so, however, the position would be inconsistent with the inclusion of an equally flourishing genre – children's games – in the syllabus of the English Folk Dance Society from its inception to the 1950s. In fact, the omission seems more likely to derive from Sharp's inability to devise a form of notation for step dancing's 'extremely complex and intricate movements'. Without a means of recording the dances, the publication of teaching manuals, on which so much of the Society's work (and Sharp's income) depended, was impossible. Clog dancing, another well established solo genre, which laboured under the dual handicap of complicated footwork and the taint of performance in the music hall, was also unrepresented.[15]

But most glaringly absent from the range of English dance traditions reproduced through the Revival were the morris dances of Lancashire and Cheshire. There were no technical grounds for non-inclusion – a simplified instruction book with a preface by Mary Neal was available as early as 1911.[16] The dances also formed an admitted part of the range of performances believed to derive from prehistoric rituals and thus represented a 'survival' of the racial heritage Sharp was dedicated to reviving. But northwestern morris was excluded from the English Folk Dance Society syllabus as a matter of conscious policy. The dances were held to be corrupt and thus 'unsuitable' for returning to national culture: 'generally speaking, the Lancashire Morris dance has come down to us, if at all, in a very degenerate condition, caused, it is said, by the extreme popularity, and urban character, of the festivities with which it is usually associated – the Wakes'.[17] This view derived from Sharp's proposal that folk dances were of two types – ceremonial and social. The implications of this division have been succinctly developed by Theresa Buckland:

Ceremonial dance was tied to the calendar; spectacular; it was performed by an elite who were all male; the dancers wore special dress;
and they appeared in conjunction with other customs. Social dance was
seen by Sharp as the direct antithesis of this. Social dance was not tied
to the calendar; it was performed by anyone of either sex; it was
choreographically simple; and no special dress was required. The consequence of this polarity was that any tradition which did not conform
to either of these two ideals was regarded as decadent... Any deviation
from Sharp's classic ideal of morris – the South Midlands tradition –
was clearly devolving from the archetype and, therefore, a modern
aberration.[18]

As in the case of his selection of West Country folksongs for
wide dissemination, Sharp privileged the dances from the area
which had provided his introduction to the genre. His personal
experience dictated what was to become the dominant form both
in the Revival and nationally. A marginalised, rural and anachronistic Folk were maintained as the source of culture; white-clad,
handkerchief-waving teams of men dancing on the village greens
of the South Country were assured a role as the embodiment of
lower-class Englishness. The ideal provided by Sharp's south Midlands archetype offered no conceptual or physical space for the
male factory workers and teams of girls who performed non-cere-
monial urban morrises at wakes and Rose Festivals in the industrial north-west. Vital and popular English dance traditions were
thus unrepresented or misrepresented in the Revival.

Styles of performance fared little better. The economic and
theoretical importance of the education system in Sharp's approach to folksong meant that adults at Vacation Schools were
used to try out the material from his latest publication for children: 'the students would sit in the hall and sing from the books of
folk songs which Sharp was editing (*English Folk-Songs for
Schools*, 1908–25). One or two might be sung as solos, but most
were in unison. It was 'boring' and 'like being back in school'.[19]
Such demonstrations of his newest products for schools to an
audience consisting largely of elementary teachers was probably an
effective form of sales promotion. And although the song tradition
represented in Sharp's fieldwork was almost entirely solo, stilted
choral performances of folksongs – 'as though they were hymns
in Sunday School' – did little more than reflect the stylistic consequences of his mechanistic approach to cultural regeneration. But

the combination of these factors at English Folk Dance summer schools year after year resulted in an identification of folksong with pedestrian performance and suitability for young children which has proved rather more durable in public consciousness than the songs themselves.

Underlying these misconceived approaches to performance, however, was a more fundamental difficulty. Although folksong was used as part of English Folk Dance Society entertainments, Vacation School and festival programmes, singing was a problematic area for the Revival. Folksong tunes were 'cast in the old modes' and represented 'the faithful expression in musical idiom of the qualities and characteristics of the nation'. The 'fatal blunder' of making 'editorial improvements' to the music was, therefore, held to be unnecessary. Though not invariably reflected in collectors' practice, 'in the precise form in which it was noted down by a competent musician from the lips of some folk-singer', the tune of a folksong called for reverential treatment and rapid assimilation among the classics through the English musical renaissance. Folksong texts, however, held far fewer attractions. Particularly in England, language is the archetypal indicator of class, and the words of songs – considered either as literature or as discourse – provided clear signs of the social status and absence of education of the singers from whom they had been collected. In contrast to the rubric applied to folk dances, therefore, precise adherence to the 'true traditional form' of songs was not advocated. Sharp edited the texts provided by the 'non-literate' Folk specifically to meet the needs of their new middle-class singers. 'No vocalist', he opined, 'would sing words that are ... ungrammatical. Nor could he, even if he would, sing accurately in dialect.'[20] Since Sharp, with his 'unique insight' into folk culture, had also seen fit to follow contemporary fashion and write piano accompaniments to folksongs, the widespread historical practice of unaccompanied singing was not encouraged by the Revival.

With little regard for the inconsistency of their position, enthusiasts who went to considerable lengths to provide special dress for dancing and took great care to follow precise instructions for revival performances of customary traditions, apparently saw nothing paradoxical in applying entirely different criteria to other genres of folk culture. Singing and dancing were treated quite separately and the question of replicating traditional vocal styles was never seriously considered. 'Our outlook on life,' W. R. W. Kettlewell proposed to 'apostles of the English Folk-song' at an EFDS Easter school at Bridport in 1930, 'our mode of expression and above all, our musical 'ear' are quite different from theirs [the Folk's] and we cannot possibly hope to recapture the atmosphere of the original ... the use of dialect and the wearing of fancy dress, when singing Folk-songs, are redundant. All we can do is to translate the original art of the Folk-singer into modern terms and adapt the songs for modern use.'[21]

Developing a national art entailed the application of criteria appropriate to art forms – a process to which, it was held, the Folk could contribute only indirectly. 'Experience has taught me', Sharp wrote for the information of members of his newly formed Society, 'that answers given by traditional dancers in response to direct questions concerning technical details of the dance must always be received with great caution.' Trustworthy information on matters of technique, he proposed, was to be found only in 'comments of this nature which dancers volunteer in the course of general conversation'.[22] Even this limited acknowledgement of expertise was denied to singers, whose age had rendered their voices 'quavering', 'thin and poor'. Kettlewell felt folksinging technique could best be acquired, therefore, by avoidance of 'un-English' traits of exaggeration, showing off, gesturing and dressing up. 'Tone colour' would then emerge naturally from good diction and concentration on telling the song's story.[23] By the time the Revival movement was fully established, field collection was believed to be virtually complete and gathering what 'little material' remained should, Sharp insisted, be restricted to those with the 'requisite experience and knowledge' – in practice himself and a handful of selected acolytes. Contact with the Folk and knowledge of their performance styles was therefore only available to the mass of Revivalists through the highly mediated channel of Sharp's publications.

But despite Sharp's 'informed' comment on the Folk's limitations as sources of objective information on their culture, his theories created ambiguities in the role of Revivalists as performers. Ignorant and uncaring though the Folk were construed to be, folk culture was in their possession. They danced the dances and sang the songs of the nation's ancestors, secure heirs of a heritage which had been prodigally abandoned by Revivalists' forebears. Given theory and practices which represented (and profited from) folk culture as a material inheritance, objectifying cultural products as 'treasure', 'wealth' or 'jewels', authentication of Revivalists as legitimate successors of the Folk was a crucial issue. It was not merely a question of justifying the need for a Revival as a source of new and better heirs to the national culture but of demonstrating ownership by developing the means to control the form of all that was involved in the reproduction of folk culture. Built into the structure and ideology of the English Folk Dance Society, therefore, was the role of expert in legitimation of performance – pre-eminently for Sharp himself, but through his *imprimatur* to the Society, its organisers and teachers. As well as graded classes with examinations, the Society also ran competitions which were adjudicated on standards and criteria set by the Society. The predilections of Revivalists, rather than reference to historical usage, were soon accepted as setting the terms for all types of performance – or even withholding their acquisition:

I should like to tell you what we have found at the Whitby Tournament. Those teams who danced to the piano, although they knew the figures of the dance perfectly, simply hadn't a chance against those teams who danced to a 'portable' instrument. This was such an obvious fact that we have now made a rule that each team shall bring its own musician who shall be part of the team, and that the use of the piano shall in all cases be avoided. And now in my own area I refuse to teach Sword dancing unless I can have a 'portable' instrument ... [24]

As Douglas Kennedy later summarised, 'We professionals are experts who owe our status to an initiation into the technical mysteries to which we only hold the key. We are the only reliable repositories of the folk dances and their mode of performance which is our precious stock-in-trade.'[25]

The Director's personal writ was all-embracing. He 'corrected' the position of dancers' arms in morris classes, apostrophised on style to entrants in Society competitions and determined the 'artistic expression' of all dances performed by the Revival:

the Country Dance is less strenuous, less stern and less detached than the morris; less involved and intense than the Sword Dance; but freer, jollier, more intimate and, in a sense, more human than either, perhaps because it is the only one of the three in which both sexes take part. It is a mannered dance, gentle and gracious, formal in a simple, straightforward way, but above all gay and sociable. The spirit of merriment, however, although never wholly absent from the dance is not always equally obvious. There are certain dances that are comparatively quiet and subdued in style, in which the normal gaiety is toned down to a decorous suavity; while between dances of this kind and those of the more light hearted variety, there are many that are emotionally inter- mediate in type. Now, it should be the aim of the dancer to feel these temperamental differences and reflect them in his manner and style. [26]

Confronted with the requirement of producing performances which were simultaneously 'mannered' and 'simple' or 'human' and 'suave' and manifesting gaiety in a non-obvious way, even Sharp's most devoted disciples seem to have failed to meet his expectations. Lavender Jones reduced his plethora of adjectives on the aesthetics of performance to noting that, for the purposes of teaching, country dances were divided into 'slow' and 'fast' and 'Mr Sharp decided which were to be done in slow times'.[27]

Sharp's influence extended beyond artistic control over the form and content of English Folk Dance Society performances. The institution which developed through the 1920s was also imbued with his views on the importance of patronage. A famous – preferably titled – name proved to be a near-essential qualification for office in the Folk Revival. Presidency of English Folk Dance Society branches was almost invariably conferred on a member of the local nobility. So assiduously was this course pursued that by 1931, of the forty branches which had a president, only three holders of the office were baldly designated Mrs, Mr or Miss. Dukes, Countesses, Dowager Duchesses, Lord Bishops, Knights and the like presided over twenty-five branches, while individuals holding a further seven academic, three civil and two military ranks accounted for the rest. Only a handful of these dignitaries, however, were members of the Folk Dance Society – they con- ferred prestige and donations, rather than offering active partici- pation. A similar pattern emerged in the National Advisory Council, through which selected numbers of the great and the good 'gave assistance' to the Society's National Executive Com- mittee. Here, as in the early Folk-Song Society, experience of performance and collection were less important criteria for mem- bership than influence in politics or the musical profession. In harmony with a Prime Minister who wrote lyrically of country smithies, plough teams and 'the eternal traditions from which we must never allow ourselves to be separated', and with the support of 'reliable' ex-ministers from the Labour Party, such as Margaret Bondfield, and high Tories like Viscount Halifax,[28] establishment ties with the Folk Revival as an embodiment of Englishness were comprehensively institutionalised.

The organisation of a mass movement was, however, less easily accommodated into Sharp's scheme for revival. Although a bewildering range of types of membership – Country, Associate, Donor, Corresponding and Ordinary – was created during the period, only a small proportion of those coming into contact with the English Folk Dance Society actually joined. It was not simply a matter of the level of the membership fee at any time. Costs of the appropriate range of clothing and footwear for dance classes and social events, travel and affording the time and charges for Vacation Schools (priced in the superior guinea rather than pounds), all limited access to full membership. And just as decisively as income, the ethos surrounding membership requirements ensured that wider participation was not encouraged. As early as 1911, Sharp had felt that the size of the movement should be limited and no further 'popularizing' adopted. 'Morris dances are not pink pills or any other quack medicine. They are art-products, and as such should be dispensed by artists and trained teachers.'[29] 'Slum girls ... with feet trained by London barrel organs' did not fit the new categories. The masses were expected to learn under the Society's supervision, rather than becoming active in its formal structures. The 'thoroughly vulgar movement' envisaged by Mary Neal formed no part of Sharp's agenda. Through the English Folk Dance Society, the Folk Revival was organised, staffed, trained and recruited among the middle classes.

Initially, these changes in the character of the Revival were not obvious to all observers. William Howells, an American writer visiting the 1913 Stratford Summer School, identified Sharp's work in terms more appropriate to the aims of the Espérance Guild:

It was a vision of Merry England which the heart could give itself to more trustingly than to any dream of the olden time when, with whatever will, England had far less reason to be merry than now. At last the sense of human brotherhood seems to have penetrated with conscience the legislature long so cold to the double duty law owes to common life. The English lawgiver has perceived that to keep people fairly good it must make them decently happy. Better wages, evener taxes, wholesomer housing, fitter clothing, are very well, but before these comes the right to a fairer part of the general cheer. It was told us that the young people who came to learn these glad tidings at Stratford were all teachers in the national schools, and that they were paid by the government for their pleasure in learning them. Perhaps I have not got it quite right, but it ought to be as I have got it.[30]

Although Howells misinterpreted the politics of the summer school, in one respect his observation was correct. An early consequence of the inclusion of folk dance in the state curriculum was a preponderance of teachers among the participants at Stratford. Here, and in the multiplying branches of the English Folk Dance Society, teachers acquiring qualifications in folk dancing began to provide significant proportions of the performers. Their presence confirmed the Society's acceptability to the educational establishment, but otherwise came to be regarded rather equivocally by the rest of the membership. What Sharp had upheld as a necessary condition for the revival of folk culture was soon represented as 'teachers aiming to improve their professional prospects' – a situation tolerable only for its substantial contribution to Society funds.

Aside from the staff of elementary schools, who were 'the young men in white flannels' and women in 'simple blue frocks' who had taken on the role of the Folk? The satirical eye describing the earnest, self-appointed committee teaching the villagers of Turnsingle 'How to be Jolly' highlighted the impact of a new but fast-growing social group – rural commuters. Dedicatedly 'doing all this for the Village', they were not 'bona-fide villagers' themselves and, as the article makes entertainingly clear, found little support among those who were.[31] Although it is a caricature, there is some evidence to suggest that the background attributed to these fictional reformers was a characteristic of the Society's new county-based organisation. The twenty-four members of Margery Howe's dance group in the Lake District in the 1930s were, she remembered, 'leading lights' of the area but very unrepresentative of 'the local 'born and bred' community ... only six were local people'. Howe's fellow dancers were also drawn from a narrow social band:

They were either people in professions or allied occupations or master

craftsmen. The farming community always gave us a wide berth ... neither could we enlist any of the many artisans, labourers, gardeners, or the domestic staff from the Castle. Most of these people danced traditionally, but could not be persuaded to become 'folk dancers'.
My personal impression has always been that the EFD(S)S, even at its most successful, has always appealed mainly to an often rather mobile sort of, as it were 'intelligentsia'.[32]

A 'romanticized passion for 'folk' culture', it was later claimed, 'was characteristic of the progressively minded within the intelligentsia of the period'.[33]

Much of the English Folk Dance Society's growth in activity in the 1920s derived from its restructuring on a county basis after the First World War. Devised by Sharp as a means of establishing the Revival in the countryside, the county organisation was funded by the Carnegie Trust, one of whose objects was making 'country life happy, bright and cheerful'. Within this structure, it was 'comparatively recent organisations' – Women's Institutes, Scout and Guide groups which were 'especially effective' in 'the re-introduction of folk-dances in village life'. The initiatives involved ranged from straightforward introductory classes and preparation for local competitions to large-scale projects such as arranging the 1921 festival in the grounds of the Earl of Bathurst's country house in 'feudal' Gloucestershire. Even before the development of the county structure, village folk dance groups were already being put forward as a solution to 'the problem of the labourer's amusement'. The first article in the first issue of the Society's *Journal* suggested that the 'psychological moment' had arrived for distributing to country people the 'keys to a spiritual kingdom' by encouraging them to take up folk dancing. In the village of Kelmscott, Mrs Sturge Gretton reported, even after a day's work, 'farm hands – carters and ploughmen' were 'thoroughly keen on their country dance': 'the peasant of to-day does take to folk dancing, takes to it ardently enough indeed to bicycle after his work – having first washed and changed into flannels – nine or ten miles, each way, to a dance'.[34]
The intentions of those 'anxious to introduce the dances into their villages' were varied. Some, like Sturge Gretton, saw it as an opportunity to develop 'genuine self expression' among the rural working class, a fulfilling alternative to 'city amusements, tangos and cinematographs' and a counter to growing rural depopulation.

Many echoed the arguments for reforming popular culture already well established in discussions of urban working-class life. Others – it was suggested, Sharp himself – saw the village as the only effective location for reviving folk dance – 'English folk art, having its roots in the country, cannot flourish if divorced too far from its origins ... the dances, when transplanted to the city, rapidly become stylised and devitalised.'[35] In general, Englishness and the appropriateness of folk dance – 'so nice and suitable' – informed perceptions of what should be encouraged as a pastime for country residents.

Means of enforcing cultural reformation were, however, limited. Sturge Gretton's initial proposal noted that 'the question we are faced with to-day is what the peasant will accept in the way of recreation, not what his masters will allow to him'. Rural classes were frequently subsidised. Wealthy residents paid the expenses of a visiting professional teacher from the English Folk Dance Society, while villagers were simply charged for tuition. Running costs were also lowered as soon as a member of the community became (or felt herself) sufficiently qualified to train others and take over the class teaching. Although resultant opportunities to extend their social life were welcomed by some organised groups or the community in general, on occasion, the 'enthusiasm' of middle-class advocates of country dancing led them to exert social pressure in a way which ultimately proved counter-productive: 'Country dancing, like other 'isms,' has been boosted in the villages, mostly on national and cultural grounds by persons who do not, perhaps, know their villagers well enough; their zeal has been magnificent, but often misdirected.'[36]

Whether overbearing or merely over-enthusiastic, the middle-class management of the Revival encountered an intensification of familiar difficulties when attempting to recruit dancers to village centres. Like the would-be folksong collectors before them, their activities necessarily brought them into close contact with members of the labouring classes. Although the role of teacher or organiser of a dance team was relatively unproblematic, dancing itself involved proximity and social interaction at an intimate level. In the early days of the Revival, this raised issues of considerable delicacy. With typical forthrightness, however, Sturge Gretton tackled the question head on. Although 'manual labour keeps the pores of the skin very open', she assured members of the English

Folk Dance Society that labourers in her evening dance group managed to 'achieve freshness equal to a gentleman's'.[37]

The 'ingrained idea' among the middle classes that the working class smelt[38] was an extreme manifestation of the realities undercutting the development of a performing consensus. As the Revival progressed, attempts to equate the Folk with contemporary villagers became fewer and complaints about the abilities of such 'untrained' performers from those 'trying to help village musicians ... develop that which lies hidden in all of us' more commonplace. By 1938, K. Marshall Jones, while confidently asserting the 'national' origin of folksongs, noted that rural novices were 'apt to trip up' when singing modal folksongs. Jones also urged the thoughtful organiser to exercise discretion in choosing songs for village use because 'while the tune may be very beautiful, the words are sometimes unsuitable'. Particularly for younger people, complete avoidance of songs containing references to blushing, love and lily white hands was strongly advised.[39] The scales in which folksongs had been recorded, and the themes and language which characterised their texts were, enthusiasts now widely accepted, entirely beyond the capabilities and appreciation of the rural working class. Despite the comprehensive formal and informal educational efforts of the Folk Revival, the inheritors of the folk tradition had again been found wanting.

Small wonder, then, that leading figures in the movement, such as Gustav Holst and Ralph Vaughan Williams, eventually concluded that 'they preferred the Morris of the Society's demonstration dancers to that of any of the traditional teams they had seen'.[40] As art forms, folk dance and song were best left to more cultivated performers, enthusiasts who had a broad range of social preferences in common and could meet easily as a group to follow their interest:

The places where Morris and Country dancing is spontaneously practised are probably not very numerous, and if they are fewer than they were, say, a hundred years ago, no conscious 'movement' from the towns is going to increase their number among rustics who have begun to prefer the foxtrot and the Charleston in village halls to the hey and the jig on the village green. It is no use trying to set the clock back in that fashion. On the other hand there is every chance that groups of people, here and there, will get together, without any ulterior motive to practise the cheerful and sociable art of folk-dancing.[41]

Vaughan Williams also came to see revived folksong as the ordained music of the middle class and middle brow, uniquely suited
to performance in the emotionally repressed, intellectually and
artistically restricted context of the bourgeois home:

In the English-speaking countries where our artistic impulses are so apt
to be inarticulate and even stifled, there are thousands of men and
women naturally musically inclined whose only musical nourishment
has been the banality of the ballad concert or the vulgarity of the
music-hall. Neither of these really satisfied their artistic intuitions, but
it never occurred to them to listen to what they called 'classical' music,
or if they did it was with a prejudiced view determined beforehand that
they would not understand it. To such people the folk-song came as a
revelation. Here was music absolutely within their grasp, emotionally
and structurally much more simple than their accustomed 'drawing
room' music, and yet it satisfied their spiritual natures and left no
unpleasant after taste behind it. Here indeed was music for the home
such as we had not seen since the days of Thomas Morley when no
supper party was complete without music when the cloth was cleared
away.[42]

Following the institution of a Folk Revival, a wave of national
regeneration did not spread outward from the schoolroom. Folk
dance became the pastime of groups who could afford to change
into flannels and knew a 'vulgar' dress when they saw one. The
'very noticeable thaw' Helen Kennedy detected among hostesses as
soon as they realised that Sharp's dance team were not 'professional dancers of the music-hall type',[43] could now be applied to
the movement as a whole. As in the proto-Revival embodied in the
Folk-Lore Society's 1891 *Conversazione*, where country gentlemen
from Staffordshire replaced the Folk in 'a careful reproduction of
the traditionary rendering' of their local 'Guisers' Play' and the
Secretary of the London Joint-Stock Bank told a folktale he had
collected in Suffolk,[44] social homogeneity became the preferred
option for English Folk Dance groupings. Taking care that the use
of dialect and absence of appropriate dress did not lead to confusion with membership of the working classes, Revival performers
could abandon convention and act out their fantasy of being the
Folk—women ostentatiously casting aside middle-class sexual
mores and ogling their partners at displays of social dancing, men
safeguarding the secrets of race by taking part in the 'fertility
rituals' of morris dancing. In a limited but none the less significant

way, the Folk Revival opened up a liberating, broader field of
physical expression to the arts and crafts orientated middle classes.

For all his proselytising, Sharp himself seems never to have had
any real enthusiasm for a popular movement. A national art music
was his first goal, and when he assumed the role of director of a
dance-based revival, his interest rapidly moved from folk tradition
to reviving entirely untraditional, mannered and elaborate, historical dances in the Playford Collection. Latterly, he mooted the
possibility of rivalling the notably modish Russian Ballet by creating a national company with a repertoire based on folk dance
forms, claiming that 'from the very beginning of the Folk Dance
movement I have hoped that it would lead to a great dance
development, possibly the foundation of an English Ballet'.[45] Making vernacular arts fit bourgeois aesthetics was the basis of his
career and the guiding spirit of the Revival which he built around
it.

Sharp had consciously chosen classical musicians, schoolteachers
and his 'personal following' among the upper middle class as the
propagators of Revival. This combination of pragmatism and
individual predilection achieved immediate success in the establishment of his version of a national movement. The effects of such
early choices, however, remained to shape the social dimensions
of the Revival as it developed throughout the rest of the century.
Local and national opinion formers were cultivated and their
wholehearted approbation won. Their wives, sisters and daughters
entered for certificates, attended vacation schools, danced in competitions, taught village classes and organised pageants with
groups of local schoolchildren trotting mechanically round Olde
Englishe maypoles. But folksong never replaced popular music in
variety theatres and folk dance failed to touch the crowds in urban
ballrooms. Those who had kept folksongs and dances in their
repertoire and the majority of the population, the industrial working classes, had no obvious role. The 'missing Folk' became the
hole at the heart of the Revival.

Notes

1 Anon., 'Teaching People How to be Jolly,' *EFDS News*, II:18 (Oct.
1928), 126–7 reprinted from the *Evening Standard*.

2 C. A. Shepperson, *Punch*, 11 Dec. 1912, p.481.

3 As for example, in Mrs [Helen] Kennedy, 'Early Days,' *EFDS News*, I:7 (May 1924), 174–7. This also details Sharp's direction of a performance of the Kirkby Malzeard sword dance using walking sticks and umbrellas as swords, whilst 'Early Days (cont),' *EFDS News*, I:9 (May 1925), 282 cites the use of evening dress in demonstration 'so as to impress on the audience the fact that it was a real social dance'. Helen (Karpeles) Kennedy (1887–1976) became interested in folk dancing as a result of attending the Stratford-upon-Avon Festival in 1909. She and her sister, Maud Karpeles, shortly afterwards began attending Sharp's classes at Chelsea Polytechnic and around 1910 formed 'a small Folk-Dance Club' which 'held weekly practices in our drawing room'. This group provided the basis for Sharp's demonstration teams and the nucleus of the early membership of the English Folk Dance Society. During the First World War, Helen Kennedy acted as Director of the EFDS in Sharp's absence in America, was appointed by the Board of Education to inspect folk dance in schools after the First World War and maintained a lifelong association with the organisation of the English Folk Dance and Song Society.

4 Douglas Kennedy, 'Mary, Lady Trevelyan 1882–1966: Obituary,' *Folk Music Journal*, I:3 (1967), 200. Douglas Kennedy (1893–1988) was introduced to folk dancing by his sister, Helen Kennedy-North, a student at Chelsea Physical Training College, and became a member of Sharp's first male morris side. He was subsequently Director of the English Folk Dance Society – later the English Folk Dance and Song Society (1925–61), Squire of the Morris Ring and President of the Folklore Society (1964–7). From 1964 he was a Vice-President of the English Folk Dance and Song Society and from 1975–7 of the International Folk Music Council (founded in 1947 by his sister-in-law, Maud Karpeles). See Roy Judge and Derek Schofield, ed., 'A Tribute to Douglas Neil Kennedy, O.B.E., 1893–1988,' *Folk Music Journal*, V:4 (1988), 520–36. He was also, with Rolf Gardiner, a founder member of the 'hidden, unofficial, band of friends and accomplices: *kinsmen in husbandry*' (later Kinship in Husbandry). This 'free association, based on loyalties and affections' which had the 'great advantages' of enfolding 'common thinking and activity whilst avoiding all the paraphernalia of democratic business' was 'able to percolate many movements and appear in different guises'. Initiated by Gardiner in 1941, its aim was 'to hammer out policies for agriculture and the rural order in the second half of the twentieth century' and combat 'the danger which imperilled the English tradition in the post-war period ... the bureaucratic or managerial Welfare State'. Rolf Gardiner, 'Can Farming save European Civilisation?' in Andrew Best, ed., *Water Springing from the Ground:*

An *Anthology of the Writings of Rolf Gardiner* (Shaftesbury: Trustees of the Estate of Rolf Gardiner, 1972), pp. 196–9.

5 Leisure (COPEC Report V), p. 132 quoted in E. R. Norman, *Church and Society in England 1770–1970* (Oxford: Oxford University Press, 1976), pp. 296–7.

6 Dr Montague Rendall, 'Personal Memories of Cecil Sharp,' *EFDS News*, II:16 (Feb. 1928), 80.

7 Sharp's speedy and vindictive marginalisation of a potential rival within the English Folk Dance Society is detailed in James C. Brickwedde, 'A. Claud Wright: Cecil Sharp's Forgotten Dancer,' *Folk Music Journal*, VI:1 (1990), 5–36. Reaction to Wright's distinctive athleticism may also underlie Sharp's description of the morris as 'an impersonal dance ... peculiarly unfitted for the exploitation of personal idiosyncrasies' in C. J. Sharp, 'Style,' *EFDS News*, I:3 (Mar. 1922), 68.

8 Raymond Williams, *The Country and the City*, (St Albans, Herts.: Granada Publishing Ltd, 1975) pp. 308–9. Further discussion of these issues is also contained in Alun Howkins, 'The Discovery of Rural England' and Peter Brooker and Peter Widdowson, 'A Literature for England,' in Robert Colls and Philip Dodd, ed., *Englishness: Politics and Culture 1880–1920* (London: Croom Helm, 1986).

9 Selections from this collection were published in a joint edition with Olive Dame Campbell as *English Folk Songs from the Southern Appalachians* (New York & London: G. P. Putnam's Sons, 1917); by Sharp alone as *Folk-Songs of English Origin, Collected in the Appalachian Mountains* (2 vols; London: Novello & Co., 1919, 1921) and *Nursery Songs from the Appalachian Mountains* (2 vols; London Novello & Co., 1921, 1923) and in an edition edited by Maud Karpeles as *English Folk Songs from the Southern Appalachian Mountains* (2 vols; London: Oxford University Press, 1932).

10 Williams, The Country and the City, pp. 308–9.

11 Roy Palmer, 'Your Dancing is Simply Glorious ...,' *English Dance and Song*, L1:1 (Apr.-May 1989), 3. At this festival, Lavender Jones's dance group did, in fact, perform a dance collected by Ella Leather, a longtime member of the Folklore Society and a published fieldworker of some repute. Jones adds however, that Leather's notation was not accepted as 'correct' by Maud Karpeles and the movements in the dance had to be completely reversed before it was allowed into the programme for performance.

12 R. Vaughan Williams, 'The Late Cecil J. Sharp,' *EFDS News*, I:8 (Nov. 1924), 219.

13 Cecil J. Sharp, *English Folk Song: Some Conclusions*, ed. Maud Karpeles (4th rev. edn, Wakefield: E. P. Publishing, 1972), p. 180.

14 London: Novello & Co., 1921–23.

15 Fuller details of this tradition and absence of its encouragement by Sharp and in the Folk Dance Revival are contained in Ann-Marie Hulme and Peter Clifton, 'Social Dancing in a Norfolk Village 1900–1945,' *Folk Music Journal*, III:4 (1978), 359–77; the same authors' 'Solo Step Dancing within Living Memory in North Norfolk,' in Theresa Buckland, ed., *Traditional Dance: Vol. I* (Crewe: Crewe & Alsager College of Higher Education, 1982), pp. 29–56; Ann-Marie Hulme, 'Recording Step Dancing,' in Theresa Buckland, ed., *Traditional Dance Vols. V & VI*, pp. 82–7; J. F. and T. M. Flett, Traditional *Step-Dancing in Lakeland* (London: English Folk Dance and Song Society, 1979) and Julian Pilling, 'The Lancashire Clog Dance,' *Folk Music Journal*, I:3 (1967), 158–79. See also A. D. Townsend, 'Cecil James Sharp as Collector and Editor of Traditional Dance,' in Buckland, *Traditional Dance Vols V & VI*, pp. 60–3 which suggests that Herbert MacIlwaine, Musical Director at the Espérance Club and Sharp's collaborator on the early morris books, developed the method of dance notation used by Sharp. At least one instructional book for clog dancing was also produced in the nineteenth century – Henry Tucker, *Clog-Dancing Made Easy: The Elements and Practice of that Art, Arranged, Simplified, and Corrected* (New York: DeWitt Publishing Co., 1874). This work, republished in 1989 by Chris Brady, Shoreham by Sea, Sussex, introduces American-style clogging, but for performance in wooden-soled clogs.

16 John Graham, *Lancashire and Cheshire Morris Dances* (London: J. Curwen & Sons Ltd, 1911). See Daniel Howison and Bernard Bentley, *The North-West Morris: A General Survey of the Traditional Morris Dance of the North West of England*, Journal Reprint no. 11 (London: English Folk Dance and Song Society, 1960), p. 15 and Michael Higgins, "A Properly Conducted Morris Dance': The Role of Jimmy Cheetham before the Great War in Oldham and Royton, Lancashire,' in Theresa Buckland, ed., *Traditional Dance: Vol. IV* (Crewe: Crewe & Alsager College of Higher Education, 1986), p. 99, n. 45 for comments on Graham's notation and Mike Heaney, *An Introductory Bibliography on Morris Dancing* Vaughan Williams Memorial Library Leaflet no. 19 (London: English Folk Dance and Song Society, 1985) for further references to works dealing with morris dance forms in Lancashire and Cheshire. Heaney also includes commentary on the 'neglect' of 'degenerate' dances from other areas outside the south Midlands arising from Sharp's comments that 'in Worcestershire and Hertfordshire and, so far as our investigation goes, in the northern counties, Morris dancing has undoubtedly fallen on evil days and become decadent' in Cecil J. Sharp and Herbert C. MacIlwaine, *The Morris Book III* (London: Novello &

Co., Ltd, 1910), p. 10.

17 Iolo Williams, *English Folk-Song and Dance* (London: Longmans, Green & Co, 1935), p. 159. Though not taught by the Society, the 'least degraded' north-western morrises were, however, sometimes included in its displays – see for example, the appearance of a team from Royton at the Albert Hall Festival in 1931, *The English Folk Dance Society Report September 1st, 1930, to August 31st, 1931* (London: English Folk Dance Society, 1931), p. 14.

18 Theresa Buckland, 'English Folk Dance Scholarship: A Review,' in Buckland, *Traditional Dance: Vol. I*, p. 11. The whole article provides a clear and stimulating overview of the development of folk dance scholarship.

19 Roy Palmer, 'Your Dancing is Simply Glorious ...,' p. 2. See also Kenneth N. J. Loveless, 'Douglas Neil Kennedy, O.B.E.: An Obituary,' *English Dance and Song*, L:1 (Apr.-May 1988), 4 for a description of the 'unsatisfactory' role of a teacher 'with the students sitting in rows, all their eyes glued to their books, while one endeavoured to teach them ...'.

20 Cecil J. Sharp, 'Preface,' *English County Folk Songs* (London: Novello & Co. Ltd, 1961) [unpaginated]. Originally published in 5 volumes, 1908–12.

21 W. R. W. Kettlewell, 'The Singing of English Folk-Songs,' *EFDS News*, II:23 (May 1930), 267. Vestiges of this stance also seem to inform more recent comments on folk and art song by Eric Crozier, the librettist of Benjamin Britten's opera *Albert Herring* – 'The difference between a Suffolk yokel singing such a folk-tune ['The Foggy Dew'] and the art-song created by Britten prompts Crozier to give a caution about translating 'Albert Herring' too realistically into Suffolk accents.' See Edward Greenfield, 'The Love that Inspired a Great Composer,' *The Guardian*, 3 June 1986, p. 9.

22 Cecil J. Sharp, 'Some Notes on the Morris Dance,' *EFDS Journal*, I:1 (1914), 6.

23 Kettlewell, 'The Singing of English Folk-Songs', p. 272.

24 Miss G. A. Hall, 'The Sword Dance,' *EFDS News*, II:21 (Sept. 1929), 218–19. Hall never mentions that, for practical and economic reasons, sword teams had historically used a 'portable' instrument to accompany their dances – her decision was apparently based entirely on a personal preference. Hall's view that such a judgement also provided a suitable basis for withholding instruction on sword dances in an area where their performance had long formed part of local culture is perhaps even more indicative of Revivalists' concept of their role as experts in legitimation.

25 Douglas Kennedy, 'The Amateurs,' *English Dance and Song*, IX:5 (June-July 1945), 44.

26 C. J. Sharp, 'Style,' *The Country Dance Book: Part VI* (London: Novello & Co. Ltd, 1922), p. 50.

27 Palmer, 'Your Dancing is Simply Glorious...,' p. 2.

28 See Martin J. Wiener, *English Culture and the Decline of the Industrial Spirit 1850–1980* (Cambridge: Cambridge University Press, 1982) pp. 98–126 for a fuller discussion of contemporary political attitudes to 'the rustic spirit of the nation' and Wal Hannington, *Unemployed Struggles 1919–1936: My Life and Struggles Amongst the Unemployed* (Wakefield: E.P. Publishing Ltd, 1973), pp. 169–74 and 203 (originally published by Lawrence & Wishart in 1936) for specific information on Margaret Bondfield in this period.

29 A. H. Fox Strangways, *Cecil Sharp* (Oxford: Oxford University Press, 1933), p. 111.

30 W. D. Howells, *The Seen and Unseen at Stratford-on-Avon: A Fantasy* (New York & London: Harper & Bros., 1914), pp. 34–5.

31 Anon., 'Teaching People How to be Jolly,' pp. 126–7. The whole article provides a concise (and entertaining) illustration of high-souled contemporary attitudes and rather less worthy practices.

32 Margery Howe, 'A Small Corner of Lakeland: Memories of the EFDS in the Thirties,' *English Dance and Song*, XLVII:3 (Autumn-Winter 1985), 20.

33 Norman, *Church and Society in England*, p. 296.

34 M. Sturge Gretton, 'Folk Dancing In and About Burford,' *EFDS Journal*, I:1 (May 1914), 2.

35 *English Folk Dance & Song Society Report For the year September 1st, 1933 to August 31st 1934* (London: English Folk Dance Society, 1934), pp. 6–7.

36 'Constant Billy', 'Folk Dancing in the Villages,' *English Dance and Song*, II:3 (Jan.-Feb. 1938), 42.

37 Sturge Gretton, 'Folk Dancing In and About Burford,' p. 2.

38 See Peter Stansky and William Abrahams, *The Unknown Orwell* (London: Paladin Books, 1985), p. 147n. for a discussion of George Orwell's claim that 'his chief impression of the working class, as he grew older, was that they smelt ... that he had been *taught* that they smelt, and that this was a lesson ingrained in all boys of his class from an early age on'. Ernest Newman's repeated association of the smell of Russian peasants with the Russian Ballet, as opposed to the fresh air and absence of smell he found in the 'clean-limbed, clear-eyed art' of Sharp's English Folk Dance Society demonstration team, also seems to bear out the wider implications of this prejudice. See 'The Week in Music' reprinted

from *The Manchester Guardian* in *EFDS News*, I:2 (Aug. 1921), 38–40.

39 K. Marshall Jones, 'The Use of Folk Song in Village Choir Training,' *English Dance and Song*, III:2 (Nov.-Dec. 1938), 19.

40 Douglas Kennedy, 'A Jubilee Symposium: 2. Folk Dance Revival, 'Folk Music Journal*, II:2 (1971), 82.

41 A. K. H. 'Music of To-Day: The Present Position of Folk Song,' *Liverpool Post and Echo*, 15 Nv. 1926, reprinted in *EFDS News*, II:13 (Jan. 1927), 15.

42 Ralph Vaughan Williams, *National Music* (Oxford: Oxford University Press, 1934), p. 69.

43 Mrs Kennedy, 'Early Days (cont),' 281.

44 See *Programme of Entertainment* for the Conversazione held at Mercers' Hall Cheapside, 5 Oct. 1891 as part of the International Folk-Lore Congress, held in the Gomme Collection, Folklore Society Archive, University College London. Running against the grain of practices in the Folk Revival, however, is a note under the heading 'Folk-Songs' which indicates that 'of the songs given by Miss Wakefield 'Sally Gray' is in the Cumberland dialect', while the experienced field collector Charlotte Burne strongly advised that folksongs 'should be without accompaniment, unless a violin only were allowed, in my opinion – at any rate not a piano!'. I am most grateful to Steve Roud, the Hon. Librarian of the Folklore Society, for information relating to this event.

45 Cecil Sharp, 'The Development of Folk Dancing,' *EFDS News*, I:6 (Nov. 1923), 145 and similar views expressed in Cecil J. Sharp, 'The English Folk-Dance Revival,' *The Music Student*, XI:12 (Aug. 1919), 449–51. For examples of ballets developed within the Folk Revival, see Anon., 'Folk-Dance Ballet at Cambridge,' *EFDS News*, no. 3 [undated, 1921–2?], 66–7; M.K. [Maud Karpeles], 'Old King Cole,' *EFDS News*, II:13 (Jan. 1927), 12–13 and performances briefly indicated in Fox-Strangways, *Cecil Sharp*, p. 193. There may also be a sense in which Sharp the nationalist was trying to assert the claims of England as a possible source for artistic development while simultaneously aiming to colonise and reform the fashionable ballet for Englishness. See Martin Green, *Children of the Sun: A Narrative of 'Decadence' in England After 1918* (London: Constable & Co. Ltd, 1977), pp. 50–61 for a discussion of the role of the *Ballets Russes* in fashionable life in England in the 1920s.

Chapter 6

'It's warmer in the street': re-interpreting culture and incorporating the Folk

it always amuses me to contrast those who now patronise folk-music with those who invented or naturally practised it.
In the days when I went ahunting folk-tunes with Mary Neal, there was, I remember, an old fellow who began a song and then, suddenly bashful, stopped. Pressed for a reason, he finally explained that 't'was a bit clumsy for girls.' A number of these songs are indeed 'a bit clumsy for girls' (not perhaps modern girls), dealing, as so many of them do before being bowdlerised, with the vicissitudes of rape and seduction. And the delivery of them, like folk-dancing, was almost always associated with a great deal of rowdiness and drinking, which, in fact, is why they were discouraged in the staid days of the nineteenth century. Anything less attuned to the earnest, high-souled young men and women who, stimulated by cocoa and sustained on buns, prance respectably around at folk-festivals I am unable to imagine.[1]

By the beginning of the 1930s, Folk culture had been fully colonised by the Revival. The Folk, on the verge of extinction at the turn of the century, could now be assumed to be non-existent. And 'save for rare and isolated instances' when 'spontaneous folk-singing on the part of country people' took place, their culture 'had died out'. Revivalists had replaced the Folk, and constructed the population of rural areas as non-Folk – failed inheritors of the Folk's culture and artistic abilities. In the absence of a living Folk, the work of collecting was impossible – but fortunately, it was also held to be unnecessary, since 'practically the whole of English folk-song' had already been recorded by 'musicians who have spent much time and money in searching out and noting down our tunes of the countryside'.[2] Now equally insulated from the field as from the recalcitrant ballroom and cinema bound urban working classes, the movement could justifiably concentrate on polishing its own aesthetic. The sum of folk culture and its reproduction were indisputedly in its control. With no one – apparently – to gainsay them, Revivalists wrote unselfconsciously of folksongs as 'our folksongs', dances as 'our folk dances'.

The English Folk Dance Society continued to enjoy broad establishment favour. Its branch officials were titled county worthies. Prominent members of the musical profession – Sir Arthur Somervell, Adrian Boult and Sir Henry Hadow political figures like H. A. L. Fisher, Margaret Bondfield and the campaigning journalist Henry Nevinson joined leading representatives of the arts world, such as Harley Granville Barker, on its National Advisory Council. Membership was still growing in country areas, and Cecil Sharp House, a prestigious and expensive national headquarters for the movement, and monument to its founder, had been opened in 1930.[3] The Society's activities included organising conferences, displays, international exchanges, competitions and festivals, as well as teaching, examining and granting certificates of proficiency in branches as far apart as Bradford and Boston, Massachusetts. Through the Revival, folk dancing had become an expected feature of village fetes and national celebrations across England, while music inspired by folksong regularly appeared on programmes in concert halls great and small. The movement was mature, widespread and formed a restricted, but accepted, part of national life.

Yet even as its hegemonic position seemed most secure and its establishment credentials ever more fully developed, fundamental premisses of the Folk Revival came into question. Although the status of the Folk as the well-spring of Englishness and national culture never came under concerted frontal assault, across a range of social, political and cultural positions there was a selective reduction in support for the institution and practices of the Revival. As the crises of the decade grew in number and intensity, established systems, whether of capitalism, democracy or art, were widely agreed to be failing.[4] New approaches were called for – youthful iconoclasts demanded the wholesale scrapping of exhausted approaches from well-connected placemen; commitment and social concern superseded hedonistic self-absorption. Unsurprisingly, therefore, as a 1938 paper for the Folk-Lore Society tersely noted, 'Tradition' had become 'unpopular at present'.[5] Meanwhile, the Revival, inured from consideration of change by self-satisfaction and a reactionary ideology embodied in the mechanistic approach of the English Folk Dance Society, continued to replicate its existing forms. In the face of worldwide economic depression and the rise of Fascist dictatorships, the carefully insulated reproduction of a synthetic art culture that was folksong and dance became less sustainable. And leaving permanent fissures, the identity of the Revival, and its institutional base in the English Folk Dance Society, fragmented.

These changes were most publicly demonstrated in what had previously been the pinnacle of the Revival's cultural success: classical music. Ralph Vaughan Williams, the English Folk Dance Society's Honorary Musical Adviser, 'held the centre stage in the 1930's in England', and the period was 'a time of achievement so far as British composers were concerned'. But even its advocates came to feel that folksong's contribution to the English musical renaissance had run its course. 'There is virtually no national music in England now, and it is significant that nobody can follow up Vaughan Williams' attempt to find the English tradition', Bruce Pattison concluded in his 1935 survey of 'Musical History'.[6] 'One English composer of genius successfully incorporated ... native nuances into a style which from the first had been unmistakably personal', Arnold Bax agreed, but otherwise, the influence of 'the era of sacred pentatonic scale and hallowed minor seventh' had not been 'very happy'. During this period, Bax added, Frederick Corder, President of the Society of British Composers (1905–18) and Professor of Composition at the Royal Academy of Music, complained of listening 'to five works of young native composers one after the other', as 'each without exception began with a figure in the latter mode.'[7] Modern culture and inadequate talent were generally identified as the roots of the problem. Like the music of any nation, the composer and folksong collector E. J. Moeran (1894–1950) proposed, 'English folk-song ... is apt to become exceedingly dull when it is handled by musicians, who, with the best intentions, possess more technical resource than inspiration, and who, by virtue of their surroundings, their sophistication and their respectability, have never experienced the feeling which gave birth to this kind of music'. Lacking the abilities of 'a Haydn or a Moussorgsky', he reported, 'the idiom of folk-song in British music' was 'submerged beneath a wave of unpopularity'.[8]

Folksong itself was no longer the revelation of pure sound and simple melody which had charmed the ears of neophyte audiences in 1907. Orthodoxy had replaced innovation and excitement. Nowadays wrote an advocate, responding to 'the jeers of academic musicians on the subject of 'folk-song cranks'', 'the thing has gone beyond the stage of being a fashionable cult' – folksongs could be 'taken for granted'. [9] In more radically modernist circles, however, not just the fashion but the role of conscious reperformance were beginning to be examined with some severity – and it struck a popular chord:

Miss Edith Sitwell has been saying unkind things about the cult of folk-songs and Morris dances among grown-up people. She thinks that this cult is not in the nature of simplicity, but in the nature of affectation. We entirely agree. These old songs and dances have a certain antiquarian interest, and there is no harm in collecting information about them, nor in reproducing some of them as curiosities or as physical exercises for the young. But when we get a 'revival' of them, when we have pale-faced intellectuals warbling and capering under the delusion that they are restoring the simple gaieties of Old England, the thing becomes ludicrous... Morris dancing has undoubtedly its value as a healthy recreation for school children. But it would be very much better left to children.[10]

The division between Revivalists and the source of the culture they sought to reproduce also led to fundamental questions:

Much of this [is] no more than the nostalgia of well-off and sophisticated people for hard physical work, for a simplicity and contact with nature which they felt they had lost. The nostalgia [is] frequently genuine; but the cure is to go out and do hard, physical work, to live simply and in close contact with nature. And yet, and yet ... was it better to be cured? Or was it better to write earthy Georgian poetry in a villa at Sevenoaks or Beaconsfield? To do one's house up with cottagey, naive wallpapers and arrange dear, simple old flowers in copper jugs? To collect round the Bechstein in Popsie's studio, with its scarlet walls, emerald ceiling and huge black 'pouffes', to sing about jolly ploughboys, tarry sailors and milkmaids dabbling in the dew?[11]

Even those who saw a dimension beyond the antiquarian in folksong and dance were no longer drawn to its reperformance on the Revival's terms. Increasingly, artists convinced of folk culture's potential as a starting point for new creative work saw a need to disassociate it from its existing institutionalised realisations. Thus, although he believed that folk dance would prove the richest source for movement in dance-drama, Tyrone Guthrie (1900–71), 'inseminated by the folk art revivalists' at Oxford and a formative influence at the Old Vic for much of the 1930s, felt that 'for the moment it had become too isolated by pedantry and too infected by amateurism'.[12] The Revival was not, he later wrote, 'a spontaneous expression of a popular need, it was sicklied o'er from its inception by the pale cast of intellectual and artistic sophistication. Also, its aspirations, as well as its roots, were firmly bedded in the past. There was something decadent in the insistence upon old tunes, old dances, the glorification of archaism for its own sake, the assumption that hand-beaten, hand-woven articles just must be better than similar articles produced by machinery. There was something plumb idiotic about dancing around Maypoles and recreating Merrie England in the public parks of Liverpool and Birmingham.'[13] To develop drama which was progressive but 'rooted in English tradition', Guthrie began a collaboration with the Group Theatre of London, founded by Rupert Doone, a former member of Diaghilev's *Ballets Russes*. Productions by the Group Theatre combined folksongs like 'King Herod and the Cock' and characters from mummers' plays with modern choreography and contemporary commentaries scripted by the poet W. H. Auden. Under the influence of Guthrie and Auden, the Group initially specialised in reworked medieval material such as *Fulgens and Lucrece*, *Launcelot of Denmark* and *The Deluge* from the Chester Mystery Cycle. Productions involving these historical sources attracted the support of longstanding theatrical associates of the Revival such as Harley Granville Barker, performers like Joan Sharp, librarian of the English Folk Dance Society and Cecil Sharp's daughter, and, most influentially, members of the Scaife family, who were also prominent in simultaneous attempts to revive folk performances at Springhead in Dorset. But in 1934, having spent some time at the Group's summer school, where maypole dancing formed an essential part of the activities, Auden wrote them an entirely original work, *The Dance of Death*, a play with a sub-text which set the Revival's practices and organisation in the context of contemporary politics:

Auden focused particularly on the Group's own yearnings for renewal and its particular dance of death. He did so by designing a mask for the Group Theatre so like its face as to be more a revelation than a disguise.

The Group did not know exactly what Auden was up to but they knew how to do what he wanted because that was what they had been doing. Like the Chorus on stage, they were middle-class folk intent on revitalizing their dust; given to arduous training, choral singing and dancing, and co-operation; idealists who sought a communal art but accepted an artistic dictator; who dreamed of an artistic colony and took refuge from perplexity in physical accomplishment; who looked for a new life in the theatre but harboured nostalgia for the mumming and melodrama of 'simpler times' ...[14]

Although T. S. Eliot felt the production was 'extremely well done' and audience reactions at two private performances were quite favourable, few aspects of the play found a positive critical response from mass circulation periodicals. Doone's view of 'the theatre as a social force' and Auden's combining the Doctor from the mummers' play and Death as a Fascist Dictator with a call for 'the 'liquidation' of the bourgeoisie by the Up-and-Coming Saints in Scarlet' proved rather too advanced for general consumption. But one section of the play's 'epic construction' was found relatively satisfactory – *The Observer*'s reviewer noted that 'the burlesque of ... Maypole-dancers' did not merely contain 'elements of good revue sketches', but offered promising material for mainstream entertainment.[15] Support for the 'new and wonderful' experiment of reviving folk dance was being replaced by conventional wisdom suggesting that 'You should make a point of trying every experience once, excepting incest and folk-dancing'.[16]

A more sustained advocacy of the value of the 'beautifully sufficient culture' that was 'the home-made civilization of the rural English' was associated with the reforming literary critics of *Scrutiny*. Founded in 1932 by a group including F. R. Leavis (1895–1978), a lecturer in English at Cambridge, '*Scrutiny* was not just a journal, but the focus of a moral and cultural crusade: its adherents would go out to schools and universities to do battle there, nuturing through the study of literature the kind of rich, complex, mature, discriminating, morally serious responses (all key *Scrutiny* terms) which would equip individuals to survive in a mechanized society of trashy romances, alienated labour, banal advertisements and vulgarizing mass media'.[17] The *Scrutiny* group's comprehensive assertion of the qualities of 'life-giving tradition' implied a far broader role for folk culture than the Revival's programme of examinations and displays:

This life, running so richly into the placing nickname and the proverbial epitome, is unmistakably the expression of a vigorous humane culture. For what is involved is not merely an idiomatic raciness of speech, expressing a strong vitality, but a traditional art of social living, with its mature habits of judgement and valuation. We must beware of idealizing uncritically, but the fact is plain. There would have been no Bunyan (as there would before him have been no Shakespeare) if in his time, with all its disadvantages from a modern point-of-view, there had not been, living in the daily life of the people, a rich traditional culture – a culture that has disappeared so completely that modern revolutionaries, social reformers and Utopists do not commonly seem to have any notion of the kind of thing that has been lost.[18]

Cecil Sharp's writings provided cardinal evidence for *Scrutiny's* theorising on this naturally creative state. Particularly in his comments on life in the Southern Appalachians, Sharp was represented as offering a comprehensive exposition of 'traditional culture':

Hearing that the English folk-song still persisted in the remoter valleys of those mountains Sharp, during the last war, went over to investigate, and brought back a fabulous haul. More than that, he discovered that the tradition of song and dance ... had persisted so vigorously because the whole context to which folk-song and folk-dance belong was there too: he discovered, in fact, a civilization or 'way of life' ... that was truly an art of social living.[19]

Scrutiny embraced an Englishness that 'was less a matter of imperialist flag-waving than of country dancing; rural, populist and provincial rather than metropolitan and aristocratic' and saw itself 'rooted in the 'English people' of John Bunyan rather than in a snobbish ruling caste'.[20] But this solidarity with the yeoman and labourer of middle England took a specific and restricted form. While nodding in the direction of 'disadvantages', 'from a modern point of view', *Scrutiny* never raised 'the penury, the petty tyranny, the disease and mortality, the ignorance and frustrated intelligence'[21] inherent in the daily life of a workhouse resident in 1906 or a seventeenth-century 'small town 'mechanick''. Considerations of social justice in the systems reproducing the 'social aspect of creative achievement' are as absent from *Scrutiny's* pages as they are from Sharp's – 'essential values', rather than 'the sordid details of everyday life' were what counted.[22] 'though overworked and underpaid', Denys Thompson assured early readers of the periodical, villagers 'enjoyed their life; they were fulfilled in their work, and their work was totally useful.'[23]

Scrutiny celebrated the tradition which Shakespeare and Bunyan 'participated in' – 'the names and racy turns of speech' which were 'organically *of*' a style that 'concentrates and intensifies the life of popular idiom'.[24] But 'the social aspect of creative achievement' was allowed no further, more developed, function. Folk culture's existence as a past condition was sufficient for the journal's theoretical requirements. Held up like a banner, its allotted role was as a depiction of former glory, to which an appreciative few might become 'sensitized' through education. Whilst producing sweeping panegyrics about 'vivid, essential' working-class life, spent practising 'numerous exciting crafts', ultimately, the journal drew on a very limited form of data to determine the way small town or village society had been lived in the past. Leavis had originally read History, but rarely engaged his expertise. Parish registers and wills, farm accounts and civic records were all eschewed in favour of contemporary language, shaped and 'intensified' in the form of published recollection, fiction, poetry and drama. For *Scrutiny* organic community was a literary phenomenon, its virtues exemplified in the works of Shakespeare, Jonson or Delony and the relations of Sir Roger de Coverley and Squire Weston with their tenants. The status of the 'social life' depicted in such works – produced for purposes far removed from displaying the artistic merits of organic community – is debatable; that fiction was preferred, and used in isolation to 'prove' *Scrutiny*'s case, leaves its central theory just so much self-reflexive assertion. In a *Scrutiny* review deploring an eighteenth-century historian's failure to take account of the contemporary significance of popular ballads, H. A. Mason complained that 'Like most academic men, he preferred the evidence of books to that of life'.[25] By this definition, Scrutineers were pre-eminently 'academic'. 'Life' – allotted a prominent role in the journal's lexicon – almost invariably occurs as a matter of report.

Commentaries on traditional culture attributed a high level of creative ability to 'folk' artists, but treated them differently to 'literary' artists. Settlers in the Appalachians and shirtmakers in Somerset remained anonymous and undifferentiated on the page, accorded less individual analysis than fictions like Gradgrind or Bitzer.[26] Sharp's fieldwork manuscripts are held at his old college in Cambridge; the songs and repertoire of named performers and 'organic communities' were therefore more than usually open to *Scrutiny*'s mature, serious and specific critical response. But the notebooks were never referred to, and a potentially significant opportunity to apply new perspectives to this area of culture went unconsidered. In its place, *Scrutiny* reiterated the well-worn lament 'traditional culture is dead ... traditional ways ... destroyed', coupled with an increasingly reactionary tirade against the 'shallow, insignificant' consumers of the 'commercial machine' (though not its owners and shareholders).

Despite espousing an "anthropological' approach to contemporary civilization', contributors to *Scrutiny* offered no critique of the unsupported generalisations on which theories of 'self-sufficient' rural life rested. Indeed, on the few occasions when the revolutionary forces of the journal applied themselves directly to consideration of inhabitants of 'organic communities', ensuing discussion was conventional to the point of cliché. While couching his description in terms of 'tradition' and 'countrymen', Adrian Bell's unlettered Sussex yokels emerge as stereotyped 'Folk' of the classic definition. Nameless, inarticulate, naive, unthinking makers of picturesquely non-standard English, their 'genius' rapidly overwhelmed by the contamination of elementary education, their creativity born of accident and confusion: 'Linguistically there is a kind of half-light in his brain, and on the impulse of an emotion words get confused with one another and fused into something new – a new shade of meaning is expressed.' Intuitive, rather than conscious reproducers of culture, countryfolk occupy a unique position outside the class system:

Comparatively, the illiterate man has few words: language is new to him; but a power within him insists on getting said what he has to say. He has to wrestle with his angel. He must feel the word almost physically, it must be born alive out of his lips... He doesn't care a jot for grammar, but only that what needs must be said, gets said somehow. Words as such don't matter to him. He enjoys and uses quite ruthlessly his freedom from class or academic restrictions.

Beset by modernity, the younger sons of the soil lose confidence in their culture and rapidly abandon it. Bell's analysis rationalises but then unhesitatingly reiterates the stereotypically heedless, failed inheritor of a glorious, unified Folk tradition whose full dereliction of cultural duty is recognised (and articulated) only by feeling members of the literate middle classes:

The first taste of education and standard English has the effect of making them acutely self-conscious. They realize (and agricultural depression helps in this) not that they stand supreme in a fundamental way of life, but that they are the last left on a sinking ship. No one decries civilization who has not experienced it *ad nauseam*. Modernity offers dim but infinite possibilities to the young countryman if only he can rid his boots of this impeding clay. Pylons, petrol pumps and other 'defacements' are to him symbols of a noble power.
The motor-bus, motor-bicycle, wireless, are that power's beckonings. But he is late, he is held hapless in a ruining countryside, everyone else is laughing at him he feels; at his heavy boots, his rough ways. Doesn't the daily paper laugh at him, and the magazine? Look at the 'comic' country articles, the illustrated jokes. The old men had their defence. They knew what they knew. But he can't stay where they are. The contentment of it is gone. Naturally he seizes on the most obvious and spurious symbols of culture first; he wants to wear low shoes and get a job behind a counter.[27]

Conforming to earlier modes of discussion, it was the recorders of traditional culture, rather than its producers and reproducers, who were individuated. In an unwitting, if timely, application of rough justice, however, a well-known name and years of widely publicised work conferred no immunity from misrepresentation when a collector came 'under scrutiny':

the exact antithesis of the attitude to the working-class that I have been considering is provided by Cecil Sharp. With no political or even cultural axe to grind, starting only from the musician's respect for the quality of the folk-songs he devoted his leisure to collecting, he was led to extend his respect to the folk-singers and all that they stood for. The process is recorded in his *English Folk-Song: Some conclusions* (1907). He was eventually able to produce evidence of a whole popular culture that but for him would have disappeared from the life of England without leaving traces by which even the archaeologist could piece it together. His virtues seem to have been threefold: he was completely unsentimental, he was intelligent enough to perceive that all cultural questions involve complex issues, and, as his singers are known to have observed, he was 'so common.'[28]

Members of the *Scrutiny* movement had much in common with Cecil Sharp, sharing his elitism, his prejudices against contempor-

ary popular culture and Arnoldian views on the instrumentality of
the education system, as well as a mutual taste for vehement
controversy. *Scrutiny*'s advocacy of the value of 'traditional culture' and 'organic communities' and Sharp's proselytising for consensus and the Folk were, in many respects, indistinguishable in
tenor and content. But the renewers of culture guiding *Scrutiny*
were dismissive and pointedly brief in their comments on Sharp's
proposals for reviving the alternative tradition they all lauded.
Scrutineers did not join morris teams and dance – 'we all know
how depressing the usual folk-dance circle is.'[29] Indeed, the journal
voiced the, by now, general derision of 'earnest townspeople la-
boriously endeavouring to learn country dances to recapture the
spirit of Olde Englande'.[30] 'Cecil Sharp was right', *Scrutiny*'s music
reviewer agreed, to emphasise 'the importance of folk-song', but
'its revival does seem artificial in an age of jazz'.[31] Like the concept
of 'organic community', the existence of traditional expressive
culture demonstrated by Sharp's collection was used as a prop to
support theorising – meanwhile, the stated and unstated processes
underlying each phenomenon remained unexplored. And, although
itself representing 'a national campaign of cultural renewal', the
Scrutiny movement put forward no proposals for broadening the
implementation of Sharp's legacy. Instead, writers in the journal
remade his discussion of culture in their own image. Ignoring his
thesis of the Folk's artistic exhaustion by 1830, they postulated a
recently existing, creative Folk, and allocated Sharp a place with
authors such as George Sturt, Richard Jefferies, Thomas Hardy
and D. H. Lawrence, in the *Scrutiny* pantheon of witnesses to 'the
folk arts of the rural civilization in its flourishing state'. Implicitly,
the 'commonness' Q. D. Leavis attributed to Sharp conferred on
him honorary membership of the Folk – though it says little for
the practice of 'close reading' that he was thus stripped of ideology
and a cultural programme and lined up with yeomanry of a
literary bent to be presented as a disinterested recorder of traditional culture.

For all its radicalism in the field of literary criticism, *Scrutiny*'s
academic analyses of folk culture rarely ventured beyond long
established theory. Early reviews and articles by the journal's
music specialist, Bruce Pattison, confirmed folksong as 'a heritage
of all classes',[32] created by a process predicated upon a *gesunkenes
Kulturgut* – 'Standards were set from above but had no difficulty

in filtering down to the people'[33] who, moreover, lived in a marginalised 'traditional culture' whose 'feeble remnants Cecil Sharp found was the reverse of a class culture'.[34] The Folk and their culture were easily distinguished from present-day decline. 'The rustics Cecil Sharpe [sic] found' were models of 'courtesy and poise', descendants of contented members of organic communities in which 'everybody had his station', and music played a very large part in traditional ways of filling leisure. This idyll was, however, swept away by the Industrial Revolution where there was 'no leisure for music, and in place of the violin and flute at the wake you have nothing now but noise and vulgarity'. Final collapse into decadence was then ensured in the twentieth century by the emergence of 'Rotarian' culture in the suburbs and 'commercialized exploitation of rhythm and sentimentality for their own sakes'.[35] In some cases, acceptance of nineteenth-century Folkloristic premisses overrode consistency with *Scrutiny*'s own positions. Upholding devolution and *zersingen* and ignoring the Scrutineers' general support for the creativity of artisans and rural labourers in organic communities, E. M. Wilson proposed that 'the lack of a current from above that could filter down and strengthen it' meant that 'our minor Folk poetry had a tendency to degenerate into nonsense'.[36] Overall, the journal propagated a version of the processes of folk culture which was outdated in terms of current work in Social Anthropology and at odds with its own pronouncements.

But *Scrutiny* was not just conventional in its treatment of traditional culture, it was also sparing. Given the centrality of the artistry of organic communities in the movement's theorising, *Scrutiny* articles devoted entirely to the study of traditional expressive culture are surprisingly few. More disappointingly still, in an area where its expertise was unquestioned, literary scholarship's most advanced practitioners of textual criticism again failed signally to offer alternatives to well-rehearsed positions. John Speirs highlighted the 'difference of vision' in separate versions of Scottish ballads and doubted that this 'arose simply from the necessity for filling up gaps in memory'. But he rapidly concluded that ballads were inherently 'impersonal', and it was to Bunyan, rather than any consideration of unknown creators of 'Poetic Diction', that he turned for corresponding genius. Moreover, while finding that the recurrence of commonplaces in a range of ballads gave them a distinctive 'richness', ultimately, he opined, the genre was by nature 'fragmentary', open to 'contagion' from broadsheets, and, of course, beyond replacement by latterday 'common people' – 'the 'ballads' that came into existence among the British troops during the war' being 'the merest drivel'.[37]

Scrutiny 'redrew the map of English literature in ways from which criticism has never quite recovered'.[38] But in the process of producing work which 'ranks with the most subtle, pioneering English criticism that the century has seen',[39] the journal uncritically reproduced illusory concepts of the Folk and folk culture, which distorted subsequent scholarship in equally decisive fashion. It is not merely that *Scrutiny*'s descriptions of 'organic communities' offered a rose-tinted or incomplete picture of pre-Industrial and rural life – contributors' fleeting admission of other emphases and a growing body of later research indicates that they did. The movement gives itself as a hostage to fortune. *Scrutiny* failed to fulfil its own promise, to undertake its self-imposed role and apply the expertise it alone was developing. For all its founders' intellectual rigour and ostensible engagement with the subject, *Scrutiny* never initiated consideration of what existed within the accepted definitions of traditional culture, let alone brought its 'courage and radicalism' to bear on its own superficial uses of such premises. The new perspectives on the processes of culture which the movement opened up were not extended from the assured high ground of 'art' to the debatable borderlands of 'informal', 'vernacular', 'traditional', 'organic' or 'folk' culture. Here, naive to the point of parody, contributors rhapsodised about a 'fulfilled' peasantry 'in touch with the seasonal rhythms' and wrote gushing reviews of the sort of books on 'old-world skills' which nowadays proliferate on the shelves of National Trust tourist centres. What Q. D. Leavis termed 'the happy ingenuousness of Mr. Adrian Bell',[40] suffused the approach of the movement as a whole.

Scrutiny's influence has long outlived – and outgrown – the movement itself. 'The fact ... that English students in England today are 'Leavisites' whether they know it or not'[41] has proved a double-edged sword – both sides of whose blade undercut progress in the study of vernacular culture. Outright advocates of *Scrutiny*'s position complacently share or vociferously compound its inadequacies; guilt by association renders the field unacceptable to the movement's critics. Setting the terms and methodology for a 'debate on the social function of literature and a critique of 'mass civilization' ... which provided the impetus and vocabulary for much later work, such as Williams's *Culture and Society* and *The Long Revolution* ...'[42] has perhaps become *Scrutiny*'s greatest disservice to cultural study. 'The wise', Raymond Williams suggested, should include in their analyses 'the experience that is otherwise recorded: in institutions, manners, customs, family memories'.[43] But Leavisite whether he recognised it or not, Williams then turned to Hardy and art literature rather than field collection for examples of what the rural working class did and said, and realised his own experience of life on the Welsh border as fiction. Sharp's definition of folksong, Williams acknowledged, was 'abstract and limiting ... based on the full rural myth of the 'remnants' of the 'peasantry'', it specifically excluded 'as not of the 'folk', the persistent songs of the industrial and urban working people, who did not fit the image but who were continuing to create, in an authentic popular culture, what it suited this period and this class to pretend was a lost world.'[44] But like the *Scrutiny* movement before him, Williams asserted the values of cultural processes he failed to elucidate systematically. 'Proper' expressive culture – that manifested in print, broadcast on television or performed in theatres, remained his central concern. Williams's illumination of what was not present in literary representations of working-class culture is an enduring achievement; exposing the sham of 'organic community' without fundamentally reconsidering what the 'authentic popular culture' of working people might comprehend defines his limitations.

The *Scrutiny* movement's concern with what was later termed 'Folklife' represents one, minor aspect of English response to a larger international development. The rise in popularity of magazines like *The Countryman* (founded in 1927), and the initiation of series of works on national traditions by Longmans whose 'English Heritage' series (begun in 1929) included *The English Country Town, The English Inn, The English Parish Church*[45] and Batsford's 'English Life' and 'British Heritage Series' (begun in 1930), distinguished by titles like *The Old Towns of England, The Old Inns of England,* and *The Parish Churches of England,* formed part of an inter-war '"back-to-the-land" cult', whose main expression was 'in the buying of books about farming and the countryside'.[46] The genre was characterised by nostalgia and at-

tempts to define national character by going 'in search of England'. In its focus on the description of ways of life, however, it
reproduced a cosy, domestic version of the growing international
preoccupation with social realism. Particularly as a result of the
artistic experimentation following the Russian Revolution, from
the late 1920s groups like the Soviet film makers Kino-Eye propagandised for cultural products which were the 'reflection of reality': 'The history of Kino-Eye has been a relentless struggle to
modify the course of world cinema, to place in cinema production
a new emphasis of the "unplayed" film over the play-film, to
substitute the document for mise-en-scene, to break out of the
proscenium of the theatre and to enter the arena of life itself.'[47]
Kino-Eye's 'Basic Watchwords' called for the complete abandoning of actors and scriptwriters:

Down with the immortal kings and queens of the screen! Long live
ordinary, mortal people, captured in the midst of life going about their
daily tasks.
Down with bourgeois fairy-tale scenarios! Long live life as it is....
Contemporary artistic drama is a hangover of the old world. It is an
attempt to mould our revolutionary reality into bourgeois forms.
Down with the scripting of life: film us unawares, just as we are.
The scenario is a fairy tale dreamed up for us by the man of letters. We
live our own lives and do not submit to anyone else's imaginings....[48]

But social realism involved more than the recording of actuality,
it also required art to manifest a social purpose. Art and politics
were comprehensively inter-related – where revolution on a national scale had not yet occurred, individuals should adopt new
ideologies and practices; only through a change in artistic perception – from individual to a group consciousness – could the 'best
work' be produced. At the same time, political allegiances had to
be realigned. In its most extreme form, 'going over' to the workers,
side of the class struggle was represented as the only means of
creating art of high quality: 'A writer today who wishes to produce
the best work that he is capable of producing, must first of all
become a socialist in his practical life, must go over to the progressive side of the class conflict ... unless he has in his everyday
life taken the side of the workers, he cannot, no matter how
talented he may be, write a good book, cannot tell the truth about
reality.'[49] Producing an art that reflected the life of the masses in

a way which was not artificial, obscure or esoteric was less easily achieved than stating its ideological necessity in the requisite 'simplistic, realistic' prose. Nevertheless, the influence of social realism in England was considerable and shaped representation in expressive forms ranging from graphic arts to music. The classic genre of social realism was, however, documentary. Here, films such as John Grierson's *Drifters* detailed the 'actuality' of the physical labour and danger of a fisherman's daily work, in combination with an implicit critique of capitalism.[50] Its overall effect was to create a more harshly mundane Folklife than that depicted in Batsford's 'English Life' series or Adrian Bell's 'English Tradition and Idiom'. Later documentaries produced by Grierson's GPO Film Unit, such as *Coal Face* and *Night Mail* (1935), for both of which W. H. Auden wrote portions of script and Benjamin Britten the music, and *Spare Time* (1939) which had a commentary by Laurie Lee, confirmed the acceptance of 'unplayed' urban working-class experience as a subject for recording. At the very time the Folk of Sharp's formulation were agreed to be safely defunct and replaced by reliable substitutes, new constructions of the processes of art began to be associated with the common people.

Film was the medium through which documentary was defined, but the possibilities of the genre soon attracted experiment in other forms of communication. Radio, with its potential for linking 'techniques drawn from cinema with a poetic style to build 'sound pictures' that appealed to the listener's inner eye', was foremost among these.[51] Initially there had been a 'prohibition of talks on controversial subjects' on the radio, but following the BBC's 'successful ... discharge of its responsibility' as 'the sole means whereby the community was kept informed at frequent intervals of the march of events' in the 1926 General Strike, the ban was lifted.[52] Concern that 'something must be done' about the social conditions arising from the Depression was rapidly met with series of talks on housing, unemployment and the state of industrial relations. Eye-witness accounts by BBC 'observers' provided telling 'sound pictures' of slum conditions in Glasgow, the East End of London and Tyneside in 1933:

Cornwallis Square – it sounds well enough doesn't it? Plane trees, Georgian houses, expensive cars, orderliness, dignity that is the sort of picture the name evokes. But Cornwallis Square hardly lives up to the name. You approach it, stumbling along a pitch dark passage which leads off a dingy alley, and you emerge into a muddy courtyard, perhaps 15 yards across. This is the square; round it, just discernible in the flare of a flickering gas light, squat a dozen misshapen houses, with a kind of verandah on wooden posts giving access to the top rooms, and making the whole place look like a collection of mud huts in an African swamp. I went into every room in those houses, and in practically every one of them lives a family. And I didn't go because I wanted to – to see one was quite enough – but because family and family begged me to come and see their surroundings. The front room was typical of the rest. It was roughly 15 feet by 12, and in it a man and a woman and nine children were gathered. They had another box of a room which was just large enough to hold a bed, and this was their home. The walls were so damp that the paper peeled off them and the ceiling was cracked and crumbling. They had to go to a tap outside for water; there was no sink. They had to share four water closets in the courtyard with other tenants of the square. They were overrun by cockroaches – blacklocks, they called them – swarms of cockroaches which poured out from the cracks and crannies in the walls and terrified the children at night, making proper sleep impossible.[53]

Increasingly, however, it was not 'observers' but the occupants of slums and workers who had lost their jobs who spoke for themselves on the radio – though the process involved was rather cumbersome:

The first programme to apply this method was *Time to Spare* [broadcast in 1934]. Felix Greene, the producer of the series, had toured the country, meeting the unemployed in their homes and clubs and selected a dozen whom he took as representative and typical to describe their experiences. Some found it difficult to write their story down though they could tell it well. When Greene tried to transcribe their words he found they spoke less freely. So he invited them to Broadcasting House, took them into a studio and got them talking. Meanwhile, unknown to them, the words were transcribed by secretaries in another room listening to them over a loudspeaker.[54]

Participants would then read their own transcribed words as a script for the live broadcast of the finished programme. Greene claimed that no editorial changes were made in the transcripts, but the question of censorship became academic when complaints about the series led to a purge and dispersal of Talks Department staff at Broadcasting House to other sections of the corporation. For the second half of the 1930s, talks from London dealt 'with

safer, less contentious topics'. In the regions, and especially the
North Region in Manchester, however, social issues and the quest
for even better means of producing 'actuality' continued to inspire
programme making. But without the mobile recording facilities
which were in use in London from 1934, radio speech in the north
was far from spontaneous or 'unplayed'. To produce the broadcasts for *Harry Hopeful*, a series depicting a fictional search for
work, D. G. Bridson the script writer, Frank Nicolls, a Manchester
clock mender who played the central character and the members
of the public taking part in the programmes had to go through a
lengthy process of location and studio work:

Together Bridson and Nicolls went to these places [different locations
in the region] and talked to the local people whom they had invited to
take part in the programmes. As Nicolls talked to them ... Bridson made
detailed notes of what they said. Later he worked this material into a
script, a copy of which was sent to each participant. A few weeks later
he and Nicolls returned with portable wireless equipment and a radio
engineer. The microphone was then set up in the homes of the participants and they each rehearsed their part with Nicholls while Bridson
listened on headphones in the car outside. Thus the speakers were
accustomed to the microphone in familiar surroundings and adjustments
could be made, if necessary, to make the script sound more natural.
Later the full cast was assembled in Manchester's main studio. After one
complete run-through came the live broadcast itself, performed before
an invited audience which included the families and friends of the
participants.[55]

For his 1938 programme *Coal*, Bridson worked with the assistance of a newly recruited student from the Royal Academy of
Dramatic Art, Joan Littlewood. He decided to base the programme
in the north-east to give an airing to the Geordie accent and 'to
tap the very rich vein of Tyneside colliery songs'. Bridson and
Littlewood spent a month at the Brancepeth Colliery in Wilming-
ton, County Durham, working in the mine and staying with
miners' families, so that 'by the time *Coal* went on the air, there
wasn't a miner at the pit who didn't know us and treat us as one
of themselves'.[56] An equal closeness was simultaneously developed
between Bridson and the mine manager – Bridson sending him the
script with a note that 'we always find it best to prepare a script
from the men's angle first and then have it vetted by the man-
agers'. *Coal* provoked a wave of sympathy throughout the country

and Bridson arranged for money donated as a result to be divided among unemployed miners and those on short time. But the levels of mediation in this and his earlier programmes fell far short of the ideals of social realism and it was with individuals and groups more closely aligned to realism's ideological sources that attempts to present 'real' working class culture were developed and reinterpreted.

The socialist movement of the period of the Second International (1890–1914) worshipped at the shrine of art; it conceived itself as a messenger of high culture, bringing education and social enlightenment to the masses. But the very reverence for high culture made socialists diffident about attempting to instrumentalise it. The absolute autonomy of art was unquestioned, and writers, painters and musicians who came into the socialist ranks were treated with exaggerated respect.[57]

From the mid-1920s, however, the role of such constructions of art was being challenged by calls for 'a proletarian outlook on life'. Bourgeois culture had to be replaced by new forms relevant to the workers, and culture itself reconstituted as a direct instrument of class struggle, rather than a life-enhancing means of superseding class differences. But the possibilities for implementing change were reduced by ideological divisions between and within political groups on the Left. From 1928 to 1935, the official policy of the Communist International (Comintern) was one of 'class against class':

Everyone who was not within the revolutionary vanguard of the working class became an actual or potential enemy of that class, and therefore, objectively, an ally of the ruling class; on the political front, social democrats were denounced as social fascists, and on the cultural front, artists and intellectuals were abused as lackeys of the bourgeoisie....

As a loyal section of the world Bolshevik party, though not without internal divisions on the matter, the Communist Party of Great Britain followed the Comintern's lead and set up revolutionary organisations parallel to existing labour movement bodies. A self-supporting autonomous 'red' world was to be created, based on the then current premiss of scientific socialism that the death knell of capitalism had already been sounded (most notably by the Wall Street crash of 1929) and that proletarian revolution followed by the coming of a soviet state was inevitably the next item on history's agenda.[58]

Consigning 'the role of raising the cultural level of the workers through contact with great dramatic art' to 'lackeys of the bourgeoisie' in the Labour Party and the Trades Unions, a range of parallel, determinedly proletarian, organisations was founded. Notable amongst these was the Workers' Theatre Movement, a 'propertyless theatre for a propertyless class', which used 'open platform' stages on the backs of lorries to give performances on street corners, in parks or at factory gates. Groups like Red Radio, Sunderland's Red Magnets, the Red Front Troupe from Dundee, Proltet, Red Dawn of Southampton and Red Flag used no scenery, props, specific costume or make-up. Instead they produced 'instant' performances to meet specific circumstances – as Ewan MacColl, a member of the Salford group, Red Megaphones, later described:

If we were due, say, to go to Wigan, in the bus on the way we'd write the sketch and we'd try it out for about half-an-hour, and then put it on at the market place by the stalls. We'd maybe be there for ten minutes before the police arrived in a van, and we'd scarper, say, to the steps of the public baths, and put it on there. Or we'd go to a factory, and occasionally we'd manage to get through a few satirical songs outside the factory gate before the police came and moved us on.[59]

A logical formalisation of these activities was *Proletkult*, the fostering of working-class creativity with the aim of producing art by and for the working class.[60] Publications such as *Left Review*, newly founded by 'Revolutionary Writers' including Hugh Mac-Diarmid, A. L. Lloyd and Amabel Williams-Ellis, specifically encouraged 'working people to send ... their work', feeling it 'reasonable to imagine that there must be a good deal of work painfully written out on old school sheets, old school books, exercise books.'[61] Demonstrably, in cases like MacColl's drama and songwriting, Julius Lipton's poetry and criticism and Lloyd's own journalism, the platform which *Proletkult* offered was used to far greater effect than *Left Review*'s patronising expectations suggest.[62] But whatever its quality, as long as 'class against class' remained Comintern policy, this type of working-class literature could be communicated only to small groups – outside factories, in workers' film clubs and through small circulation magazines. Concern at the isolation of the proletariat from other 'revolutionary elements' began to be voiced, and in 1935, the Seventh Comintern pragmatically endorsed the need for a 'Popular Front' – 'a device to build political unity among democratic forces, linking

worker and bourgeois across barriers of social class, in order to
mount domestic and international resistance to the greater common enemy of fascism and the authoritarian Right'.[63] As well as
promoting some concerted action across the Left, the Popular
Front also opened new, larger fields of communication to realist-
inspired experiment; middle-class writers and composers – Auden,
Britten, Michael Tippett and Alan Bush produced large-scale public works for working-class organisations such as the Workers'
Music Association and the Trades Unions;[64] at the same time,
mass audiences were given access to 'a self-consciously proletarian
aesthetic' through collaborations like Littlewood, MacColl and
Lloyd's work with institutions such as the BBC in Manchester and
London.

Kino-Eye's statement of social realism turned everyday life into
culture. Through their 'Basic Watchwords', 'Ordinary, mortal
people ... going about their daily tasks' were transformed into an
art form – not as reified by the individual, sensitive perception of
an artist but exactly as lived. Its premisses were, and remain,
controversial. They occasioned massive contemporary dissention
over 'realism', 'naturalism', 'stylisation' and the impossibility of a
workers' art in a capitalist society – and today, their absence of
consideration of mediation, selectivity and editing appears problematic and naive. But however flawed in practice, Kino-Eye's
'Watchwords' encapsulated a process which decisively affected
attitudes to working-class culture and its recording. In the context
of their influence on the documentary movement, working-class
life in town and country was not accorded different treatment –
kazoo bands playing 'Rule Britannia' in urban Lancashire were
filmed under the same construction of 'life' as the traditional
routine of the herring fleet. Popular culture and folklife were
desegregated and equally revealed as involving 'ordinary, mortal
people ... going about their daily tasks'. And although *Proletkult*
in England never had the institutional base it acquired in Germany
or America, its incorporation into the Popular Front ensured that,
as a subject of art, the work of the post office sorter could join
that of the ploughman. Moreover, the ability of both types of
workers to express themselves creatively could not be discounted.
Long-established conceptions of aesthetics were comprehensively
challenged. How long could the premiss of an artistically deficient
working class be maintained in the face of productions by Unity

Theatre, Theatre of Action and Theatre Union, writing which
eschewed modernism in favour of the creative use of folkloric
materials, and a criticism convinced of the artistic superiority of
'the home-made civilization of the rural English'? By 1939, Olive
Shapley, another of the innovative radio producers based in Manchester, was using mobile recording equipment 'to get ... people I
met to tell in their own words something of what their life is like'
and assuring listeners to the Northern Region of the BBC, 'All the
records you'll hear were made without script or rehearsal.'[65] Even
in the case of programmes where speakers' experiences were specifically chosen to be 'representative', their expression was individual – the concept of an undifferentiated, anonymous, common
people became less tenable.

Like other contemporary groupings, the Folk Revival was affected by the existence of these developments. As mass media
presented people to each other more directly, the place of the
expert collector, decisively interposed between the Folk and Revival performance, shed its mystique. And at the same time, more
open social manners and a gradual rise in living standards reduced
barriers to inter-class communication – fear of approaching the
'uninstructed' Folk became less of a 'perplexity' for would-be
collectors. But in other respects, the past still continued to shape
contemporary perceptions. Englishness provided the context
through which all aspects of the rural were produced and interpreted. A tide of publications presented photographic evidence and
reported conversations indicating that the gramophone and com-
pulsory education had not wholly eradicated the mythic countryman. Working-class inhabitants of country areas were seen and
presented in terms deriving from earlier formulations of the embodiment of national character. The possibility that the Folk still
existed among the rural working class became more certain. But
despite this limited realignment in the normative definitions of the
Folk and their culture, the effects of operational processes such as
social realism remained unassimilated. There was an increasing
disjunction between what was said and believed about the Folk
and the reproduction and recording of cultural traditions. A comprehensive reconsideration of the implications of developing ideas
and practices on the part of those institutions specialising in the
study of tradition, such as that undertaken by the Soviet folklorist
Yuri Sokolov, was becoming an urgent necessity.[66]

Intellectually, however, the English Revival offered a continuing example of self-regulating arrested development. Sect-like in its avoidance of critical examination of its basic premisses, the English Folk Dance Society in the 1930s saw little need to incorporate changes in scholarship and practice, even where these impinged directly on its organisation and working methods. Fieldwork had become the primary source of data for both Anthropology and Folkloristics in the same period – the first full-scale anthropological expedition and the Folk-Song Society both having their beginnings in 1898. But this simultaneous methodological shift was not accompanied by parallel theoretical realignments. In Anthropology, field research eventually led to 'the adoption of a more relativistic attitude to other societies'. The search for origins and attempts 'to 'place' others on a universal hierarchy' were succeeded by empirical observation and an acceptance of the transience of theory.[67] Although as early as 1910, folklorists were aware of the criticism that their methodology involved 'recklessly pulling up 'items' of folklore by the roots to set them beside other items, similarly uprooted, from other social systems and other stages of culture', they continued to work comparatively and interpret data from field research in a framework of cultural evolution.[68] Folklore's institutions and area of study, in fact, provided a convenient bolt-hole for anthropologists who were incapable or unwilling to accept changing methods and theory – 'Students of social anthropology are, in this country and in America, so busily engaged in demonstrating the 'functional' unity of any given culture that they are apt to ignore the processes by which its component elements came in the first place to be associated together' insisted a die-hard cultural evolutionist in a 1937 anthropological article for *Folk-Lore*.[69] Drawing Folkloristics' wagons into a still tighter circle, Professor J. H. Hutton, member of the Folk-Lore Society Council and Indian Civil Service (retired), warned, 'The functional school has a valuable (though not exclusive) part to play in social anthropology, but the extension of its principles to folklore will give rise to some misgivings.'[70] The amalgamation of the English Folk Dance Society and the Folk-Song Society in 1932 reinforced the Revival's existing conservatism by formally taking the movement into the ambit of already static Folkloristic scholarship. And though the Folk-Lore Society turned down a simultaneous 'approach' to amalgamate and join in a 'national centre for Folk Art' based at Cecil Sharp House,[71] even after 1932 the societies maintained a united theoretical front, had a number of prominent members in common and arranged joint lectures.

In such an intellectual context, the apparently outward-looking practice of European exchange visits fostered by the newly conjoint English Folk Dance and Song Society proved less than fruitful. Following Sharp's definition, the vast majority of European dances were classified as 'social', and thus unworthy of note. At the same time, well prepared by his and Folkloristics' advocacy of survivals theory, revivalists promptly discovered *The Golden Bough* 'unrolled before our eyes – for all those who indeed had eyes to see'[72] in the few 'primitive rituals' other European nations could display. The Continent was found to offer little which might shake the movement's preconceptions of theoretical rectitude and practical superiority, as the 1939 report on the International Folk Dance Festival in Stockholm succinctly indicated:

The E.F.D.S. *[sic]* represented England and teams of dancers were sent by Belgium, Denmark, Esthonia, Finland, France, Germany, Holland, Latvia, Norway, Rumania, Scotland and Sweden. The English programme had more variety than that of any other team and much interest was shown in the Yorkshire and Northumberland Sword Dances and the two types of Morris Dance. Rumania was the only other country that presented men's dances.[73]

Internally, the dissention caused by the Executive Committee's attempts to break Sharp's copyright monopoly influenced attitudes to new ideas on field collection. Noting that some gaps in the range of recorded English social dance had been detected, the Society's National Executive Committee sent a Memorandum to the September 1937 meeting of the Branch Council, asking for branches' 'co-operation' in encouraging the 'collection of Folk Song and Dance Material'. Mindful of existing problems, though less than tactfully, they also added that collectors would be 'invited to assign their rights to the Society on suitable terms'. Captain Kettlewell of the Oxford and County Branch fired off a broadside against all such innovations, opposing the adoption of the Executive Committee's scheme on the grounds '(a) that it was unusual for collectors to be invited to assign their rights; (b) that it was unnecessary, since the ground had already been well covered and recent re-collections had been of no material value; and (c) that the proposal was unimportant, no one, in fact having been hampered in the past by private control of material and the position being likely to remain unchanged if the Society acquired control'. Faced with such a barrage, the Executive made a tactical withdrawal for 'further study' and a re-presentation at the next meeting. In January 1938, the Memorandum was brought forward and eventually adopted, though various prominent and longstanding Oxford branch members resigned from the National Executive.[74] By January 1939, the English Folk Dance and Song Society was in a position to consider asking members to provide minor additions to its repertoire from their own collection. Responding dynamically to the cultural innovation of the times, the Society implicitly accepted that 'remnants of the Folk' had 'survived' into the late 1930s.

When the BBC took a 'broad look' at 'the question of national interests' in the early 1930s and funded broadcasts to the empire, folk music dominated their preliminary list of recorded programmes. Of the ten programmes which included music, five made use of folk material – Manx traditional airs, Old English songs and choruses, 'A Pageant of English Life', Scottish traditional music and a children's programme with 'traditional songs and choruses, written round the Robin Hood legend'.[75] Across the ideological spectrum – in the service of consolidating the empire, or as a means of combating the results of capitalism's decline, Englishness continued to be represented through images of traditional dance and in traditional music:

George Lansbury, a lifelong Londoner and deputy leader of the [Labour] party, saw throughout his career a solution to unemployment in home land-cultivation. The resettlement of the countryside was more for him, however, than an economic matter; it touched on some of his deepest emotions. 'I just long,' he wrote in 1934, 'to see a start made on this job of reclaiming, recreating rural England. I can see the village greens with the Maypoles once again erected and the boys and girls, young men and maidens, all joining in the mirth and foll of May day.'[76]

But, for the majority of the population, the contemporary form of the Revival failed to reproduce these almost universally accepted symbols. Observers highlighted the distance between synthetic re-creations and the social reality from which the performances derived – 'the revival of folk-songs and folk-dances as present entities is necessarily an artificial thing, in that our civilisation has nothing in common with the civilisation that gave them birth.' They questioned whether established definitions were sustainable – 'A popular hymn-tune, a dance-tune, a music-hall tune that has become embedded in popular consciousness is in the real sense far more the folk-music of today than anything resuscitated from the seventeenth or eighteenth centuries.'[77] Those whose disenchantment was grounded in personal experience pointed to the English Folk Dance and Song Society's exclusivity and its continuing failure to create a popular movement at a time of heightened social awareness:

Mr. Wright moved the following resolution which was seconded by Miss Naylor:-
'That Cecil Sharp House, both in method and in spirit, is insufficiently popular in its appeal.'
Speaking to the resolution, MR. WRIGHT said that he had attended classes and parties at Cecil Sharp House for some two years and felt very strongly that the building failed to take the place that it should as a community centre. The Society's scale of fees and membership subscription debarred a large proportion of London citizens from using the facilities at Cecil Sharp House and the building appeared to be in the hands of a coterie who did not seem to feel any responsibility for propaganda for folk ritual. Mr Wright urged that to be successful, folk dance and song must be associated with social activities; the Society must go out to social centres and recruit for Cecil Sharp House. Demonstrations were of little value unless followed up by active propaganda. Mr. Wright spoke of the success of another movement with which he was associated, which took drama and literature into the public houses, which were in England natural social centres for the people. He urged the Society to try and find out what it could do on similar lines, particularly in the immediate environs of Cecil Sharp House. In discussion, it was suggested that the teaching of folk dancing in Elementary Schools hampered recruiting for the Society. It was also suggested that recruiting in London might successfully be carried out by a team of working class people with a musician.[78]

Closing the decade in the spirit in which the English Folk Dance and Song Society had started it, Frank Howes, the Chairman of the Society's National Executive Committee pointed out to the 1938 Annual General Meeting that 'much of Mr. Wright's criticism was pertinent, although not in his opinion, all applicable'. When put to the vote, the motion was lost and its content publicly ridiculed in the following issue of the members' magazine.[79]

Notes

1 Francis Toye, *For What We Have Received: An Autobiography* (London: William Heinemann Ltd, 1950), pp. 98–9.

2 This and previous quotation from E. J. Moeran, letter to *The Musical Times*, Mar. 1931, p. 254 reprinted in Lewis Foreman, *From Parry to Britten: British Music in Letters 1900–1945* (London: B. T. Batsford Ltd, 1987), p. 145.

3 *The English Folk Dance Society Report for September 1st, 1930, to August 31st, 1931* (London: English Folk Dance Society, 1931), p. 5. In the light of current debates on the future of Cecil Sharp House, the Report's comments on the possibility that Cecil Sharp House ran the risk of 'embarrassing the Society's very existence by a continual demand on its resources' seems remarkably prescient.

4 See Valentine Cunningham, *British Writers of the Thirties* (Oxford: Oxford University Press, 1989), particularly pp. 36–44 for extensive documentation of 'observers of every stripe' 'grimly sensing and declaring a crisis'; and further examples in Samuel Hynes, *The Auden Generation: Literature and Politics in England in the 1930's* (London: Faber and Faber Ltd, 1976), pp. 78, 81, 83, 89, etc. and studies in Ian Clark, Margot Heinemann, David Margolies and Carole Snee, *Culture and Crisis in Britain in the Thirties* (London: Lawrence and Wishart, 1979).

5 A. M. Hocart, 'In the Grip of Tradition,' *Folk-Lore*, XLIX (Sept. 1938), 258. After examining contemporary reaction to the abdication crisis of 1936 and the phenomenon of dictatorship, however, Hocart ultimately concluded that English culture and society were as tradition-bound as they had ever been.

6 *Scrutiny*, III:4 (Mar. 1935), 377.

7 Arnold Bax, *Farewell, My Youth* (London: Longmans, Green & Co., 1943), p. 17. Whether the 'one English composer of genius' Bax (1883–1953) referred to was Vaughan Williams is a moot point.

8 Moeran, *Musical Times*, p. 254.

9 A.K.H., 'Music of To-Day: The Present Position of Folk Song,' *Liverpool Post & Echo*, 15 Nov. 1926 reprinted in *EFDS News*, II:13 (Jan. 1927), 15.

10 Anon., 'Current Topics: Morris Dancing,' *Sheffield Telegraph*, 28 Sept. 1926, p. 6.

11 Tyrone Guthrie, *A Life in the Theatre* (London: Columbus Books

Ltd, 1987), p. 36 (originally published by Hamish Hamilton Ltd in 1960).

12 See Michael J. Sidnell, *Dances of Death: The Group Theatre of London in the Thirties* (London: Faber and Faber Ltd, 1984), p. 32. Discussion of the Group Theatre in this period is based on information in Sidnell and Robert Medley's more discursive, personal account published in *Drawn from the Life: A Memoir* (London: Faber and Faber Ltd, 1983), particularly pp. 117, 130–68.

13 Guthrie, *A Life in the Theatre*, p. 39.

14 Sidnell, *Dances of Death*, p. 75.

15 Ivor Brown, 'The Dance of Death,' *The Observer*, 6 Oct. 1935.

16 In *Farewell My Youth*, p. 17, Bax cites this as the comment of 'a sympathetic Scot', but the remark is (inevitably) also popularly attributed to Sir Thomas Beecham.

17 Terry Eagleton, *Literary Theory: An Introduction* (Oxford: Basil Blackwell Publisher Ltd, 1983), p. 33.

18 F. R. Leavis, 'Literature and Society,' *Scrutiny*, XII:1 (winter 1943), 8. I am most grateful to John Brown for his perceptive and generous discussions of Leavis.

19 *Ibid.*

20 Eagleton, *Literary Theory*, p. 37.

21 Raymond Williams, *Culture and Society 1780–1950* (Harmondsworth, Middx: Penguin Books Ltd, 1961), p. 253.

22 Bruce Pattison, 'Music in Decline,' *Scrutiny*, III:2 (Sept. 1934), 202.

23 Denys Thompson, 'A Cure for Amnesia,' *Ibid.*, II:1 (June 1933), 7.

24 Leavis, 'Literature and Society,' p. 8.

25 H. A. Mason, 'Eighteenth Century Musical Taste: Review of *A General History of Music* by Charles Burney,' *Scrutiny*, IV:1 (June 1935), 427.

26 See F. R. Leavis, *The Great Tradition* (Harmondsworth, Middx: Penguin Books Ltd, 1962), pp. 259–83. Originally published by Chatto & Windus 1948. Leavis's late conversion to Dickens makes the comparison even more disproportionate.

27 All quotations from Adrian Bell, 'English Tradition and Idiom,' *Scrutiny*, II:1 (June 1933), 4–9. Bell's insistence that footwear plays a decisive role in the peasantry's abandonment of folk culture does, however, add an entirely new premiss to the thesis.

28 Q. D. Leavis, 'Lady Novelists and the Lower Orders,' *ibid.*, IV:2 (Sept. 1935), 132.

29 Frank Chapman, 'Rural Civilization: Review of *The Open Air,*

An Anthology of English Country Life by Adrian Bell,' *ibid.*, V:2 (Sept. 1936), 219.

30 Frank Chapman, 'Review of *Totem: The Exploitation of Youth* by Harold Stovin,' *ibid.*, IV:1 (June 1935), 448.

31 Bruce Pattison, 'Music and the Community: Review,' *ibid.*, II:4 (Mar. 1934), 400.

32 Bruce Pattison, 'Musical History,' *Ibid.*, III:4 (Mar. 1935), 374.

33 Bruce Pattison, 'Music in Decline,' *Ibid.*, III:2 (Sept. 1934), 202.

34 Pattison, 'Musical History,' p. 375.

35 *Ibid.*, pp. 369–77.

36 E. M. Wilson, 'Mr. Maughan and Spanish Literature: Review of *Don Fernando* by W. Somerset Maughan,' *ibid.*, IV:1 (June 1935), 211.

37 John Speirs, 'The Scottish Ballads,' *ibid.*, IV:1 (June 1935), 35–44.

38 Eagleton, *Literary Theory*, p. 32.

39 *Ibid.*, p. 43.

40 Q. D. Leavis, 'Lives and Works of Richard Jefferies,' *Scrutiny*, IV:4 (Mar. 1938), 440.

41 Eagleton, *Literary Theory*, p. 31.

42 Iain Wright, 'F. R. Leavis, the *Scrutiny* Movement and the Crisis,' in Clark, et al., *Culture and Crisis in Britain in the Thirties*, p. 38.

43 Williams, *Culture and Society*, p. 248.

44 Raymond Williams, *The Country and the City* (St Albans: Granada Publishing Ltd, 1975), p. 309.

45 This series also included *English Music* by Vaughan Williams and *English Folk-Song and Dance* by Iolo Williams.

46 Roy Lewis and Angus Maude, *The English Middle Classes* (1949) quoted in Martin Weiner, *English Culture and the Decline of the Industrial Spirit 1850–1980* (Cambridge: Cambridge University Press, 1981), p.73. Weiner also notes (p. 186) that 'Country Life' began to be listed separately in the *Subject Index to Periodicals* in 1926.

47 Dziga Vertov, speech given in Paris as part of his 1929 European tour, quoted in Jay Leyda, *Kino: A History of the Russian and Soviet Film* (London: George Allen & Unwin Ltd, 1960), p. 176.

48 Dziga Vertov, 'Provisional Instruction to Kino-Eye Groups' reprinted in Christopher Williams, ed., *Realism and the Cinema* (London: British Film Institute and Routledge and Kegan Paul Ltd, 1980), pp. 25–6.

49 Edward Upward, 'Sketch for a Marxist Interpretation of Literature,'in *The Mind in Chains: Socialism and the Cultural Revolution*, ed. Cecil Day Lewis (London: Frederick Muller, 1937) quoted in Cunningham, *British Writers of the Thirties*, p. 212.

50 *Drifters* was premiered in London in the same showing as Sergei

Eisenstein's archetypally realist *Battleship Potemkin*. Both Eisenstein and
Vertov attended the premiere. For additional discussion of the documen-
tary movement in England at this time see Nicholas Pronay and D. W.
Spring, *Propaganda, Politics and Film, 1918–1945* (London: Macmillan
Press Ltd, 1982); Alan Lovell and Jim Hillier, *Studies in Documentary*
(London: Secker and Warburg and the British Film Institute, 1972); Don
Macpherson, ed., *Traditions of Independence: British Cinema in the
Thirties* (London: British Film Institute, 1980); Stephen G. Jones, *The
British Labour Movement and Film, 1918–1939* (London: Routledge
and Kegan Paul Ltd, 1987); Forsyth Hardy, *John Grierson: A Documen-
tary Biography* (London: Faber and Faber Ltd, 1979); Derek Paget, *True
Stories?: Documentary Drama on Radio, Screen and Stage* (Manchester:
Manchester University Press, 1990); Paul Swan, 'John Grierson and the
G.P.O. Film Unit 1933–39,' *Historical Journal of Film, Radio and
Television*, III:1 (1983), 19–34 and works cited in other notes on
documentary and social realism. Concern to 'produce quality films,
accurately portraying British life' also underlay the setting-up of British
National Films, a company co-founded by J. Arthur Rank, which made
feature films such as *Turn of the Tide* (1935), a dramatisation of life in
the fishing community of Robin Hood's Bay in North Yorkshire.
   51 Paddy Scannell, 'The Stuff of Radio: Developments in Radio
Features and Documentaries Before the War,' in John Corner, ed.,
Documentary and the Mass Media (London: Edward Arnold (Publishers) Ltd, 1986), p. 2.
   52 *The BBC Year Book 1933*, p. 22.
   53 Howard Marshall's report on conditions in South Shields published in *The Listener*, 18 January 1933, pp. 73–4, reprinted in Scannell,
'The Stuff of Radio,' pp. 8–9. For additional contextualising information, see the admirable Paddy Scannell and David Cardiff, *A Social
History of British Broadcasting: Volume I 1922–1939* (Oxford: Basil
Blackwell Ltd, 1991), pp. 134–52.
   54 Scannell, 'The Stuff of Radio,' p. 10.
   55 *Ibid.*, p. 15.
   56 *Ibid.*, p. 18 quoting D. G. Bridson, *Prospero and Ariel* (London:
Victor Gollancz, 1971), p. 69.
   57 Raphael Samuel, 'Introduction: Theatre and politics,' in Raphael
Samuel, Ewan MacColl and Stuart Cosgrove, *Theatres of the Left
1880–1935: Workers' Theatre Movements in Britain and America* (London: Routledge and Kegan Paul Ltd, 1985), p. xvii.
   58 Colin Chambers, *The Story of Unity Theatre* (London: Lawrence
and Wishart Ltd, 1989), p. 26. See also Jim Fyrth, 'Introduction: In The
Thirties,' in Jim Fyrth, ed., *Britain, Fascism and the Popular Front*

(London: Lawrence and Wishart Ltd, 1985), pp. 9–29 for more detailed discussion of the implications of 'Class against Class' and its ultimate replacement with the tactic of a 'Popular Front'.

59 Ewan MacColl, 'The Grass Roots of Theatre Workshop,' trans-cibed in Samuel, 'Theatres of the Left,' p. 46 and summarised (with some additional detail) in Howard Goorney, *The Theatre Workshop Story* (London: Eyre Methuen Ltd, 1981), p. 3.

60 For further discussion of the influence of *Proletkult*, see H. Gustav Klaus, 'Socialist Fiction in the 1930's: Some preliminary observations,' in John Lucas, ed., *The 1930's: A Challenge to Orthodoxy* (Brighton: Harvester Press Ltd, 1978), pp. 13–41.

61 John Lucas, 'An interview with Edgell Rickword,' in Lucas, *The 1930's*, p. 5.

62 See Lucas, 'An interview with Edgell Rickword,' pp. 5–6 for names and comments on 'talented' proletarian writers, and Julius Lip-ton, 'A Few Remarks about Proletarian Poetry – With Some Notes on Bourgeois Poetry,' *Poetry and the People*, III (1938), 12–18 for Lipton's criticism and views on *Proletkult*.

63 Helen Graham and Paul Preston, 'The Popular Front and the Struggle Against Fascism,' in Helen Graham and Paul Preston, ed., *The Popular Front in Europe* (Basingstoke: Macmillan Press Ltd, 1987), p. 4.

64 See John Hasted, *Alternative Memoirs* (Itchenor, W. Sussex: Greengate Press, 1992), p. 37–51 for the background to the founding and examples of the repertoire of the Oxford Workers' and Students' Choir, Ian Watson, 'Alan Bush and Left Musik [sic] in the Thirties,' *Gulliver*, IV (1978), 80–90 for a rather undifferentiated discussion of the interaction of music and politics in the period and Margot Heine-mann, 'The People's Front and the Intellectuals,' in Fyrth, *Britain, Fascism and the Popular Front* , pp. 157–86 for a more informative examination of political activism and all areas of intellectual life. I am most grateful to John Hasted for providing me with a copy of his uniquely informative memoirs.

65 Olive Shapley, script of *Canal Journey*, 25 Aug. 1939 reprinted in Scannel, 'The Stuff of Radio,' pp. 20–1.

66 See Y. M. Sokolov, *Russian Folklore* (translated by Catherine Ruth Smith; Detroit: Folklore Associates, 1971), particularly pp. 3–39. To the great detriment of Folkloristic study, theories dealing with the interaction of tradition and creativity and issues relating to the definition of 'the Folk' and 'the people' highlighted by Sokolov in *Russian Folklore* (published in the Soviet Union in 1938 and first published in English by the American Council of Learned Societies in 1950) have only recently

been developed in the West. Still more regrettably, soon after the publication of Sokolov's work, changes of literary policy under Stalin led to its replacement by other, less 'internationally oriented' textbooks in the Soviet Union.

67 Brian V. Street, *The Savage in Literature* (London: Routledge & Kegan Paul, 1975), p. 16.

68 See Charlotte Sophia Burne, 'Presidential Address: The Value of European Folklore in the History of Culture,' *Folk-Lore*, XXI (1910), 18–36 for an extensive defence of continuing this approach.

69 John Layard, 'Labyrinth Ritual in South India: Threshold and Tattoo Designs,' *ibid.*, XLVIII (June 1937), 116.

70 J. H. H[utton], 'Review of *The Irish Countryman: An Anthropological Study* by Conrad M. Arensberg,' *ibid.*, XLVIII (Sept. 1937), 320.

71 *English Folk Dance Society Report 1930 to 1931*, p. 7.

72 Violet Alford's revealingly expressed recollections should be read in full in 'A Jubilee Symposium: 4. Foreign Relations,' *Folk Music Journal*, II:2 (1971), 95–8.

73 *The English Folk Dance and Song Society Report September 1st, 1938, to August 31st, 1939* (London: English Folk Dance and Song Society, 1939), p. 10.

74 See Minutes of Fifteenth Meeting of the Branch Council, 25 Sept. 1937 and Minutes of Sixteenth Meeting of the Branch Council, 10 Jan. 1938, *English Folk Dance and Song Society Report Sept 1st, 1937, to Aug 31st, 1938* (London: English Folk Dance and Song Society, 1938), pp. 24–5 and pp. 27–30. For subsequent resignations see Minutes of Seventeenth Meeting of the Branch Council, 24 Sept. 1938 and Minutes of Eighteenth Meeting of the Branch Council, 9 Jan. 1939, *English Folk Dance and Song Society Report September 1st, 1938, to August 31st, 1939*, pp. 23–4 and 27. For an EFDS *(sic)* offer to 'do anything in can to help' a British Film Institute project to 'collect and preserve' films of 'British Customs', see Anon., 'Film Records of British Customs,' *English Dance and Song*, II:4 (Mar.-Apr. 1938), 66.

75 *BBC Year Book 1933*, pp. 263–71.

76 Quoted in Wiener, *English Culture and the Decline of the Industrial Spirit*, pp. 122–3.

77 Toye, *For What We Have Received*, p. 98.

78 *English Folk Dance and Song Society Report 1937 to 1938*, pp. 22–3.

79 See 'letter' from 'Beatrice Catchpole' to 'Mrs Waghorn' in *English Dance and Song*, II:3 (Jan.-Feb 1938), 39.

Chapter 7

'Pressing charges': rediscovering the Folk and expanding the Revival

Representatives of the Travelling Morrice first called on Sharp, who was then a dying man, meaning to fortify him with their confidence in the good reception his printed versions of the 'Morris' would receive in the villages of their origin. Sharp told me after the interview that he felt rather like a suspected person visited by the flying squad who had decided not to press a charge before collecting supporting evidence from certain elderly persons who would be able to help them with their enquiries.[1]

Throughout the 1930s, to the outside world, the Revival maintained unassailable self-assurance abroad and refusal to be swayed by passing trends at home. Public mockery and accusations of preciousness were ignored or met with naive counter-claims that folk dancers were not 'cranks' or 'peculiar people who meet together in odd places to practise their obscure and not altogether reputable art'.[2] Despite amalgamation with the Folk-Song Society, the conjoint organisation had fewer full members at the end of the decade than the English Folk Dance Society could muster in 1930–31.[3] The attractions of rival leisure activities were, however, still discounted. The burgeoning and fashionable keep-fit movement would, it was comfortably assumed, 'ultimately lead to a wider use of folk dancing';[4] while any productive relationship between reviving folksong performance and the popularity of community singing was denied, because 'Folk song has always been an individual and private rather than a public form of self-expression and the success of a folk song revival is not therefore to be measured by the extent to which folk song figures in programmes of 'community singing".[5] Internally, however, ac-

knowledgement of the Revival's difficulties began to emerge early
in the 1930s. Discreetly phrased questions were raised within the
English Folk Dance and Song Society about Sharp's legacy of
institution – 'Even before his death the organisation had grown
into a complicated piece of machinery and during recent years an
impartial observer might have questioned whether the machinery
was not, in fact, crippling the Society's work'[6] and practice –
'Possibly, in concentrating upon co-operation with the school and
school teacher, we have not hitherto, paid sufficient attention to
the natural social groupings of town life'[7] – as the English Folk
Dance and Song Society responded to a form of challenge it could
not easily dismiss. For the first time in twenty years, a competing
approach to reviving the performance of folk dance and song was
being put forward with force and consistency and from close to
home. Advocates of the Revival who were at odds with the English
Folk Dance and Song Society's methods, approach and ideology
set out a detailed, insiders' critique which became increasingly
difficult to counter:

there is much criticism to be levied against it [The English Folk Dance
Society]. For in the course of years, it has grown to be an academic
institution with all the limitations of the academic mind. It has a
rigorous monopoly of the English folk dance forms, intrusion upon
which is apt to be curiously resented. Its averred aims are to uphold a
scientific body of technique, a purity of tradition, which will be strong
enough to withstand every degenerative or corruptive influence. But in
the pursuit of this very aim, it has set shackles on the feet of the
movement, manacles on its hands. The technique upheld by the E.F.D.S.
is nothing like the traditional technique of the English villages, though
the Society is the first to wish it. The technique evolved by the Society,
is actually something quite new, a style copied from people, who for the
most part, have derived their idea of the dance from the descriptions of
those who saw it in its old age and decrepitude. This was inevitable, but
what was not inevitable, was that the exponents of the revival should
delude themselves into believing that their style was the only endurable
and correct one. After all is there any really vital health or virtue in a
fixed and standardized technique? Assuredly very little if we consider it.
For a dynamic art of this kind, is at root the antithesis of rigidity, and
of its very nature bound up with relentless experiment. If the folk dance
movement were really healthy in England today, there would be five,
ten, nay, twenty separate movements, each pursuing its own ends, and
its own salvation, in friendly rivalry with its neighbour, and no doubt

there would be an annual congress, for comparison of methods etc. and a loose federation of cooperation, and further there would be room for a purely scientific body whose aim would be to preserve a pure academic style, a very useful thing in its way. But the real aims of the movement are last and least those of the archaeologist: the dance is to be a living art form, a great instrument of health and purification, a communal dynamic. Yet since among English people, there never was any lack of restraining elements, the reformer is compelled to drive the dagger of his ideal up to the hilt of imprudence, to achieve even a moiety of his hopes.[8]

The twenty-one-year-old imprudent enthusiast whose first book contained this iconoclastic call for reform of the Revival was Rolf Gardiner (1902–71), editor of *Youth: An International Quarterly of Young Enterprise* and a recent graduate of Cambridge. Gardiner was the great-nephew of the folksong collector George B. Gardiner and had been drawn into the Revival by dance at school and the influence of his uncle, the composer Henry Balfour Gardiner. Despite such distinguished establishment credentials, Rolf Gardiner had already broken Sharp's monopoly on contact with the Folk by joining with friends to take folksong and dance performances into villages and re-collecting in areas of Sharp's fieldwork.[9] The results were striking. Particularly through his association with the Travelling Morrice, a dance group deliberately formed outside Society auspices, it became apparent to Gardiner that the Folk Dance Society's policy that 'contact with the living tradition' was 'mainly a matter for its Director', had resulted in a style of dancing amongst EFDS teams which was easily distinguished from the 'traditional technique of the English villages'.[10] Gardiner felt that this – and the Society's programme as a whole – was mistaken. In place of rigid criteria, he argued for a pluralist approach in which the practice of 'drawing an artificial distinction between 'traditional' performers and imitators' could be abandoned and a range of styles allowed to develop naturally. 'No one would deny the great works of the 'E.F.D.S.'', Gardiner conceded, 'It has collected and published under Mr. Sharp's direction a vast number of dances and songs, it has trained a vast number of teachers, and held schools of instruction, it has disseminated far and wide an art form, which people of every class and occupation, have rejoiced to possess, and it has been instrumental in bringing no mean measure of real creative joy, to a people tired and sickened by the destructive squalidness and soullessness of our mechanical civilization.' But, he insisted, the Society had 'become respectable, and respectability in England is the death warrant of any vital enterprise'. What was needed to bring folk dance back to life and restore its cultural function was a recognition of its ritualistic genesis. Only through folk dancing could art and religion – 'the attitude of ecstasy, of worship' – be evoked to 'complete us modern townbred persons'.[11]

The Travelling Morrice offered the first systematic questioning of the Revival as conceived by Cecil Sharp since the battles with Mary Neal before the First World War. Founded in 1924 by Gardiner and Arthur Heffer (1900–31), who had met at a Folk Dance Society Christmas vacation school at Chelsea College in 1919, the membership of the Travelling Morrice was largely drawn from Oxford and Cambridge graduates. Looking back, Gardiner saw 'the motive behind the movement' as nothing less than the overthrow of the existing ideology of Revival performance. Dancing for demonstrations and examinations was too far removed from the original purpose of the performances. 'Unless we can subordinate the dance to motive again,' he had proposed, 'it will become about as silly as it often looks.'[12]

As an institution and in its practices, Cecil Sharp's Revival was conceived as the converse of Mary Neal's. In rejecting the existing form of the Revival, the Travelling Morrice therefore came – by chance and design – to echo some of the ideas about performance which had been characteristic of the Espérance movement. It also attracted support from former Espérance adherents, among them Francis Toye, Conrad and Miriam Noel and Mary Neal herself. The founders of Travelling Morrice 'were impatient,' Gardiner recalled, 'and felt with Mr. Francis Toye that much of the talk about traditional steps was putting a false stress on the matter. 'The spirit is what matters, the spirit and again the spirit.''[13] A further strand shared with Espérance was the group's approach to 'remaining old dancers': 'we have all devoured Mr. Sharp's accounts of his experiences... But how many of us have been right through the country; have talked to the old people, the Taylors, the Prateleys, the Hitchmans, have danced their own dances to them?'[14] Although presented as picturesquely dialected 'characters', 'Old Harry Taylor of Longborough, an octogenarian, with

gleaming eye, met us.... 'Skuse me lardin in surr, but thic-yer be a skew-karnered dance' was his comment on one item of our repertoire',[15] the 'veteran dancers' of Travelling Morrice accounts are named and individuated and their experienced reflections on dancing taken seriously. Overall, the Travelling Morrice's concept of Revival required a shift in concern from what was performed to those who did the performing, from the precise reproduction of a recorded dance to the expressive possibility of dancing arising from a knowledge of recorded dance.

Pre-eminent in their position, however, was the reconstitution of 'motive'. What was revived dance for? Sharp's prescription of precise replication of the forms of folk culture to produce a renewed national culture was rejected in favour of what had previously been an entirely abstract theoretical concept. With the development of the Travelling Morrice, recreating the hypothesised 'original' motivation for ceremonial dance became the rationale for its revival. In Heffer and Gardiner's formulation, contemporary performers of morris and sword dances were revealed as exponents of an inherited ritual of masculinity and priestly brotherhood. Through its rebellious attempts to break free of the 'freezing' of performance in 'sterile demonstrations' of technical and grammatical skill, the Travelling Morrice offered a new and dynamic future for the Revival. And though it shared some of the policies of the Espérance movement, in many other respects its basis was new and distinct. For its two founders, and most notably for Rolf Gardiner, this 'political act of the younger generation' had wide implications:

To Arthur Heffer and myself, with bonds of friendship that led our minds to sweeping views of our time, the deeper result of the Travelling Morrice, we hoped, would be the achievement of a *sense of purpose and direction*, not merely in the folk dance revival but in the whole life of our generation, the generation which had experienced the nightmare of the First World War, and had now before it the problems of the aftermath and the prospects of an England never to return to the sunlit comforts of pre-1914....
Speaking for myself, those tours were instruments of a sense of direction and purpose which I wanted to find and instil in my half-hearted contemporaries. I had a roving commission in those years, and was soon embroiled in youth movements, then a potent force for reconstruction in a bewildered post-war world. Through those experiences I saw Europe threatened by the huge upper and nether millstones of a mech-

anised America, and a revolutionary Russia. Could Europe, the Hellas of the modern civilisation, be saved from the collision of these giants of materialism? Could we form a union of the younger generation in northern Europe, between the historically varied yet kindred people of the North Sea and Baltic? That was the central idea that emerged from the tours in 1926 and 1928.... But to the members of the Travelling Morrice, this was going too far. Perhaps the majority were indeed profoundly sceptical of mixing up the morris with other things? My retort was, and still is, that the morris always has been mixed up with other things, and that to isolate it as a pastime unrelated to some wider purpose or context is to emasculate it and make it meaningless.[16]

And as Gardiner later revealed, whatever its differences over foreign affairs, the Travelling Morrice was united in rejection of specific aspects of the hegemony of the Revival at home:

they were none of them altogether satisfied by the jurisdiction of that august body in which, now that the Oxford heroes were dead, ladies had such a preponderently [sic] large say... They furthermore rather resented having to learn masculine dances from feminine instructions, and if they attended the Vacation Schools of the Society it was primarily for the purpose of coming into closer contact with Mr. Sharp's personality and of dancing under the leadership of his chief remaining dancer, Douglas Kennedy. Perhaps the tacit conspiracy of these positions drew them closer together.[17]

Gardiner was an activist whose call to youth to challenge and revolutionise moribund institutions was characteristic of the 1930s. Equally typical was his association with politics – firstly with Guild Socialism and then rapidly, through his interests as a Germanist, with Fascism. 'Every nation to-day', he wrote in 1932, 'requires a form of Fascism to rescue it from the pitfalls of its own self-sufficiency.'[18] In Gardiner's case, the form of statist, anti-capitalist Fascism advocated was inextricably connected with his developing concepts of a revived folk dance. Folk culture was, after all, not the Folk's, but 'ours' – the race's – and should therefore, serve the race's needs. Revitalising customary performances, Gardiner believed, would restore old, lost values underlying 'organic unities' of leadership, community, expressive culture and spirituality. Gardiner's membership of ultra-reactionary groups like English Mistery, 'an anti-democratic back-to-the-land organisation', and English Array, 'a ruralist school for leadership'[19] led him to promote ideas of the 'lost secrets' of government associated with William Sanderson's concept of 'statecraft':

The Secret of Memory, as opposed to the mere paraphernalia of learning; the Secret of Race, on which was based the hereditary transmission
of memory (here the experience of stockbreeders was of great importance); the Secret of Government based on tradition; the Secret of Power,
which, like the other Secrets, had been destroyed by 'industrial ideals';
the Secret of Organisation, based on service; the Secret of Property (with
feudalism being the ideal); and the Secret of Economics, which was
destroyed by the 'moneyed interests'.

Sanderson, whose work was the inspiration for the English Mistery, also presented clear policies on genetics and race. He divided
races into two types – those who 'differ very widely from us both
in character and tradition' and 'Norwegians, Danes, Dutch and
other people of North-West Europe' who were 'near to us in race
and tradition'.[20] Virulently anti-Semitic, 'the proper breeding of
Britons' and 'the proper development of traditions' were at the
heart of his group's beliefs.

Gardiner's assimilation of these views soon found practical extension in an attempt to develop a neo-feudal estate at Springhead
in Dorset.[21] Here, a programme combining 'the tending of cultural
relations between England and other countries in northern Europe', 'the development of Land Service camps' and 'the cultiva-
tion of musical forms of community refreshment and thanksgiving'
was initiated. It produced a highly cost-effective restoration of his
'tumbled-down farmlands' by unemployed industrial workers and
Aryan visitors, and the creation of 'a calendar of festivals and
celebrations ... connected with the economic endeavours of the
community'.[22] The folk and specially composed songs and dances
performed at Springhead festivals symbolised and reinforced its
social relations. These Gardiner saw in terms of 'the German *Bund*
– a kinship based on common experiences, common forms, common hopes'. In true feudal spirit, however, the common herd were
spared the complexities of a formative role in the Springhead
Bund. The uncultured, Gardiner proposed, were unsuited to the
task of developing folksongs and dances by themselves – 'artistic
leadership is an aristocratic function and each grade of society
needs its appropriate level of expressions, its applicable forms'.

But Gardiner's concept of the future of performance was not
merely a matter of ruling out the working class on the grounds of

ability, there was also the question of protecting them from too close an association with the peril that was folk dance – 'these forms sometimes have an inherent evocative power which must be controlled by responsible and initiated leadership.' Gardiner's view of this leadership was as grandiose as it was secretive: 'Avoiding spectacular publicity, they will remould the small units of the body politic ... they will exert their power in the lanes and hamlets of England, their authority will be anonymous as the seasons.'[23] To propagate his ideas, in 1932, Gardiner joined with 'a consultative body of friends' to form 'The Springhead Ring':

we differed from other members of our generation who became asphyxiated by the gas of the intellectual life around them. We were certainly less clever than they, less talented; our virtue if we had one was that we were not so frightened either of inward disturbance or of ecstasy as they; we refused to accept the stale, flat and unprofitable religion of the day, scientific scepticism, as our guide. Finally, perhaps, some of us had intensely vivid memories, racial or spiritual, of the past. Nostalgia was to a very high degree a spur to action. The music of an older Europe, the culture of pre-industrial England, the wonder of landscapes haunted by the ghosts of a remote past, here were some of the tutors of our inspiration. And these values were experienced not solely in the course of beholding and listening but in that of vivid activities ...[24]

Following discussions through the winter of 1933, in June 1934 some of the same individuals also set up 'The Morris Ring'. This organisation, conscious of what Vaughan Williams saw as 'the honour and responsibility' of preserving 'the aristocrat of the English folk dance', was intended to fill a gap in EFDS work on the revival of folk dance. 'The missing element was the essential unit of the ceremonial dance, a coherent group of performers, learning, practising and dancing together.'[25] The Morris Ring organised two or three 'gatherings' each year, 'at which men from various Clubs may meet and dance together'. Continuing a practice which pre-dated the formation of the Morris Ring, each spring one of these meetings was held at Thaxted in Essex, where members danced to the church of Conrad Noel, founder of the Catholic Crusade, a 'radical (or reactionary)' group which 'combined a kind of communism with medievalism and Anglo-Catholicism'.[26] An ideological tossed salad, in which High Anglican and Folk ritual co-existed with the politics of the revolutionary Left and Fascist Right, the groups meeting at Thaxted were unified by attempts to involve receptive members of the working class (though not the bourgeoisie) in spiritually fulfilling, craft-oriented ruralism. Through his links with such a range of variously motivated initiatives, however, Gardiner the charismatic innovator was well placed to influence the future of the Revival.

In 1936, Gardiner proclaimed that the Morris Ring was 'beginning to rescue the Morris from the movement', from 'the wimbly young men of the suburbs', the physically deficient 'concave-chested, bespectacled suburbans prancing over the schoolroom floor'. Through the Morris Ring, he wrote, the morris dance was becoming 'itself again' – 'the communion rite of clubs and 'secret societies,' of lazy rascals, roisterers and scallyways, of princes among these'. Pre-eminently, the Morris was being recovered as 'the dance of men, sworn to manhood, fiery ecstasy, ale, magic and fertility', of men who met together 'to pitch camp, to sleep in the grass, to cook the breakfast, to sweat over the hills with the impedimenta of an expedition, and then to dance in blazing noon or at the going down of the sun'. 'To be genuine', Gardiner asserted, the dance had to be subordinated 'to the real needs of our time' – to the development of an initiated *Männerbund* which would 'make themselves vehicles of the arcane powers', 'form the nucleus of a new organic society' and become the leaders of a renewed English culture.[27]

Gardiner's views found a ready echo in some sections of the English Folk Dance and Song Society. As Douglas Kennedy, a consistent advocate and early 'Squire' of the Morris Ring later summarised, the style of dancing developed in the Revival was 'flamboyant and fussy', thus 'there had always been a camp rebelling against artistic grooming, and it became more vocal as time went on'.[28] Sharp's influence was still considerable, but inevitably it was diminishing with the passing of time after his death. So just as the paradoxes and inconsistencies of his organisation and method were becoming increasingly apparent, the possibility for voicing dissent grew. Indeed, in concert with the movement's embattled insistence on the validity of cultural evolution, Gardiner's atavistic appeals to restore the active ritual status of the morris dance seemed to call for greater ideological orthodoxy than Sharp had applied. Nor was an association with the politics of the extreme Right a particular bar to credibility within the movement. Through most of the 1920s and 1930s, *The Morning Post*, which had unfailingly supported Sharp's version of the Revival, was the mouthpiece of the 'Diehard' group of Conservative extremists,[29] while Lady Ampthill, the President of the English Folk Dance and Song Society throughout the 1930s, was the wife of the President of the 'ultra Conservative' National Party.[30] More generally, the Society's incorporation into the establishment and its manifest Englishness attracted many whose views were extremely reactionary, as well as some – such as Evelyn Sharp, Conrad Noel and George Lansbury, who were closer to the spirit of Blatchford's 'Merrie England'. The Morris Ring's aura of hearty good fellowship in the outdoors also accorded with the 1930s fashion for fitness, youth movements, sunbathing and hiking – 'people in shorts were everywhere'.[31] Manly and modern, Gardiner accurately delineated the inherent weaknesses of Sharp's version of the Revival and put forward an attractive programme of restoration, combining greater convergence with accepted theory and a developmental role for an elite of 'initiated' performers in which acts of revival became, rather than depicted, cultural identity.

As he makes clear, however, Gardiner's solution to the theoretical and practical questions surrounding Revival performance was shaped by a number of influences. Unlike his predecessors, his theories on the function of customary performance were drawn not directly from James Frazer's detailed exposition of the workings of cultural evolution in *The Golden Bough* but from a more recent hybrid of art and science. Gardiner was an effusive admirer of the writer D. H. Lawrence – whom he ostentatiously cited as a correspondent, frequently quoted and tried to recruit to the Revival as (inevitably) a member of a sword dance team.[32] Lawrence's novels, with their creative assimilation of Frazer's theories and Freudian premisses of the all-pervading influence of sex, offered a particularly attractive new openness on issues that nineteenth-century Folkloristics had only obliquely implied and Sharp delicately circumlocuted as 'associated in some occult way with the fertilization of all living things, animal and vegetable' of which 'mating was the obvious symbol'.[33] His writings provided an explicated, full-frontal updating of the combination of rural-sexual metaphor and anti-industrialism inspiring the Revival's concepts of 'village survivals of ancient fertility rituals'. But Lawrence's novels offered more than an extended literary redaction of existing theories. His later works, particularly *The Plumed Serpent* (1926), which dealt with a revival of ancient religion in Mexico, developed primitivist themes of race, phallicism and male calling to male. And it was these that Gardiner deployed to modify the Revival's dominant ideology of cultural evolution and produce an overall rationale for performance.[34] The resultant view of men's dance provided a marked contrast to Sharp's concept of 'grace and dignity, instinct with emotion gravely restrained':

The actual technique of the Sword-dance calls for less of individual skill than a perfect cooperation, a perfect subjugation of the minds and bodies of the several dancers to the pure purpose of the group, bodies and minds must think and move instinctively as the mind and body of man, but of a man of superhuman power, there are none of the complex coordinated movements of hand and foot, the perfect unstrained muscular control of the Morris dancer, demanded here, but agility and presence of mind, and perfect fitness of body, and above all an emotional unity, which with the fierce excitement of the dance seems to set in voltaic commotion every electron in the souls and bodies of the dancers, till all five, six, or eight, of them, as the case may be, are consumed, as it were, by one fluid, electric, purging, flame of ecstasy, an exaltation, a cathartic frenzy, impossible to convey in words to one who has not experienced it.[35]

Clearly, dance implied a coming together of more than minds.

The social formation Gardiner chose as a vehicle for his theories was also influenced by developments outside the existing ideology of the Revival. Though his Fascism differed somewhat from that of the Nazis, Gardiner's views manifested a number of the characteristics of *Freikorps* officers – men from 'semifeudal' backgrounds, who formed 'roaming, largely autonomous armies each commanded by its own charismatic leader' which 'served the cause of domestic repression' in Germany in the 1920s and provided a fertile recruiting base for National Socialism.[36] From his preoccupation with male bonding and belief in the efficacy of rural work camps to details like the apparent namelessness of his wife, Gardiner's writings overtly evoke models in the 'free Buende of the pre-Nazi period'.[37] Inherent in the German form was a corollary which Gardiner also took over into the Morris Ring – the *Freikorps* were an all-male association, created 'to escape women', and with a pervasive underlying view of women and women's bodies as a contaminating threat. Dancing supermen – perfect physical specimens, spending their leisure time camping together, willing to subjugate their minds and bodies to 'the pure purpose of the group' and whose joint performance climaxed in 'one fluid, electric, purging, flame of ecstasy' were Gardiner's version of this brotherhood. But although their dances were 'hallowed' to 'the promotion of fertility', Gardiner's lexicon comprehensively excludes women – masturbatory display, rather than potentially productive coupling – emerges as his rationale. Women, linked in his writing with night, elemental unreason, silence, obedience, the subconscious, absence of ethics, blood and faeces[38] are neither wanted nor necessary to such a context: 'I think we all shared a private rage at 'women's morris', – 'werris' we called it'.[39] The historical terms for performers of morris had been 'molly' or 'morris dancers' – under Gardiner's new rubric they were renamed 'morris men'.

That the sources of Gardiner's theories were unedifying is not in question, but their significance lies in the process of their conflated application at this point in the Revival's development. Divided over the Sharp copyright issue, ridiculed and no longer fashionable, failing to compete effectively with alternative types of leisure activity, the movement was losing impetus and direction. Gardiner's bonhomie and frankness were attractive. His clarity and fundamentalism offered a revision of purpose which was broadly welcome. Underlying these, for the initiated, was his fantasist's lure of the great big secret – arcane powers and a destiny as the natural aristocracy when the new order was established. Given the Revival's ideology, Gardiner's elitism in the English lanes was infinitely preferable to joining the working classes in London pubs and turning Cecil Sharp House into a community centre.

But was the movement capable of the required change? A far more effective cultural dictator than was produced in Europe in the 1930s, Sharp's concepts of the past, present and future of folk performance were virtually guaranteed canonical status in the systems of the Revival he had removed all challengers to make his own. Enduring replication of his ideology and the structures for its maintenance were built into his version of the movement. During his lifetime, Sharp forbade sympathetic Folk Dance Society staff members like Douglas Kennedy from participating in Gardiner's German tours, and work with Travelling Morrice. And after his death, the only construction available for alternative views within the Revival was as modifications, additions or slight corrections to the founder's minor oversights. Without wholesale abandonment of the legacy of a venerated national figure and begetter of the Revival, what scope was there for reorganisation? The answer was to multiply and colonise, rather than publicly change the existing system. Leaving Sharp's hegemony overtly unchallenged, the movement was instead apparently expanded to accommodate a distinct but related group. Then, institutionalised through the foundation of the Morris Ring, and networked through the Ring's 'very friendly and complementary relationship' with the English Folk Dance and Song Society, Gardiner's formulations were bequeathed as a continuing legacy of belief, attitude and practice to the Revival as whole. Their effect was to give focus to a longstanding, generalised unease about the membership of the movement. As *The Dance of Death*, Auden's replay of the Revival as political allegory, unerringly discerned, introduction of 'the doctrines of D. H. Lawrence as well as Hitler' had radical implications for the membership of the movement – 'It's about the girls. Man must be the leader whom women must obey.'[40]

Women had long been a 'problem' for the Revival. A combination of pragmatism and socio-cultural context led to women's forming the core of the Folk Dance Society's founding group and predominating in its membership and organisation. Despite the growing popularity of ballroom dancing, culturally, particular interest in dance was perceived as slightly effeminate in men but one of the more acceptable forms of leisure activity for women. From the inauguration of the Folk Dance Society, in pursuit of his educational aims, Sharp had deliberately sought to recruit numbers of women primary school teachers to the movement. This bias was later intensified by the effects of losses of men in the First World War. But the issue of women's forming the majority in Society activities was not simply a matter of equity of numbers. Potentially, folk dancing with its classes, performances and competitions offered women more than a 'suitable' hobby or source of additional professional qualification. The Revival was constructed on the premiss that teaching folk dance was a patriotic duty to culture. And since male participation in dance had some inherent ambiguities, and providing worthy pastimes for the community was historically a preserve of the genteel female, setting up and taking part in folk dance classes emerged as a form of national service especially suited to 'ladies'. Overall this created a situation where male dominance of the day-to-day existence of the movement was only uncertainly operative. For women of all classes, the comparative absence of men in the Revival offered a small area of external autonomy, satisfaction and personal achievement in a culture which still saw woman's place as the home, her role as an adjunct of men. More specifically, however, such conditions left 'artistically-inclined' middle-class women with the opportunity of taking up a full or part-time career in professional teaching with the English Folk Dance and Song Society – a job which involved travel, diversity, relative independence and the chance to exercise authority in management.[41] But though it was recognised that 'every woman who really cares for Folk Art must feel the call of the Morris and glory in its disciplined vigour and restraint', the first issue of the *EFDS Journal* had questioned the 'advisability of women dancing Morris dances in public demonstrations'. 'Morris dance is a man's dance and a ceremonial dance, and the flick of a woman's skirt only intensifies that indefinable something in her temperament which robs the Morris of its predominant feature, viz., the portrayal of strong emotions under absolute control combined with manly vigour and easy dignity.' If women must dance morris in public, the article concluded, they should keep a suitably manly stiff upper lip while doing so and wear 'simple' dresses in dark or neutral, non-feminine colours.[42] From the foundation of the Society, therefore, the presence of women as members, leaders and most fundamentally, as non-men,had been surrounded by question.

But theory and practice were often at odds in the movement's approach to women's dancing. At Sharp's suggestion, members of the Espérance Girls' Club had been the first morris dancers of the Revival, and dances in the first edition of *The Morris Book* were notated from the performance of Florence Warren, an Espérance member. Some early expressions of doubt about women's morris emerge, therefore, as products of the English Folk Dance Society's incarnation as the mirror image of Espérance and its seamstresses, rather than the result of theoretical doubts about the gender of the dancers. Sharp prefaced his report of Joseph Druce's comment 'Girls have got things for their use and men have got things for their use, and the Morris is for men', with the view that it reflected Druce's scorn for the prominent part taken by women in 'the present Revival of morris dancing'. And while providing historical examples of women's morris from village tradition, he firmly added that these were 'short-lived': 'the Morris was a man's dance'.[43] In other respects, however, his attitude was equivocal. His correspondence with Alice Gomme indicates that the formation of a demonstration side of male morris dancers was prompted by Perceval Lucas as a response to Mary Neal's introduction of a 'team of young men, friends and relatives of the [Espérance] girls' in January 1910, rather than at Sharp's own suggestion. But although he wrote that he was 'very anxious to have a man's side at my command', it took him two years to produce one, and in the meantime he apparently saw no difficulty in combining discussion of the origin of morris dances in 'nature ceremonies' with the information that he 'took the Chelsea girls up to Huddersfield and Halifax on Friday and Saturday and they danced really superbly'.[44] Similarly, the mixed side which had provided illustrations for Sharp's early lectures was prudishly discontinued when newspapers reported admiration for its 'coquettish question and answer', rather than on grounds of 'authenticity'. Even in Sharp's inner circle, there was an absence of complete theoretical agreement on the maleness of morris – his friend E. Phillips Barker holding that the presence of men dressed as women in a number of dance traditions represented roles from which women had been 'ousted' when agriculture and its cults 'passed from the women's province into the men's'.[45] And Sharp himself felt that tradition and Revival should be accorded different treatment:

The Morris is, traditionally, a man's dance. Since, however, it was revived a few years ago it has been freely performed by women and children. Although this is not strictly in accordance with ancient usage, no great violence will be done to tradition so long as the dance is performed by the members of one sex only; none but the pedant, indeed, would on this score debar women from participation in a dance as wholesome and as beautiful as the Morris.[46]

Moreover, although Gardiner reported that it was Sharp's 'pessimism' that deterred him from acting against 'werris', the position of a male director of a Society composed almost entirely of women was not without its compensations:

Girls hung over the edge of the gallery to wave to friends just discovered below; girls on the window-sills called greetings to others who had

climbed up on the ladders and bars of the gymnastic apparatus; girls ran about looking for chairs or song-books.
Some one began to clap, and the hall rang with the welcome of six hundred folk-dancers to their chief. The white-haired Director appeared on the platform and smilingly acknowledged the greeting. He struck a chord on the piano and silence fell; he announced, 'Number One,' and began to play a rippling accompaniment.... 'He's our Prophet' – she leaned across to Ruth. 'We all love him!'[47]

Decisive repudiation of women's participation in morris and sword dance was, therefore, a later development, forming a minor cultural aspect of the counteraction which followed women's attaining the vote and a measure of personal and financial independence after the First World War. The start of Gardiner's campaign for all-male morris coincided with a moral panic, orchestrated by the popular press, surrounding questions of female sexuality and the existence of a generation of 'surplus women'.[48] In the Revival, its acceptance marked a long-term shift in hegemonic control which served to reduce the autonomy and status of women in all areas of the movement – as Gardiner later admitted: 'women flocked to the schools and dominated the Society's branches. Men were in a hopeless minority. It was a most unnatural state of affairs.'[49] Unfocused concerns about the suitability of women performing 'male ritual dances' then crystallised, as underlying cultural mysogyny and current public hysteria were given a 'legitimate' expression in Gardiner's demands for greater theoretical rectitude – especially as this was coupled with the provision of an 'appropriate' alternative to women performers in the shape of the Morris Ring.

But as the 1930s progressed, women were not merely denied a role in sword and morris, they were increasingly marginalised as participants in other forms of dance. The Folk Dance Society had already warned them not to show too much expertise and 'betray their virtuosity' if they wanted more men to attend country dance classes. Sharp's writings characterised social dance as less significant than 'ancient ceremonial' performances, and women's status was reduced because it was the only form they could 'legitimately' take part in. In the 1930s, these pre-existing factors were linked with an explicit English Folk Dance and Song Society policy of refusing to provide country dance teaching for all-women classes and a practice of allowing women to join in events involving social dancing only if they could produce a male partner. Women were therefore multiply disadvantaged – the dances they could perform were merely 'recreational' and of relatively low status; as individuals or as part of a single-sex group, they were debarred from the opportunity of taking a full part in many of the Society's weekend, summer schools, parties and other social activities; and more subtly, if they attempted to find the requisite male partner, this was represented as 'eagerness to entrap'. The implication of a man-hungry horde, ever on the lookout to 'secure' a 'reluctant' man to dance with them, underlay many 'light-hearted' descriptions of women's participation at Revival events, where, 'overwhelmed by numbers', men with 'sinking hearts' succumbed to 'a bevy of fair damsels'.[50] The Society's policy was reportedly implemented 'to attract a larger proportion of men', but its effect was to marginalise and discriminate against women already well aware of the demographic results of war. As a member of the English Folk Dance and Song Society or the Morris Ring, any man, however inexperienced or inexpert a dancer, was to be preferred to a woman.

Sharp was no feminist – determinedly anti-suffrage, his attitude to women ranged from an urbane clubman's disdain for female folly to downright unpleasantness in his dealings with Mary Neal. Aside from any consideration of his standing as founder-director, his view that 'no great violence' was done to tradition by women's performance in the Revival might therefore, have been expected to carry considerable weight with the Morris Ring and its supporters. With a small number of exceptions, however, it was women who put up the most consistent defence of Sharp's legacy in the Revival and attempted to maintain the structure and procedures he had personally formulated. As a tactic, claiming solidarity with their male founder rather than asserting the value of their participation on their own account had a number of possible advantages. Women as women were under attack – reiterating that their role in the movement had been determined and verified by its originator linked their position with his. Potentially, it also shifted the argument from questions of gender, in which they were disadvantaged, to that of maintaining orthodoxy – a guiding principle of the movement.

Defending a significant role for women in the Revival at this time, however, involved dimensions beyond a relatively uncomplicated advocacy of long-established practice. At a time when tradition was 'unpopular' and fomenting revolutionary change a near-requirement of activists in any organisation, an appeal to keep up the status quo was easily construed as a perverse obstruction of the grain of the times, unimaginative, restricting and timid. The Revival was misdirected, stagnating in a morass of convention and respectability, claimed supporters of the Morris Ring, and women clinging on to a mistaken bureaucracy were largely responsible for keeping it there. That women liked and wanted to keep their status and independence, that they might have preferred dancing with a female partner in a single-sex group, or simply enjoyed dancing for its own sake, irrespective of the gender of their partner, were never considered as explanations of their opposition. Meanwhile, those who might otherwise have agreed a continuation of the English Folk Dance and Song Society's existing approach were warned that women's stated views should not be taken at face value. Maintaining that his comments were 'nothing if not complimentary to the ladies, bless them', Gardiner suggested that women were saying 'no' to progress in the form of a reconstituted motive for men's dance, when what they really meant was 'yes'. Despite reporting 'a female voice' at the 1935 International Folk Dance Conference which proclaimed 'We do not like all this talk of magic; we do not want fertility!', he concluded 'They in their hearts want what we want more than anyone; look how they kindle at the show of any genuine touch of real manhood!'[51] Dancing in all forms 'naturally' involved sex and, 'naturally', 'real men' should be in charge of it.

Paradoxically, the Revival's ethos of traditionality also made women's case more difficult to argue. Having failed in its attempt to replace contemporary popular culture with folk alternatives, the movement had institutionalised the genteel and nostalgic. Typified by events such as the 'Folk Masque' staged by its Gloucestershire and Bristol Branch 'in the beautiful garden of Goldney House, Clifton', where 'Morris and Country dances, folk-songs and ancient customs' were 'skilfully woven' into 'a charming little pageant', the English Folk Dance Society of the 1920s offered a target, rather than a cause for the radical.[52] From 1924, moreover, the Woodcraft Folk provided a separate, identifiably socialist, context for those who might wish to use folksong and dance as one of the means to 'pass on to our children the desire to work

for that International comradeship and understanding that alone
will bring to the world unity and peace'. So as the ideological
polarisation of the 1930s intensified, the majority of overtly political, artistic and intellectually innovative approaches to folk culture were consciously located outside the English Folk Dance and
Song Society. The individuals who continued to support the idea
of a Folk Revival within the Society during this period were
therefore more than usually predisposed to support Gardiner's
reactionary stereotypes: 'A 'return to masculinity' is an unthinkable concept, for masculine is defined by the present tense. But in
clothes, in attitude and in everything else, to be safely feminine –
to 'retain' her femininity – a woman must look to the distant
past.'[53]

   This combination of dynamics proved impossible for some leading women members of the Society to overcome, and they actively
confirmed the movement's preconceptions about the attitudes and
motivation of 'the ladies'. 'We were not, however, unduly de-
pressed by these minor misfortunes,' wrote Helen Kennedy of the
collapse of a portion of the stage during her first public performance, 'because we had secured real men to take part in the
Country dances, and such a thing had never been done before. I
use the word 'secured' advisedly,' she thoughtfully expanded for
those who might otherwise have missed the point, 'as the men
were friends who had been dragged in, for, although they knew
very little about the dances, they were men.'[54] The Morris Ring
also had its female supporters – favoured with a brief opportunity
to join men in their exclusive dances, Gardiner's friend Gladys
Hall breathlessly confirmed to an audience of fellow teachers the
wonders of performing with manly implement in hand:

the first time I danced with the North Skelton Team, it was a revelation
to me. I thought I knew quite a lot about sword dancing, but I realised
then that I did not know the first thing. I went in to the dance with my
mind a blank, feeling I should always be going in the wrong direction,
but I hadn't been in many minutes when I realised that neither I nor the
men who were dancing mattered in the least degree, that it was the
SWORD, and the SWORD only, that mattered. You felt absolutely that
they were holy things to be borne carefully and reverently.[55]

By suggesting to members of such a sub-culture that 'real' women
were distinguished by their appreciation of 'real' men, therefore,

Gardiner both reinforced existing attitudes and provided a handy source of dismissal for anyone who attempted to counter his proposals. Men who disagreed could be attacked as gender traitors, 'seduced' like gullible serving girls: 'Whatever species of dyspeptic 'cannibal' has been seducing the mind of our good Francis Fryer with all this blarney about 'mixed Morris sides'? The Morris has surely suffered enough emasculation to provide sufficient example of maltreatment and misuse. And yet here is our enthusiast handing over the remains on a platter of indeterminate sex.'[56] Women were in a double bind, guilty of biological and cultural failure. If they opposed the Morris Ring, they could not be 'real' women, and were therefore also 'unfeminine'. Moreover, while men reputedly gained masculinity by performing in single sex groupings, no matter how they looked or acted women lost femininity by dancing with other women.

Campaigning to keep a significant place in the Revival whilst maintaining consonance with such attitudes, therefore, involved complex negotiations. As had often been the case in hegemonic struggles in the Revival, presenting an appropriate appearance emerged as a major battleground – length and fullness of skirt and fit of bodice became the weapons. 'If you're going to do morris,' wrote the novelist Elsie J. Oxenham in the early 1920s, 'you'll have to get into a tunic, you know! Morris in a frock, or in a blouse and skirt, would be too awful for words!'[57] In the 1930s, this approach was answered with a consciously reversed form – if women were to be debarred from morris and 'domination in the Branches', they needed to be got into frocks as soon as possible. And not just any frocks – the coveted blue demonstration dresses used by the Society from its earliest days would no longer do. Now long waisted and unfitted, they gave little evidence of the 'shapely whole' of 'a woman with a good figure'. Fortunately, a 'natural' opportunity for change soon arose. English women dancers, it seemed, had been compared very unfavourably with foreign performers in national costume who had taken part in the International Folk Dance Festival of 1935. A crisis meeting of the National Executive had taken place and the first issue of *English Dance and Song* was used to invite proposals for a home-grown national dress to be used for demonstration performances.[58] The Society's problem was clear cut – women were letting the side down and their appearance needed to be reconstituted. But Violet

Alford, who had dutifully suggested a national costume that was
'graceful', with a 'flared and full skirt' and a 'neatly fitted bodice'
for women, also took the opportunity to complain of male dancers
in 'untidy and featureless flannels, which across the Channel call
forth surprised and amused remarks ... and which, except on grass,
impart a peculiarly washy aspect'.[59] Nela Bower, the editor of
English Dance and Song, then advanced the argument by suggesting that men's choice of costume was detrimental to the whole of
men's dance:

we see men in flannels and baldricks, hot but unflagging, as they appear
in quick succession in a morris, a country, a sword dance, and a set run
from Kentucky, giving what is often an excellent trailer of the variety
of English folk dancing, but scarcely, we venture to suggest, showing
the real thing. For these breathless men have no time to change their
clothes. They are using the different dances as contrasting turns to make
variety. They are not allowing each tradition to stand by itself and to
appear in its own atmosphere enhanced by its own dress.

Pausing only to designate an appropriate costume for rapper
dancing, 'whether for men or women', she turned to the question
of suitable styles for women's dress, contrasting two memories:

One is that of a team of young women who danced well but whose line
was completely spoilt by their appearance in bare arms and long full
skirts. The other is a team of the twelve to fourteen year old daughters
of traditional dancers. They wore short dark 'gym' tunics and stockings
and white blouses with full sleeves and collars. Their dress enhanced
their delightful dancing which was no mere copy of their fathers and
brothers as was proved by the feminine swish of their brief skirts.[60]

Bower's editorial touched on all the public facets of women's case
in the struggle for hegemony. Women as well as men, she implied,
could appropriately perform 'ceremonial dances' – and what was
more, the Folk offered no objections to their daughters and sisters
making up teams to do so. Appearance was important, but high
artistic standards could be associated with short skirts, just as the
much reviled gym tunic could be more aesthetic and feminine than
long dresses and a display of bare flesh. But even in this clear
assertion of the values of women's participation, a separate category of performance, defined by gender stereotype, was
presented as a reference point for revivalists. And in consequence,
Bower's closing argument that 'since the variety of woman's

beauty is so great, it may be a pity to strain it into a standard garment' loses much of its force.

As embodied in their 'official' dress, Revival attitudes to women offered a marked contrast to clothes worn for other pastimes in the 1930s. The costume of satin shorts and blouses which formed the demonstration dress of the Women's League of Health and Beauty, a contemporary single-sex group applying a more supportive construction of the feminine, caused Prunella Stack, the League's co-founder, to comment to readers of *English Dance and Song* in 1938: 'Used to our bare black-and-white uniforms, you look a little overdressed to me! Why do the women wear stockings and the men long shorts, instead of short ones?'[61]

More radically still, Francis Fryer, maintaining his advocacy of mixed morris in spite of Gardiner's insinuations, suggested that 'mixed sides and teams could nowadays easily dress the sexes alike'.[62] To an organisation in which women's appreciation of the freedom and independence associated with moving about in gym tunics was rapidly losing out to a requirement of long full skirts for all types of performance, the prospect of women dancers in trousers seems to have been unthinkable.[63] Although in the outside world, shorts and 'pyjama suits' were the height of fashionable leisure wear, and despite the fact that 'counterfeit men' had taken part in the Folk Dance Society ballet 'Old King Cole' as late as 1927, any hint of female bifurcation was suppressed in Society performances in the 1930s. Women revivalists were not to be seen as 'wearing the trousers' literally or metaphorically.

Attempts to redress the reallocations in hegemony on other grounds were hampered by an equal absence of a well-defined position from which women might argue with confidence. In the late 1920s, Evelyn Sharp attacked changes based on 'motive' at their apparent source by suggesting that social dance was also traceable to 'the old rites that form the background of all dancing' – 'the ceremonial dance round the sacrificial victim', and 'sun worship': might not dances where men and women partnered each other 'have something to do with a marriage rite?'[64] Her proposals shared many premises with the theory of the ritual origin of children's dancing games put forward by her colleague on the English Folk Dance Society Executive Committee, the folklorist Alice Gomme.[65] Gomme's views were, at the time, still very widely accepted, and a genesis in prehistoric religious belief chimed with the Society's insistence on the validity of cultural evolution. But Evelyn Sharp's tentative description of her theorising as vague speculation and lingering prejudice against her 'Nealite' past combined to reduce her writing's effectiveness. Despite resort to the ultimate weapon – supporting comment from Maud Karpeles that 'although it has for many generations been danced purely as a means of social and artistic recreation, Cecil Sharp believed that it had its origin in the processional and ring dances which at one time formed part of the May Day ritual'[66] – a ritual origin for social dancing was never accepted Society theory.

Nor was Evelyn Sharp's case helped by the fact that Mary Neal herself had recently changed her stance on women's morris. One of the more mystical of the youth movements originating in the 1920s was the Kibbo Kift Kindred, 'a scheme of youth training which would enable the individual, from infancy to manhood, to recapture the primitive phases of human development; exploration, hunting, conflict, invention and so on. The idea was that a new elite, drawn preferably from the 'children of the slain', would be created which would be physically and mentally superior to its predecessors.' The Kibbo Kift had its founding meeting at the house of Neal's lifelong friends from the Espérance Club, Emmeline and Frederick Pethick-Lawrence, and initially drew its membership from Utopian socialists and adherents of the Social Credit movement, among them the young Rolf Gardiner.[67] Although the Labour group withdrew in 1924 to set up the Woodcraft Folk, Gardiner had stayed with Neal that summer, signing her visitors' book in his Kibbo Kift persona 'Rolf the Ranger, KK'. 'We had', she wrote shortly afterwards, 'some wonderful talks. He has got the real spirit of the morris as a priest's dance of ritual and discipline. He propounded ideas to me of what a man's life should be under the influence of such a ritual.' Despite her conversion, however, Neal was still shrewd enough to recognise that proposals that morris and sword dances 'were the remains of a purely masculine ceremonial, and that they represented a ritual of discipline for war and sex expression' might well be accepted within the Revival if propounded by Gardiner, 'a very virile and beautiful youth'. If put forward by her, such high flown exotica would be seen as 'silly old maid's nonsense'.[68]

Self-censorship, inability to resolve the paradoxes of their conservative attitudes and institutionalised misogyny all contributed

to the matrix hampering women's defence of their share of hegemony. But critically, attempts to justify their position were characterised by absence of any specific discussion of the significance
of their contribution to the existence of the movement. Women's
experience as dancers, members, organisers and theorists of the
Revival was unrepresented in the debate. Morris tours were recorded in Society and Ring publications in exhaustive detail, and
Gardiner overflowed with lyricism for men's performance:

His erect carriage, masculine grace and splendid arm-movements evinced
an Attic power: see the bigness of the half-rounds, with the beautiful
arms-apart movement on the jump, the 'caesura' – check – before the
galley ... to see him do that jig was to watch a dancer in whose body
every muscle and limb worked in complete harmony, resulting in a
picture of beautiful strength and kingly presence in movement.[69]

But description of women's response to dance is most extensively
present in popular fiction:

Gasping with amazement, Mary found herself dancing; found herself
instinctively keeping time to the music found herself enjoying this new
thing as she had enjoyed nothing for years. The movements, simple as
they were, demanded all her thought; she was desperately determined
not to spoil Jen's dance by being clumsy and forgetful; awkward and
stiff she felt, indeed, but fortunately without the faintest idea how
awkward she seemed to her partner.
At the moment she could think only of what she must do next; of
running or skipping; right hand or left. For a wild agonised second she
did not know how to skip; then it came to her suddenly. She was not
sure if she had ever skipped in her life before, but she had watched
children, and she found her feet discovering what to do. Any thought
at all beyond her feet and hands was given to the astounding incredible
fact that she, Mary Devine, was dancing; had danced 'up the line,' and
was beginning to go down again. Then, to her horror, she discovered
that nearly everything she had learned with such difficulty must be
reversed; over first instead of under, and the swing in the opposite
direction. Jen laughed at her dismay, and gently kept her right.[70]

The support from her female partner, the 'kindly encouragement'
of her female teacher, the jokes and companionship of her female
fellow students all serve to bring shabby-genteel Mary Devine,
thirtyish, unmarried and leading a narrow, joyless, pointless existence, into a new, more satisfying and enjoyable life. But though
they reportedly existed in overwhelming numbers in the move-

ment, the significance of the Revival for archetypal performers of
'werris' such as this is scarcely touched on in the publications of
the English Folk Dance Society. Women's qualities, their contribution and their potential had no official existence.

The official view of the English Folk Dance and Song Society
was that a preponderance of women was a problem whatever their
status and wherever they were to be found. After Sharp's death,
the benefits of a large professional membership was untapped, as
women teachers working for additional qualification in folk dance
were repeatedly dismissed as using the Society 'for their own ends'.
For all their complaints, however, the Society's policy makers put
forward no innovative proposals for development of the Revival
by reforming this extensive channel to the education system –
teachers were simply blamed for taking part in the movement as
they found it. Future prospects in education were still further
diminished by the introduction of the policy of mixed couples 'as
the only right method of country dancing'. Strict application of
this rule then meant that 'the E.F.D.S. could obviously take only
a partial interest' in dance at single-sex teacher training colleges –
a course of action which rapidly led to Society classes being
replaced by identical teaching from less doctrinaire non-Society
specialists.[71] As performers or members, the large number of
women in the English Folk Dance and Song Society during the
1930s were patronised and ridiculed as 'hundreds of jolly women
in gym-slips persuading the few men that they had dragooned to
move the piano onto the grass to gather ye peascods'.[72] And in
contrast to the single-sex composition of the Morris Ring, their
forming a majority in the Society was constructed as a source of
diminished status for women themselves and the movement they
had joined:

In the successful rural centres there is the balanced proportion of men
and women dancers which is essential to the permanent re-establishment
of the country dance in every day life ... In the cities and towns the
position is far less encouraging and this year in particular [1933–34] has
proved a period of exceptional difficulty. There exists in the towns a
very large number of enthusiastic and experienced dancers; there persists
a demand for personal instruction, especially among women; but what
is conspicuous by its absence is the social group of men and women
meeting together to dance for recreation.... The stronghold of the
E.F.D.S. [sic] in the majority of towns remains the dusty, draughty drill

hall with its questionable piano and its complete absence of warmth, gaiety and decoration, where some twenty or thirty women in every-day dress await the arrival of the visiting teacher.[73]

Women had the most at stake in the existing form of the Revival and, in the reformation which followed Gardiner's initiatives, experienced the brunt of the losses. To take the most prominent example, Sharp's closest collaborator, Maud Karpeles (1885–1976), led the fight to retain the Sharp family's share of copyright, tirelessly propagandised for his version of the movement and ensured that his plans for collecting and publishing were continued after his death. She was, her most perceptive obituarist noted, 'impelled ... to project into futurity the dogma and interpretations of Cecil Sharp'.[74] Concentrating her efforts on her role as his literary executor, she 'turned some attention to her own research only after she had edited and re-edited Sharp's material for publication, written and re-written his bibliography.'[75] But although Karpeles was 'ranked after Sharp' in the Society's hierarchy during his lifetime, and had been intimately associated with his work in dance and song in the Revival since 1909, it was Douglas Kennedy, her less experienced brother-in-law, whose involvement had been limited to 'weekend' dance, who was designated Director in succession to Sharp.[76] Karpeles's administrative ability was not in question – she had a 'natural inclination to the procedure and language of committee government' and with Kennedy and Ralph Vaughan Williams formed the directorate making up the Folk Dance and Song Society's Board of Artistic Control. Later she became honorary secretary of the committee, organising the 1935 International Folk Dance Festival and Conference, which in turn led to her role as co-founder and secretary of the International Folk Music Council in 1947.[77] During the 1930s, she made two major collecting trips to Newfoundland and also published extensively:

in the decade following Sharp's death, with other claims on her time [Karpeles] brought out *The English Country Dance*, nine volumes in a graded series, with dance notations, 1926–34; four parts of Sharp's dances from Playford's Dancing Master, some 160 in all, re-edited in 1927; a re-edition of Sharp's 'Incidental Music and Dances' for *A Midsummer Night's Dream*, with dance notations added, 1930... These, be it noted, were in addition to the work on the Appalachian and Newfoundland volumes. She undertook at the same time, with A. H. Fox Strangways as co-author, a full-length biography of Cecil Sharp.[78]

But her devotion to Sharp and his work is treated as faintly ridiculous. She was alternately patronised as Sharp's 'little secretary-lady', "the little foot-page,' out of that ballad ... she sits at his feet, in her tunic, and flies off if he wants anything, almost before he's asked for it',[79] and presented as an archetypal battleaxe – 'the feeling was at times that he was 'under the thumb of Miss Karpeles", she 'was sometimes irreverently known as 'Mrs Sharp".[80] Latterly, her interest in 'ghost and fairy lore' provoked the comment that 'she considered herself somewhat fey',[81] an imputation of arch otherworldliness which Gardiner's highly coloured strainings on the wonders of masculinity deserved but never seemed to produce. Karpeles was also allotted the well-rehearsed female role of carrying the burden of fault. 'Maud's hand on the helm' was reportedly both responsible for the 'great disproportion of women' in the Revival and the reason for which 'the Society soon found itself in a rut' after Sharp's death.[82] Uniquely in a movement for which its founder's pronouncements assumed near-religious significance, Karpeles's and other women's advocacy of Sharp's policies was represented as a failing. Following the ascendancy of the Morris Ring viewpoint, Karpeles, the foremost woman organiser of the Revival, was left with little option in her career but to turn her attention from dance to song scholarship – an area of secondary specialism, but one in which she again established a leading position. Though their involvement with the Revival shows some parallels in this respect, however, assessment of the characters of its two leading proponents remains markedly different. Sharp was autocratic, dedicated, conservative, opinionated and is revered; Karpeles was autocratic, dedicated, conservative, opinionated and is derided.

Ostensibly, the work and sphere of influence of the Morris Ring was quite separate from that of the English Folk Dance and Song Society. The function of the Morris Ring was 'to perform a task which the EFDSS could not do', by taking 'ceremonial dance ... beyond the classroom'. For its part, the English Folk Dance and Song Society was to adopt 'a diminishing role in relation to the ceremonial dance'.[83] In practice, the Ring's effect on the dominant ideology of the Revival was far less restricted. Drawing on her Diplomas of the University of London and of the Chelsea College of Physical Education (1937), in an official Society publication, Sibyl Clark offered the following advice on folk dance in schools to teachers in 1956:

If in a mixed school dancing is continued when there is a disinclination on the part of boys and girls between 12 and 14 to dance together in Country dancing, Morris or Sword dancing could be introduced as part of the lesson, with the boys making their own sets and the girls doing the same. The problem here is that girls at this age have a greater facility for picking up new things and better co-ordination than have boys of the same age; but if the teacher allows the boys to set the pace, they will have caught up with and passed the girls within six months, provided they had not been made too conscious of their slowness in the early stages. As Morris and Sword dances are men's dances, it is important that here the boys should have preferential treatment.

'Man must be the leader whom women must obey' had become overt English Folk Dance and Song Society policy in 'ceremonial' and social dance, and throughout its organisation. The re-alignment of hegemonic control was complete: 'There should be social training from the start. The boys should be the dominant partners and take the lead; the boys are responsible for the safety and comfort of their partners. The girls should learn from the beginning to allow their partners to lead them and to hand them into place, and never go their own way regardless of the boy, however sure they may be that *they* are right and their partner wrong.'[84]

Gardiner and his supporters had called for reform of the Revival, but elitism, a reactionary ideology and internecine struggles produced change which was regressive rather than developmental. As the world outside moved towards mixed sex, companionate groupings and equality, the Revival completed the shifts in its hegemony which set up a male elite drawn from the professions and 'Varsity', confirmed the exclusion of the working classes from its organisation and policy and institutionalised the most patronising excesses of Edwardian 'chivalry'. Dismissing contemporary theory, the creation of a fundamentalist annexe in the Morris Ring and displacing blame for the movement's stagnation to its women members all served to intensify the Revival's academic isolation. At the same time, the most basic of its practical functions, the teaching and performance of dance of all types, was increasingly obfuscated by Douglas Kennedy's introduction of the concept of 'anacrusis' – a confused principle of rhythmic momentum which was deployed talismanically as a cure for the Society's self-conscious, arty style. (Prunella Stack's suggestion that Society dancers should 'smile *often* instead of occasionally' would probably have

been a more effective aid to relaxation and certainly involved far
less pretension.) With 'support from the educational world diminishing' and unable to comprehend the 'general public' that broadcasting and mass culture was now addressing, the Revival finally
experienced its own 1930s crisis. At its Annual General Meeting
on 3 December 1938, Lady Ampthill's 'Opening Remarks from the
Chair' consisted of a reminder 'that the Society's great need was
for more members', whilst for the Executive Committee, Mr Tabor
'drew particular attention to the serious deficit on the year's
working' and highlighted 'the falling revenues of the Society'. The
Sharp copyright battle reached its bitter climax, but victory for the
Executive Committee was accompanied by pointed comments
from the floor on their absence of integrity. Belated attempts to
expand the movement had met with mixed fortunes – a policy of
affiliating non-Society groups to the organisation had been initiated and led to an increase in numbers taking part in dancing
under its auspices, but the transfer had not effected the desired
growth in membership for the EFDSS. Executive Committee parties for specially invited groups who were new to folk dance
produced a 'lady guest' who commented on the 'fun' associated
with an absence 'of negroid 'numbers' and dismal 'blues'', but
apparently made no headway in 'getting on a par' with ballroom
dancing, which was their main aim.[85] And despite high levels of
unemployment, there were 'openings in the country for qualified
part-time and whole-time teachers and organisers' of folk dance.
Symbolising all the limitations inherent in the institutionalised
version of the Revival was the near-halving of attendances at
graded classes at Cecil Sharp House – the number participating in
the mechanism for attaining a quality-controlled reproduction of
folk culture at the centre named after its originator fell from 1,265
in 1937–8 to 892 in 1938–9.[86] By the end of the decade, Douglas
Kennedy, the Director of the English Folk Dance and Song Society,
reportedly 'considered emigration to America, which seemed to
offer more prospects for revival'. As Kennedy's obituarist noted,
however, events outside the Society's control intervened – 'the War
prevented this move.'[87]

Unlike the First World War, which had delayed rather than
changed Sharp's plans for Revival, the Second World War had a
marked effect on the development of the movement. Propaganda
designed to bolster morale and build a consensus among those

experiencing 'The People's War' drew heavily on images of national identity. 'A country lane', 'a cottage small beside a field of grain' were not just the popular song's convenient encapsulation of 'what we're all fighting for' but were presented as Englishness itself – in their absence, the song claimed, there could be no nation. Moreover, as the war intensified, Englishness took on an additional function. 'The Southcountry', its rolling hills and village greens reflecting priorities set by nature rather than current events, offered a timeless and indestructible, conceptual retreat to those whose uncertain present was bombing raids, the rubble of destroyed cities, factory production lines and foreign battlefields.[88] More familiar and long-established in popular imagination than many objective realities, Englishness was reified in films, radio programmes, stage presentations and a range of publications – a fugue on hedgerow, manor, field and cottage suggested a various, but reassuringly identifiable destination for psychological escape. And, implicitly at least, on every village green there was a maypole.

Just as the landscape of Englishness fulfilled an additional role in the reproduction of dominant culture, its inhabitant, the mythic countryman, was also publicly re-interpreted to meet the needs of wartime consensus: 'In periods of acute social change and insecurity, popular cultural forms have a threefold function. They provide reassurance for marginal groups by according them a symbolic presence, they produce pleasure for the audience by temporarily resolving real tensions in their lives, and they clarify confusions about moral or social boundaries.'[89] Through the medium of broadcasting, pre-existing modes of social realism were combined with the emergent reform of Englishness to create a consensus which embraced the marginalised Folk and gave them a voice – at one of the darkest periods of the war, 'Country Magazine', a programme with the brief of giving 'country people and their war-work ... their rightful share of publicity', was initiated:

It is interesting to look back on 1942. On May 1st, Hitler and Mussolini were in conference in Austria. On the 2nd the Japanese captured Mandalay. On the 3rd the first Country Magazine was broadcast.
The aim was to create a better team spirit between people working in factories and people working in fields; we wanted to remind men and women living under great strain in the cities that the people in the

country were doing their best to help. We hoped to let them know that
the countryside had its own problems, all the way from looking after
homeless children to ploughing under shell-fire.[90]

In keeping with the image of a nation unified in its struggle against
an anti-democratic foe, in the studios of 'Country Magazine' Lob
and Hodge mixed with their social superiors, evolved differing
persona (and genders) and acquired individual voices:

So the farmer, the farm worker, the butcher, the baker, the saddler, the
huntsman, the squire, the doctor, the retired colonel, the vet, the Home
Guard, Uncle Tom Cobley and all, together with their womenfolk, could
and did rub shoulders in the studio and broadcast, not what the
producer might want them to say, but what they themselves wanted to
say. There was never the slightest suggestion of importing a countryman
to London to put him on a pin and let him wriggle in front of the
microphone for the amusement of the town listener.
Having started on such lines, the rest was easy. Country Magazine just
ran away on its own momentum, if you like on quality, the quality of
the country people. Not the prehistoric country people who then existed
in the minds of the majority of listeners, but the country people of the
times, real people, each an individualist ...[91]

The programme, broadcast on alternate Sundays, was 'a success
from the word 'go'', and during the 1940s held the record of
longest unbroken run in British broadcasting. A major part of its
appeal, its advocates claimed, was its policy of including 'a
country song' halfway through each edition. This decision was
made in the face of some opposition – 'I confess that in the
beginning I deplored it', noted A. G. Street, doyen of country
writers and the programme's first compere. Though he agreed he
had since been proved 'hopelessly wrong', the programme's producer, Francis Dillon, was at pains to distance 'Country Magazine's' broadcasts of 'country songs' from the general run of
folksong performance. Dillon also identified the Revival's responsibility for folksong's poor reputation with devastating clarity:

Sharp's intentions, it is recorded, were of the purest, but after noting
them faithfully, the old songs were served up in simplified form to
schools and the sort of singers who could just manage them for a
concert, until men and women who could really sing them in the proper
style were ashamed to, and folk song became associated with floppy ties
and folksy get-togethers. Inevitably the decoration had to be cut, the
alterations to *tempi* provoked the gibe 'nothing succeeds like six-eight',

and after the words had been given a necessary clean up, they were sprinkled with unnecessary lavender water and then minced.[92]

In contrast to the English Folk Dance and Song Society's view that folksong 'had died out', 'Country Magazine' proclaimed that songs had been 'discovered in almost every county in the land'. Its musical arranger, Francis Collinson, recorded pub singers at the 'Eel's Foot' in Suffolk, hurdle makers in Dorset and Harry Cox in his woodshed. But it wasn't simply that the Society's assertions about the death of folksong had been proved wrong, 'Country Magazine' challenged the whole approach to folk music which the Revival had established. Despite amalgamation with the Folk-Song Society, very little informed discussion of folksong was presented to English Folk Dance and Song Society members. Performance fared no better – Sharp's dictates on impersonal, undecorated singing with constant *tempi* and unvarying dynamics still held good for the generality of individuals. Pre-war Society 'Folk Music Festivals' were competitive events with a large choral element, while Cecil Sharp House concerts offered an aimless mix of madrigals, classical music, arranged folksongs from around the world and accompanied works from Sharp's published collection. Conversely, 'Country Magazine's' position was grounded in an intellectual and social appreciation of folksong, which was neither academically pretentious nor quaintly sentimental. The programme also adopted a far broader definition of the genre than was admitted by the Revival:

Forty years ago Cecil Sharp said that if the songs were not collected at once it would be too late. Even for England this was an underestimate of the vitality of folk songs. In Scotland a great part of the art of folk singing and the craft of ballad making live on in certain stout hearts. Hear Willie Kemp sing the old timeless ballads, the great Hamish Henderson singing his own creations, which include such notable favourites of the North African forces as 'Farewell ye banks o' Sicily' and 'Mak' your mind up, Farouk'. Hear also Hector Maciver rousing the English pubs to anger with his beautiful renderings of the proper Hebridean songs. He does not use the Kennedy Fraser transcriptions. In Ireland too, folk singing and ballad making are not yet dead, although powerful preservation societies are bent on their destruction.

Of course, the proper style of singing the folk song has gone beyond hope of revival, in accordance with the law of decay to which all ancient usages are subject. Only a few men in Britain still have it, and if the ordinary listener heard them sing he or she would not be impressed although it might give the more intelligent pause to know that almost any of the leading composers in Britain would gladly sit on the floor of Harry Cox's woodshed for as long as he cared to sing to them.

Quite apart from the merit of the songs themselves, this old style has a carefully placed decoration, a beautifully judged phrasing, an exact control of highly complex rhythm and a singing tone which requires no accompaniment. There is also a high nasal style which called for modifications in the tune (following invariable laws) and was not as pleasing, although very popular still with the older men.[93]

'Country Magazine' took a progressive view of folksong and its performance, but as its discussion of the 'decay' of style shows, it also maintained some elements of the devolutionary premisses of standard Folkloristic theorising. And, despite exploratory efforts, the programme did not succeed in fostering its own sympathy with older singing styles and song content in its listeners – transcriptions sung by trained singers were what was usually broadcast:

Now and again we have used recordings of the genuine folk songs in Country Magazine to no applause whatever. As a rule we use a 'straight' version, but we do give the proper tunes in the proper *tempo* and as far as B.B.C. policy permits, since we are not broadcasting in the Third Programme, the proper words. The singing we entrust to the finest vocalists we can find who can be relied upon to get the words over clearly without loss of vocal quality.[94]

The ideology and practices of 'Country Magazine' were shaped by the requirements of building consensus during the war. Its talks and interviews with 'your country cousins at every financial and social level' and from all parts of the British Isles reproduced the image and values of representing a unified nation. But the programme's format, with its guest list of mole catchers and university lecturers, basket makers and circus performers, as well as innumerable farm workers, and its stance on social issues – combining careful attention to inclusion of the role of women with positive discussion of nationalisation and Trades Unions – had much broader implications. Pre-war technological developments which permitted greater flexibility of radio presentation carried forward social realism's concern for actuality into a period where aspects of its ideological stance coincided with the national interest and official policy on the media in general:

There is no doubt that films came increasingly to use realistic settings and to spotlight ordinary people as the war went on... Realism in setting and character was a deliberate policy prescribed for the industry by the Ministry of Information, encouraged by the influential critics and opinion-formers of the high-brow press, the documentary movement and the native film culture and willingly introduced by patriotic film-makers... [95]

Thus whilst perpetuating the dream landscape of Englishness, the exigencies of creating wartime propaganda gave England's inhabitants voices and faces with a meaningful present. This conjunction was, moreover, incorporated in broadcasts of 'Country Magazine' after the war and in its televised version. In common with other propagandistic interventions in popular culture, such as the films *This England* and *Tawny Pipit*, 'Country Magazine' linked the rural myth with depictions of democratic action. In their explicit concern for giving 'their rightful share of publicity' to the life of the working class, these more obvious reproductions of national images also shared the intentions of works like *The Common Touch* and the film version of Walter Greenwood's novel on unemployment in Salford, *Love on the Dole*. Here, 'the misery and waste of the 1930s' were depicted in 'patriotic films, [in which] there is an undercurrent of radicalism, a determination that the end of the war should also mean the beginning of a new and better society'.[96]

The value of working-class culture and a heroic role for the lower classes was incorporated into post-war constructions of Englishness:

What of the people who inhabit this legacy of England? Their different occupations and surroundings set their mark on them. The Cockney is alert, quick in his movements, volatile, and always witty. The farm worker is slow-moving, stolid, and possessed of a sardonic humour. Sailors and road transport drivers show the same wrinkles round the eyes, due to staring ahead into the night for long periods. Railway workers are very like farm workers in speed of movement and habit of mind. The trains go fast enough; their job is to see that accidents are few and far between. Speech, of course, varies from county to county. From the 'Wot cheer, mate?' of the Cockney to the 'How bist?' of Dorset; from the soft U of Devon to the harsher dialect of Northumberland; and from the sweet 'Love' and 'Honey' of Lancashire to the rasping 'Bor' of East Anglia.

But with all these differences of habit and speech English people from
north to south and east to west have one thing in common – they will
not permit anyone to throw his weight about unduly, no matter what
his wealth or how high his position. Thus when Hitler began his Fascist
salute, the London taxi-drivers hailed each other with it in derision.
Years before the war, when the news reels showed Mussolini strutting
across the cinema screen, audiences in town and country greeted him
with derisive laughter. They subject their own leaders to the same
salutary discipline, the colonel, the sergeant-major and the mother-in-
law are traditional figures of fun on their music-hall stage. They elect a
town council, and thereafter refer to them in conversation as the 'town
scoundrels'.[97]

A. G. Street's introduction to *England Today* makes careful initial
reference to 'he and she' and prefaces a collection of photographs
with captions which link the English 'pageantry' of the Yeomen of
the Guard with that of 'folk traditions' like the Bacup Coconut
dancers and the Hocktide celebrations at Hungerford; the education section shows state and public schools and technical education, and has a special feature on vocational training for women.
Popular culture – from fairs, greyhound racing and ballroom
dancing to athletics, Christmas mumming plays and the annual
procession of the Vintners' Company – appears as an equally
valuable part of the 'glorious inheritance ... that has been handed
down to the English of today'.
    Folk and popular culture, urban and rural life, had been accom-
modated in a reproduction of national identity which marginalised
the Revival's central theories and faced it with apparently unavoid-
able paradoxes. Reports of the death of folksong had been found
to be an exaggeration, though the discovery owed nothing to the
diligence of Revival fieldworkers and much to professional uses of
technology and mass media – phenomena which were, reputedly,
antithetical to tradition and all it stood for. In the arts, forms of
dance and drama were being developed which drew on Revival
collectors' work but deliberately eschewed the methods of performance advocated by the Revival and were at pains to distance
themselves from it. Even within its own institutional ranks, the
price for hegemonic control had been the development of a group-
ing which required greater adherence to fundamentalist principles
on the part of others, whilst abrogating the distinction between
Revival and traditional performance for itself. The Revival's long-

established certainties were being disproved or discarded as no longer meaningful. As the Second World War drew to a close, it seemed the Folk had outlived the organisations intended to promote their culture's continued existence.

Notes

1 Douglas Kennedy, 'A Jubilee Symposium: 2. Folk Dance Revival,' *Folk Music Journal*, II:2 (1971), 88.

2 R. C. Davison, 'Making London Dance,' *EFDS News*, II:18 (Oct. 1928), 111.

3 See *The English Folk Dance Society Report September 1st, 1930, to August 31st, 1931* (London: English Folk Dance Society, 1931), p. 9 and *The English Folk Dance and Song Society Report September 1st, 1938, to 31st August, 1939* (London: English Folk Dance and Song Society, 1939), p. 6.

4 *The English Folk Dance and Song Society Report September 1st, 1936, to August 31st, 1937* (London: English Folk Dance and Song Society, 1937), p. 21.

5 *The English Folk Dance and Song Society Report September 1st, 1933, to August 31st, 1934* (London: English Folk Dance and Song Society, 1934), p. 6. This conclusion and the rejection of an association between reviving folksong performance and community singing should, however, be read in the context of T. P. Ratcliff's 'Foreword' to the *News Chronicle Song Book* (London: News Chronicle Publications, ND [1937?]), p. 3 – 'With this Song Book the 'News Chronicle' hopes to encourage and bring back singing in our homes. Then Community Singing will take care of itself.' The 'Foreword' also makes clear that Novello and Curwen, the major publishers of folksong, were actively involved in 'suggesting' material for inclusion (with the large body of 'National Song') in community song books. For a brief history and indication of the role of the BBC and mass circulation newspapers in fostering the movement, see the entry for 'Community Singing' in Percy A. Scholes and John Owen Ward, ed., *The Concise Oxford Dictionary of Music* (2nd edn, London: Oxford University Press, 1964), pp. 122–3.

6 *The English Folk Dance and Song Society Report September 1st, 1931, to August 31st, 1932,* (London: English Folk Dance and Song Society, 1932), p. 3.

7 *English Folk Dance and Song Society Report 1933 to 1934*, p. 6.

8 Rolf Gardiner, *The English Folk Dance Tradition: An Essay* (Hellerau: Neue Schule Hellerau, 1923), pp. 28–9.

9 See C.H.O.S. [Christopher Scaif], 'A Test of Folk song,' *EFDS*

News, I:4 (Nov. 1922), 95–8; A. B. Heffer, 'The Tour of the Travelling Morrice,' *ibid.*, I:9 (May 1925), 247–60 and Kennedy, 'A Jubilee Symposium: 2. Folk Dance Revival,' p. 88.

10 Sharp seems to have recognised this, and as early as 1911 had felt it necessary to 'warn' his followers before taking them to see morris dancing in Bampton for the first time 'that the dances we should see would be very different from those he had taught us because he had noted them from an older and better generation of dancers'. Maud Karpeles, 'Letter – Traditional Form,' *English Dance and Song*, XVII:4 (Feb.-March 1953), 124.

11 Gardiner, *The English Folk Dance Tradition*, pp. 29–31.

12 Rolf Gardiner, 'The Travelling Morrice and the Cambridge Morris Men,' p. 10, offprint (from *Springhead News Sheet*, winter solstice 1961?), held in Vaughan Williams Memorial Library, English Folk Dance and Song Society, Cecil Sharp House, P7145 AS 14. I am most grateful to Malcolm Taylor, the Librarian at VWML for bringing this article to my attention and for his unfailing courtesy and informed assistance in dealing with many requests.

13 Rolf Gardiner, 'A Brief Account of the Travelling Morrice,' *North Sea and Baltic*, New Series no. 4 (high summer 1938), 76. Gardiner notes that the account was written in 1928.

14 Heffer, 'The Tour of the Travelling Morrice,' p. 248.

15 Gardiner, 'The Travelling Morrice and the Cambridge Morris Men,' p. 10.

16 *Ibid.*, pp. 10–11. For a German assessment of Gardiner's artistic work at this time see 'Rolf Gardiner,' in Hinrich Jantzen, *Namen und Werke*, vol. 1 (Frankfurt a.M.: DIPA, 1972), pp. 77–81. I am most grateful for the help of Dr Jurgen Dittmar and Barbara James of the Deutsches Volksliedarchiv in Freiburg for their assistance in obtaining the latter reference and additional information on Gardiner and the *Wandervogel*.

17 Gardiner, 'A Brief Account of the Travelling Morrice,' p. 75.

18 Rolf Gardiner, *World Without End: British Politics and the Younger Generation* (London: Cobden-Sanderson, 1932), p. 33.

19 For discussion of the background to these organisations, see G. C. Webber's admirably clear *The Ideology of the British Right 1918–1939* (Beckenham: Croom Helm Ltd, 1986), pp. 60–2 and 150 and George Thayer, *The British Political Fringe: A Profile* (London: Anthony Blond Ltd, 1965), pp. 104–13 (the latter is particularly good on the influence of the "Muck and Mysticism' school of political thought' on post-war Fascism and neo-Nazism); for further information on Gardiner's ideology, see the section devoted to him in R. Griffiths,

Fellow Travellers of the Right: British Enthusiasts for Nazi Germany 1933–39 (London: Constable & Co. Ltd, 1980), pp. 142–6, Malcolm Chase's succinctly illuminating 'This is no Claptrap: This is our Heritage,' in Christopher Shaw and Malcolm Chase, ed., *The Imagined Past: History and Nostalgia* (Manchester: Manchester University Press, 1989), pp. 128–46 and Gardiner's own works cited here. It should, however, be noted that the works Gardiner published in Germany contain elements not manifested in his English-language books, notably (and despite his mother's Jewish ancestry), anti-Semitism and other forms of racism – as for example comments on Jews as 'restless Ahasueruses' who 'brought the smell of Asia with them in their beards', see his 'Die deutsche Revolution von England gesehen,' in *Nationalismus von Ausland gesehen* published in Berlin in 1933, pp. 15–18

20 Griffiths, *Fellow Travellers of the Right*, pp. 317–8 summarising and quoting William Sanderson, *Statecraft* (London: Methuen, 1927), pp. 9–58. The latter work clearly demonstrates the extent of Gardiner's ideological debt to Sanderson, who was also co-publisher of Gardiner's *World Without End*.

21 The ideas underlying the purchase and restoration of Springhead are set out in detail in Rolf Gardiner, *England Herself: Ventures in Rural Restoration* (London: Faber and Faber Ltd, 1943), particularly pp. 57–77 and 125–46, from which all quotations on these subjects are taken.

22 See Gardiner, *England Herself*, pp. 57–71. Further details of Gardiner's proposals to introduce neo-feudalism and permanent Land Service Camps 'outside the economic machine' are contained in his 'Estates as Pivots of Regional Development: Memorandum of evidence submitted to Lord Justice Scott's Committee on Land Utilization in Rural Areas,' reprinted as Appendix 3 in the same work, pp. 153–64 and his chilling 'The Triple Function of Work Camps and Work Service in Europe,' *North Sea and Baltic*, (harvest 1937), new series no. 2, Springhead reprinted in Andrew Best, ed., *Water Springing from the Ground: An Anthology of the Writings of Rolf Gardiner* (Springhead, Dorset: Trustees of the Estate of the late H. Rolf Gardiner, 1972), pp. 109–25.

23 Gardiner, *World Without End*, p. 38, from which all quotations on *Bund* are taken. Gardiner, *England Herself*, pp. 18, 29, 30, 45 also contains examples of song texts written by and for the national leadership-in-waiting which, in the light of Gardiner's views on the need for aesthetic leadership, may instructively be compared with 'folksong' texts created by the rural working class.

24 Rolf Gardiner, *England Herself*, pp. 61–2. Christopher Scaif,

Gardiner's 'chief colleague' in the Springhead Ring, was also associated with Gardiner, Douglas Kennedy, Adrian Bell, Edmund Blunden, Arthur Bryant and others in 'Kinship in Husbandry' (for details see Earl of Portsmouth [Gerald Wallop], *A Knot of Roots: An Autobiography* (London: Geoffrey Bles, 1965), p. 86, Best, *Water Springing from the Ground*, pp. 198–9 and Webber, *The Ideology of the British Right*, pp. 155). As a close friend of Tyrone Guthrie and brother of two of its leading members, Scaif was also linked with the Group Theatre of London – see particularly Robert Medley, *Drawn from the Life: A Memoir* (London: Faber and Faber Ltd, 1983), pp. 89 and 192–3.

25 Walter Abson, 'Fifty Years of the Morris Ring,' *English Dance and Song*, XLVI:2 (1984), 11 and p. 12, quoting Vaughan Williams's address to the Morris Ring in February 1936.

26 Martin J. Weiner, *English Culture and the Decline of the Industrial Spirit 1850–1980* (Cambridge: Cambridge University Press, 1981), p. 166.

27 Rolf Gardiner, 'Mixed Morris Sides,' *English Dance and Song*, I:2 (Nov. 1936), 27 and *World Without End*, pp. 33–40 [passim].

28 Douglas Kennedy, 'A Jubilee Symposium: 2. Folk Dance Revival,' *Folk Music Journal*, II:2 (1971), pp. 85–6. For Kennedy's formative role in the Morris Ring, see Arthur L. Peck, 'The Foundation of the Morris Ring,' *English Dance and Song*, X:5 (1946), 62.

29 See Webber, *The Ideology of the British Right*, pp. 20–3 and 158; and Francis Toye, *For What We Have Received: An Autobiography* (London: William Heinemann Ltd, 1950), pp. 196–8. Toye was music critic of the *Morning Post*.

30 Webber, *The Ideology of the British Right*, p. 142 and 158.

31 See Griffiths, *Fellow Travellers of the Right*, p. 143 and Cunningham, *British Writers of the Thirties*, pp. 161–5. *Youth*, the periodical Gardiner edited, was among the first to note that 'German youth movements have lit the beacon-lights of a new civilisation and culture' and to print photographs of naked German youths plunging into swimming pools.

32 See Harry T. Moore, ed., *The Collected Letters of D. H. Lawrence* (2 vols; London: William Heinemann Ltd, 1962), II, p. 928. Eventually, however, Lawrence decided that 'the young man who does Morris dances and all that' was 'very nice, but not much in my line'. *Ibid.*, p. 1038.

33 Cecil J. Sharp and Herbert C. Macilwaine, *The Morris Book I* (2nd edn, London: Novello and Co. Ltd, 1912), pp. 11–13. For the influence of Frazerian theories in Lawrence's writing, see Phillip L. Marcus, "A healed whole man': Frazer, Lawrence and Blood Conscious-

ness,' in Robert Fraser, ed., *Sir James Frazer and the Literary Imagin-ation: Essays in Affinity and Influence* (Basingstoke: Macmillan Press Ltd., 1990,) pp. 232–52.

34 'In *The Plumed Serpent* we are given an allegory of the renewal of a sterile, stagnant people. We are shown how they are quickened out of their coma by life-giving action, symbols and words. How a few men and women dare to make themselves vehicles of the arcane powers.... *Ramon* and *Cipriano* form the nucleus of a new organic society in Mexico. Is their experiment valid for British conditions? The answer is, Yes, with a difference. We must go warily.' Gardiner, *World Without End*, p. 36.

35 Gardiner, *The English Folk Dance Tradition*, p. 12.

36 See Klaus Theweleit, *Male Fantasies* (Cambridge: Polity Press, 1987), particularly pp. ix-xii and 3–63. Gardiner frequently visited the eastern areas of Germany at the time when the *Freikorps* were most active there.

37 Gardiner, *England Herself*, p. 44.

38 Gardiner, *World Without End*, pp. 39–40.

39 Gardiner, 'The Travelling Morrice and the Cambridge Morris Men,' p. 10.

40 See Hynes, *The Auden Generation*, pp. 95 and 128 and Sidnell, *Dances of Death*, p. 83.

41 Teachers were generally employed by the branch, though they could also make extra income by taking individual and additional non-Society classes. The Society's view of the genteel nature of the work ('artistic' and not vulgarly well paid) was succinctly described in Anon., 'Wanted – More Teachers,' *English Dance and Song*, III:1 (Sept.-Oct. 1938), 9. Training for teaching was, however, only available at Cecil Sharp House in London. As advertisements in *The Dancing Times* throughout this period also confirm, the overwhelming majority of teachers of other forms of dance were women.

42 Florence Golding, 'What Shall We Wear?' *EFDS Journal*, I:1 (May 1914), 14–15.

43 Cecil J. Sharp, 'Some Notes on the Morris Dance,' *ibid.*, I:1 (May 1914), 7–8.

44 See letters from Cecil Sharp to Alice Gomme on 10 Feb. 1910 and 20 Feb. 1910, held in the Vaughan Williams Memorial Library, Cecil Sharp House. Roy Judge, 'Mary Neal and the Espérance Morris,' *Folk Music Journal*, V:5 (1989), 545–91 gives details of the appearance of Sharp's men's rapper side at Oxford on 16 Feb. 1911 and his morris side on 27 Feb. 1912.

45 E. Phillips Barker, 'Two Notes on the Processional and the Morris

Dance,' *EFDS Journal*, I:2 (Apr. 1915), 38–44.

46 Cecil J. Sharp and Herbert C. MacIlwaine, *The Morris Book: I* (2nd edn; London: Novello and Co. Ltd, 1912), p. 42.

47 Elsie Jeanette Oxenham, *The Abbey Girls in Town* (London & Glasgow: Collins, ND [1920s], pp. 74–5.

48 For an extended discussion of this phenomenon, see Billie Melman, *Women and the Popular Imagination in the Twenties: Flappers and Nymphs* (London: Macmillan Press Ltd, 1988).

49 Gardiner, 'The Travelling Morrice and the Cambridge Morris Men,' p. 10.

50 See for example the description of the 'fun' at a Folk Dance Society social at Loughborough College in G. Stevenson, 'Initiation of a Novice,' *English Dance and Song*, II:3 (Jan.-Feb. 1938), 42–3.

51 Gardiner, 'Mixed Morris Sides,' p. 27.

52 See 'A Folk Masque,' *EFDS News*, I:10 (1925), 333.

53 Susan Brownmiller, *Femininity* (London: Paladin Books Ltd, 1986), p. 62.

54 Mrs Kennedy, 'Early Days,' p. 175.

55 Miss G. A. Hall, 'The Sword Dance,' *EFDS News*, II:21 (Sept. 1929), 217.

56 Gardiner, 'Mixed Morris Sides,' p. 37.

57 Elsie J. Oxenham, *The Abbey Girls Again* (London & Glasgow: Collins, ND [1920s]), p. 168.

58 *English Dance and Song*, I:1 (Sept. 1936), 9. Thirty-eight entries were received and the competition, judged by Lady Ampthill, Sir Augustus Daniel and Mr Douglas Kennedy, was won by Miss Margaret Clarke of London 'for her series of designs for a dress of thin material, to be worn with or without a covering coat, and with or without a cape'. The design was not illustrated and was, to protests about constant change from branches, replaced by a dirndl, blouse and 'coatee' the following year, see *English Folk Dance and Song Society Report 1938 to 1939*, pp. 25–6.

59 Violet Alford, 'National Costume,' *English Dance and Song*, I:3 (1937), 59.

60 Anon. [Nela Bower], 'On Dress,' *ibid.*, II:5 (May 1938), 75.

61 Prunella Stack, 'As Others See Us: 1. The Women's League of Health and Beauty,' *ibid.*, III:1 (Sept.-Oct. 1938), 9. For further details of the Women's League of Health and Beauty, see Jill Julius Matthews' excellent 'They had Such a Lot of Fun: The Women's League of Health and Beauty Between the Wars,' *History Workshop*, XXX (autumn 1990), 22–54.

62 Francis Fryer, 'Mixed Morris Sides,' *English Dance and Song*, I:3

(1937), 59. Fryer's proposal was not without precedent. Young women in knee britches took part in turn-of-the-century north western morris performances and also appeared as 'counterfeit men' in Espérance-inspired displays of 'mixed' morris – see the engaging 1911 photograph of 'The Spirella Folk Dancers', young women from the Spirella Corset Factory in Letchworth, half of whom danced in smocks and knickerbockers. I am most grateful to Pat Pickles of Wakefield for drawing my attention to this item in her personal collection of postcards and photographs.

63 The freedom associated with wearing short skirts for dancing is a constant theme of Elsie J. Oxenham's factually-based novels about the early Revival, see for example *The Abbey Girls Again*, p. 71 and the whole chapter devoted to 'Mary-Dorothy's Gym Tunic', pp. 169–79. For attitudes to bifurcation, see Brownmiller, *Feminity*, pp. 57–8.

64 Evelyn Sharp, *Here We Go Round: The Story of the Dance* (London: Gerald Howe Ltd, 1928), pp. 67–8.

65 See particularly Alice Bertha Gomme, 'Memoir on the Study of Children's Games' read at the Folk-Lore Society on 16 March 1898 and reprinted in *The Traditional Games of England, Scotland, and Ireland* (2 vols; New York: Dover Publications Inc., 1964), pp. 458–531.

66 Cecil J. Sharp, *The Country Dance Book: Part 1*, ed. Maud Karpeles (2nd edn; London: Novello & Co. Ltd, 1934), p. 7.

67 Paul Wilkinson, 'English Youth Movements, 1908–30,' *Journal of Contemporary History*, IV:2 (1969), 19–23.

68. See letter from Mary Neal to Clive Carey, 9 August 1924 reprinted in Judge, 'Mary Neal and the Espérance Morris,' 575 and Mary Neal, 'The Broken Law,' *The Adelphi*, XVI (Jan. 1940), 149–50.

69 Gardiner, 'The Travelling Morrice and Cambridge Morris Men,' p. 9.

70 Oxenham, *The Abbey Girls Again*, p. 141. For a recent consideration of the role of dancing in all–women groups see Angela McRobbie, *Feminism and Youth Culture: From Jackie to Just Seventeen* (Basingstoke: Macmillan Education Ltd, 1991), pp. 55–8.

71 'Report of the Annual Staff Conference 1937' session on 'Folk Dancing in Training Colleges', pp. 30–2. Typescript held in Vaughan Williams Memorial Library, Cecil Sharp House.

72 Peter Kennedy, 'Random Memories of an English Dancing Master,' *English Dance and Song*, XLVII:1 (spring 1985), 15.

73 *Report of the English Folk Dance and Song Society 1933 to 1934*, p. 6.

74 Margaret Dean-Smith, 'Dr Maud Karpeles, O.B.E.: 12 November 1885–1 October 1976,' *Folklore*, LXXXVIII:1 (1977), 111.

75 Carole Henderson Carpenter, 'Forty Years Later: Maud Karpeles in Newfoundland,' in *Folklore Studies in Honour of Herbert Halpert: A Festschrift*, ed. Kenneth S. Goldstein and Neil V. Rosenberg (St John's, Newfoundland: Memorial University of Newfoundland, 1980), p. 120.

76 This transition is generally presented as a natural progression – 'Sharp remained the Director until his death in 1924, when he was succeeded by Mr. Douglas Kennedy' (Iolo Williams, *English Folk-Song and Dance* (London: Longmans, Green & Co. Ltd, 1935), p. 188) – or as the result of Sharp's choice: 'Cecil Sharp had asked him [Kennedy], shortly before his death, to give up his University post as a biologist, and to lead the Society' (Fr Kenneth N. J. Loveless, 'Douglas Neil Kennedy, O.B.E.: An Obituary,' *English Dance and Song*, L:1 (Apr.-May 1988), 2). Elsewhere, however, a more complex picture emerges – 'A Board of Artistic Control was appointed consisting of Dr. Vaughan Williams, Douglas Kennedy, and Maud Karpeles, and the following year the direction of the Society was put into Douglas Kennedy's hands' (A. H. Fox Strangways, *Cecil Sharp* (Oxford: Oxford University Press, 1933), p. 197); whilst Douglas Kennedy himself recorded the existence of an interim administration arising from a lack of confidence within the English Folk Dance Society's National Executive Committee following the loss of 'Sharp's personal hand on the wheel' – 'We had relied on [Sharp] for so long, and for so many guidelines, that all felt the need to import an experienced administrator, at least temporarily. Our choice fell on Sharp's friend Paul Oppé.... So we offered to co-opt him as our Chairman. To our relief, he readily accepted .... ' (transcript of Douglas Kennedy's taped comments in Peter Kennedy, 'Do They Still Need Us?' *English Dance and Song*, LI:2 (July-Aug. 1989), 10). Oppé, Sharp's collaborator in his last work, did not remain in office.

77 For additional detail see Maud Karpeles, 'The International Folk Music Council: Twenty-One Years,' *Yearbook of the International Folk Music Council*, I (1969), 14–32 and Klaus Wachsmann, 'In Memoriam: Maud Karpeles (1885–1976),' *ibid.*, VIII (1976), 9.

78 Bertrand H. Bronson, 'Maud Karpeles (1886–1976),' *Journal of American Folklore*, (Apr.-June 1977), 460.

79 Elsie J. Oxenham, *The Abbey Girls Go Back to School* (London & Glasgow: Wm Collins Sons & Co. Ltd, 1949), p. 174 (originally published in 1922).

80 Roy Palmer, 'Your Dancing is Simply Glorious...,' *English Dance and Song*, LI:1 (Apr.-May 1989), 3.

81 Carpenter, 'Forty Years Later: Maud Karpeles in Newfoundland,' p. 116.

82 See Douglas Kennedy, 'Obituary: Dr Maud Pauline Karpeles, O.B.E. 1885–1976,' *Folk Music Journal*, III:3 (1977), 292–3 and Loveless, 'Douglas Neil Kennedy,' p. 2.

83 Walter Abson, 'Dancer,' in 'A Tribute to Douglas Neil Kennedy, O.B.E., 1893–1988,' *Folk Music Journal*, V:4 (1988), 522.

84 *English Folk Dancing for Schools: A Book of Advice for Teachers with Instruction and Tunes for 14 Dances* (London: The English Folk Dance and Song Society, 1956), pp. 5 and 6.

85 Anon., 'Practical Propaganda,' *English Dance and Song,* II:3 (Jan.-Feb. 1938), 44.

86 All information taken from *English Folk Dance and Song Society Report 1938 to 1939.*

87 Loveless, 'Douglas Neil Kennedy,' p. 3.

88 See Weiner, *English Culture and the Decline of the Industrial Spirit*, pp. 76–7 and Jeffrey Richards, 'National Identity in British Wartime Films,' in Philip M. Taylor, ed., *Britain and the Cinema in the Second World War* (Basingstoke: Macmillan Press Ltd, 1988), pp. 42–61.

89 Sue Harper, 'The Representation of Women in British Feature Films, 1939–45,' in Taylor, *Britain and the Cinema in the Second World War*, p. 168.

90 Donald McCullough, 'Foreword,' in Francis Dillon, ed., *Country Magazine: Book of the BBC Programme* (London: Odhams Press Ltd, ND [1949]), p. 7.

91 A. G. Street, 'Introduction,' *ibid.*, p. 10.

92 Dillon, *ibid.*, p. 137.

93 *Ibid.*, pp. 137–9.

94 *Ibid.*, p. 139.

95 Jeffrey Richards, 'Wartime British Cinema audiences and the Class System: the case of 'Ships With Wings' (1941),' *Historical Journal of Film, Radio and Television*, VII:2 (1987), 139.

96 Robert Murphy, 'The British Film Industry: Audiences and Producers,' in Taylor, *Britain and the Cinema in the Second World War*, p. 37. For discussion of *This England* and *Tawny Pipit* see Richards, 'National Identity in Wartime Films,' *ibid.*, pp. 44–8.

97 A. G. Street, 'Introduction,' *England Today in Pictures* (London: Odhams Press Ltd, 1947), pp. 5–16.

Chapter 8

Anthems from Eden

The lyric and glee songs of England put together like icons by shepherds and farm workers all seem to tell part of the same story: meetings, partings, young men taken away to fight wars they didn't understand.... But today's England has a special generation: from grammar schools and housing estates, from techs and universities are coming enough young men and women with a clear historical and prophetic vision of themselves, enough now to continue the story: no propagandist is going to fool them, or government coerce them. They know that they will inherit the best of their tradition ...[1]

'When this war ends', wrote Douglas Kennedy in 1944, 'the E.F.D.S. will have the chance to stage its second revival.'[2] Reflecting the plans for wide-ranging institutional change put forward by the various Reconstruction Committees set up by the Coalition Government as victory became more certain, the proposals for 'post-war organisation and policy ... thrashed out by the Executive Committee' of the English Folk Dance and Song Society called for renewal and identifiable progress. 'Starting all over again', Kennedy suggested, could be an advantage – 'if past mistakes can be rectified and improved methods adopted and applied.' A range of policy changes was therefore proposed. The Society's work of training dancers and callers would obviously continue, but far more attention would be paid to developing musicians' skills: 'Before this war good folk dance musicians were few and far between.... The second revival of folk dancing can only be successful if a high level of vital and infectious dance music is set and maintained.' In future the Society aimed to foster 'a rich diversity of local styles and variants' of dance. 'Ritual ceremonial dance', including 'Lancashire Morris', would be encouraged and 'ideally the Society should aim at reviving each Morris tradition in the locality where it belongs'. The Morris Ring had been 'wound up on the outbreak of war'. But Kennedy, who had been elected Squire in 1939 and was also the Director of the English Folk Dance and Song Society, remained in office, foreseeing that the Ring would 'get rolling as its members are demobilised'. His leading position in both organisations gave him unique power to synthesise Morris Ring and Society policies:

What of the women? Are they to dance the Morris in the second revival, and the Sword dance? Nobody can now stop them. They have created a feminine interpretation which can and has at times been developed into a performance of great beauty. But performances in public should be regulated so that nothing is shown to weaken the status of the dance as a man's dance....
But it is over the Country Dance that we shall have to watch our step in this second revival.... I personally feel very strongly the Country Dance as a party dance only gets a square deal when the company that takes the floor is equally mixed men and women. For some dances this condition is less important than it is for others, and less harm is done if the company that takes the floor is not evenly balanced. But the desirable condition for all dances is, of course, a man to every woman.... I suppose people feel differently about women dancing together in couples. I mind that much more than I do a team of women in a Morris or Sword dance which, if danced with artistry, I am always prepared to accept. Probably that's quite personal to me.

Overall, though, the greatest change proposed was in the Society's policy on song:

The Folk Songs in comparison with dances have not received enough attention. The conditions that are right for singing are not necessarily those that are right for a dance-party, even a party of an informal nature. Folk Music Festivals are admirable for encouraging the trained choirs and singers, but I would also like to see song gatherings which had a touch of the smoking concert or even of the old-time Music Hall, where the singing can be spontaneous and uninhibited. Anyhow, in the second revival the folk songs must be given a square deal.

But the future of the Folk Revival could no longer be wholly determined by the idiosyncrasies of the Director of the English Folk Dance and Song Society – or even members of its National Executive, branches and related organisations. Radio had given a countrywide audience an experience of folksongs and their performers which owed little to the organisation founded by Cecil Sharp. The 'vitality' of 'country songs' and interviews revealing their significance in the lives of people who sang them offered a prosaically convincing alternative to the arch stereotypes of the earlier Revival. And the Revival itself was ceasing to consist solely of events and performances mediated by the English Folk Dance and Song Society and the Morris Ring. Despite continuing assertions of hegemonic status as 'the only authoritative bodies in England devoted to folk music', responsible for the fact that English 'folk thrives around the country' and 'has spread throughout the world', control of the reproduction of Folk culture had passed beyond the institutions of Sharp's form of the movement.[3]

The war had provided acceptability and a national platform for songs of anti-Fascist resistance – and initially left-wing groups such as the Workers' Music Association, Clarion Ramblers and various Co-Operative Society choirs were the only performers whose repertoires contained suitable material.

After 1939 [the Workers' Music Association] was swept forward with the tide of war and its consequent cultural awakening. Large scale concerts, directly concerned with the war effort and with aid to China and the Soviet Union, were organised at the Albert Hall every year. At one such gathering the performers included Michael Redgrave, the London Philharmonic Orchestra and a choir of voices drawn from (among others!) Birmingham Clarion Singers, Croydon Operatic Society, Goldsmith's Choral Union, Kodak Factory Choir, the Royal Choral Society and the W.M.A. singers. The programme was, as usual, entrusted to the W.M.A.

National songs in a range of languages, 'folk-songs, madrigals, freedom songs, variety numbers and some classical pieces', as well as newly composed political songs were the standard fare at concerts and broadcasts devised by such organisations. The construction of folksong as a purely aesthetic category, isolated from current events and needs, had become less clear-cut. Additionally, towards the end of the war, in fulfilment of its object of presenting 'to the people their rich musical inheritance', the Workers' Music Association brought out the Keynote Series, low-priced paperbacks dealing with music, culture and history. The fourth of these was *The Singing Englishman* by A. L. Lloyd, an attempt to clear away contemporary 'misunderstanding' of English folksongs by relating them 'to the times and circumstances they were made up in'. Lloyd offered a history which dealt with 'the common people' rather than the Folk, and a view of folksong – 'the peak of cultural achievement of the English lower classes' as 'something that came out of social upheaval'. What was more, *The Singing Englishman* presented a discussion of the development of folksong which made no reference to Sharp's definition.[6] A cultural history devoid of 'the tired clichés of the Sharp school' seemed to be in prospect.

Beyond the confines of such interest groups, however, was an infinitely larger public, with experiences shaped by six years of war. Evacuation, conscripted land work and military bases in rural areas brought substantial numbers of the town-bred population into contact with agricultural communities. As a result, country life and work became rather less easily idealised. At the same time, the spirit of city dwellers enduring nightly bombing raids, coupled with recognition of the importance of factory production for the war effort, reduced the ground for attacks on town life and industrialisation. Propaganda aimed at fostering consensus had stressed a nation historically at one in its concern to promote democracy and equality. But the pragmatic image-building of war-time public relations was not the only source of contemporary perceptions of egalitarian unity. The population which emerged from 'the Peoples' War' was the first to have entered it with a full adult franchise, to have been subject to such a broad span of military and civil mobilisation and to have faced equal dangers on the battlefield and on the home front. The peace was therefore consciously 'the People's' too – and the consequences of this were wide ranging. Attitudes which supported the introduction of more equitable health and education systems and the nationalisation of basic industries also confirmed the value of folk culture as a democratic aspect of national culture. Reflecting the changed status of the people, Folklore research emphasising the role of named individuals, historical record and uncensored material came to the fore; new organisations to study the Folk were inaugurated; folksong, in its field or non-classical performance became sought after and fashionable; folk dance, particularly the North American Square dance, became the rage. A demotic culture, more broadly defined and contemporary than Leavis's artisanate, pre-industrial middle England, less rosily arcadian than Morris's world of hand-crafts and milkmaids, excited scholars and public alike with its emerging possibilities.

The events and processes which shaped the 'second revival' are, therefore, far less an unforeseen and dramatic intervention in culture than the Folk Revival's own myths suggest. To date the start of the post-war movement from 1951 and attribute its cause to the arrival from America of the musicologist Alan Lomax is to ignore *The Singing Englishman* and all the developments arising in theatre, music and radio from the 1930s – to say nothing of the English Folk Dance and Song Society's 1944 policy statement. That the Revival underwent some realignment after the war is indisputable, but positing a 'Folk Song Revival' as a distinct entity, unrelated to earlier ideology and practice in the movement to replace the Folk, is not borne out by contemporary sources or later events. Indeed in many respects, the post-war Revival has been a prisoner of its pre-war past, constantly regurgitating relict ideologies of the 1920s and 1930s. And in the long term, although its institutions ceased to hold a monopoly on performance, the cultural thesis Sharp created to necessitate a Revival proved monumentally durable – outlasting most attempts at innovation by ensuring they were either sidelined as not relevant or macerated until they conformed with established positions.

Immediately after the Second World War, however, the possibilities for change and development appeared to be more open than at any time since the Revival was first conceived. The English Folk Dance and Song Society embarked on a programme of organisational reform, and was reportedly committed to an approach which promised that 'there will not be one official dogma, but an infinity of variegated vital forms which will be right for those who are sincerely expressing them'.[7] Enthusiasts for folksong from left-wing choirs were finding opportunities to perform in smaller groups or as soloists. Some were also writing new songs. Their models owed nothing to the secular religiosity of earlier hymns of labour, with their images of sturdy workers reaping just rewards while the larks sang above, but derived from the narrative, direct and unashamedly popular American political tradition.[8] Meanwhile, not content with merely putting forward an alternative history of folksong, Lloyd also had innovative proposals for new sources of collection. Taunting both folklorists 'who have made of folklore a quaint parsonage affair, or something to be wrapped up in a lot of dark anthropological hoo-ha' and

'Comrade Cleverdick' for suggesting 'you can't have folk in a capitalist society', he outlined an entirely untouched area for fieldwork:

Nobody, to my knowledge, has been around the mines and the mills and among the fettlers and the professional footballers, collecting the stories and sayings which must certainly abound in such jobs ... a folklore anthology should be a great funny tragic heroic lusty tender brutal and essentially everyday affair. So much an everyday affair, indeed, that it strikes one, if some people would put their anthropological books away for a moment, and take a walk round Woolworth's, say, they might learn a bit more about folkways than they'd bargained for. Comrade Cleverdick might tag along.[9]

Working within more conventional definitions, in 1946, the English Folk Dance and Song Society sponsored its first commercial recordings of 'authentic folk music performed by traditional ... instrumentalists', featuring William Kimber and George Tremain playing 'ceremonial dance tunes'.[10] Access to other forms of 'authentic' performance was also widened. Reflecting the internationalism fostered by wartime alliance-building and post-war co-operation, a range of institutions to promote research and performance across national boundaries were inaugurated. From 1947, events in neighbouring countries such as the International Eisteddfodau held at Llangollen and the Edinburgh Festival brought polished and increasingly spectacular examples of non-native Folk genres to public notice in England through attendance, newsreels and broadcasts.

Public enthusiasm was not limited to new organisations – the English Folk Dance and Song Society also benefited. 'Evidence of the increased interest in folk dancing and singing is reflected in the number and variety of persons who either write or call at Cecil Sharp House to find out 'what it is all about'' reported the Society's magazine of March 1947, noting with satisfaction that membership had risen by almost twenty per cent since 1946.[11] But this growth in popularity was to prove double-edged – the Society was rescued from its pre-war decline, but only at the cost of a comprehensive loss of hegemonic control:

Throughout its history the E.F.D.S. has enjoyed a quasi monopoly, the field of folk music being thought too arid to attract competitors. That peaceful scene has given place to another. Folk music is now popular.

An old song may become a smash hit overnight. Square dancing might easily become as much of a racket here as it threatens to do in the United States. The commercial dance world, which has already been browsing thoughtfully on the fringes of the field, is now making deep raids.[12]

More importantly, content and style of all aspects of 'folk' performance were no longer assessed by the standards of the Society's 'Headquarters demonstration team' and fulfilment of its agreed syllabus. Professionalism, and the demands of a mass audience reaching far beyond the pre-war avant garde, challenged its long-established aesthetic and limited repertoire. From the late 1940s, the Society's reproductions of folk culture jostled with state ensembles of trained and choreographed performers offering determinedly entertaining propaganda for governments in the Communist bloc. Meanwhile, capitalism, in the form of products of the American recording industry, provided more obvious commercial competition. Unrelated at all but the most basic level of nomenclature, a multiplicity of dominant and sub-cultural constructions contested definition as folksong, folk music and folk dance.

Challenges to English Folk Dance and Song Society control were not just limited to performance genres – a second front was also opened up in scholarship and the principles of Revival. Tradition and how to revive it were at the heart of A. L. Lloyd's earliest considerations of folksong. He concluded *The Singing Englishman* by looking forward to a time when there was 'no longer any special distinction between the composer and the rest of his fellowmen' – only then, he proposed, could a 'great body of fine folksong that is bound close to our social life and the times we live in and the way we go about our work' be created. But until such conditions were achieved, Lloyd insisted, the separation of traditional music from 'social life' meant that a Folk Revival was impossible. And all that those who tried to 'make a living thing' of folksong produced was 'a recital of the popular songs of the past'.[13] More conventional arguments from longstanding oppositional voices within the movement were also given fresh impetus. Following her attendance at the formation of the United Nations Educational, Scientific and Cultural Organization (UNESCO) in November 1946, Maud Karpeles convened a conference in London in September 1947 which led to the founding of the International Folk Music Council.[14] The Council's aims emphasised the role of folk music in the promotion of 'understanding and friendship' between nations and encouraged wide-ranging scholarship, fieldwork and performance. Not entirely coincidentally, however, the organisation also provided Karpeles, its Honorary Secretary, with an autonomous base to question developments in the postwar English Folk Dance and Song Society. Karpeles's stance was grounded in maintaining 'artistic merit' and performances 'worthy of the great inheritance which has been delivered into our keeping'. Her disaffected eye ranged over contemporary morris dancing ('it can best be described as foot-flapping') and country dancing ('what one chiefly misses is the sense of gaiety') to song (mistakenly presented as 'raw and uncouth'). The Society Sharp had founded, Karpeles indicated with undisguised contempt, was abandoning his legacy of ideas and practices in favour of innovation for its own sake and a populist approach based on misrepresentation and lowered standards.[15]

The first major controversy of the post-war Revival, however, was a specialist manifestation of a far greater national debate. American films and popular music had enjoyed widespread success in England before and during the war, but with the coming of peace the range and type of expressive culture made available from America extended in a way that threatened to overwhelm native products. With Tennessee Williams's *Streetcar Named Desire* and Arthur Miller's *Death of a Salesman* drawing full houses for a new, bleaker drama and variety performers like Danny Kaye taking the Palladium by storm, 'by 1949, it began to seem that in theatrical terms at least Britain was now on the way to becoming the 49th State'.[16] No longer offering recontextualisations of European forms and concerns, new generically American types of music and dance also proved to have striking appeal:

In April, 1948 ... the all-American *Oklahoma!* exploded across the vast stage of Drury Lane, and in the words of the sober critic, Harold Hobson, shook 'London up more than anything that has hit it since the first flying bomb'. Thirty-eight days later, *Annie get Your Gun* opened at the Coliseum. For two years, through the dismal succession of 'cuts' and crises, these two robust American musicals with their zestful dancing, youthful high spirits, and bright primary colours cast their spell over the London scene. Between the Convertibility Crisis and the Devaluation Crisis, *Oklahoma!* cheered up 2,200,000 British citizens – and continued to pack them in. Whistled by bus conductors, booming from radios, reverberating in bathrooms, 'Oh, what a beautiful morning!', 'Doin' what comes nat'r'lly', 'The Surrey with the fringe on top' echoed on down the Forties and into the Fifties.[17]

Dynamic, innovative, slick and irreverent, American presentations contrasted sharply with the inconsequential drawing-room comedies, sweetly-pretty musicals and remnants of music hall filling the generality of English stages. At a time of increased rationing and dragging, bitter winters, the tension between the colour and vivacity of these imports and resentment of yet more 'overpaid, oversexed' Yanks 'over here' was not easily accommodated:

An endless procession of American stars of 'stage, screen and radio', marched into the spotlight, hugged the microphone, and made their little speech about how fine it felt to be back again with the 'wunnerful English people' who could 'take it' in the Blitz. Most of them received a rapturous welcome. Yet if the offerings were greedily consumed, they nevertheless left a curious, indefinably unpleasant, after-taste....
As military, financial, cultural bonds grew tighter, and 'Anglo-American' became an ever more valid adjective, the old love-hate relationship grew more tortuous, intense and ever-present; the old strand in the pattern of our history flared out in new and angrier colours. Resentment about the money the American performers were taking out of the country was loudly voiced. British reporters, interviewing visiting American sportsmen, would inquire caustically about the poundage of steaks brought over in their baggage. In a jaundiced book entitled *What the English think of Us*, Fred Vanderschmidt, London correspondent of *Newsweek*, estimated and opinion polls bore him out – that one in every three Englishmen were 'more or less antagonistic to anything that came from America from Buicks to businessmen'.[18]

In this climate, Douglas and Helen Kennedy resumed proselytising for a type of dance they had first introduced to England in 1938. 'During its forty years' campaign on the side of the set dances,' proclaimed an unashamedly revisionist Douglas, 'the English Folk Dance Society only became effective during the last ten, when it shifted its ground and concentrated upon simple dance forms and public opinion was once again leaning in the direction of set dancing.' 'American Square Dances', he concluded provocatively, 'are the modern living embodiment of the folk tradition.'[19] Square dances, with a caller to remind participants of the moves and all the advantages of association with Western films and hit musicals, held far more attraction for the dancing public than the complex 'little ballets' of the Playford Collection, which had been the standard fare at the Society's 'social dances'. From 1948, a series of broadcasts of 'Country Dance Parties' featured 'The Square Dance Band', with Douglas Kennedy as caller and drummer. The programmes brought the dances to a national audience, and played a significant part in the development of the 'Square Dance Boom' of 1951–2, when Cecil Sharp House was 'inundated' with 'demands for 'callers', for 'square dance bands', for the right music and tutors to coach callers' and lengthy queues waited for the doors to open at EFDSS dances in Birmingham. At the same time, transatlantic influence was also extending into folksong, as radio programmes for troops stationed in Europe brought more special-ist American music to English listeners. Recordings of blues and other forms of 'race' music, 'hillbilly', political and 'folk' material had become increasingly available in America during the 1930s. And from the early 1940s, the possibilities for their commercial exploitation throughout the United States were greatly expanded.[20] Compared to folksongs for schools – or even folksongs as sung by Peter Pears post-war broadcasts and records featuring Burl Ives or groups like the Weavers came as a revelation. Their repertoires of catchy tunes, with lyrics directly related to everyday experience, had a broad, non-elitist appeal that was social as well as vocal. The status of 'specialist performers' which pigeonholed the Folk, classical musicians and self-defined experts from the English Folk Dance and Song Society, did not seem to apply to the smiling, unclassifiable singers of 'On Top of Old Smokey' and their encour-aging invitations to 'sing along'. In the short term, this combina-tion of developments led to Square dancing becoming a country-wide craze. More lastingly, the guitar began its progress towards domination of the accompaniment of popular song and English audiences for a plethora of new types of American-derived music increased in size and enthusiasm.

Like the issue of American influence itself, responses to this new wave of interest in 'folk' were not easily reconciled. An inrush of attention and potential recruits revitalised and enlarged the scope of the Revival. But at the same time, their presence highlighted the limitations of its current organisation. A monthly 'Folk Song Club' for 'Members and their friends who would like to hear and sing

Folk Songs' was inaugurated at Cecil Sharp House in 1949 and a similar small club was also set up by the English Folk Dance and Song Society in Birmingham. But singers like Harry Boardman, whose enthusiasm for folksong had developed through listening to Northern Region radio programmes, American forces broadcasts and contact with the Workers' Music Association, found themselves involved in all the formalities of becoming 'certified folk singers' when they attempted to work with the 'official' institutions of the Revival in Manchester.[21] Still more incongruously, at Cecil Sharp House, A. L. Lloyd's capabilities were recognised with a first prize (of eight shillings) in the Solo Singer section of a 1948 Folk Music Festival Competition. Every type of club member from ex-Marines to jive fans, reported an Essex Youth Club Leader, had become 'converted' after hearing a record of Bing Crosby 'calling a Square'. Subsequent weekly dances at the Ewell Youth Centre were 'a great romp, they take turns in calling, they invent their own dances ..., then they find that other English Community Dances give them even greater chances of expression and we are well on our way to adding the whole of the Community Dance Book to our repertoire'. The Leader doubted whether the Club could take matters any further by themselves and felt it was time to start introducing the 'keener people' to the local Society branch.[22] What reception their 'sheer joy in movement' then met with was not recorded – but official pronouncements were far from encouraging. Classes, competitions and making thoroughly sure people were 'doing it properly' were the English Folk Dance and Song Society's predictable means of dealing with their new found popularity. In particular, Douglas Kennedy warned, undue enthusiasm was to be avoided at all costs: 'It is only too easy to mishandle this square dancing, to emasculate it and to put people off for a generation. There is also a real danger that the shy and silly dancers will romp them and the clever ones will elaborate them. Their appeal depends on simplicity and restraint in performance.'[23] Presenting a 'programme of simple traditional country dances and squares [which] hardly varied from week to week' and ensuring that he was there at festivals to 'use the break' and impose a curfew when 'so many dancers got wound up and would have gone on all night',[24] Kennedy finally proved himself a true inheritor of Sharp's Directorial mantle.

A Revival based on privileging 'set dances', whether American

Squares or English country dances, proved less easy to justify to longstanding members of the English Folk Dance and Song Society than to the public at large. Sharp had concentrated on teaching dances from the Playford Collection 'because he regarded these as of higher artistic quality than the living traditional dances', a speaker at 1947 Annual General Meeting of the Society complained, adding that 'the present policy of the Executive Committee, designed to increase the popularity of English folk song and dance is not in keeping with the teaching of Cecil Sharp, nor is it likely to attract to the Society permanently enthusiastic Members and Associates'.[25] The Executive maintained its stance, but opinion within the Society was split. At least one member resigned because 'he could not stomach the Morpeth Rant' and Kennedy later maintained that the Society 'lost its opportunity' to obtain full benefit from the Square dance boom because it was 'divided as to whether English folk dance should include American variants'.[26]

But questions of American influence, aesthetics and maintaining consonance with Sharp's approach were less significant in the long term than the transformation of Kennedy's personal difficulties with gender into an Executive policy on social dance. As the Society began to promote festivals and summer schools again, clear guidelines were given on the suitability of applicants for tickets: 'Acceptance of entries will be determined by the need to keep the numbers of men and women equal ... preference will be given to entries made as mixed couples.'[27] Kennedy unashamedly confirmed that his intransigence on mixed couples drove 'a rather large army of unpartnered girls' away from Square dances at Cecil Sharp House. But, determined to maintain the 'natural virility attracting the young men of today', he justified this as a means of protecting the genre from 'emasculation' and encouraging more 'chaps' to attend. Others, though, saw the policy from an entirely different viewpoint:

Mr Korner then moved:- (b) 'The rule "Mixed couples only on the floor" should not be enforced at Members' social evenings.'
In support of the resolution, Mr. Korner said that the rule which had been imposed at the Members' Square Dances on the second Saturday of the month operated unfairly against women Members, as it prevented them from enjoying the same benefits as male Members, although they paid the same subscription. Mr. Ingerson, in seconding the resolution, said that the rule had not been enforced for all dances at the first

Members' Square Dance which he had attended, but exception was taken to the publication of the rule on the Square Dance leaflet.[28]

The motion was carried, but the prospect of recognising that the same membership fees as men should provide women with the same membership rights as men proved too revolutionary for the Society's hierarchy to cope with. It was 'an essential condition' of the holding of additional Members' Dances that the Master of Ceremonies should have 'the authority to insist on 'Mixed couples only the floor'', reported an unsigned notice in the next issue of *English Dance and Song*. And since the motion had shown that individuals were not 'prepared to accept the inequity of mixed couples' as a price for 'the enjoyment of the corporate body', the additional dances were to be abandoned forthwith.[29] Although women dancing together had long been an unremarked aspect of behaviour in dance halls and ballrooms throughout the country, its existence in English Folk Dance and Song Society performances was uniquely and increasingly controversial. In 1944, Douglas Kennedy proposed that mixed couples were a 'desirable condition', but that it was less important for some social dances than for others. By 1946, however, he had reached the conclusion that their occurrence should be a matter for dissembling and shamed concealment:

we must face the fact that at this present stage the bulk of our most active Members are women. It is inevitable that any event arranged for our Members is likely to be overborne by women. This can only right itself in time if more men are recruited. Once a man is bitten with the folk dance virus he is not daunted by being in a minority. While we cannot deprive the majority of their right to enjoy the dances we can enlist their aid to help with recruiting of men. How? By concealing their present disproportion behind the curtain of the 'private' type of event while we continue to encourage the growth of men's Morris and Sword and mixed teams of Country dancers so that the Society can more frequently appear in public and do more recruiting.[30]

The 1952 decision on Members' Square dances cancelled even this limited acknowledgement of the rights of the majority – the desirable condition of mixed couples had become 'essential'. Recruitment, 'the main object of the E.F.D.S.', was defined as 'the active enrolment of a Member or an Associate', and by this, Kennedy wrote, 'I mean rendering down an ordinary chap into a dancer'.

The Society's message was clear: the only worthwhile members were men, and men were a prime requisite for 'perfect' performances: 'When the Society is 'on show' the conditions must be as near perfect as local circumstances permit. The Morris and Sword dances are to be shown by men and the social dances by mixed couples. If these conditions are not possible, then the Society must refrain from publicly performing...' The ultimate statement on social dance and the Revival in this period, however, seemed to remove the need for consideration of women as partners altogether – though, like the masturbatory imagery of Rolf Gardiner, it opened the question of precisely which usage of the term 'male member' was intended: 'The so-called 'social' dance has rediscovered the springs of rhythm centred in the body. The physical pole has been elevated and freed to pulsate with great liberality. So free indeed is each dancer that expression is no longer directed at a partner, except in casual conversation.'[31]

In the area of dance revival, the English Folk Dance and Song Society's much vaunted 'starting all over again' soon involved a re-assertion of its most reactionary views and policies. It quickly became clear that the promised post-war 'rectification' of 'past mistakes' did not encompass any permanent change of approach to the majority of the Society's members. Events followed a wearily familiar pattern – hardening of attitudes to women in social dance was accompanied by a revisiting of the great costume crisis. Festival dress, which Kennedy had decreed should be abandoned in 1946, began a process of reinstatement, at his instigation, in 1949.[32] 'Women's dresses have been severely criticised both at Stratford and at the Albert Hall, and cutting comparisons have been made between them and the men's Morris Dress', he reported. Yet again a 'neat waist and full skirt', lace, mittens, 'collarettes' and Englishness were invoked to encourage women to 'participate in the approval and admiration always accorded our Morris Men but so far never given to us'. Even so, the Society's eventual choice of dress for women, circular felt skirts and black waistcoats, seems extraordinarily perverse. When the skirts flared out during the dance – as heavy circular skirts will – the resultant extensive additional display of lady members' persons led to the rapid introduction of 'the festival tube', a straight, white underskirt which limited potential embarrassment – and movement. But such practicalities aside, in a Society constituted to safeguard

English tradition the costume's design – owing more to 'Old Heidelberg' than 'Olde England' – also provoked even 'loyal and most ardent' members to point out:

The dances we do are traditional, handed down to us. The men of our Society when performing at functions, festivals or for their own pleasure wear the traditional costume, as our forefathers wore it. Why then do the ladies of our Society wear those felt skirts (which invariably hang badly) and black waistcoats? This is no more traditional costume than if they wore a bikini and looks a cross between an Austrian-Swiss-Bavarian costume – and with the addition of a few sequins would do for an Ivor Novello musical!... Will someone, please, before it is too late and we look like a Ruritanian chorus, design a traditional frock for ladies so that they are in keeping with our Morris men. Our grandmothers never wore a felt skirt and bolero....[33]

Circular skirts had been chosen because they were today's fashion, responded the editor of the members' journal and 'the Society has always felt that folk dancing belongs to to-day'. On the contemporaneity of male dancers' knee breeches, however, the editor was unaccountably silent. Overall, as far as its women members were concerned, the tradition the Society seems most willingly to have upheld during much of the twentieth century was misogyny.

But if only superficial change could be seen in the performance of folk dance, folksong was undergoing a transformation. The source of these changes is generally presented as the political Left – 'As far as Europe is concerned,' Lloyd proposed in an article for *Marxism Today*, 'Britain is probably unique in the degree in which it depends on folk-melody for its present-day political songs.' As a whole, he suggested more modestly, 'the present revival in folk music shows some left-wing political colouring'.[34] Subsequent writers have been less tentative. 'In fact', Harker concluded in his study of 'fakesong', changes in the movement were another manifestation of the Comintern's popular front strategy begun in the 1930s, 'the history of the Second Folksong Revival ... was closely involved with the cultural policy of the CPGB [Communist Party of Great Britain]'.[35] On the contrary, countered a longstanding participant, Communist direction of the Revival was 'a myth'. 'Far from being a dastardly plot orchestrated from somewhere behind the walls of the Kremlin ... the apparatchiki of the Communist Party of Great Britain had no understanding of what Ewan [Mac-Coll] and Bert [A. L. Lloyd] and other members were on about, and they would probably have tried to stop it if they had.'[36] Was the post-war Revival a 'CPGB strategy of winning some sort of hegemony' for its supporters? Even taking the Square dance boom into account, was the movement significant enough for its control to be of political concern? As founder members of the extreme right-wing group 'Kinship in Husbandry', Douglas Kennedy and Rolf Gardiner had certainly numbered the Revival among the 'many movements' it was important to 'percolate'. And arguably, Kennedy's post-war populism and reorganisation of the English Folk Dance and Song Society on a national basis, concentrating its management in his hands, was part of this strategy.[37] So why should the extreme Left not have taken a similar view and attempted to act on it? For both Left and Right, it was not so much political parties as specialist organisations with a pre-existing interest in folk culture which seem to have been motivated to become involved in the Revival. Under all the circumstances, the proposal that any single organisation was responsible for the initiation and development of the movement – or even its 'cultural policy' – is simplistic in the extreme.

A complex of events and attitudes was producing an entirely fresh approach to the way that songs were sung – taking them beyond the classroom and concert hall into a developing new field of activity. Chronologically, the availability and increasing acceptance of 'authentic' performance was among the earliest influences for change in singing style. Collecting begun for wartime broadcasting had revealed that 'Folk' of the classic definition – Louie Hooper, who had sung for Cecil Sharp, Harry Cox, the Copper family, whose songs appeared in Volume One of the Folk-Song Society's *Journal* – were not merely alive but, like numbers of less well known 'tradition bearers', still singing and playing.[38] Social realism, with its emphasis on actuality, was now thoroughly institutionalised within the mass media. And this, in combination with the obvious popularity of programmes like 'Country Magazine' and its spin-off, 'The Postman Brings Me Songs', encouraged the BBC to develop its approach to folksong, using field recordings rather than re-voiced material in its programmes. In television, this led to series such as 'Ballad Hunter' in 1953, which featured Alan Lomax with Bob Cann, Margaret Barry, Charlie Wills, Harry Cox, Bob Roberts and Jeannie Robertson.[39] But its most ambitious expression was the 'scheme for the collection, in recorded form, of folk music, local speech and custom in the British Isles and Ireland', launched by BBC radio in 1952. Introducing the project, Marie Slocombe, Head of the BBC Recorded Programme Library and a member of the International Folk Music Council, laid particular emphasis on the implications of the 'improved technical means' provided by the BBC: 'sound recording adds a new dimension; the actual style and personality of the performer can be preserved, as well as some of the subtleties of tune and rhythm which defy notation, and the living tradition can be studied and experienced by a wider public in a much more direct and vivid way.'[40] No longer carefully limited to the select few surrounding 'the Director', 'folksongs' as performed by 'the Folk' at last became accessible to a mass audience.

'Authentic' performance and a widening range of American music were also preoccupying jazz enthusiasts at this time. Compared to the heavily orchestrated 'romantic ballads' and cutesy novelty songs which dominated the English 'Top Twelve', the sparse arrangements and 'realistic' lyrics of American vernacular music had much to recommend them. And in many respects, for a 'thinking' audience, jazz represented an ideal contemporary synthesis, embracing fashionable American culture whilst avoiding the taint of its commercial excesses. But the application of jazz fans' views on authenticity and vulgar popularity resulted in a strain of purism which eschewed 'contemporary sounds' – dismissed as 'rabble-rousing stuff which relies for its effect on single note-honking and frenetic riffs' – in favour of 'declining forms of Negro popular music'.[41] 'The differences between the English bands of 1956 and the Negro bands of 1900–1925 are great, yet many English musicians insist that their sole aim is to re-create this sound,' was the warning of a visiting American blues guitarist, concerned at 'the vehement insistence on the part of many English musicians upon authenticity, upon non-commerciality'. 'They are not playing as themselves but as antiquarians and archaeologists.'[42] So despite the creation of an audience 'educated' by record reviews, published interviews and the activities of musicians like Chris Barber, who featured Big Bill Broonzy, Sonny Terry and Brownie McGhee and Sister Rosetta Tharpe on his tours, growing experience did not lead to a broader approach. The American repertoire offered in performance at jazz concerts in England was selective and limited: 'specialist audiences rarely understood or

paid much attention to contemporary forms of black music and
often distorted the nature of the music they did like. Big Bill
Broonzy had played for years in Chicago with small groups –
piano, harmonica, bass and drums – but in England was encouraged to play acoustic guitar with no other accompaniment, which
he obligingly did.'[43]

English jazz bands reproducing late nineteenth- and early twentieth-century American music began to proliferate from just after
the war, but similar groupings of folk musicians were rather
slower to form. American models had themselves only recently
developed and were of specific type – in the United States in 1946,
Oscar Brand recalled, 'there were few groups singing folk songs
and ballads. Most of the singers were soloists, although the politically minded or religious singers often sang together for spiritual
stimulation.'[44] But for English performers who were interested in
the repertoire of pre-war American 'politically minded' bands such
as the Almanack Singers, the difficulties of obtaining amplification
equipment suited to an informal vocal style, or even the requisite
instruments, were the immediate bar to performance, as John
Hasted, an early enthusiast, found:

Bob Hinds, a merchant seaman, had brought the Almanacs 78 rpm
record 'Talking Union' for me to hear in 1946. I at once wanted to
make music like this. But it was years before I could even got [sic] hold
of a folk guitar, let alone find other people with similar aspirations.
Eventually I found folklorist Bert Lloyd, and asked him if he wanted to
start an Almanac group in England. To my astonishment his voice
dropped about an octave, and he said very quietly 'Passionately'.[45]

Hasted had to make his own twelve-string guitar out of an old
six-string and acquire 'folk guitar' technique 'from Pete Seeger's
cyclostyled documents, and from listening to records'. Ultimately,
however, he and Lloyd, together with Neste Revald and Jean
Butler, an American who 'had plenty of experience singing with
five-string banjo for American Unions and had often performed
with the Almanacs', formed an English counterpart, the Ramblers,
around 1952.[46]

The Ramblers lasted only a couple of years, but their influence
long outlived them. As performers, their instrumentation, style and
repertoire provided domestic prototypes for the new music of the
regenerating Revival.[47] Their introduction of the American prac-

tice of linking political songs and folksongs in concerts for Trades Unions was also of wider significance. Semi-classical, choral performances of 'artistic' librettos had been the accepted mode for political expression in song, but the emergence of directly relevant music of informal style mounted a successful challenge to orthodoxy. Massed voices suddenly seemed 'rather out of place in the post-war world', and although jazz bands provided much of the music for the marches organised by the Campaign for Nuclear Disarmament, it was folksong which became synonymous with 'protest'. Increasing musical contacts with Trades Unions generated new songs[48] and fostered the innovative research Lloyd had first suggested in 1946. In pioneering collections like Lloyd's *Come All Ye Bold Miners*, published in 1951, and Ewan MacColl's *The Shuttle and Cage* three years later, the musical traditions of groups outside those defined as 'Folk' became accessible for Revival performance:

There are no nightingales in these songs, no flowers – and the sun is rarely mentioned.... They should be sung to the accompaniment of pneumatic drills and swinging hammers, they should be bawled above the hum of turbines and the clatter of looms for they are songs of toil
...
Few of these songs have ever appeared in print before, for they were not made with an eye to quick sales – or to catch the song-plugger's ear, but to relieve the intolerable daily grind....
The folklore of the industrial worker is still a largely unexplored field and this collection represents no more than a mere scratching at the surface. A comprehensive survey of our industrial folk-song requires the full collaboration of the Trade Union movement. Such a survey would, undoubtedly, enrich our traditional music.[49]

A genre of 'anthems to an industrial age', collected from and reflecting the 'work, poverty, hunger and exploitation' of miners, railway workers and weavers was being formulated and reproduced.

Specifically 'folk' material became increasingly available particularly through performances on radio and television. But common interest in 'authentic' American music meant that audiences for folk and jazz were often identical, or brought together by appreciation of the 'country blues' repertoire of Huddie Leadbetter and Big Bill Broonzy and the work of itinerant songmakers such as Woody Guthrie. Broadcasts and concerts of 'Ballads and Blues', featuring Humphrey Lyttelton's jazz band and folksongs from British and American singers such as Jean Ritchie, Ma Rainey, Alan Lomax, Isla Cameron, Lloyd and MacColl enjoyed 'huge successes'.[50] Shared ideology also created links between performers of the two musics – Lyttelton joined Lloyd as a Vice-President of the Workers' Music Association and prominent jazz and folk musicians appeared on the same platform at political events.[51] Mirroring the bias prevailing in English jazz circles, the songs favoured among folk enthusiasts for transatlantic music were untypical of American singers' repertoires as a whole – 'the blues had covered a wide range of topics but particularly relationships with women, the British folk audience was interested primarily in the songs that expressed some kind of protest or criticism against the American social system'.[52] Interaction reinforced the values jazz and folk fans and performers shared, and the resultant idiom was idiosyncratic – privileging 'the authentic', selected oppositional themes and anachronistic musical styles. But the concepts of song and performance emerging from this context have been reproduced in the Folk Revival until the present day. The broader range of blues has been only grudgingly accommodated, its performers (mainly soloists) accepted principally on the grounds of their musicianship and 'authentic' approach to a traditional American genre. Moreover, early inconsistency has since been compounded by obfuscation, as what had essentially been operational choices based on personal enthusiasms and ideology were later recast as 'academic' definitions of folksong, 'Industrial Song' and a 'policy' for Folk Revival performance.

With far less instrumental intent, the jazz-folk idiom also provided the vehicle for the first large-scale recruitment of enthusiasts for folksong revival outside the English Folk Dance and Song Society. The catalyst which took 'the entire folk heritage of the United States' beyond the confines of a specialist audience was Skiffle. Although Skiffle was reportedly introduced by the Original London Blues Blowers in 1947, was played at performances by the Crane River Jazz Band from 1949 and regularly formed part of Ken Colyer Jazz Band sets in the early 1950s, it was only when the two Skiffle tracks from a 1954 album by Chris Barber's Band were issued as a 'novelty single' in 1956 that the genre took off.[53] 'Rock Island Line' by Barber's banjo player, Lonnie Donnegan, sold over a million copies and became the first British pop record to get into the American Top Ten. As a musical form, Skiffle, with its chunking guitar, tea-chest bass and rattling washboard accompaniments, enjoyed only a brief, highly commercialised boom in the mid-1950s. 'The kings of entertainment and publicity are seeking to make it nothing more than a fashionable craze', complained Hasted, an early devotee, 'the real music is being strangled in a welter of skiffle clothes, skiffle outfits (with specially designed washboards) and skiffle toilet rolls.'[54] Skiffle assumed far greater significance in the Folk Revival however – as contemporaries soon recognised: 'skiffle awakened the consciousness of young people in Britain to lead them on to the folk music revival. In that, it served its purpose. Now it is as dead as a dodo.'[55] An accessible, 'do-it-yourself' music, the legacy the Revival inherited from Skiffle was thousands of young enthusiasts 'left around with guitars', keen to continue playing and increasingly aware of the 'huge jazz and folk repertoire' available to them.[56]

The 'folk repertoire', and how to perform it, became an increasing pre-occupation of new recruits to folksong revival. Since the movement's inception, Sharp's own predisposition, and the background of the majority of English Folk Dance and Song Society members, had made applying the techniques of art song voice production to a disparate range of British and foreign 'folksongs' the agreed approach to singing. Unaccompanied song was felt to be 'too difficult' for most singers – and audiences – so a piano was a fixed accessory of performance. In 1952, however, following Lloyd's acceptance on to the Editorial Board of the Society's *Journal*, the English Folk Dance and Song Society sponsored two records of MacColl's unaccompanied singing. The results were reviewed by Lloyd, who assured readers that more and more singers 'have come to feel that the conventional platform performances from the printed arrangement does less than justice' to folksong. He proposed that the future of song in the Revival rested on striking a new balance between authenticity and art:

Conscious that the immediate future of English folk-song is in the hands, or rather the mouths, of the 'revivalists' rather than the 'survivalists,' a growing number of singers are listening carefully to recordings of live performances of genuine traditional singers, and trying to absorb and reproduce the characteristics of folk-song in its workaday clothes. They try to sing in a style which is acceptable as a 'performance' to ordinary audiences, and which, at the same time, stays as close as possible to the traditional manner.[57]

Lloyd's arguments had won over Douglas Kennedy, who felt that attempts to move away from 'conventional performance, as given on the concert platform, toward the unaccompanied informal rendering of the countryman' was finding 'an ever-growing public'. In an article in *English Dance and Song*, Kennedy described a concert by 'some of the Society's best known musicians – Nan and Brian Fleming-William, Jean Forsyth and Patrick Shuldham-Shaw', devised and played 'with a fine sense of balance and proportion', contrasting it with a relatively impromptu evening of 'raw folk songs' presented by Jean Richie, Seamus Ennis, Lloyd and MacColl. 'Nothing quite like it', he averred, 'has been heard before at Cecil Sharp House.' The Director avoided drawing the obvious conclusion himself, preferring instead to print as part of his column a letter from 'a young and thoughtful Member of the Society' whose opening salvo was more than adequate to the task – 'The *ceilidhe [sic]* at Cecil Sharp House on April 15th should have demonstrated to all those present the superiority of unaccompanied, unedited versions of folk songs over the edited accompanied versions which have been published or recorded.'[58] Such an attack on the principles of folksong performance as laid down by Cecil Sharp could not be allowed to pass unchallenged. Maud Karpeles, eternally prepared to champion 'the old ways', used a broadcast celebrating the founder's birthday a few months later to draw attention to the fundamental artistry of traditional singers, who only sang 'to give expression to the music that lies within'. 'I mention this,' she expanded pointedly, 'because now-a-days folk song is so often thought of as something raw and uncouth ...' Ms Karpeles then 'kindly offered' the script of her talk for publication in *English Dance and Song*.[59]

Despite considerable suspicion on one side, and monumental lack of interest on the other, attempts to integrate differing approaches to folksong were set in train. Many of the efforts to do this were associated with contributors to the folk music magazine, *Sing* – notably its editor, Eric Winter, A. L. Lloyd and Fred Dallas. *Sing*, the first publication embodying the ideology of the new wave of song revival, was founded by members of the London Youth Choir and affiliated to the Workers' Music Association. Aiming to 'play an important role in the struggles of the British people for

peace and socialism', *Sing*'s first editorial in 1954 offered a clear
statement of 'the task which this magazine sets itself': 'The songs
which are produced in the course of man's struggle for a better
life have not always been written down. This may not have done
any harm to the songs but it has certainly restricted their value
and importance. Today there is a need for the distribution of such
songs, of immediate and topical interest, as widely as possible,
particularly among young people.'[60] While it acknowledged other
musical influences, the editorial highlighted oppositional song's
'roots' in 'the traditions of English, Welsh, Scottish and Irish folk
songs, together with those of other countries'. *Sing*'s intention was
'to print examples of these traditions, so that performers can
ground themselves in their heritage'. However, almost all of the
songs published in the early run of the magazine were newly
composed, or merely set to traditional tunes. Then in the summer
of 1955, a request for comments from readers suggested slightly
different priorities. A correspondent from Bradford praised 'the
invaluable aid of your material to struggling provincial groups',
but proposed that in future, to give a firm lead to those 'active in
producing' such songs, 'traditional material should be given pride
of place'.[61]

A new accommodation was, in fact, already being reached. Winter
and Dallas had joined Lloyd as members of the English Folk Dance
and Song Society and were involved in moves to consolidate not
just the music but the institutional resources of the Revival. Writing
in *English Dance and Song*, Dallas praised the contributions of
Douglas and Peter Kennedy in putting 'the fifth word of our Society's
name back into its proper prominence'. Studies by 'folklorists' such
as Lloyd, Hasted and MacColl, programmes like 'As I Roved Out'
and the Society's wonderful library of field recordings could, he
proposed, all be used to turn 'lots of young people going around
with guitars and banjos', 'singing on the streets, in the pubs, in the
coffee bars, and in the newly created 'skiffle clubs'' into 'a really
hefty revival', 'something that strikes strong roots, and has a lasting
effect on our national tradition'.[62] In October 1957, an 'English
Folk Music Festival' was organised at Cecil Sharp House. Intended
'to enable singers and players to compare methods of interpretation
and standards of performance', it brought together representatives
of the English Folk Dance and Song Society, Revival performers
of all types, and 'genuine traditional singers'. The resultant collision

of cultures made plain the divisions within the major groups as well as differences between them. 'Not everybody at the English Folk Music Festival agreed about style and interpretation', was *Sing*'s understated conclusion – the magazine itself offering 'three personal comments from SINGers who attended'. Dallas pointed to a split in the new Revival's ranks – 'The festival brought out into the open the cleavage of opinion between those, like us, who believe that non-traditional singers like us should nevertheless perform in the nearest approximation to a traditional style they can manage, and the others who talk glibly of 'impersonating traditional singers''. 'Imitation' of well known Revival, rather than 'traditional', singers drew Lloyd's fire. 'Certain singers show great skill and assiduity in impersonating' he reported, claiming to have heard stylistic hybrids as unlikely as 'a lady MacColl and a male Isla Cameron' – 'If they transferred half that doggedness towards creating a personal performance, we should all gain.' The three 'SINGers' were, however, unanimous in their condemnation of aspects of the English Folk Dance and Song Society's approach. In keeping with the Society's past practice, the Festival was part concert, part competition, and it was with the competitive element that the greatest controversy arose. There was no unanimity among the four adjudicators selected by the Society, Dallas felt – Peter Kennedy judged entries 'on one set of standards, based on his study of traditional singers', while the other three worked 'in a completely opposite direction'. Entirely unversed in 'traditional singing styles', the majority of judges did not conceal their 'impatience with venerable traditional singers'. 'It looked at one time as if Dr Northcote was going to rap on his glass as if to say he would take the other five or so verses as read', Winter observed, appealing for 'a non-competitive festival next year'. Adjudicators' comments on diction, voice production, stance and the tone of 'the various rude things said by Dr Sydney Northcote to some of Britain's finest traditional singers, venerable old gentlemen who should have been treated with more respect', meant that angry scenes followed several competition performances. In summing up, Lloyd pointed to the many lessons to be learned by the Society and performers, not least that 'when listening to folk song performers, genuine or revival, adjudicators have to be looking for a different set of artistic virtues from those immediately recognised by the singing teacher'. Disputes continued – Douglas Kennedy maintained that 'the 'modern' folk singer who uses the conversational method is, unless extremely skilful, in danger of singing to himself and failing to capture his hearers and communicate his message'. At subsequent festivals, though, judging what Kennedy termed 'traditional ancients' according to the 'standards of the concert platform' was abandoned. And, moving into areas pioneered by the new wave of Revivalists, later festivals were opened to 'any kind of performance', including 'original items in the English traditional manner'. But new positions were taken on both sides. Winter ended his critique of the 1957 event by concluding that the appropriate place to discuss how an urban singer should 'sing a traditional song without impersonating' was 'the meetings and councils of the Society'.[63] Although enlarged by new voices and concepts, Revivalists' role as experts in legitimation was reaffirmed.

Changes emerging from the first English Folk Music Festival in 1957 were a late development compared to the effects of the first Edinburgh Festival on the Folk Revival in Scotland. The absence of any aspect of 'traditional Scottish culture' in the programme of the 1947 Festival led enthusiasts for folksong to organise 'informal ceilidhs' in private houses.[64] Success promoted repetition. National consciousness, fostered by the work of creative writers and institutions such as the School of Scottish Studies, concerts, a series of Edinburgh Labour Festivals and the sheer attraction of the music itself, subsequently drew increasing audiences 'hungrily absorbing this 'new' musical experience'. Scotland had, enthusiasts pointed out, a 'fantastic tradition of popular culture', represented by singers of 'the great Scottish ballads', including John Strachan and Jeannie Robertson, whose style was 'obviously authentic' and 'age-old'. There was also the later, more informal genre of songs reflecting the experience of farm workers, initially brought to Revival notice in the performances of Jimmy MacBeath. But the range of material performed in the Revival was not limited to bothy ballads or 'the muckle sangs'. Particularly after the Skiffle boom – led, Scots were quick to report, by Lonnie Donnegan of Glasgow – American music enjoyed wide success. Indeed for many English audiences, appearances by Scottish 'cowboys' like Alex Campbell gave the first chance of hearing classic Appalachian, Union or Woody Guthrie songs in live performance. As in England, political subjects generated topical songs, but the related issues of nationalism and the Scottish language provided broader fields of contact with audiences – and the roles of collector and song writer of folksong were equally enhanced by the status of Hamish Henderson at the School of Scottish Studies. Street songs and children's rhymes too added a racy, vernacular irreverence to the Scottish repertoire that English Revivalists' selection of 'authentic' and political songs could not, at first, match. Unimpeded by the deadening prescriptions and staid image of Sharp's Revival and despite the worst excesses of 'The White Heather Club', the Scottish Revival projected a drive and continuity with living tradition that seemed to have eluded its English counterpart.

Unsurprisingly then, as the English Revival grew in popularity, Scottish singers and songs were arguably more prominent than English. Regular appearances on television by Alex and Rory McEwan, Robin Hall and Jimmie Macgregor brought Scottish Revival song to a vast non-specialist public. As, until then, the most frequently televised English 'folksinger' had been Elton Hayes a light tenor whose 'rollicking songs' with 'riddle-de-day' choruses featured on children's programmes, the contrast – and resulting appeal – were marked. For singers keen to emulate television or Revival favourites, a Scottish repertoire was also more easily acquired. Most compilations – *Come All Ye Bold Miners*, *The Shuttle and Cage*, *The Singing Island* – contained Scottish material, while *Scotland Sings* and *101 Scottish Songs* were not just more varied and closer to contemporary taste than the larger English collections of Sharp and Baring-Gould but cheaper and widely available.[65] 'Irish Songs of Resistance' had been one of the Workers' Music Association's earliest recordings and performers such as Dominic Behan, Margaret Barry and Michael Gorman and the McPeake Family recorded for English labels and appeared regularly in London. Most English singers included Irish songs in their repertoire, but their range was rather more limited: 'rebel songs' and 'rousing choruses' were its main constituents.[66] Overall, the status of the Scottish 'big ballads', and the formative influence of 'English Scots' like MacColl in London and Ian Campbell in Birmingham, gave their music an advantage. As a result, in the later 1950s and early 1960s, if an English Revivalist announced the performance of a 'traditional' song, it would frequently have been collected in Scotland.

Despite the growing role of Scottish song, however, the major formative influence on repertoire during this period was still

American. Songs by 'Woody' and 'Leadbelly', particularly in performances by Pete Seeger, were enormously popular and widely
copied. But the Revival's espousal of American culture was more
than usually problematic. The American music reproduced by the
English Revival – a folk tradition demonstrating the creative abilities of black and white working people, a history of oppositional
songs supporting Trades Unions and Civil Rights – represented all
that the section of the movement proselytising for songs of struggle
could aspire to. But outside this supportive mutuality, America
represented a new imperialism – 'send the Yanks back home again'
wrote MacColl in 1955, in a song hymning international friendship and berating the American atomic bomb.[67] More seriously, as
the influence of the Cold War and Joseph McCarthy, its witchfin-
der general, grew ever more pervasive, the United States became a
source of government sponsored repression and blackmail. The
first issue of *Sing* already carried a warning:

Not many of us will be familiar with SING's big brother 'Sing Out' a
song magazine which has given the progressive movement in the United
States such stalwart service. And although very few copies arrive here,
the numbers from Sing Out are frequently performed in Britain. But
victimisation of professional singers is very serious in [the] U.S.A. The
top-line recording group 'The Weavers' has been refused all engage-
ments and can no longer hold together. Their leader, Pete Seeger ...
contributes songs to the current Sing Out.[68]

Unsubstantiated allegations of twenty-year-old sympathies with
any radical cause were sufficient to have individuals defined as
'subversive'. To the compilers of 'blacklists' competing to sell their
wares, ever-increasing numbers of 'secret Reds' and the inclusion
of famous names gave an edge over 'less comprehensive' publications from rival organisations – and attracted necessary publicity.
Unfortunately for the American Folk Revival, the Weavers had just
put a series of records into the charts and formed part of a
movement which, throughout the 1930s and 1940s, had provided
music for picket lines and at benefits for left-wing causes. They
offered easy and numerous targets. Over the next twelve years,
'blacklists' ruled what might or might not be publicly presented in
America – songs and singers were banned, concerts and record
contracts cancelled and performers were required to affirm their
patriotism by giving evidence about their own and their friends'

political affiliations. 'We, as artists, must protest an act that seeks to compel the performer to bargain for his livelihood with other values than his talent' wrote a defiant Theodore Bikel, on behalf of the Arts Chapter of the American Jewish Congress.[69] But the policy continued – and its effects were not restricted to America. The State Department confiscated Paul Robeson's passport, making it impossible for him to travel outside the country. In 1957, eight years after his last English appearance, the only way the Workers' Music Association could hear its Vice-President in concert in London was by amplifying a performance given over transatlantic phone lines.[70] Other 'subversives' were not allowed to enter America – MacColl had to cancel a lengthy tour and 'lost about £7000', when he was refused a visa to work there in 1961. The following year he, Lloyd, Humphrey Lyttelton and Benjamin Britten sponsored British concerts to raise money for Pete Seeger's legal costs in an appeal against imprisonment for contempt of Congress. Seeger's crime was to refuse to discuss his political affiliations but to tell the Un-American Activities Committee he was 'no less a patriot' because his opinions were 'different'. For the English movement, which that same year had seen almost all its best known writers and singers involved in providing music for the Campaign for Nuclear Disarmament's march to Aldermaston in opposition to government policies on defence, the spread of American culture held ever fewer attractions.[71]

If doubt was beginning to surround American music, the nature of the 'authentic' English repertoire was apparently becoming clearer. Growing interest in performance was creating a demand for material less manicured than Sharp's arrangements for piano. But the last substantial publication of folksongs had been Alfred Williams's *Folk Songs of the Upper Thames* in 1923 – and that had contained no music. So from the beginning of the 1950s, publications which reproduced and themselves modified the movement's assumptions became available. And through this process, a changed focus of performance emerged. Competitions and unison voices singing bowdlerised texts from Sharp's and Vaughan Williams's published collectings, gave way to soloists and small groups. Works such as Margaret Dean-Smith's *Guide to English Folk Song Collections*, *The Penguin Book of English Folk Songs* and Stan Hugill's near-comprehensive volume of maritime work-songs opened up the possibilities of creating a repertoire from

thousands of songs.[72] Decisions on 'singability' were increasingly
the performer's, rather than the choice of the Director enshrined
in a syllabus. Any interested individual was now also encouraged
to collect songs, using mechanical recording wherever possible, to
reproduce the style of singing and give 'an accurate record of the
subtleties of rhythm, intonation and ornamentation'.[73] Potentially,
revival performers could acquire songs directly from the Folk by
oral transmission in the classic manner. But even for those who
learned from other sources, a new aesthetic, repertoire and performance style was being shaped.

Interest in 'authentic' song was not limited to esoteric debates
on style among English Revivalists. Folk was becoming popular,
and echoing Douglas Kennedy during the Square Dance Boom,
Lloyd warned that 'the amusement industry', which had paid it
little attention in the past, 'begins to feel that money is to be made
from the folk song revival'. The perennially contentious issue of
copyright was again coming to life and reaching areas unknown
in Sharp's day:

At present, here as in America, every other folknik and city-billy who
makes a record is claiming copyright on the items he sings, even if he
'collected' them from a library book or off someone else's records. Or
if he doesn't, his agent will. Some American agents do this even in face
of their own singers' protests. And in Britain a small concert agency
recently attached its copyright tag to items learnt from the singing of
Jean Robertson, without a word to the lady. The situation reaches its
extreme in the remark of an American visitor to our shores, who
roundly announced: 'I want to be in a position to block the use of these
songs', with the implied rider: 'Unless I get something out of it.'[74]

In England, the publisher of a songbook on the travelling life
attached her copyright to traditional songs including 'The Rocks
of Baun', 'The Shooting of his Dear', 'The Twa Corbies' and
'Edward'. Commercial pressures in America were such, Oscar
Brand reported, that a large record company had listed him as the
author of 'The Battle Hymn of the Republic' and even as the
composer of 'Old King Cole', though 'actually, it was old when
London Bridge was still a plank and 'Beowulf' was the Book of
the Month'. And it was all legal: 'The laws are producing a
situation in which one group copyrights a song and another group
records the same song and then copyrights it for themselves. The
record companies pay each group the required two cents royalty

fee. The status quo often deprives the original singer of any recompense, and usually ignores the claim of the original collector.'[75] The balance between collector and informant, Lloyd claimed, was changing – somewhat:

in the old days ... the collector descended on the countryside and took from the comparatively uneducated, unsophisticated and socially inferior peasantry whatever they had to offer in the way of home-grown or home-preserved culture, without giving thought to the informants' own rights to their material. Generations of villagers might have preserved a ballad for centuries or a Negro washerwoman might have made a song up yesterday, but once the collector had it, then it was his song, and any other claim would be laughable. This situation is altering rapidly now that, all over the world ... the humble informant is no longer likely to be intimidated by the collector's collar and tie. He is himself likely to be moving towards the orbit of professional music-[making], if he is an able performer. As example, when an obscure convict sang 'Goodnight, Irene' to a folk-song collector, the collector felt himself free to copyright the song. The song became a hit, but not before the convict himself had become a well-known public performer, wishing to exploit his own song. (The confusion was resolved out of court, to the collector's advantage).

In fact, in many respects, matters had become worse as a result of the new situation. Collectors at the turn of the century had 'merely' expropriated and sold the cultural products of the Folk, but the new acceptability of 'authentic' performance left the Folk themselves open to treatment as commodities – 'We should like to thank all those who guided us to the 'storehouses' [traditional singers].... We hope they will be rewarded by seeing the names of their own particular singers ... and by hearing younger folksingers quoting their names with reverence.'[76] For some 'source singers', requests to appear in concerts or at festivals brought status – though the 'performance syndrome' and transformation into 'entertainers' could serve to alienate them from their home culture.[77] Others, well known as performers in their own communities, made the transition to larger events with relative ease. But it is repertoire rather than experience of performance which marks out the Folk. And at least one elderly 'source', whose previous performances had been limited to singing to her children in her own village kitchen, shyly refused to perform when brought to a city for the first time and faced with a large room full of strangers. 'I've paid for her to come and she'll damn well sing', was the caring response of the collector and concert organiser. And, isolated and unhappy, the woman was pressured into singing. The new 'reverence' for the Folk was all too often a veneer for old condescensions and the view that, as 'containers' of the national culture, the Folk had a bounded duty to perform and Revivalists had a right to require them to do so.

However provided, increasing exposure to 'authentic' performance at concerts and in field recording emphasised the discrepancies between what had been published as 'folksong' and 'folksong' as sung by the Folk:

It had long been known to editors of songs from the 'peasantry', as they had formerly been called, that while the tunes were often of rare beauty and purity, the words were far from acceptable to the taste of the polite world. The verse was irregular, and grammar was often so unconventional as to be ludicrous. Worse still, there were in traditional verse none of the taboos, especially with regard to sex, which were taken for granted in the public utterance of the educated. Nor was it simply a matter of taboos in the negative sense. Not only did folk songs contain overt references to fornication and pregnancy, there was a quite shameless delight and interest in the details of these matters.[78]

To match the conversational style of singing, non-standard grammar and pronunciation, there was now a folksong manifesting 'little or none of the archness and evasion characteristic of courtship among the refined' – a 'lively, vigorous traditional verse, sturdy, resourceful, direct, humorous and natural'. Folksong enthusiasts (and others) had found 'The Foggy Dew', the first song to receive widespread hearing in unexpurgated form, a revelation. *Sing* published four versions of it, 'ink flowed and typewriter ribbons grew faint' in literary discussion of its title, and for a time 'The Foggy Dew' became a symbol of the 'new approach' in folksong. Though 'to the facile it is just naughty', Reginald Nettel proposed in 1954, 'the popularity of this song is due not merely to the beauty of the tune but to its vision of the nature of man'.[79] Discovering that such unselfconscious, 'exciting and virile poems' were attached to folksong's 'indisputably marvellous' tunes, would, John Brunner suggested, finally change the image of the Revival and Revivalists – 'For too many people for far too long a time, an English folksong has implied a group of slightly eccentric people – the women with glasses, out-of-fashion dresses and in-

credible buns of hair, the men with a slightly glassy-eyed, dedicated look – trolling out inferior late Victorian verse adaptations
to a tinkly piano accompaniment.'[80] The difficulties of eradicating
stereotypes of this kind were not to be underestimated – especially
when other sections of the Revival seemed to be conspiring to fulfil
them. In its uncensored forms, 'Blow Ye Winds in the Morning' is
a *Schwanklied*, telling of a resourceful girl who escapes from a
would-be rapist by hoodwinking him into taking her to the safety
of home by making a combined appeal to his lust and greed. To
illustrate the superiority of folksongs' 'true poetry' – and the
difference between them and the 'poor hack verses' produced by
Victorian bowdlerisers – Brunner printed a stanza of an 'authentic'
text of the song which detailed the girl's tempting offer. A few
months earlier, 'Blow Ye Winds in the Morning' had also appeared in *A Jubilee Book of English Folk-Songs*, published by the
English Folk Dance and Song Society in joint celebration of the
Diamond Jubilee of the Folk-Song Society and 'the ever-growing
popularity of folk songs since the first steps were taken to preserve
them sixty years ago'. The version of the song presented by the
Society was complete with piano accompaniment, but its text
consisted of four stanzas dealing with the girl and aggressor's
meeting, and a footnote referring readers to Thomas Percy's *Re-
liques of Ancient English Poetry*, first published in 1765, 'where
the rest of the verses may be found'.[81]

The new frankness also failed to impress a number of authorities
outside the movement. Bringing all the 'mature, discriminating,
morally serious' powers of late period Scrutineering to bear on this
innovative turn in 'the folk arts', David Holbrook knew what he
didn't like:

In England the pre-occupation with folksongs seems to lapse at times
into a false cult of commonness, with bawdiness for its own sake
(witness the popularity of *The Foggy Dew* which is cherished for its
innuendo rather than its tenderness). The folksong movement, too,
seems foolishly bent on endeavouring to pretend that the tradition
persists, and that what persists reveals more accurately the tastes of 'the
people' than what is in published collections such as those of Cecil
Sharp. Inevitably this leads to the publication, side by side with the great
folksongs, of a good deal of rubbish by way of working men's songs,
and the resurrection of a good deal of bawdy stuff of poor quality (as
in James Reeves' *The Idiom of the People*). The confusion does not

assist the possibilities of the threads of popular poetic and musical culture being picked up in our time, because it implicitly denigrates popular taste.[82]

More seriously, from the 'progressive' wing of the Revival, Hasted, as a singer and collector, raised a lone ideological objection to the role of 'bush ballads' in repertoire:

English folk songs (but to a much lesser extent the Scots and Irish) include a very large number of narrative love songs 'I saw a pretty fair maid..... I took her behind the bushes .... about nine months being over .... a warning to you all (or *maybe* we live in the happiest content of life). 'For example, in Reeves' 'Idiom of the People' nearly one in three songs is of this type or closely related.

We live in an age when such songs are well received by certain audiences, for reasons probably different from the ones which originally made the songs popular. So the singer naturally chooses a goodly number of such bush ballads for his programme. We might almost say that the English folk song revival was in danger of being diverted into roll n' run, just as the American folk song movement was to some extent diverted into rock n' roll.

But the issue is more serious than this. The songs are usually written from the man's point of view, and thus male supremacy is subtly perpetuated in an age when other cultural forces are breaking it down. When a singer gets a girl into trouble, it is always her fault! And in some country districts, traditional singing has largely degenerated into roll n' run; some of the songs are fine ones, but some are down to the level of the classic *Ball of Yarn*. Idiomatic suggestion makes this type of song popular, and such suggestion is more effective than bald statement, because it lets the audience in on the 'presumed' joke.[83]

But it was not just the humour of 'bush ballads' which promoted their popularity. Beyond the appeal of innuendo, complex resonances and hegemonic negotiations were making this particular form of 'authenticity' attractive to new recruits to the Revival.

The majority of the unbowdlerised transcriptions becoming available during the later 1950s had been notated at the turn of the century. They reflected both the concerns of the elderly rural singers sought out by collectors of the time and the pastoral imagery of the eighteenth- and earlier nineteenth-century broadsides which had influenced their repertoires. The resultant songs were both lyrical and forthright, and for many Revivalists, this combination proved to have even more appeal than the spare romance of American vernacular:

I think it was the first time A. L. Lloyd had visited the Princess Louise; it was then still a skiffle centre, and had not gone over to out-and-out folk music....

Bert was brought forward and introduced; he looked thoughtful (in a certain way he has which one might almost call mischievous, were he not so essentially dignified), and then he addressed the audience.

'Well, everyone seems to have been singing American songs, so I'm going to sing some English songs. And they're going to be love songs.' The audience composed itself to listen; one could see an attitude which indicated they were prepared to look politely interested but reserved the right to feel bored. And Bert sang about seven bawdy songs in a row – *My Husband's Got No Courage In Him* was the best – and the audience loved it.[84]

Lloyd's choice of erotic songs evoked the dream landscape of Englishness – stonecutters and pretty maids on May mornings or drifting golden afternoons; sailors and sweethearts pairing and parting against a seaside backdrop as vivid as a memory of a childhood holiday. Lloyd himself drew attention to the 'shade of stern reality that comes over the sunny scene' as the actuality of lovers' fate is worked out. As Wise Uncle Bert he deflated the priapic with a reminder that often 'with songs of sexual content, behind the joke there is a problem and fear.'[85] 'The real', however, is barely discernible in the texts – many were, Lloyd admitted, 'sentimental narratives as conventional as any girls' magazine story'. As writer of sleeve notes and 'world expert on British folk song', it was Lloyd's construction of 'readings' that carried the main force of his songs' veracity. Always on hand with a historical example of a disguised female drummer, a reconstruction of the 'ritual sense of the custom ... declining into horseplay by Henry VII's time', or a telling note about the singer and a European variant of her song, even the most insubstantial of Arcadian idylls was surrounded by a confirmatory welter of 'relevant' facts or affirmation of its psychological truth. Then there was the sex. Ever-ready young women and ever-potent young men generally offer good value to singers and audience at any time. A sexual element in humour which ridicules authority is ancient – intercourse was not invented in the 1960s – but a need to comment graphically on their existence became more pressing then. 'Authenticity' was coming to be identified with erotic or bawdy song –

these were, after all, the elements which had been suppressed in earlier published texts. And if folksong's reality was sometimes shocking, or not quite respectable, to the 'special generation', clear-sighted inheritors of 'the best of their tradition', it was the truth.

And an even greater authenticity began to be formulated. 'How long since tunes like this sparkled on the London stage?', asked Johnny Ambrose in a review of a Theatre Workshop production of December 1955. 'Where are the modern pops to match Mr Froggie and Long John and I wonder when I shall be married?... Where the lilting lyric and the rippling rhythm that run like a rich vein of glinting gold through the good earth of folk song?'[86] The answer was, in *Big Rock Candy Mountain*, the most comprehensively 'folk' and almost completely American musical by Alan Lomax. It was recognised that there was 'a wonderful world of music and song, of gaiety and humour, of sharp satire and sheerest fantasy' in Lomax's play and in American music in general. The contribution to the development of the English Revival of American performers like Pete Seeger, Peggy Seeger or Lomax, creator of the role of media celebrity collector, was welcomed. American songs were still sung by prominent English singers – MacColl recorded a cover version of Merle Travis's chart-topping, 'Sixteen Tons' in 1956.[87] But the pre-eminence of American music in the English Revival was beginning to be eroded. The search for an accommodation with the English Folk Dance and Song Society was modifying the construction of 'authentic' to privilege English music at the very time that persisting anti-Americanism and the Cold War were creating tensions that the left wing of the Revival could no longer override with high-minded calls to internationalism. As MacColl later recalled, 'a Revival that was based on ... the indigenous culture' had become 'necessary'.[88] 'Sing covers the field of song you are interested in' ran an announcement to the magazine's readers in the spring of 1957. 'We are always hearing that too many performers rely on American material. But there's a load of British material untapped ... and many American songs have British ancestors worth reviving.'[89] And, in its next issue, for the first time *Sing* gave a MacColl recording a less than glowing review:

This is our home-grown version of Sixteen Tons. We'd have liked it more if we hadn't become accustomed to Pete Seeger's magnificent

singing of American worksongs. Let's put it this way: if this were a
Scottish miners' song, MacColl's version would have a ring and a beat
and an authenticity that no American singer could touch – even Pete.
But this song was born in a Kentucky coalfield. Both singing and
accompaniment lack, understandably, the smell of American coal-dust.
The other side of the record bears out this argument perfectly. Here
MacColl is on his own ground, and the emotional quality and under-
standing that is lacking in his Sixteen Tons is here in full measure.[90]

Changing assumptions about what kinds of folksong were appropriate for the English Revival, and how they should be performed, became a matter of (sometimes vehement) public debate.
But simultaneously, an even more significant contribution to the
development of the Revival was coming into being with barely a
passing comment. One of the factors that distinguished the movement in the post-war era was the emergence of a separate economic and social base for creating, reproducing and disseminating
the practice and ideology of performance – the folk club. But what
were the sources of this important innovation? How did folk clubs
begin? In 1989, MacColl was very sure of the facts:

One of the most interesting developments of the folk revival was the
growth of the club movement. It had begun in London with the opening
of the Ballads and Blues Club at the Princess Louise, a pub in High
Holborn. The year was 1954....
Resident performers in the club included Bert [Lloyd], Seumus Ennis,
Fitzroy [Coleman], Peggy [Seeger] (after 1956) and myself.[91]

But in January 1959, Brunner's appreciative comments on Lloyd's
performance of bawdy songs had indicated that Lloyd first performed at the Princess Louise in 1958, when it was 'still a skiffle
centre, and had not gone over to out-and-out folk music'. Or,
setting aside the date, if the Princess Louise is to be proposed as
the first club, where does that leave the Good Earth Club, putting
on folksong rather than Skiffle in 1954, but with (reputedly)
admittance by invitation only, or the 'Folk Song Club' inaugurated
in 1949 at Cecil Sharp House or the Birmingham Folk Song Club
formed by Eddie Cassidy for the English Folk Dance and Song
Society, which had been 'running since the end of the war'?[92]
Perhaps Harry Boardman's response to a question on when he
started the first folk club in Manchester gives the clearest answer:

... in 1954. We didn't even know the term 'folk club'. It didn't exist.

There was a classical guitar session in a Manchester pub called the Guitar Circle, so Lesley [Boardman] and I thought of starting a 'folk circle'. I sang mainly MacColl and Lloyd songs. There was a friend of ours – a taxi driver – who was obsessed with Leadbelly songs, and there was Pauline Hinchcliffe from the Derby area who sang English and Appalachian songs. I was not even aware of MacColl's 'Ballads and Blues' club until 1957.[93]

The institutions which came to be known as 'folk clubs' were the result of a process rather than a single act of foundation. Individuals got together to sing folksongs, with or without the assistance of the English Folk Dance and Song Society, left-wing choirs adapted their repertoire and settled in a pub, existing jazz or Skiffle clubs with folk performers split or were transformed into 'out-and-out' folk clubs over time.[94]

   Relative consensus on the kind of activity that constituted a 'folk club' seems to have been reached by 1957 – 'Most SING readers will have heard a skiffle group, but fewer will have been to a skiffle *club*. There aren't so many yet where this kind of music is played in the evening. How can you start a skiffle and folksong club in your part of the world? This is certainly the time to start one. You will need to build your group first.'[95] Hasted's practical and encouraging article demonstrates that much of the organisational format of Skiffle clubs was simply transferred to folk music without alteration. From the choice of pubs as a location to the roles of residents and floor singers, folk clubs' debt to Skiffle is clear. Even the aim of trying 'to rebuild a living, urban people's music, and an audience for it', was, in Hasted's view, identical. The processes bearing on the decision to start the Topic Folk Club in Bradford in November 1956 were fairly typical of this approach:

The club was formed when the choir at St Chrysostoms in Bolton Road broke up and the members decided to form a club to enable them to carry on singing....
1956 was the year of Aldermaston marches, CND, self entertainment, skiffle and the American influenced folk boom.... Amidst all this, the Topic Folk Club was formed, taking its name from the record company to give it identity.... The first paid guest at the club was Rambling Jack Elliot from America.[96]

The existence of 'a group' as the core of folk clubs was also a common factor. The Ian Campbell Folk Group developed out of

a 'sort of skiffle group' in Birmingham in 1958, and the Spinners
setting up in Liverpool the same year, both founded their own
clubs. Elsewhere, the chance discovery of the existence of one club
encouraged the formation of another – Rotherham's first folk club,
for example, was founded as a result of Stan Crowther's visit to
Bradford Topic after a CND demonstration in 1957.[97] Difficulty
in finding suitable songs in the early stages of this development
were in some cases marked – one night at the Bradford Topic, for
lack of alternatives, 'The Good Reuben James' was reportedly
sung seven times by different people. At the Oxford Heritage
Society in 1958, a group of undergraduates sang five songs from
the same, newly released, Weavers' record. For members of provincial clubs at least, the mutuality of singing and joining in with
inspiring songs was often more significant and desirable than the
polished presentation typical of 'commercial' entertainment. But
early folk club performances were not entirely amateur. A small
number of professional singers acted as paid 'residents' in London
clubs, circulating as paid 'guests' in and outside London on nights
when their own clubs were not running. Along with new songs,
their appearances evidenced the nature of the performance skills
and approach associated with 'being a folksinger'. Implicitly, the
frequency of visits and close contact inevitable in a movement
initially characterised by low numbers, scattered locations and
small premises meant that 'stars' were comprehensively accessible
– in the place of performance, in style and, since they usually
stayed in the houses of folk club members after a booking, in
human terms. Gossip about 'the scene', personal familiarity and
the shared nature of performance left little perceived gap between
professional singer and club member. And such intimacy promoted
a level of identification which was extremely attractive. In its
'What's On and Who's Singing' column in September 1959, *Sing*
listed only nine English folk clubs – Manchester Wayfarers, Liverpool Spinners, the Topic in Bradford and six in London. Though
all the lists are undoubtedly incomplete, an expansion to thirty-six,
including four separate clubs in Birmingham and two in Manchester by September 1961, with a leap to seventy-eight, spread across
the country from Newcastle to Worthing, Plympton to the Isle of
Man by May 1962, indicates something of the momentum of the
process.[98]

What attracted people to the movement in the mid-1950s and

early 1960s? As folk clubs began to spread across the country, their membership and performers were initially recruited among left-wing activists, bohemian remnants of wartime Fitzrovia and the masses of young enthusiasts attracted to the American vernacular music of the Skiffle boom. The Campaign for Nuclear Disarmament, and its youth wing YCND, brought many people into contact with oppositional folksong and, eager to hear more, large numbers then joined local folk clubs. Other left-wing organisations, such as the Woodcraft Folk and Christian Socialist groups, also included folk music in their social events and often familiarity encouraged participation in the Revival.[99] But the excitement of discovery of a new music and the source of its attraction which Edwardian enthusiasts had managed to convey, rarely appears in accounts of this further rediscovery. That it existed is easily established – 'One hearing', said Eric Winter, of his first encounter with folksong via the London Youth Choir, 'and that was it. I said sign me up, I'm in!'[100] It is only in retrospective evocations that the excitement of the new club movement emerges: a dive your parents would never approve of, a 'sweaty, scruffy, smoke-filled basement room', subversive songs and their even more subversive singers – bohemians 'with scant regard for middle-class conventions, who exploded through life trailing a string of girlfriends, ex-wives, children, friends, foes and a host of apocryphal legends.'[101] The contrast with suburbia, the bland pop of a Mecca Ballroom or table tennis at the Youth Club could not have been greater – or more enticing.

The proliferation of folk clubs was associated with a number of changes in the character of the Revival. From 1944, direct or indirect sponsorship by the Workers' Music Association had influenced the ideology of the new wing of the movement and provided it with a small but adequate internal communications network. Revival activists such as Winter and Hasted, performers like Leon Rosselson, Shirley Collins and Hylda Sims had been in the WMA-sponsored London Youth Choir, and WMA classes and summer schools encouraged Dolly Collins's and Harry Boardman's existing interest in folk music. *The Singing Englishman*, *The Shuttle and Cage* and *Sing*, which reproduced part of the 'new' repertoire, were all the result of the linkage between the Association and the Revival. Most influentially of all, by providing models of performance, the WMA's record company, Topic, was a major factor in shaping the style as well as choice and availability of material appropriate to folksong. Initially, Topic had put out folk music in a range of styles – early issues included choral folksongs from the Warsaw Festival, Jack Elliot's 'Songs of Woody Guthrie', an LP of songs and poems commemorating the twentieth anniversary of the Spanish Civil War and MacColl and Lloyd's 'authentic' sea songs and shanties. These records were, however, produced in limited editions for subscribers only. Then in 1956, when Bill Leader took over as production manager of Topic, a new commercial approach was adopted: it included a specific policy on folksong and the decision to sell to the general public:

> Despite the current interest in folk music no record label in this country has a consistent policy towards it. It is welcome news therefore, that Topic will initiate a 'Blue Label' towards the end of the year. This series will cover folk music and music which owes its development to oral tradition, music created by people in their work and relaxation.... The series, which will sell at approximately 16s. a disc, will be prepared under the guidance of experts in the field and will cover international as well as British songs.[102]

Though the relationship was not always smooth-running – Hasted clashed with WMA hierarchy over his introduction of small groups and a changed repertoire – performers and material reproducing the Association's ideology offered the earliest source of identity to Revivalists attempting to define folk clubs and what should be sung in them and how it should be sung. The English Folk Dance and Song Society, Lloyd felt, had certainly not been equal to this task – 'Most of the participants in the revival are outside the orbit of the E.F.D.S.S., and are sometimes hostile to it, feeling rightly or wrongly that the Society (whose President is Princess Margaret) is too closely tied to the Establishment. Thus, the English Folk Dance and Song Society is in a dilemma, being neither a truly popular body nor yet a learned society proper.'[103] Whether new recruits to the movement knew – or cared – who was President of the English Folk Dance and Song Society is a moot point. How many had even heard of the Society is probably a more relevant question. But whether the WMA or the Cultural Committee of the CPGB was now proving more effective in overseeing 'the preservation, study and performance of folk music in England' is equally doubtful. The movement was growing rapidly

– small and hidebound, the WMA as an organisation or a source
of ideology meant little to the erstwhile fans of Lonnie Donnegan
now crowding into folk clubs. Pointing to the work of 'a modern
ballad-maker like Cyril Tawney whose entire output is unpoliti-
cal', Sydney Carter highlighted the existence of 'modern folk
songs' which were '*not* about the H-bomb, the Colour Bar, Capital
Punishment or Greedy Landlords'. He then added that a recent
summary of the 'main pre-occupations of the folk, as judged by
their balladry, were ... Sex, snobbery and murder'.[104] 'Man's
struggle for a better life' was not a necessary constituent of
'authentic' English folksong. And folk clubs which embraced the
'pre-occupations of the folk' rather than vestigial remains of the
cultural popular front of the Communist Party were now being
founded.

As the institutions where the ideology of the Revival was reproduced in performance, folk clubs became a major site of hegemonic negotiations in the movement. Outside the Revival, the
changed approach to folksong had not always been greeted with
approval – 'It is surprising ... to hear the talent of skilled singers
of folksongs such as Isla Cameron and Ewan MacColl wasted on
the crudities, rhythmical and emotional, of a wireless programme
such as *The Ballad of John Axon*: here the folky-progressive and
the emotional exploitation of the *Daily Mirror* meet.'[105] But even
'insiders' like Francis Collinson, whose involvement ran from collecting songs from Harry Cox for 'Country Magazine' to membership of the staff of the School of Scottish Studies, admitted to
shock at seeing the field of English folksong 'used for the exploitation or exposition at least, of class distinction and class prejudice
and the representing of England as a land of struggle of worker
against employer and master against man'.[106] Such reactions were
comprehensively satirised in a consideration of 'Politics, S*x and
the Folk Revival' which appeared in *Folk Music*, a new Revival
magazine:

Time was when the earnest seeker after beauty could wander undis-
turbed through the realm of poesy, hand in hand with the artless muse
of [the] people. The poisoned air of the teeming city would be left
behind and soon the poor wanderer, sloughing off his grosser self,
would find himself in sylvan glades basking in pure sunlight and shy
glances from purer maidens whose raven tresses put the night to shame.
Then did the smalle birds sing right lustilie and gentle shepherds took

time off from gathering primroses to raise their voices in praise of it all, their sweet songs rivalling the golden notes of the wild carolling black-bird.

Alas, how changed it all is! Time's withered hand has touched the raven tresses, the maidens have become bolder than was their wont and the banks of the quiet, purling streams, where once sprang the tiny blue milkwort and the asphodel, are now littered with abandoned maiden-heads; worst of all, the gentle shepherds have fled before the hordes of loud-voiced plebs wearing pit-boots and arguing politics.[107]

But though this might (without undue exaggeration) have repre-sented the view of romantics, reactionaries or the wilder tea-danc-ing sections of the English Folk Dance and Song Society, the article had reportedly been prompted by none of these. The target of the writer's ridicule was the wording of a Folk Club membership card:

To call Folksong & Ballad, Newcastle, a club or a society would tend to mislead since it differs considerably from that which is usually associated with these terms. In this organisation it is sought to combine the sincere and even scholarly approach of the society with the infor-mality of the club. Unlike many organizations involved in the current revival of interest in folk music, Folksong and Ballad, Newcastle, main-tains a strict impartiality to current politics and to the associated national and international problems.

Other clubs were equally didactic. A 'Tradnight' 'strictly for tradi-tionalists' from which 'non-trad instruments were barred' was running in London by 1959. Its organiser, Frank Purslow, felt the EFDSS view of folksong 'was fuddy-duddy', but he was equally unhappy about the emphasis on politics in other institutions.[108] A different approach still was adopted by the Ballads and Blues Club. Here political songs were welcome. But, inspired by his new American partner, Peggy Seeger, who 'found it difficult to keep a straight face when she heard cockneys and Liverpudlians singing Leadbelly and Guthrie songs' and perhaps learning from *Sing*'s cool response to his own recording of 'Sixteen Tons', MacColl and the resident singers at the Club 'decided on a policy: that from now on residents, guest singers and those who sang from the floor should limit themselves to songs which were in a language the singer spoke or understood. We became what began to be known as a 'policy club'.[109]

Although by now couched in terms of traditionality, it was the concept of authenticity formulated in the jazz-folk milieu of the late 1940s which was actually reproduced through 'policy clubs'. Over a decade later, in the Folk Revival, the same privileging of anachronistic styles of performance and accompaniment were applied to English 'traditional' music with a large measure of approval, but few concessions to logic. Take the case of 'traditional songs'. Most accounts of the Folk's singing reported unaccompanied performances. In consequence, some 'policy clubs' refused to admit musicians who arrived with guitars. In others, a gentle hiss went round the room when someone entered carrying a guitar case and they were 'encouraged' not to use it. As late as 1984, a band which played entirely 'traditional' material encountered objections on 'policy' grounds because they used electronic instruments.[110] Yet, unaccountably, no 'policy clubs' seem to have refused to accept a performer who sang with concertina accompaniment. The concertina was, after all, 'authentic' – old(ish), used by the Folk (sometimes) and, most of all, unsullied by modernity. And what of the choice of songs? Again, the influence seems to have been American. In America, the 'catholicity of the neo-folksinger's repertory' was claimed to be 'little short of breathtaking'. With only slight exaggeration, Gershon Legman suggested, 'no one would today be surprised to hear' a singer perform a programme consisting of a Child ballad, followed by a Palestinian children's round, an Argentinian tango, an expurgated version of 'John Anderson My Jo', 'a suggestive version' of 'I Gave My Love a Cherry' and 'a Japanese boatmen's song in Japanese'. But whilst eclecticism might reasonably be found wanting on aesthetic grounds, Legman's objections lay elsewhere. Such a repertoire did not reflect the 'consonant' material of 'a real folksinger'.[111] Equally, though Peggy Seeger 'had a sizeable repertoire of songs in French, Russian, Spanish and Italian', it was mainly the fact that the songs were from 'an alien culture or lifestyle' that led to Seeger and MacColl's feeling 'no real sense of identity with them' and adopting a 'policy'.[112] 'Authentic' repertory, therefore, was that of the 'real' traditional singer, singing of 'what he knows about and cares about'. But what defined 'consonance' and an 'alien lifestyle'? What was a consonant repertory for an American coffee house performer, who as a member of a technologically complex society had a world of musical cultures on record and in print to draw on? Was it necessarily the same as that of a 'traditional' singer? The repertoires of 'traditional' singers had never been fully explored by folksong collectors, who had very clear ideas on what they did not want to record. Whether the full range of songs known by any 'traditional' singer were 'consonant' or not, was simply undemonstrable. And how could the 'lifestyle' of say, a Salford-bred man, whose background was in Agit-Prop Theatre and who now made a living writing, recording and performing songs for the twentieth-century mass media be 'identified' with an eighteenth-century woman like Anna Brown of Falkland, daughter of the landed gentry and academia, late and genteelly married to a retired military chaplain, who incidentally was found to know some ballads?

As a policy of authenticity was reproduced and negotiated in the maturing folk club movement, tensions between 'traditional' and 'contemporary' song grew. It was not just a rejection of the newly written 'commercial folksongs' which a second generation of American singers were bringing to England, and the pop charts. Mistrust of all aspects of commercial popular culture was endemic to the Revival, as much an article of faith for Sir Hubert Parry at the foundation of the Folk-Song Society as it was latterly for Sharp and MacColl, Mary Neal and Lloyd or Douglas Kennedy and Gardiner. In pursuit of authenticity, the movement was turning on itself – 'polarised around two main viewpoints which we might call 'pop' and 'ethnic'. The basic problem dividing them is that of the relationship of the body of folk music we have inherited ... to the joy of continuing the folk process in a changing world' – 'the problem of relating the past and the present, the traditional and the topical'.[113] As presented by the 'ethnic' lobby, the preoccupations of the authentic folksongs were 'sex, snobbery and murder', political songs demanded 'more commitment than your traditional singers are prepared to give'. Traditional singers' political stance was 'generally hard-bitten, anarchic, sceptical' with a 'mean, distrustful attitude toward furriners'.[114] How was this to be reconciled with the creation of 'songs of immediate and topical interest', which would 'play an important role in the struggles of the British people for peace and socialism'? John Foreman felt it could be done – modern topical songs did not 'need the merits of a song that has lasted for centuries and looks fair for a few more. Like egg and chips, it's hot from the pan, and tomorrow you'll still be hungry for more.' What was more, Foreman proposed, topical songs had roots – 'we can easily overlook the fact that old folk forms flowed into music halls and from these almost directly into folk clubs ... the making of topical songs has grown steadily out of the past.'[115] The view found little favour, but then there was less to challenge or admire in a genre that was no longer guaranteed to be oppositional – 'overt political commitment has become a commercial cliché. When a protest meeting in Trafalgar Square is used as an opportunity for Donovan to plug his latest single, the wheel has turned full circle.'[116] A repressively macho social realism also limited the appeal of other 'non-authentic' forms. MacColl and Lloyd continued to proselytise for 'Industrial Songs' – editing hymns to male struggles in heavy industry from the past or political battles in the present. But somehow, the industries worth researching and writing about were never catering or nursing, hairdressing or office work, and only the heroic was celebrated. As subjects for consideration in song, as writers who might draw on their concerns or experience, as club members in a pub-based movement or performers attempting to reproduce its agreed repertoire, women had no obvious role among the 'plebs in pitboots arguing politics'. Meanwhile, 'authentic' songs, bawdy and Arcadian, historical and locally relevant, in apparently boundless supply were being discovered in libraries or recorded from 'traditional singers'. For clubs with a 'traditional policy', the whole of folk culture, plays, dances and crafts as well as music and song, was available to be lived and reproduced. Compared to the thin, ephemerality of topical song, members of traditional policy clubs saw themselves as the inheritors of the totality of 'authentic' folk culture. It was their responsibility to carry on where the Folk left off. And the Folk, by definition, re-created, rather than innovated.

Folk clubs were the generators of the Revival in the late 1960s and the culmination of the movement to replace the Folk. Through the later 1960s and into the 1970s, they became a way of life – a major source of a Revival sub-culture expressed in vaguely historical styles of dress and vernacular artefacts, in performances among a close and known community with shared identity, beliefs, rituals and values. Clubs ran concerts and ceilidhs, organised trips to Revival and 'traditional' events and published songs and magazines – even made their own records. Members formed associated bands, dance teams and mummers' groups. Federations of clubs arranged block bookings with specialist agents for increasing numbers of professional and semi-professional performers as the movement provided an economic base as well as a hobby for enthusiasts. Festivals proliferated, offering club members the chance to live the Revival lifestyle for days at a time and acquire approved technical skills through workshops and contact with professional performers. In pursuit of more authentic traditional material, club members researched and photographed and taped, and as they did so they became increasingly aware of the theoretical writings of nineteenth-century folklorists and their modern counterparts. Survivals theory was given a new lease of life in pamphlets on local mumming plays and public announcements before performances of 'ritual' dances. The movement had never been as widespread and active. But for all its apparent innovation and variety, the Revival was hidebound by historical theory. Determinedly reproducing a policy of authenticity, it became a more effective vehicle for Sharp's views than the English Folk Dance Society of the 1920s. Typifying all that had set the Revival on a return to the past was its most valued theoretical statement on folk culture, A. L. Lloyd's *Folk Song in England*. Published in 1967, the new work accepted the survivals theory Lloyd had dismissed in 1946 as 'a lot of dark anthropological hoo-ha' and approvingly reproduced Sharp's 1907 definition of folksong in its entirety. If this meant that 'Industrial Song', Lloyd's main innovation in the field, could not be counted as 'folksong proper', Lloyd reported himself content. The problem obviously lay with the genre of Industrial Song, rather than the formulation of any aspect of Sharp's theory. The Folk Revival had succeeded, folksongs were known and sung, folk dances of all types danced, but unless its fundamental concepts of the Folk and folk culture were rejected, the movement had no possibility for development.

Notes

1 Sleeve notes from Shirley and Dolly Collins, *Anthems in Eden* (Harvest HVL 754, 1969).

2 Douglas Kennedy, 'Where Do We Go from Here?,' *English Dance and Song*, IX:2 (Dec. 1944), 13–15 from which all quotations are taken. Despite twelve years of amalgamation and the promise of an imminent 'square deal' for song, in common with other prominent members of the English Folk Dance and Song Society, Kennedy still refers to the future of the 'E.F.D.S.'.

3 Comments from Douglas Kennedy, *English Folk Dancing: Today and Yesterday* (London: G. Bell & Sons Ltd, 1964), p. 7 and an English

Folk Dance and Song Society Press Release on the Society in the 1990s quoted in Anon., 'People, Misc...,' *Folk Roots*, XIII:4 (Oct. 1991), 13, with the laconic note 'This may come as a surprise to many readers!'

4 Eric Winter, 'Achievement: The Story of Twenty One Years,' *Sing*, III:6 (Feb.-Mar. 1957), 82–3. I am most grateful to Eric Winter for copies of early numbers of *Sing*.

5 See various examples discussed in Ernst Herman Meyer, 'The Singers of Battersea,' in P. M. Kemp-Ashraf and Jack Mitchell, ed., *Essays in Honour of William Gallacher* (Berlin: Humboldt University, 1966), pp. 181–4. For a study of the origin and uses of one newly created song see Richard Raskin, "Le Chant des Partisans': Functions of a Wartime Song,' *Folklore*, CII:1 (1991), 62–76.

6 A. L. Lloyd, *The Singing Englishman: An Introduction to Folksong* (London: Workers' Music Association, ND [1944]). Albert Lancaster Lloyd (1908–82) a writer, singer, broadcaster and lecturer on ethnomusicology, whose publications and contributions to the recording of folksongs (as performer, writer of sleeve notes, patron of younger singers and source of songs) have been of considerable influence in shaping attitudes and repertoires within the Revival from the 1940s to the present. Lloyd's complete reversals of view on the relevance of Revival and 'Industrial Song', as well as his editorial practices and acceptance of a role in the hegemony of the English Folk Dance and Song Society, have raised questions, notably from Harker. For substantial discussion of Lloyd's work, see Dave Harker, *Fakesong: The Manufacture of British 'folksong' 1700 to the Present Day* (Milton Keynes: Open University Press, 1985), pp. 231–53 and the same author's *One For the Money: Politics and Popular Song* (London: Hutchinson & Co. Ltd, 1980), pp. 150–85 and the following papers in Ian Russell, ed., *Singer, Song and Scholar* (Sheffield: Sheffield Academic Press, 1986): Leslie Shepard, 'A. L. Lloyd – A Personal View,' pp. 125–32; Roy Palmer, 'A. L. Lloyd and Industrial Song,' pp. 133–44; Vic Gammon, 'A. L. Lloyd and History: A Reconsideration of Aspects of *Folk Song in England* and some of his other Writings,' pp. 147–64, and David Arthur, 'A. L. Lloyd 1908–82: An Interim Bibliography,' pp. 165–77. I am most grateful to Dave Arthur, who is currently working on a biography of A. L. Lloyd, for his unstinting generosity with information and time on the subject of Lloyd's work and his own early experiences in the Revival.

7 Douglas Kennedy, 'The Amateurs,' *English Dance and Song*, IX:5 (June-July 1945), 45.

8 See for instance, the wide range of rural imagery and hymn-like features of the contents of *Labour's Song Book* (London: I.L.P. Publi-

cation Department, 1931). For an example of the post-war activities and repertoire of a left-wing choir, see comments on the Workers' Music Association Singers and London Youth Choir in John Hasted, *Alternative Memoirs* (Itchenor, W. Sussex: Greengates Press, 1992), pp. 100–04 and 108–17. The musical range and approach of the American Folk Revival at the time is best exemplified in Waldemar Hille, ed., *The People's Song Book* (New York: Boni and Gaer, Inc., 1948).

9 A. L. Lloyd, 'This 'Folk' Business: Review of *The American People* by B. A. Botkin,' *Our Time*, Sept. 1946, pp. 44–6.

10 HMV B9539, HMV B9519, HMV B9520, HMV B9578, HMV B9579, HMV B9669, HMV B9670, HMV B9671, HMV B9672. These were produced in co-operation with His Master's Voice in November and December 1946, May 1947 and May 1948, probably as a result of Maud Karpeles's preparatory work for setting up of the International Folk Music Council (see below). At the same time, the English Folk Dance and Song Society also bought up and took over sales of Maud Karpeles's 1937 recordings of Phil Tanner (R.101 and R.102) which Columbia had deleted. See Norman Fraser, ed., *International Catalogue of Recorded Folk Music* (Oxford: For UNESCO by The International Folk Music Council, 1954), pp. viii, 154–5 and 196–7. Recordings of Harry Cox were also made during the 1930s, but in common with many later EFDSS recordings were apparently available to members only. I am very grateful to Malcolm Taylor of the Vaughan Williams Memorial Library at Cecil Sharp House for information relating to recordings by Harry Cox and Phil Tanner.

11 From 2,024 to 2,431; see A. H. Swinson, 'Editorial,' *English Dance and Song*, XI:1 (March 1947), 3.

12 D. N. Kennedy, 'The Director Writes: Copyright in Folk Music,' *ibid.*, XVI:2 (Sept. 1951), 42.

13 Lloyd, *The Singing Englishman*, p. 68.

14 An outline of the formation and early development of the IFMC appears in Maud Karpeles, 'The International Folk Music Council: Twenty-One Years,' *Yearbook of the International Folk Music Council: Volume I* (1969), pp. 14–32.

15 See for example comments in Maud Karpeles, 'Traditional Form,' *English Dance and Song*, XVII:4 (Feb.-March 1953), 124; 'New Members' Page: Talk Broadcast by Maud Karpeles,' *ibid.*, XVIII:4 (Feb.-March 1954), 114 and 'A Jubilee Symposium: 5. Past and Present,' *Folk Music Journal*, II:2 (1971), 99–101 which offer counter-arguments to Douglas Kennedy's 'The Director Writes: Traditional Form,' *English Dance and Song*, XVII:3 (Dec. 1952–Jan. 1953), 76–7; 'The Director Writes: In the Raw,' *Ibid.*, XVIII:3 (Dec. 1953–Jan. 1954), 77–8 and 'A

Jubilee Symposium: 2. Folk Dance Revival,' *Folk Music Journal*, II:2 (1971), 80–90.

16 Harry Hopkins, *The New Look: A Social History of the Forties and Fifties in Britain* (London: Secker & Warburg Ltd for the Readers Union, 1964), pp. 106–8.

17 *Ibid.*, pp. 106–7.

18 *Ibid.*, p. 109. Vanderschmidt's *What the English Think of Us* was published in 1948 by Quality Press.

19 D. N. Kennedy, 'The Director Writes: The Square Dance Comes Back,' *English Dance & Song*, XVI:4 (Feb.-March 1952), 109.

20 The process as it related to folksong is detailed with commendable frankness in Oscar Brand, *The Ballad Mongers: Rise of the Modern Folk Song* (NP: Minerva Press, 1962). See Charlie Gillett's unsurpassed *The Sound of the City* (rev. edn; London: Souvenir Press Ltd, 1983), pp. 5–22 for specific introduction and the book as a whole for background to other forms.

21 For details see Derek Schofield, 'A Lancashire Mon,' *Folk Review*, (Apr. 1975), 4–9.

22 Kenneth G. Baker, 'Correspondence,' *English Dance and Song*, XII:2 (Mar. 1948), 34. I am also grateful to Kathleen Page for her vivid and detailed account of the Square Dance Boom in Sheffield. Interview with the author, 12 Mar. 1992.

23 Kennedy, 'The Director Writes: The Square Dance Comes Back,' p. 109. All additional quotations on Square dancing are from his *English Folk Dancing*, p. 28.

24 Kennedy, 'The Director Writes: In the Raw,' p. 77.

25 D. Kennedy, 'The Policy of the Executive Committee,' *English Dance and Song*, XII:3 (June 1948), 35 and 43.

26 See Kennedy, 'The Square Dance Comes Back,' p. 111 and *English Folk Dancing Today and Yesterday*, p. 28.

27 *English Dance and Song*, XI:1 (Mar. 1947), 7. Notes accompanying details of festivals at Bexhill, the National Festival and Summer School.

28 *English Folk Dance and Song Society Annual Report 1951*, pp. 20–1.

29 See announcement in *English Dance and Song*, XVI:4 (Feb.-March 1952), 108.

30 'Douglas Kennedy, 'Notes on Recruiting,' *ibid.*, X:6 (1946), 74.

31 Douglas Kennedy, 'A Jubilee Symposium: 2. Folk Dance Revival,' *Folk Music Journal*, II:2 (1971), 90.

32 See for example Douglas Kennedy, 'Festival Dresses – to start you thinking,' *English Dance and Song*, XIII:2 (Feb.-March 1949), 25 and

V[iolet] A[lford], 'Your Festival Dress – Two More Ideas,' *ibid.*, XIII:3 (May 1949), 42. In the light of Alford's 1937 criticism of male morris dancers' dress, it is not clear whether her final comments are the result of forgetfulness or irony.

33 Mrs D. D. Anne Teagle, 'What Should Ladies Wear?,' *ibid.*, XXI:1 (Sept.-Oct. 1956), 31–2.

34 A. L. Lloyd, 'The Folk-Song Revival,' *Marxism Today*, June 1961, pp. 170–1.

35 Harker, *Fakesong*, p. 250.

36 Karl Dallas, 'MacColl – the Man, the Myth, the Music,' *English Dance and Song*, LI:4 (Christmas 1989), 11.

37 See Rolf Gardiner, 'Can Farming save European Civilisation?,' in Andrew Best, ed., *Water Springing from the Ground: An Anthology of the Writings of Rolf Gardiner* (Shaftesbury: Trustees of the Estate of Rolf Gardiner, 1972), pp. 196–9. For the, post-war reorganisation of the EFDSS, see Douglas Kennedy, 'The Amateurs,' *English Dance and Song*, IX:5 (June-July 1945), 44–5.

38 For details of Louie Hooper, see Douglas Cleverdon, 'Adventures in Recording – 2,' *ibid.*, VIII:4 (Apr.-May 1944), 27–8.

39 Roy Harris, 'Bob Cann,' *Folk Review*, IV:11 (Sept. 1975), 16–17.

40 Marie Slocombe, 'Round Britain with a Recording Machine: The BBC as Collector,' *English Dance and Song*, XVII:1 (Aug.-Sept. 1952), 12–13.

41 Gillett, *The Sound of the City,* pp. 257–8 and including quotation from Humphrey Lyttelton.

42 Nicky Thatcher, 'An American at the Court of Queen Elizabeth,' *Sing*, III:5 (Dec. 1956–Jan. 1957), 73–4.

43 Gillett, *The Sound of the City*, p. 260.

44 Brand, *The Ballad Mongers*, p. 106.

45 Hasted, *Alternative Memoirs*, p. 121.

46 *Ibid.*, pp. 124–27. I am also most grateful to Dave Arthur for additional detail on Lloyd's part in the Ramblers – personal communication, 14 May 1992.

47 The Ramblers' repertoire included 'The Duples Strike' (John Hasted), 'Are You Going Off to War, Billy Boy?' (Traditional adapted by 'The Ramblers'), 'Go Home Yankee' (John Hasted's adaptation of the German 'Go Home Ami'), 'Hoist the Window, let the dove come in' (Negro spiritual collected by A. L. Lloyd), 'Poor Working Man' (Henry Mitchell), 'I dreamed I saw Paul Robeson' (Henry Mitchell, John Hasted and George Peters), 'Johnny has Gone for a Soldier' (traditional collected by John and Alan Lomax) and 'Johnny I hardly knew You' (traditional), as well as established British and American political/Union

songs such as 'Banks of Marble', 'The Union Maid' and 'Hold the Fort'. Information taken from 'Youth Sings for Peace: Songs sung by The Ramblers' (duplicated words and music printed and published by Workers' Music Association c.1952). The same songs also featured in the repertoire of the London Youth Choir, a much larger group, affiliated to the Workers' Music Association, which was formed in 1951 'to participate in the Berlin Youth Festival'. Hasted was its conductor.

48 For examples, see Wal Hannington, 'The Happy Engineers', *Sing*, II:1 (Mayday Supplement 1955), 20 and Fred Dallas, 'We Try to Build the Union', *ibid.*, II:6 (Feb.-March 1956), 88 and foregoing details of new material written for the Ramblers and the London Youth Choir.

49 Ewan MacColl, 'Preface', *The Shuttle and Cage: Industrial Folk-Ballads* (London: Workers' Music Association, 1954) from which subsequent quotation is also taken. I am most grateful to Clare Gilliam of the Vaughan Williams Memorial Library, Cecil Sharp House for assistance with copies of this publication. Ewan MacColl [James Miller] (1915–89) actor, writer and singer. As his autobiography makes clear, MacColl had no contact with the Folk Revival in England until 1951. In the following ten years, however, he made a considerable mark, performing and broadcasting in Britain and America. From 1961, he increasingly withdrew from the broader English Revival to work within self-defined limits (see for example the exchanges in *Sing*, V:4 (Aug. 1961), 65; VI:4 (Dec. 1961), 34 and VI:6 (Feb. 1962), 56 and Ewan MacColl, *Journeyman: An Autobiography* (London: Sidgwick & Jackson Ltd, 1990), pp. 339–41). He remained a lifelong Communist and controversialist. MacColl recorded extensively – and though his distinctive singing style clearly influenced a number of younger singers, his actor's habit of performing in 'appropriate' accents reduced his effectiveness. As an innovator in Agit-Prop theatre, and writer of plays, prose and songs, his work was notable. But his most celebrated creation, the 'Radio Ballads' (begun in 1957), jointly produced with Peggy Seeger and Charles Parker, owed far more to pre-war North Region programmes than MacColl ever chose to acknowledge. His widely credited role as the 'founding giant of the Folk Music Revival' seems to be based on insistent personal publicity rather than any documentary evidence. For a standard view, see Michael Grosvenor Myer's obituary article, 'Breathing New Life into Folk Song and the Theatre,' *The Guardian*, 24 Oct. 1989, p. 39.

50 See brief description in MacColl, *Journeyman*, p. 275.

51 Robin Denselow, *When the Music's Over: The Story of Political Pop* (London: Faber and Faber Ltd, 1989), p. 23.

52 Both quotations from Gillett, *The Sound of the City*, p. 260. See

also Peter Narvaez, 'Blues,' in Graham C. Garnett, ed., *A Hundred Years on Record: An Appreciation of Recorded Sound* (London: The Rococo Group, 1989), pp. 102–4 for a valuable summary of Country Blues forms and their relationship with other genres of traditional song.

53 I am most grateful to Paul Adams for details of the above performances, to Eric Winter for extensive information about the background to folk music and Skiffle in London in this period, and to both for their ever-generous, witty and informative responses to my many enquiries. Additional discussion is based on Gillett, *The Sound of the City*, pp. 259–60 and Robin Denselow, 'Folk-Rock in Britain,' in Dave Laing, Karl Dallas, Robin Denselow and Robert Shelton, *The Electric Muse: The Story of Folk into Rock* (London: Eyre Methuen, 1975), pp. 141–2.

54 John Hasted, 'A Singer's Notebook,' *Sing*, IV:2 (June-July 1957), 22.

55 E[ric] W[inter], 'Review of Brian Bird, *Skiffle* published by Robert Hale, 1959,' *ibid.*, V:1 (Sept. 1959), 7.

56. Among those who 'drifted' into folk via Skiffle were singers and musicians such as Dave Swarbrick (see *ibid.*, VI:11 (July 1962), 118), Martin Carthy (see *Folk Review*, (March 1975, pp.4–8), Frankie Armstrong (*ibid.*, June 1975, pp.4–7), Robin and Barry Dransfield (*ibid.*, April 1978, p.4), as well as club and festival organisers such as John Heydon (*ibid.*, July 1975, pp.7–8). Hasted's *Alternative Memoirs*, pp. 136–7 lists the personnel of twelve London Skiffle groups many of whom then moved into the Folk Revival, including his own Ramblers Skiffle Group with Redd Sullivan and (from time to time) Shirley Collins. Interestingly, Harker, *One For the Money*, p. 151, notes that MacColl formed a Ramblers Skiffle Group with Lomax, Peggy Seeger and Shirley Collins.

57 A. L. Lloyd, 'Recent Recordings,' *English Dance and Song*, XVII:2 (Oct.-Nov. 1952), 52–3. Reviews of Ewan MacColl, 'Lord Randall'/'Van Diemen's Land' HMV B10259 and 'Sir Patrick Spens/Eppie Morrie' HMV B10260, 'recorded under the auspices of EFDSS'.

58 See Douglas Kennedy, 'Folk Songs Raw and Civilised,' *ibid.*, VIII:1 (Aug.-Sept. 1953), 26–7 and 'The Director Writes: In the Raw,' pp.77–8.

59 Karpeles, 'New Members' Page: Talk Broadcast by Maud Karpeles,' p. 114.

60 Anon. [John Hasted], 'Editorial: Something to Sing About,' *Sing*, I:1 (May-June 1954), 2. The first issue contained 'The Atom Bomb and the Hydrogen!', words and music by Leon Fung; 'The Bird with a Leaf

in her Beak', words and music by Geoff Skeet which had been awarded second prize in the Bucharest Festival Music Competition; 'On Top of No Smoking', an anonymous (later reprinted as adapted John Hasted) parody of 'On Top of Old Smokey' protesting about the 1954 Budget; 'Robin Hood', tune 'Traditional', words by the boys of Mayflower School, Poplar; 'Talking Rearmament,' words by John Hasted 'in the traditional [American] Talking Blues style, spoken against a guitar accompaniment'; 'I Won't Clean Your Windows Today', words by Joe Balby, music by John Hasted, social comment in music hall style; 'The Ballad of Jomo Kenyatta', words by Johnny Ambrose, music adapted from the 'Negro folksong' 'Poor Lazarus'; 'Arian', 'a traditional Korean Song', English words by Arthur Kevess, reprinted from '*Sing*'s big brother', the American magazine *Sing Out*. Two short-lived earlier magazines, the original *Keynote* and *Folk*, contained articles but no songs.

61 Alex Eaton, 'Letter,' *Sing*, II:3 (June-July 1955), 34. A former member of a Young Communist League Choir, Eaton was one of the founders of the Topic Folk Club in Bradford in November 1956 and went on to record (with John Hasted) 'The Collier's Rant' and 'The Row between the Cages' (TRC 106) for Topic Records in 1957.

62 Fred [Karl] Dallas, 'How Can We Help the Folk Song Revival,' *English Dance and Song*, XXI:2 (Nov.-Dec. 1956), 71–2

63 See *Sing*, IV:2 (June-July 1957), 27 for EFDSS announcement and A. L. Lloyd, Eric Winter and Fred Dallas, 'Made in Britain,' *ibid.*, IV:4–5 (Dec. 1957), 52 and 57 for remaining quotes from 'SINGers'. Douglas Kennedy's comments appeared in his 'A Fourth Folk Festival,' *ibid.*, VI:10 (June 1962), 107. I am also grateful to Norma Waterson for additional information on the Festival.

64 For specific details of the first Edinburgh Festival and its aftermath, see Ailie Munro, *The Folk Music Revival in Scotland* (London: Kahn & Averill, 1984), pp. 50–4, and p. 18 for the view of 'several authorities with long memories of the Scottish revival' that Sandy Bell's Bar (the Forest Hill Bar) in Edinburgh was 'where it all started ... singing, discussion and the making of plans'. Further considerations of the Revival in Scotland are published in Hamish Henderson, 'Scots Folk-Song Today,' *Folklore*, LXXV (spring 1964), 48–58; Francis Collinson, *The Traditional and National Music of Scotland* (London: Routledge and Kegan Paul Ltd, 1966); Sheila Douglas, 'The Ballad on the Scottish Folk Scene,' in Georgina Boyes, ed., *The Ballad Today: History, Performance and Revival* (Doncaster & Addiscombe: January Books, 1985), pp. 36–42 and Ailie Munro, 'The Role of the School of Scottish Studies in the Folk Music Revival,' *Folk Music Journal*, VI:2 (1991),

132–68.

65 A. L. Lloyd, ed., *Come All Ye Bold Miners: Ballads and Songs of the Coalfields* (London: Lawrence and Wishart Ltd, 1952); Peggy Seeger and Ewan MacColl, ed., *The Singing Island: A Collection of English and Scots Folksongs* (London: Mills Music Ltd, 1960);Ewan MacColl, *Scotland Sings* (London: Workers' Music Association, 1953); Norman Buchan, ed., *101 Scottish Songs* (Glasgow: Wm Collins Sons & Co. Ltd, 1962).

66 And of course there were 'rebel songs' with rousing choruses. *Sing*'s policy of presenting songs of struggle meant that *Songs of the Easter Rising, Irish Songs of Resistance* and Dominic Behan's family tradition of Republicanism were particularly well represented. For examples of records of Irish material during the period, see Patrick Galvin, 'Irish Songs of Resistance', Topic Records T3 and T4, 1956; Margaret Barrie *[sic]*, Michael Gorman and Willy Clancy, 'Irish Songs and Dances', Topic Records T7, 1956; 'Folk Song Today' (compilation by Peter Kennedy, including track by McPeakes) His Master's Voice DLP 1143, 1957 and Dominic Behan, 'Irish Songs', Topic 10T28, 1959 and 'Finnegan's Wake', Collector JE11, 1959.

67 Ewan MacColl, 'For Peace and Lasting Friendship,' *Sing*, II:1 (May Day Supplement), 18–19.

68 Anon. [John Hasted], 'A Singer's Notebook,' *ibid.*, I:1 (May-June 1954), 11. Particularly through his live appearances in England, Seeger had drawn audiences to folk music and been an inspiration to many English Revival performers. See Brand, *The Ballad Mongers*, pp. 57–230 for an outline of his work during the period under discussion.

69 Brand, *ibid.*, p. 139. See pp. 122-39 for a detailed examination of the effects of blacklists on the Folk Revival in America.

70 See Anon., 'Discussion: Review of Paul Robeson's Trans-Atlantic Concert, Topic 10T17,' *Sing*, IV:6 (Oct. 1958), 73.

71 Anon., 'Aldermaston: Glesca Eskimos,' *ibid.*, VI:9 (May 1962), 95. Among the performers listed were Anti-Polaris Singers from Scotland – 'The Glesca Eskimos', Nigel Denver of the Glasgow Folk Club, 'Mrs Josh Macrae', Maurice Blythman (Thurso Berwick) and Gordon McCullogh. Groups included The Ian Campbell Folk Five, the London Fesival Singers, the WMA Singers and members of the Unity Theatre Club. Members of the Editorial Board of *Sing* attended the march – Winter being 'again in charge of music.' John Foreman, Colin Wilkie and Shirley Hart, Bob Davenport, Lloyd, MacColl and Peggy Seeger appeared at concerts on the route.

72 Margaret Dean-Smith, *A Guide to English Folk Song Collection 1822–1952* (Liverpool & London: University Press of Liverpool in

association with the English Folk Dance and Song Society, 1954). The 'Introduction' also offers an excellent concise account of the history of folksong study in England; Ralph Vaughan Williams and A. L. Lloyd, ed., *The Penguin Book of English Folk Songs* (Harmondsworth, Middx: Penguin Books, 1959) and Stan Hugill, *Shanties from the Seven Seas: Shipboard Work-Songs and Songs used as Work-Songs from the Great Days of Sail* (London: Routledge & Kegan Paul Ltd, 1961).

73 Maud Karpeles and Arnold Baké, *Manual for Folk Music Collectors* (London: International Folk Music Council, 1951), p. 10. See also Peter Kennedy, 'Collector's Corner, Part 2,' *English Dance and Song*, XXI:1 (Sept.-Oct. 1956), 27–8.

74 This and subsequent quote from Lloyd appears in his 'Who Owns What in Folk Song?' *English Dance and Song*, Special Edition (New Year 1961), 15–18. Details of the copyright claims on 'Edward', etc. appear in Anon., 'Book Review: *The Roving Songster,' Ballads & Songs*, no. 6 (ND [1965]), 22.

75 Brand, *The Ballad Mongers*, pp. 214–15.

76 Peter Kennedy, ed., *Folk Songs of Britain and Ireland* (London: Cassell & Co., 1975), p. viii.

77 For full discussion and thoughtful comments on this see Ewan MacColl and Peggy Seeger, *Till Doomsday in the Afternoon: The Folklore of a Family of Scots Travellers, the Stewarts of Blairgowrie* (Manchester: Manchester University Press, 1986), pp. 31–7.

78 This and subsequent quotation from James Reeves, *The Idiom of the People: Traditional English Verse Edited with an Introduction and Notes from the Manuscripts of Cecil J. Sharp* (London: William Heinemann Ltd, 1958), p. 8. Other contemporary collections of unexpurgated texts are James Reeves, *The Everlasting Circle: English Traditional Verse from the Mss of S. Baring-Gould, H. E. D. Hammond and George B. Gardiner* (London: William Heinemann Ltd, 1960) and V. de Sola Pinto and A. E. Rodway, ed., *The Common Muse: An Anthology of Popular British Ballad Poetry XVth-XXth Century* (London: Chatto and Windus Ltd, 1957).

79 Reginald Nettel, *Sing a Song of England: A Social History of Traditional Song* (London: Phoenix House Ltd, [ND 1954]), p. 10. See also A. L. Lloyd, *Folk Song in England* (London: Panther Books, 1969), pp. 215–17 (originally published by Lawrence and Wishart Ltd, 1967) for comments on literary explanation of the song's title.

80 John Brunner, 'Shakespeare Spake: Review of James Reeves, *The Idiom of the People,' Keynote*, I:1 (Jan. 1959), 4. I am most grateful to Dave and Heather Bradley for the loan of this publication.

81 *A Jubilee Book of English Folk-Songs: Selected by Kenneth*

Loveless and Arranged for Unison Voices and Piano by Imogen Holst
(London: Oxford University Press, 1958), p. 19. Douglas Kennedy's
'Preface' commends Holst's 'modern treatment' of the songs.

82 David Holbrook, *English for Maturity: English in the Secondary
School* (Cambridge: Cambridge University Press, 1961), pp. 107–8. I am
most grateful to John Brown for bringing this work to my attention.

83 John Hasted, 'A Note About Bush Ballads,' *Keynote*, I:1 (Jan.
1959), 16. Unfortunately, there are aspects of Hasted's illustrations of
his autobiography which present difficulty in this respect.

84 John Brunner, 'Shakespeare Spake: Review of James Reeves, *The
Idiom of the People*,' *ibid.*, p. 5.

85 Lloyd, *Folk Song in England* – these and subsequent quotations
in the paragraph are from the chapter on 'The Lyrical Songs and Later
Ballads', pp. 176–316.

86 'In the Big Rock Candy Mountains,' *Sing*, II:6 (Feb.-Mar. 1956),
90.

87 On a single for Topic Records (TRC 98), the company set up by
the Workers' Music Association.

88 Munro, 'The Role of the School of Scottish Studies in the Folk
Music Revival,' p. 135 quoting her interview with MacColl of 9 Aug.
1988.

89 Anon., *Sing*, IV:1 (Apr.-May 1957), 9.

90 J[ohnny] A[mbrose], 'Discussion: New Topics,' *ibid.*, III:1 (Apr.-
May 1956), 10.

91 MacColl, *Journeyman*, p. 286.

92 See A. H. Swinson, 'Folk Song Club,' *English Dance and Song*,
XIII:1 (Jan. 1949), 4; John Hasted, 'A Singer's Notebook,' *Sing*, I:6 (ND
1955), 129; Robin Stubbs, 'A Singer's Notebook: Birmingham Scene,'
ibid., VI:2 (Oct. 1961), 15 and David Arthur, 'Isabel Sutherland (1921–
1988), '*English Dance and Song*, LI:3 (Oct. 1989), 14. For further
details of the development of the folk club movement, see the issues of
Club Folk held in the Harker Collection, Centre for English Cultural
Tradition and Language.

93 Schofield, 'A Lancashire Mon,' p. 5.

94 For examples of the mixture of music offered see the advert for
a Studio Skiffle Night with the City Ramblers and guest artists at the
Princess Louise, promising a programme including 'Worksongs, Ballads,
Blues, Union songs, Stomps', *Sing*, III:1 (Apr.-May 1956), front inside
cover, and the advert for the Forty-Four Skiffle and Folksong Club,
featuring the John Hasted Skiffle and Folksong Group with 'Blues-
singers, Folksingers' as 'Guest Artists', *ibid.*, back outside cover.

95 John Hasted, 'A Singer's Notebook,' *ibid.*, III:5 (Dec. 1956–Jan.

1957), 70.

96 Anon., 'Folk News,' *Tykes News*, Sept.-Nov. 1981, pp.43–5.

97 I am very grateful to Stan Crowther, Sheila Cameron, Les and Betty Carman and Tony McDool for the opportunity to share their longstanding enthusiasm for folk music and extensive knowledge of the Revival in Rotherham and the rest of Britain.

98 Anon., *Sing.*, V:1 (Sept. 1959), 7. In 1961 and 1962, 'What's On and Who's Singing' were included with the magazine as loose leaf duplicated sheets. In the totals given, I have not counted choir rehearsals, concerts or festivals.

99 I am particularly grateful to Malcolm Fox, Steve Roud, Martin Carthy and Dave Brady [Bradley] for information on their experiences of becoming involved in the Revival during this period.

100 Interview with Eric Winter, 21 Apr. 1992.

101 Dave Arthur, 'Soho – Needless to Say: A Life of Russell Quaye,' *English Dance and Song*, XLVI6:3 (autumn-winter 1984), 2. The introduction to the article offers one of the best evocations of the excitement of early folk and Skiffle clubs.

102 E[ric] W[inter], 'Discussion: Topic Folk Song Label,' *Sing*, V:4 (Oct.-Nov. 1956), 51. The main 'expert in the field' involved in the preparation of Topic records was Lloyd.

103 Lloyd, 'The Folk-Song Revival,' p. 171.

104 Sydney Carter, 'Political Songs will Never be Top Pops,' *Sing*, VI:3 (Nov. 1961), 20. For a Folk Club member's view see Alan Bell, 'Leftwing Folk: Some Reactions to Leon Rosselson,' *Folk Review* III:5 (Mar. 1974), 11.

105 Holbrook, *English for Maturity*, p. 108.

106 Francis Collinson, 'Review of *Folk Song in England* by A. L. Lloyd,' *Folk Music Journal*, I:4 (1968), 270.

107 This and subsequent quotation from Jack Speedwell, 'Politics, S*x and the Folk Revival,' *Folk Music*, I:5 (1965), 13–15.

108 Anon., 'What's on and Who's Singing', *Sing*, V:1 (Sept. 1959), 7 and personal communications, Eric Winter, 30 November 1986 and 21 April 1992. I am also extremely grateful to Toni Arthur for her timely assistance with other details of the organisation of the Club.

109 MacColl, *Journeyman*, pp. 287–8.

110 Personal communication, Bernie Forkin of 'Caught on the Hop', 3 Feb. 1991.

111 Gershon Legman, 'Folksongs, Fakelore, and Cash,' *Ballads & Songs*, no. 6 (ND [1965]), 4. Reprinted from *The Horn Book*, originally published in 1964.

112 MacColl, *Journeyman*, p. 287.

113 John Foreman, 'Topical Songs,' *Folk Scene*, no. 9 (July 1965), 18.

114 The descriptions are drawn from Carter, 'Political Songs will Never be Top Pops,' p. 20, John Marshall, 'Folk Song as a Political Weapon,' *Folk Scene*, No. 10 (Aug. 1965), 11 and Legman, 'Folksongs, Fakelore and Cash,' p. 4.

115 Foreman, 'Topical Songs,' 19.

116 Marshall, 'Folk Song as a Political Weapon,' p. 11.

Bibliography

Abrahams, Roger D. and Foss, George. *Anglo-American Folksong Style*. Englewood Cliffs, New Jersey: Prentice-Hall Inc., 1968.

Abson, Walter. 'Fifty Years of the Morris Ring.' *English Dance and Song*, XLVI:2 (1984), 11–12.

Ackerman, Robert. *J. G. Frazer: His Life and Work*. Cambridge: Cambridge University Press, 1987.

Alford, Violet. 'National Costume.' *English Dance and Song*, I:3 (1937), 59.

A[lford], V[iolet]. 'Your Festival Dress – Two More Ideas,' *English Dance and Song*, XIII:3 (May 1949), 42.

Alford, Violet. *Introduction to English Folklore*. London: G. Bell and Sons Ltd, 1952.

Alford, Violet. *Sword Dance and Drama*. London: Merlin Press, 1962.

Alford, Violet. 'A Jubilee Symposium: 4. Foreign Relations.' *Folk Music Journal*, II:2 (1971), 95–8.

Anon. 'Folksong in Somerset.' *Fabian News*, July 1904, 26.

Anon. 'English Folk-Music in Dance and Song: Report on Conference held at The Goupil Gallery, 5 Regent Street, Thursday, November 14th, 1907 – 8.30 p.m.' Unpublished verbatim transcription of conference proceedings, Keith Chandler Collection.

Anon. 'Folk-Dance Ballet at Cambridge.' *EFDS News*, no. 3 [undated, 1921–2 ?], 66–7.

Anon. 'The Collecting of Folk Dances and Songs.' *EFDS News* II:16 (Feb. 1928), 67.

Anon. 'Teaching People How to be Jolly.' *EFDS News*, II:18 (Oct. 1928), 126–30. [Reprinted from the *Evening Standard*.]

Anon. *Labour's Song Book*. London: I.L.P. Publication Department, 1931.

Anon. 'Report of the Annual Staff Conference 1937.' Typescript held in Vaughan Williams Memorial Library.

Anon. 'Film Records of British Customs.' *English Dance and Song*, II:4 (Mar.-Apr. 1938), 66.

Anon. [Nela Bower]. 'On Dress.' *English Dance and Song*, II:5 (May 1938), 75.

Anon. 'Wanted – More Teachers.' *English Dance and Song*, III:1 (Sept./Oct. 1938), 9.

Anon. *The Story of the English Folk Dance and Song Society* Leaflet no. 12; Rev. edn. London: EFDSS, 1974. Wortley Collection.

Arthur, David. 'Soho – Needless to Say: A Life of Russell Quaye.' *English Dance and Song*, XLVI:3 (autumn-winter 1984), 2–5.

Arthur, David. 'Isabel Sutherland (1921–1988).' *English Dance and Song*, LI:3 (Oct. 1989), 14–15.

Barker, E. Phillips. 'Two Notes on the Processional and the Morris Dance.' *EFDS Journal*, I:2 (Apr. 1915), 38–44.

Barker, E. Phillips. 'Cecil James Sharp.' *EFDS News*, I:8 (Nov. 1924), 202–10.

Barlow, Michael. 'George Butterworth and the Folksong Revival.' *English Dance and Song*, XLVII:3 (autumn-winter 1985), 10–11.

Bax, Arnold. *Farewell, My Youth*. London: Longmans, Green & Co., 1943.

Bell, Adrian. 'English Tradition and Idiom.' *Scrutiny*, II:1 (June 1933), 45–50.

Bell, Alan. 'Leftwing Folk: Some Reactions to Leon Rosselson.' *Folk Review*, III:5 (Mar. 1974), 11.

Bertrand, H. Bronson, 'Maud Karpeles (1886–1976).' *Journal of American Folklore* (Apr.-June 1977), 455–64.

Besant, Walter. *The Alabaster Box*. London: Thomas Burleigh, 1900.

Best, Andrew, ed. *Water Springing from the Ground: An Anthology of the Writings of Rolf Gardiner*. Shaftesbury: Trustees of the Estate of Rolf Gardiner, 1972.

Bird, John. *Percy Grainger*. London: Elek Books Ltd, 1976.

Blatchford, Robert. *Merrie England*. London: Clarion Press, 1894.

Booth, Michael R. *Victorian Spectacular Theatre 1850–1910*. London: Routledge & Kegan Paul Ltd, 1981.

Bourne, Henry. *Antiquitates Vulgares*. Newcastle: For the author, 1725.

Boyes [Smith] Georgina. 'Literary Sources and Folklore Studies in the Nineteenth Century: A Re-assessment of Armchair Scholarship.' *Lore and Language*, II:9 (1978), 26–39.

Boyes [Smith] Georgina. 'Chapbooks and Traditional Plays: Communication and Performance.' *Folklore*, XCII:2 (1981), 208–18.

Boyes, Georgina, ed. *The Ballad Today: History, Performance and Revival*. Doncaster and Addiscombe, Surrey: January Books, 1985.

Brand, Oscar. *The Ballad Mongers: Rise of the Modern Folk Song.* NP: Minerva Press, 1962.

Brickwedde, James C. 'A. Claud Wright: Cecil Sharp's Forgotten Dancer.' *Folk Music Journal,* VI:1 (1990), 5–36.

Broadwood, Lucy E. 'On the Collecting of English Folk-Songs.' *Proceedings of the Royal Musical Association* (1904–5), 14 Mar. 1905, pp. 89–90.

Broadwood, Lucy E. and Fuller – Maitland, J. A. *English County Songs.* London: J. B. Cramer & Son Ltd, ND [1892].

Brownmiller, Susan. *Femininity.* London: Paladin Books Ltd, 1986.

Brunner, John. 'Shakespeare Spake: Review of James Reeves, *The Idiom of the People.*' Keynote, I:1 (Jan. 1959), 4–8.

Buchan, Norman, ed. *101 Scottish Songs.* Glasgow: Wm Collins Sons & Co. Ltd, 1962.

Buckland, Theresa, ed. *Traditional Dance: Vol. I.* Crewe: Crewe & Alsager College of Higher Education, 1982.

Buckland, Theresa, ed. *Traditional Dance: Vol. II – Historical Perspectives.* Crewe: Crewe & Alsager College of Higher Education, 1983.

Buckland, Theresa, ed. *Traditional Dance: Vol. IV.* Crewe: Crewe & Alsager College of Higher Education, 1986.

Buckland, Theresa, ed., *Traditional Dance: Proceedings of the Traditional Dance Conference Vols. V & VI.* Crewe: Crewe & Alsager College of Higher Education, 1988.

Burke, Peter. *Popular Culture in Early Modern Europe.* London: Temple Smith, 1978.

Burne, Charlotte Sophia. 'Presidential Address: The Value of European Folklore in the History of Culture.' *Folk-Lore,* XXI (1910), 18–36.

Burne, Charlotte Sophia, ed. *The Handbook of Folklore.* Rev. edn. London: The Folklore Society, 1957. [Originally pub. 1914.]

Campbell, Mrs Olive Dame and Sharp, C. J. *English Folk Songs from the Southern Appalachians.* New York & London: G. P. Putnam's Sons, 1917.

Campbell, Ian. 'Illusion and Reality.' *Sing,* X:1 (June 1967), 10–11.

Carter, Sydney. 'Pop Goes the Folk Song.' *English Dance and Song* (New Year 1961), 3.

Carter, Sydney. 'Political Songs will Never be Top Pops.' *Sing,* VI:3 (Nov. 1961), 20.

Cawte, E. C. *Ritual Animal Disguise: A Historical and Geographical Study of Animal Disguise in the British Isles.* London: Folklore Society, 1978.

Cawte, E. C., Helm, Alex and Peacock, N. *English Ritual Drama: A Geographical Index.* London: Folklore Society, 1967.

Chambers, Colin. *The Story of Unity Theatre*. London: Lawrence and Wishart Ltd, 1989.

Chandler, Keith. 'Morris Dancing at Spelsbury: An Analytical Essay.' *Oxfordshire Local History*, I:7 (1983), 2–13.

Chapman, Frank. 'Rural Civilization: Review of *The Open Air, An Anthology of English Country Life* by Adrian Bell.' *Scrutiny*, V:2 (Sept. 1936), 219–20.

Cheesman, Tom, ed. *Recent Ballad Research*. 2 vols. London: Folklore Society Library, 1990.

Clark, Ian, Heinemann, Margot, Margolies, David and Snee, Carole. *Culture and Crisis in Britain in the Thirties*. London: Lawrence and Wishart, 1979.

Clark, Sibyl. *English Folk Dancing for Schools: A Book of Advice for Teachers*. London: English Folk Dance and Song Society, 1956.

Cleverdon, Douglas. 'Adventures in Recording – 2.' *English Dance and Song*, VIII:4 (Apr.-May 1944), 27–8.

Collinson, Francis. *The Traditional and National Music of Scotland*. London: Routledge and Kegan Paul Ltd, 1966.

Colls, Robert and Dodd, Philip, ed. *Englishness: Politics and Culture 1880–1920*. London: Croom Helm, 1986.

'Constant Billy'. 'Folk Dancing in the Villages.' *English Dance and Song*, Jan.-Feb. 1938), 42.

Corner, John, ed. *Documentary and the Mass Media*. London: Edward Arnold (Publishers) Ltd, 1986.

Cox, Gordon. 'The Legacy of Folk Song: The Influence of Cecil Sharp on Music Education.' *British Journal of Music Education*, VII:2 (1990), 89–97.

Cunningham, Valentine. *British Writers of the Thirties*. Oxford: Oxford University Press, 1989.

Dallas, Fred [Karl], 'How Can We Help the Folk Song Revival.' *English Dance and Song*, XXI:2 (Nov.-Dec. 1956), 71–2.

Dallas, Karl. 'MacColl – the Man, the Myth, the Music.' *English Dance and Song*, LI:4 (Christmas 1989), 11–14.

Davin, Anna. 'Imperialism and Motherhood.' *History Workshop Journal*, V (spring 1977), 9–65.

Davison, R. C. 'Making London Dance.' *EFDS News*, II:18 (Oct. 1928), 111.

Dean-Smith, Margaret. *A Guide to English Folk Song Collection 1822–1952*. Liverpool & London: University Press of Liverpool in association with the English Folk Dance and Song Society, 1954.

Dean-Smith, Margaret. 'The Life-Cycle Play or Folk Play: Some Conclusions Following the Examination of the Ordish Papers and Other

Sources.' *Folklore*, LXIX (1958), 237–53.

Dean-Smith, Margaret. 'Dr Maud Karpeles, O.B.E.: 12 November 1885–1 October 1976.' *Folklore*, LXXXVIII:1 (1977), 110–11.

Denselow, Robin. *When the Music's Over: The Story of Political Pop*. London: Faber and Faber Ltd, 1989.

Dillon, Francis, ed. *Country Magazine: Book of the BBC Programme*. London: Odhams Press Ltd, ND [1949].

Donellan, Philip. 'Subversion from the 'Other Room': Appreciation Ewan MacColl.' *The Guardian*, 26 Oct. 1989, p. 39.

Dorson, R. M., ed. *Peasant Customs and Savage Myths: Selections from the British Folklorists*. 2 vols. London: Routledge and Kegan Paul, 1968.

Eagleton, Terry. *Literary Theory: An Introduction*. Oxford: Basil Blackwell Publisher Ltd, 1983.

Elbourne, R. P. 'The Question of Definition.' *Yearbook of the International Folk Music Council*, VII (1975), 9–29.

Finnegan, Ruth. *The Hidden Musicians: Music-Making in an English Town*. Cambridge: Cambridge University Press, 1989.

Foreman, John. 'Topical Songs.' *Folk Scene*, no. 9 (July 1965), 18–19.

Foreman, Lewis. *From Parry to Britten: British Music in Letters 1900–1945*. London: B. T. Batsford Ltd, 1987.

Forrest, John. *Morris and Matachin: A Study in Comparative Choreography*. Sheffield: Centre for English Cultural Tradition & Language, 1984.

Fox Strangways, A. H. 'Cecil Sharp: Obituary.' *EFDS News*, I:8 (Nov. 1924), 232–3. [Originally pub. *The London Mercury*.]

Fox Strangways, A. H. *Cecil Sharp*. Oxford: Oxford University Press, 1933.

Fraser, Robert, ed. *Sir James Frazer and the Literary Imagination: Essays in Affinity and Influence*. Basingstoke: Macmillan Press Ltd, 1990.

Fryer, Francis. 'Mixed Morris Sides.' *English Dance and Song*, I:3 (1937), 59.

Fyrth, Jim, ed. *Britain, Fascism and the Popular Front*. London: Lawrence and Wishart Ltd, 1985.

Fuller-Maitland, J.A., 'The Beginning of the Folk-Song Society', *Journal of the Folk-Song Society*, VIII:7 (1927), 46–7.

Gammon, Vic. 'Folk Song Collecting in Sussex and Surrey, 1843–1914.' *History Workshop Journal*, X (autumn 1980), 61–89.

Gammon, Vic. 'Seeger and MacColl Revisited.' *English Dance and Song*, XLV:3 (autumn-winter 1983), 23–4.

Gardiner, Rolf. *The English Folk Dance Tradition: An Essay*. Hellerau:

Neue Schule Hellerau, 1923.

Gardiner, Rolf. *World Without End: British Politics and the Younger Generation.* London: Cobden-Sanderson, 1932.

Gardiner, Rolf. 'Mixed Morris Sides.' *English Dance and Song*, I:2 (Nov. 1936), 27.

Gardiner, Rolf. 'A Brief Account of the Travelling Morrice.' *North Sea and Baltic*, New Series, no. 4 (high summer 1938), 75–80.

Gardiner, Rolf. *England Herself: Ventures in Rural Restoration.* London: Faber and Faber Ltd, 1943.

Gardiner, Rolf. 'The Travelling Morrice and the Cambridge Morris Men' (Offprint from *Springhead News Sheet*) winter solstice 1961?, held in Vaughan Williams Memorial Library, P7145 AS 14.

Gilchrist, Anne G. 'Let us Remember.' *English Dance and Song*, IV:6 (July.-Aug. 1942), 62–3.

Gillett, Charlie. *The Sound of the City.* Rev. edn. London: Souvenir Press Ltd, 1983.

Girouard, Mark. *The Return to Camelot: Chivalry and the English Gentleman.* New Haven & London: Yale University Press, 1981.

Golding, Florence. 'What Shall We Wear?' *EFDS Journal*, I:1 (May 1914), 14–15.

Goldstein, Kenneth S. and Rosenberg, Neil V., ed. *Folklore Studies in Honour of Herbert Halpert: A Festschrift.* St John's, Newfoundland: Memorial University of Newfoundland, 1980.

Gomme, Alice Bertha. *The Traditional Games of England, Scotland and Ireland.* 2 vols. New York: Dover Publications Inc., 1964. [Originally pub. 1894–98.]

Gomme, George Laurence. *Folk-Lore Relics of Early Village Life.* London: Elliot Stock, 1883.

Gomme, G. L. *The Handbook of Folk-lore.* London: Folk-Lore Soceity, 1890.

Gomme, Sir Laurence and Lady. *British Folk-Lore, Folk-Songs, and Singing-Games.* London: National Home-Reading Union, ND [1916].

Goorney, Howard. *The Theatre Workshop Story.* London: Eyre Methuen Ltd, 1981.

Goorney, Howard and MacColl, Ewan, ed. *Agit-Prop to Theatre Workshop: Political Playscripts 1930–50.* Manchester: Manchester University Press, 1986.

Graham, Helen and Preston, Paul, ed. *The Popular Front in Europe.* Basingstoke: Macmillan Press Ltd, 1987.

Graham, John. *Lancashire and Cheshire Morris Dances.* London: J. Curwen & Sons Ltd, 1911.

Grainger, J. H. *Patriotisms Britain: 1900–1939.* London: Routledge and

Kegan Paul, 1986.

Grainger, Percy. 'Collecting with the Phonograph.' *Journal of the Folk-Song Society*, III:3 (May 1908), 147–242.

Graves, Perceval. *Irish Literary and Musical Studies*. London: Elkin Mathews, 1913.

Graves, Alfred Perceval. 'Ireland's Share in Folk Song Revival.' *Journal of the Irish Folk Song Society*, XIV (Apr. 1914), 19–21.

Green, Martin. *Children of the Sun: A Narrative of 'Decadence' in England After 1918*. London: Constable & Co. Ltd, 1977.

Gretton, M. Sturge. 'Folk Dancing In and About Burford.' *EFDS Journal*, I:1 (May 1914), 1–3.

Griffiths, R. *Fellow Travellers of the Right: British Enthusiasts for Nazi Germany 1933–39*. London: Constable & Co. Ltd, 1980.

Grosvenor Myer, Michael. 'Breathing New Life into Folk Song and the Theatre.' *The Guardian*, 24 Oct. 1989, p. 39.

Groves, Reg. *Conrad Noel and the Thaxted Movement: An Adventure in Christian Socialism*. New York: Augustus M. Kelley, 1968.

Guthrie, Tyrone. *A Life in the Theatre*. London: Columbus Books Ltd, 1987. [Originally published by Hamish Hamilton Ltd, 1960.]

H., A. K. 'Music of To-Day: The Present Position of Folk Song.' *EFDS News*, II:13 (Jan. 1927), 15. [Reprinted from *Liverpool Post and Echo*, 15 Nov. 1926.]

H[utton], J. H. 'Review of *The Irish Countryman: An Anthropological Study* by Conrad M. Arensberg.' *Folk-Lore*, XLVIII (Sept. 1937), 320–1.

Hall, Miss G. A. 'The Sword Dance.' *EFDS News*, II:21 (Sept. 1929), 216–18.

Hamer, F. B. 'The Hinton and Brackley Morris.' *Journal of the English Folk Dance and Song Society*, VII:4 (Dec. 1955), 205–16.

Hannington, Wal. *Unemployed Struggles 1919–1936: My Life and Struggles Amongst the Unemployed*. Wakefield: E.P. Publishing Ltd, 1973. [Originally pub. Lawrence & Wishart, 1936.]

Hardy, Forsyth. *John Grierson: A Documentary Biography*. London: Faber and Faber Ltd, 1979.

Harker, David. 'Cecil Sharp in Somerset: Some Conclusions.' *Folk Music Journal*, II:3 (1972), 220–40.

Harker, David. *One For the Money: Politics and Popular Song*. London: Hutchinson & Co. Ltd, 1980.

Harker, David. 'May Cecil Sharp be Praised?' *History Workshop*, XIV (autumn 1982), 44–62.

Harker, David. *Fakesong: The Manufacture of British 'Folksong' 1700 to the Present Day*. Milton Keynes: Open University Press, 1985.

Harris, Roy. 'Bob Cann.' *Folk Review*, IV:11 (Sept. 1975), 16–17.

Harrison, W. *Ripon Millenary*. Ripon: W. Harrison, 1892.

Hartman, Mary and Banner, Lois, ed. *Clio's Consciousness Raised: New Perspectives on the History of Women*. New York: Harper & Row, 1974.

Hasted, John. 'A Singer's Notebook,' *Sing*, I:1 (May-June 1954), 11.

Hasted, John. 'A Note About Bush Ballads,' *Keynote*, I:1 (Jan. 1959), 16–17.

Hasted, John. 'A Singer's Notebook.' *Sing*, IV:2 (June-July 1957), 22.

Hasted, John. *Alternative Memoirs*. Itchenor, W. Sussex: Greengate Press, 1992.

Heaney, Mike. *An Introductory Bibliography on Morris Dancing*. Vaughan Williams Memorial Library Leaflet no. 19. London: English Folk Dance and Song Society, 1985.

Heffer, A. B. 'The Tour of the Travelling Morrice.' *EFDS News*, I:9 (May 1925), 247–60.

Helm, Alex. *The Chapbook Mummers' Plays: A Study of the Printed Versions of the North-West of England*. Ibstock, Leics: Guizer Press, 1969.

Henderson, Hamish. 'Scots Folk-Song Today.' *Folklore*, LXXV (spring 1964), 48–58.

Heydon, John. 'Herga.' *Folk Review*, (July 1975), 7–8.

Hille, Waldemar, ed. *The People's Song Book*. New York: Boni and Gaer, Inc., 1948.

Hitchcock, Gordon, ed. *Folk Songs of the West Country Collected by Sabine Baring-Gould*. Newton Abbot: David and Charles, 1974.

Hobsbawm, Eric and Ranger, Terence, ed. *The Invention of Tradition*. Cambridge: Cambridge University Press, 1983.

Hocart, A. M. 'In the Grip of Tradition.' *Folk-Lore*, XLIX (Sept. 1938), 258–69.

Holmes, Edgar. *What Is and What Might Be: A Study of Education in General and Elementary Education in Particular*. London: Constable, 1911.

Holst, Imogen. *Gustav Holst: A Biography*. London: Oxford University Press, 1969.

Holst, Imogen. 'Gustav Holst's Debt to Cecil Sharp.' *Folk Music Journal*, II:5 (1974), 400–3.

Honko, Lauri. 'The Kaleval and Myths.' *Nordic Institute of Folklore Newsletter*, XII:4 (1984–5), 2–3.

Hopkins, Harry. *The New Look: A Social History of the Forties and Fifties in Britain*. London: Secker & Warburg Ltd for the Readers Union, 1964.

Howe, Margery. 'A Small Corner of Lakeland: Memories of the EFDS in the Thirties.' *English Dance and Song*, XLVII:3 (autumn-winter 1985), 18–20.

Howells, W. D. *The Seen and Unseen at Stratford-on-Avon: A Fantasy.* New York & London: Harper & Bros., 1914.

Howes, Frank. *Man, Mind and Music: Studies in the Philosophy of music.* London: Secker and Warburg, 1948.

Howes, Frank. *The English Musical Renaissance.* London: Martin Secker & Warburg Ltd, 1966.

Howes, Frank. *Folk Music of Britain and Beyond.* London: Methuen & Co Ltd, 1969.

Howison, Daniel and Bentley, Bernard. *The North-West Morris: A General Survey of the Traditional Morris Dance of the North West of England.* Journal Reprint no. 11. London: English Folk Dance and Song Society, 1960.

Howkins, Alun. *Whitsun in 19th Century Oxfordshire.* History Workshop Pamphlets no. 8. Oxford: History Workshop Pamphlets, 1973.

Hugill, Stan. *Shanties from the Seven Seas: Shipboard Work-Songs and Songs used as Work-Songs from the Great Days of Sail.* London: Routledge & Kegan Paul Ltd, 1961.

Hulme, Ann-Marie and Clifton, Peter. 'Social Dancing in a Norfolk Village 1900–1945.' *Folk Music Journal*, III:4 (1978), 359–77.

Hunt, Ken. 'Shirley and Dolly Collins.' 2 parts. *Swing Fifty-One*, I:1 (1979), 4–19 and I:2 (1980), 6–29.

Hynes, Samuel. *The Auden Generation: Literature and Politics in England in the 1930's.* London: Faber and Faber Ltd, 1976.

Inglis, K. S. *Churches and the Working Classes in Victorian England.* London: Routledge & Kegan Paul, 1963.

Irwin, Colin. 'English Folk Revival: The Early Years 1957–1961.' *The Southern Rag*, V:3 (Jan.-Mar. 1984), 23–5.

Irwin, Colin. 'English Folk Revival: The Boom Years 1962–1967.' *The Southern Rag*, V:4 (Apr.-June 1984), 15–18.

Jacobs, Joseph. 'The Folk.' *Folk-Lore*, V (1893), 233–8.

Jones, Gareth Stedman. *Outcast London: A Study in the Relationship Between Classes in Victorian Society.* Oxford: Oxford University Press, 1971.

Jones, K. Marshall. 'The Use of Folk Song in Village Choir Training.' *English Dance and Song*, III:2 (Nov.-Dec. 1938), 19–20.

Jones, Stephen G. *The British Labour Movement and Film, 1918–1939.* London: Routledge and Kegan Paul Ltd, 1987.

Joseph, Nathan. 'Revival or Standstill.' *Folk Scene*, no. 9 (July 1965), 27–9.

Joyce, P. *Work, Society and Politics: The Factory North of England 1860–1890.* Brighton: Harvester Press Ltd, 1980.

Judge, Roy. 'A Branch of May.' *Folk Music Journal*, II:2 (1971), 91–8.

Judge, Roy. 'Mary Neal and the Espérance Morris.' *Folk Music Journal*, V:5 (1989), 545–91.

Judge, Roy. 'May Day and Merrie England.' *Folklore*, CII:2 (1991), 131–48.

Judge, Roy and Schofield, Derek, ed. 'A Tribute to Douglas Neil Kennedy, O.B.E., 1893–1988.' *Folk Music Journal*, V:4 (1988), 520–36.

Karpeles, Maud. 'Old King Cole.' *EFDS News*, II:13 (Jan. 1927), 12–13.

Karpeles, Maud. 'English Folk Dances, their Survival and Revival.' *Folk-Lore*, XLIII (1932), 123–41.

Karpeles, Maud. 'Letter – Traditional Form.' *English Dance and Song*, XVII:4 (Feb.-Mar. 1953), 124.

Karpeles, Maud. 'New Members' Page: Talk Broadcast by Maud Karpeles.' *English Dance and Song*, XVIII:4 (Feb.-Mar. 1954), 113–15.

Karpeles, Maud. *Cecil Sharp: His Life and Work.* London: Routledge & Kegan Paul Ltd, 1967.

Karpeles, Maud. 'The Distinction between Folk and Popular Music.' *Journal of the International Folk Music Council*, XX (1968), 9–12.

Karpeles, Maud. 'The International Folk Music Council: Twenty-One Years.' *Yearbook of the International Folk Music Council: Volume I* (1969), 14–32.

Karpeles, Maud. *An Introduction to English Folk Song.* London: Oxford University Press, 1973.

Karpeles, Maud and Baké, Arnold. *Manual for Folk Music Collectors.* London: International Folk Music Council, 1951.

Keel, Frederick. 'The Folk Song Society 1898–1948.' *Journal of the English Folk Dance and Song Society*, V:3 (1948), 111–127.

Kemp-Ashraf, P. M. and Mitchell, Jack, ed. *Essays in Honour of William Gallacher.* Berlin: Humboldt University, 1966.

Kennedy, Douglas. 'Where Do We Go From Here?' *English Dance and Song*, IX:2 (Dec. 1944), 13–15.

Kennedy, Douglas. 'The Amateurs.' *English Dance and Song*, IX:5 (June-July 1945), 44–5.

Kennedy, Douglas N. 'Notes on Recruiting.' *English Dance and Song*, X:6 (1946), 73–4.

Kennedy, Douglas N. 'The Policy of the Executive Committee.' *English Dance and Song* XII:3 (June 1948), 35–43.

Kennedy, Douglas. *England's Dances: Folk Dancing Today and Yesterday.* London: G. Bell & Sons Ltd, 1949.

Kennedy, Douglas. 'Festival Dresses – to start you thinking.' *English*

Dance and Song, XIII:2 (Feb.-Mar. 1949), 25.

Kennedy, Douglas. 'The Director Writes: Copyright in Folk Music.' *English Dance and Song*, XVI:2 (Sept. 1951), 41-2.

Kennedy, Douglas N. 'The Director Writes: The Square Dance Comes Back.' *English Dance and Song*, XVI:4 (Feb.-Mar. 1952), 109-11.

Kennedy, Douglas N. 'The Director Writes: Traditional Form.' *English Dance and Song*, XVII:3 (Dec. 1952-Jan. 1953), 76-7.

Kennedy, Douglas. 'Folk Songs Raw and Civilised.' *English Dance and Song*., VIII:1 (Aug.-Sept. 1953), 26-7.

Kennedy, Douglas N. 'The Director Writes: In the Raw.' *English Dance and Song*, XVIII:3 (Dec. 1953-Jan. 1954), 77-8.

Kennedy, Douglas N. 'The Director Writes: The Re-birth of Folk Music.' *English Dance and Song*, XXI:2 (Nov.-Dec. 1956), 39-41.

Kennedy, Douglas N. 'The Director Writes: Local Tradition.' *English Dance and Song*, XXII:1 (Sept.-Oct. 1957), 3-5.

Kennedy, Douglas N. 'Rocking the Morris.' *English Dance and Song*, (New Year 1961), 4-7.

Kennedy, Douglas. 'A Fourth Folk Festival.' *Sing*, VI:10 (June 1962), 107.

Kennedy, Douglas. *English Folk Dancing: Today and Yesterday*. London: G. Bell & Sons Ltd, 1964.

Kennedy, Douglas. 'Mary, Lady Trevelyan 1882-1966: Obituary.' *Folk Music Journal*, I:3 (1967), 200-01.

Kennedy, Douglas. 'A Jubilee Symposium: 2. Folk Dance Revival.' *Folk Music Journal*, II:2 (1971), 80-90.

Kennedy, Douglas. 'Obituary: Dr Maud Pauline Karpeles, O.B.E. 1885-1976.' *Folk Music Journal*, III:3 (1977), 292-3.

Kennedy, Douglas. 'Cecil Sharp and Mary Neal.' *English Dance and Song*, LI:1 (Apr.-May 1988), 5.

Kennedy, Mrs [Helen]. 'Early Days.' *EFDS News*, I:7 (May 1924), 172-7.

Kennedy, Mrs [Helen]. 'Early Days (cont).' *EFDS News*, I:9 [ND], 277-83.

Kennedy, Mrs [Helen]. 'Early Days (concluded).' *EFDS News* I:10 (1925), 325-32.

Kennedy, Michael. *The Works of Ralph Vaughan Williams*. London: Oxford University Press, 1964.

Kennedy, Paul and Nicholls, Anthony, ed. *Nationalist and Racialist Movements in Britain and Germany Before 1914*. St Antony's/Macmillan Series. Oxford & London: Macmillan & St Antony's College, 1981.

Kennedy, Peter. 'Post-War Planning.' *English Dance and Song* IX:3

(Feb.-Mar. 1948), 22–3.

Kennedy, Peter, ed. *Folk Songs of Britain and Ireland*. London: Cassell & Co., 1975.

Kennedy, Peter. 'Random Memories of an English Dancing Master.' *English Dance and Song*, XLVII:1 (spring 1985), 15.

Kennedy, Peter. 'Do They Still Need Us?' *English Dance and Song*, LI:2 (July-Aug. 1989), 10–11.

Kettlewell, W. R. W. 'The Singing of English Folk-Songs.' *EFDS News*, II:23 (May 1930), 267–72.

Kidson, Frank. 'English Folk-Song.' *The Musical Times*, 1 Jan. 1908, 23–5.

Kidson, Frank. *A Garland of English Folk-Songs*. London: Ascherberg, Hopwood & Crew Ltd, ND [1926].

Kidson, Frank and Neal, Mary. *English Folk-Song & Dance*. Cambridge: Cambridge University Press, 1915.

Laing, Dave, Dallas, Karl, Denselow, Robin and Shelton, Robert. *The Electric Muse: The Story of Folk into Rock*. London: Eyre Methuen, 1975.

Layard, John. 'Labyrinth Ritual in South India: Threshold and Tattoo Designs.' *Folk-Lore*, XLVIII (June 1937), 115–82.

Leavis, F. R. 'Literature and Society.' *Scrutiny*, XII:1 (winter 1943), 2–11.

Leavis, F. R. *The Great Tradition*. Harmondsworth, Middx: Penguin Books Ltd, 1962. [Originally pub. Chatto & Windus, 1948.]

Leavis, Q. D. 'Lady Novelists and the Lower Orders.' *Scrutiny*, IV:2 (Sept. 1935), 112–32.

Legman, Gershon. 'Folksongs, Fakelore, and Cash.' *Ballads & Songs*, no. 6 (ND [1965]), 4.

Leyda, Jay. *Kino: A History of the Russian and Soviet Film*. London: George Allen & Unwin Ltd, 1960.

Lipton, Julius. 'A Few Remarks about Proletarian Poetry – With Some Notes on Bourgeois Poetry.' *Poetry and the People*, III (1938), 12–18.

Lloyd, A. L. *The Singing Englishman: An Introduction to Folksong*. London: Workers' Music Association, ND [1944].

Lloyd, A. L. 'This 'Folk' Business: Review of *The American People* by B. A. Botkin.' *Our Time*, Sept. 1946, pp.44–6.

Lloyd, A. L. 'Folk-Songs of the Coalfields.' *Coal*, May 1951, pp. 26–7.

Lloyd, A. L., ed. *Come All Ye Bold Miners: Ballads and Songs of the Coalfields*. London: Lawrence and Wishart Ltd, 1952.

Lloyd, A. L. 'Recent Recordings.' *English Dance and Song*, XVII:2 (Oct.-Nov. 1952), 52–3.

Lloyd, A. L. 'Who Owns What in Folk Song?' *English Dance and Song*,

Special Edition (New Year 1961), 15–18.

Lloyd, A. L. 'The Folk-Song Revival.' *Marxism Today*, June 1961, pp.170–1.

Lloyd, A. L. *Folk Song in England*. London: Panther Books, 1969. [Originally pub. Lawrence & Wishart Ltd, 1967.]

Lloyd, A. L. 'Towards a Distinction Between 'Popular' and 'Folk' – A bit of History.' *Club Folk*, Mar.-Apr. 1970, 8–11.

Lloyd, A. L., Winter, Eric and Dallas, Fred. 'Made in Britain.' *Sing*, IV:4–5 (Dec. 1957), 52 and 57.

Loveless, Kenneth N. J. 'Douglas Neil Kennedy, O.B.E.: An Obituary.' *English Dance and Song*, L:1 (Apr.-May 1988), 2–4.

Lovell, Alan and Hillier, Jim. *Studies in Documentary*. London: Secker and Warburg and the British Film Institute, 1972.

Lucas, E. V. *London Lavender*. London: Methuen & Co. Ltd, 1912.

Lucas, John, ed. *The 1930's: A Challenge to Orthodoxy*. Brighton: Harvester Press Ltd, 1978.

Lytton, Neville. *The English Country Gentleman*. London: Hurst & Blackett Ltd, ND.

MacColl, Ewan. *Scotland Sings*. London: Workers' Music Association, 1953.

MacColl, Ewan. *The Shuttle and Cage: Industrial Folk-Ballads*. London: Workers' Music Association, 1954.

MacColl, Ewan. *Journeyman: An Autobiography*. London: Sidgwick & Jackson Ltd, 1990.

MacColl, Ewan and Seeger, Peggy. *Till Doomsday in the Afternoon: The Folklore of a Family of Scots Travellers, the Stewarts of Blairgowrie*. Manchester: Manchester University Press, 1986.

MacKenzie, John M. *Propaganda and Empire: The Manipulation of British Public Opinion 1880–1960*. Manchester: Manchester University Press, 1984.

MacKenzie, Norman and Jeanne. *The First Fabians*. London: Quartet Books, 1979.

Mackenzie, Pat and Carroll, Jim. 'Obituary: Ewan MacColl 1915–1989.' *Folk Music Journal*, VI:1 (1990), 121–4.

Mackenzie, Midge. *Shoulder to Shoulder: A Documentary*. Harmondsworth, Middx: Penguin Books Ltd, 1975.

Mackerness, E. D. 'The Yardley Gobion Morris.' *Journal of the English Folk Dance and Song Society*, VII:4 (Dec. 1955), 216–17.

Mackerness, E. D. *A Social History of English Music*. London: Routledge & Kegan Paul, 1964.

Macpherson, Don, ed. *Traditions of Independence: British Cinema in the Thirties*. London: British Film Institute, 1980.

Mann, John Edgar. 'Random Thoughts on Identity.' *Folk Review*, V:2 (Dec. 1975), 20–5.

McRobbie, Angela. *Feminism and Youth Culture: From Jackie to Just Seventeen*. Basingstoke: Macmillan Education Ltd, 1991.

Marshall John, 'Folk Song as a Political Weapon,' *Folk Scene*, no. 10 (Aug. 1965), 11.

Martinengo-Cesaresco, Countess [Evelyn]. *Essays in the Study of Folk-Songs*. London: J. M. Dent and Sons Ltd, ND [1886].

Mason, H. A. 'Eighteenth Century Musical Taste: Review of *A General History of Music* by Charles Burney.' *Scrutiny*, IV:1 (June 1935), 427.

Matthews, Jill Julius. 'They had Such a Lot of Fun: The Women's League of Health and Beauty Between the Wars.' *History Workshop*, XXX (autumn 1990), 22–54.

Medley, Robert. *Drawn from the Life: A Memoir*. London: Faber and Faber Ltd, 1983.

Melman, Billie. *Women and the Popular Imagination in the Twenties: Flappers and Nymphs*. London: Macmillan Press Ltd, 1988.

Middleton, Richard. *Studying Popular Music*. Milton Keynes: Open University Press, 1990.

Miller, Edward Kerr. 'An Ethnography of Singing: The Use and Meaning of Song Within a Scottish Family.' Unpublished PhD dissertation, University of Texas at Austin, 1981.

Miller, Jimmy. 'MacColl and Myth.' *Mole Express*, XLVI (Oct. 1975), 20.

Mitford, Mary R. *Sketches of English Life & Character*. Edinburgh & London: T. N. Foulis, 1909. [Originally pub. 1824–32.]

Moore, Harry T., ed. *The Collected Letters of D. H. Lawrence*. 2 vols. London: William Heinemann Ltd, 1962.

Moran, Dave. 'The Condition of MacColl's Folk Music.' *Folk Scene*, No. 18 (June 1966), 23–6.

Morton, A. L., ed. *Political Writings of William Morris*. London: Lawrence & Wishart Ltd, 1984.

Munro, Ailie. *The Folk Music Revival in Scotland*. London: Kahn & Averill, 1984.

Munro, Ailie. 'The Role of the School of Scottish Studies in the Folk Music Revival.' *Folk Music Journal*, VI:2 (1991), 132–68.

Neal, Mary. *The Espérance Morris Book: Part I A Manual of Morris Dances, Folk-Songs and Singing Games*. 3rd edn, London: J. Curwen & Sons Ltd, 1910.

Neal, Mary. *The Espérance Morris Book: Part II Morris Dances, Country Dances, Sword Dances and Sea Shanties*. London: J. Curwen & Sons Ltd, 1912.

Neal, Mary. 'The National Revival of the Folk Dance: no. III – Present Day Interpreters of the Folk Dance.' *The Observer*, 3 Dec. 1911, p. 20.

Neal, Mary. 'The Broken Law.' *The Adelphi*, XVI (Jan. 1940), 147–50.

Nettel, Reginald. *Sing a Song of England: A Social History of Traditional Song.* London: Phoenix House, ND [1954].

Newman, Ernest. 'The Folk-Song Fallacy.' *English Review*, V (1912), 255–68.

Newman, Ernest. 'The Week in Music.' *EFDS News*, I:2 (Aug. 1921), 38–40. [Reprinted from *The Manchester Guardian*.]

Norman, E. R. *Church and Society in England 1770–1970.* Oxford: Oxford University Press, 1976.

Olson, Ian A. 'The Influence of the Folk Song Society on the Greig-Duncan Folk Song Collection: Methodology.' *Folk Music Journal*, V:2 (1986), 176–201.

Oxenham, Elsie Jeanette. *The Abbey Girls in Town.* London & Glasgow: Collins, ND [1920s]

Oxenham, Elsie J. *The Abbey Girls Again.* London & Glasgow: Collins, ND [1920s]

Oxenham, Elsie J. *The Abbey Girls Go Back to School.* London & Glasgow: Wm Collins Sons & Co. Ltd, 1949. [Originally pub. 1922.]

Paget, Derek. *True Stories?: Documentary Drama on Radio, Screen and Stage.* Manchester: Manchester University Press, 1990.

Palmer, Roy. 'Your Dancing is Simply Glorious ...' *English Dance and Song*, LI:1 (Apr.-May 1989), 2–3.

Parker, Anthony. *Pageants: Their Presentation and Production.* London: Bodley Head, 1954.

Parry, Sir Hubert. 'Inaugural Address.' *Journal of the Folk-Song Society.* Nendeln, Liechtenstein: Kraus Reprint, 1975. [Originally pub. 1898.]

Pattison, Bruce. 'Music and the Community: Review.' *Scrutiny*, II:4 (Mar. 1934), 399–404.

Pattison, Bruce. 'Music in Decline.' *Scrutiny*, III:2 (Sept. 1934), 198–205.

Pattison, Bruce. 'Musical History.' *Scrutiny*, III:4 (Mar. 1935), 369–77.

Peck, Arthur L. 'The Foundation of the Morris Ring.' *English Dance and Song*, X:5 (1946), 62.

Pedersen, Rita and Andersen, Flemming G., ed. *The Concept of Tradition in Ballad Research: A Symposium.* Odense: Odense University Press, 1985.

Pegg, Bob. 'New Facts in Child Murder Case.' *Club Folk*, II:6 (Nov.-Dec. 1969),12–14.

Pickering, Michael. *Village Song and Culture: A Study Based on the*

Blunt Collection of Song from Adderbury North Oxfordshire. London: Croom Helm, 1982.

Pickering, Michael and Green, Tony, ed. *Everyday Culture: Popular Song and the Vernacular Milieu.* Milton Keynes: Open University, 1987.

Piggott, Stuart. *Ruins in a Landscape: Essays in Antiquarianism.* Edinburgh: Edinburgh University Press, 1976.

Pilling, Julian. 'The Lancashire Clog Dance.' *Folk Music Journal,* I:3 (1967), 158–79.

Pinto, V. de Sola and Rodway, A. E., ed. *The Common Muse: An Anthology of Popular British Ballad Poetry XVth-XXth Century.* London: Chatto and Windus Ltd, 1957.

Pronay, Nicholas and Spring, D. W. *Propaganda, Politics and Film, 1918–1945.* London: Macmillan Press Ltd, 1982.

Prynn, David. 'The Clarion Clubs, Rambling and the Holiday Associations in Britain since the 1890's.' *Journal of Contemporary History,* XI (1976), 65–77.

Raskin, Richard. "Le Chant des Partisans": Functions of a Wartime Song.' *Folklore,* CII:1 (1991), 62–76.

Reeves, James. *The Idiom of the People: Traditional English Verse ... from the Manuscripts of Cecil J. Sharp.* London: William Heinemann Ltd, 1958.

Reeves, James. *The Everlasting Circle: English Traditional Verse from the Mss of S. Baring-Gould, H. E. D. Hammond and George B. Gardiner.* London: William Heinemann Ltd, 1960.

Rendall, Montague. 'Personal Memories of Cecil Sharp.' *EFDS News,* II:16 (Feb. 1928), 79–80.

Rowe, Doc. '*With a Crash and a Din Comes the Morris Dancer in: A Celebration of Fifty Years of The Morris Ring 1934–1984.* NP: The Morris Ring, 1984.

Russell, Dave. *Popular Music in England 1840–1914: A Social History.* Manchester: Manchester University Press, 1987.

Russell, Ian, ed. *Singer, Song and Scholar.* Sheffield: Sheffield Academic Press, 1986.

S[caif], C[hristopher] H. O. 'A Test of Folk Song.' *EFDS News,* I:4 (Nov. 1922), 95–8.

Samuel, Raphael, ed. *Peoples' History and Socialist Theory.* London: Routledge & Kegan Paul Ltd, 1981.

Samuel, Raphael, MacColl, Ewan and Cosgrove, Stuart. *Theatres of the Left 1880–1935: Workers' Theatre Movements in Britain and America.* London: Routledge and Kegan Paul Ltd, 1985.

Sanderson, William. *Statecraft.* London: Methuen, 1927.

Scannell, Paddy and Cardiff, David. *A Social History of British Broadcasting: Volume I 1922–1939*. Oxford: Basil Blackwell Ltd, 1991.

Schofield, Derek. 'A Lancashire Mon.' *Folk Review*, Apr. 1975, pp.4–9.

Schofield, Derek. 'Nibs Matthews – 50 Years a Dancer.' *English Dance and Song*, XLVII:3 (autumn-Winter 1985), 2–6.

Schofield, Derek. "Revival of the Folk Dance: An Artistic Movement': The Background to the Founding of the English Folk Dance Society in 1911.' *Folk Music Journal*, V:2 (1986), 215–19.

Seeger, Peggy and MacColl, Ewan, ed. *The Singing Island: A Collection of English and Scots Folksongs*. London: Mills Music Ltd, 1960.

Sellors, Frank. 'William Bolton.' *English Dance and Song*, XLVIII:1 (spring 1986), 30–1.

Sharp, Cecil J. *A Book of British Song for Home and School*. London: John Murray, 1902.

Sharp, Cecil J. 'Folk-Songs Noted in Somerset and North Devon.' *Folk-Song Journal*, II:6 (1905), 1–60.

Sharp, Cecil. *English Folk-Song: Some Conclusions*. Taunton: Barnicott & Pearce, 1907.

Sharp, Cecil J. 'Some Characteristics of English Folk-Music.' *Folk-Lore*, XIX (1908), 132–46.

Sharp, Cecil J. 'A Guild of Morris Dancers.' *The Morning Post*, 1 Apr. 1910, p. 5.

Sharp, Cecil. 'English Folk-Dances.' *The Morning Post*, 10 May 1910, p. 6.

Sharp, Cecil. "The Folk-Song Fallacy': A Reply.' *English Review*, V (1912), 542–50.

Sharp, C. J. *Folk-Singing in Schools*. London: The English Folk Dance Society, 1912.

Sharp, Cecil J. 'Some Notes on the Morris Dance.' *EFDS Journal*, I:1 (May 1914), 6–8.

Sharp, Cecil J. *Folk-Songs of English Origin, Collected in the Appalachian Mountains*. 2 vols. London: Novello & Co., 1919, 1921.

Sharp, Cecil J. 'The English Folk-Dance Revival.' *The Music Student*, XI:12 (Aug. 1919), 449–51.

Sharp, C. J. *English Folk Songs*. London: Novello & Co. 1921–23.

Sharp, Cecil J. *Nursery Songs from the Appalachian Mountains*. 2 vols. London: Novello & Co., 1921, 1923.

Sharp, C. J. 'Style.' *EFDS News*, I:3 (Mar. 1922), 67–9.

Sharp, Cecil. 'The Development of Folk Dancing.' *EFDS News*, I:6 (Nov. 1923), 145.

Sharp, Cecil J. *English Folk Songs from the Southern Appalachian Mountains*, ed. Maud Karpeles. 2 vols. London: Oxford University

Press, 1932.

Sharp, Cecil J. *The Country Dance Book: Part 1*, ed. Maud Karpeles. London: Novello & Co. Ltd, 1934.

Sharp, Cecil J. *English County Folk Songs*. London: Novello & Co. Ltd, 1961. [Originally pub. in 5 volumes, 1908–12.]

Sharp, Cecil. *English Folk-Songs: Some Conclusions*, ed. Maud Karpeles. Wakefield: E.P. Publishing Ltd, 1972.

Sharp, Cecil J. and MacIlwaine, Herbert C. *The Morris Book: A History of Morris Dancing with a Description of Eleven Dances as Performed by the Morris-Men of England*. London: Novello & Co. Ltd, 1907.

Sharp, Cecil J. and MacIlwaine, Herbert C. *The Morris Book III*. London: Novello & Co., Ltd, 1910.

Sharp, Cecil and MacIlwaine, Herbert C. *The Morris Book*. 2nd rev. edn London: Novello & Co. Ltd, 1912.

Sharp, Cecil J. and Marson, Charles L. *Folk Songs from Somerset*. Taunton: The Wessex Press, 1904.

Sharp, Evelyn. *Here We Go Round: The Story of the Dance*. London: Gerald Howe Ltd, 1928.

Sharp, Evelyn. *Unfinished Adventure: Selected Reminiscences from an Englishwoman's Life*. London: Bodley Head Ltd, 1933.

Shaw, Christopher and Chase, Malcolm, ed. *The Imagined Past: History and Nostalgia*. Manchester: Manchester University Press, 1989.

Sidnell, Michael J. *Dances of Death: The Group Theatre of London in the Thirties*. London: Faber and Faber Ltd, 1984.

Slocombe, Marie. 'Round Britain with a Recording Machine: The BBC as Collector.' *English Dance and Song*, XVII:1 (Aug.-Sept. 1952), 12–13.

Smith, Paul and Widdowson, J. D. A., ed., *Traditional Drama Studies: Volume I*. Sheffield: Centre for English Cultural Tradition and Language & Traditional Drama Research Group, 1985.

Sokolov, Y. M. *Russian Folklore*, translated by Catherine Ruth Smith, Detroit: Folklore Associates, 1971. [Originally pub. in the Soviet Union in 1938.]

Solway, Richard. 'Counting the Degenerates: The Statistics of Race Degeneration in Edwardian England.' *Journal of Contemporary History*, XVII (1982), 137–64.

Speedwell, Jack. 'Politics, S*x and the Folk Revival.' *Folk Music*, I:5 (1965), 13–15.

Speirs, John. 'The Scottish Ballads.' *Scrutiny*, IV:1 (June 1935), 35–44.

Stack, Prunella. 'As Others See Us: 1. The Women's League of Health and Beauty.' *English Dance and Song*, III:1 (Sept.-Oct. 1938), 9.

Stevens, F. L. *Through Merrie England*. London: Frederick Warne &

Co. Ltd, 1928., 1–3.

Stevenson, G. 'Initiation of a Novice.' *English Dance and Song*, II:3 (Jan.-Feb. 1938), 42–3.

Stewart, Bob. *Where is Saint George: Pagan Imagery in English Folksong*. Bradford-on-Avon, Wilts: Moonraker Press, 1977.

Storch, Robert D., ed. *Popular Culture and Custom in Nineteenth-Century England*. London & Canberra: Croom Helm, 1982.

Street, A. G. 'Introduction,' *England Today in Pictures*. London: Odhams Press Ltd, 1947.

Street, Brian V. *The Savage in Literature*. London: Routledge & Kegan Paul, 1975.

Stubbs, Robin. 'A Singer's Notebook: Birmingham Scene,' *Sing*, VI:2 (Oct. 1961), 15.

Sughrue, Cindy. 'Continuity, Conflict and Change: A Contextual and Comparative Study of Three South Yorkshire Longsword Dance Teams.' Unpublished PhD dissertation, University of Sheffield, 1989.

Swan, Paul. 'John Grierson and the G.P.O. Film Unit 1933–39.' *Historical Journal of Film, Radio and Television*, III:1 (1983), 19–34.

Taylor, Philip M., ed. *Britain and the Cinema in the Second World War*. Basingstoke: Macmillan Press Ltd, 1988.

Teagle, Mrs D. D. Anne. 'What Should Ladies Wear?' *English Dance and Song*, XXI:1 (Sept.-Oct. 1956), 31–2.

Thatcher, Nicky. 'An American at the Court of Queen Elizabeth,' *Sing*, III:5 (Dec. 1956–Jan. 1957), 73–4.

Thayer, George. *The British Political Fringe: A Profile*. London: Anthony Blond Ltd, 1965.

Theweleit, Klaus. *Male Fantasies*. Cambridge: Polity Press, 1987.

Thompson, E. P. 'Folklore, Anthropology and Social History.' *Indian Historical Review*, III:2 (1978), 247–66.

Thompson, Denys. 'A Cure for Amnesia.' *Scrutiny*, II:1 (June 1933), 2–11.

Toye, Francis. 'Some Folk-Music.' *Vanity Fair*, 12 May 1910, pp. 585–6.

Toye, Francis. *For What We Have Received: An Autobiography*. London: William Heinemann Ltd, 1950.

Turner, Victor W. *The Ritual Process: Structure and Anti-Structure*. Harmondsworth, Middx: Penguin Books, 1969.

Tylor, Edward B. *Primitive Culture*. 2 vols. London: John Murray, 1871.

Underdown, David. *Revel, Riot and Rebellion: Popular Politics and Culture in England 1603–1660*. Oxford: Oxford University Press, 1985.

Vidler, Alec R. *The Church in an Age of Revolution: 1789 to the Present Day*. Harmondsworth, Middx: Penguin Books, 1980.

Watson, Ian. 'Alan Bush and Left Musik [sic] in the Thirties.' *Gulliver*, IV (1978), 80–90.

Watson, Ian. *Song and Democratic Culture in Britain: An Approach to Popular Culture in Social Movements*. London: Croom Helm, 1983.

Webber, G. C. *The Ideology of the British Right 1918–1939*. Beckenham: Croom Helm Ltd, 1986.

Wiener, Martin J. *English Culture and the Decline of the Industrial Spirit 1850–1980*. Cambridge: Cambridge University Press, 1981.

Wilgus, D. K. *Anglo-American Folksong Scholarship Since 1898*. New Brunswick, New Jersey. Rutgers University Press, 1959.

Wilkinson, Paul. 'English Youth Movements, 1908–30.' *Journal of Contemporary History*, IV:2 (1969), 19–23.

Williams, Christopher, ed. *Realism and the Cinema*. London: British Film Institute and Routledge and Kegan Paul Ltd, 1980.

Williams, Iolo A. *English Folk-Song and Dance*. London: Longmans, Green & Co., 1935.

Williams, R. Vaughan. 'The Late Cecil J. Sharp.' *EFDS News*, I:8 (Nov. 1924), 219–20.

Williams, Ralph Vaughan. *National Music*. Oxford: Oxford University Press, 1934.

Williams, Ralph Vaughan and Lloyd, A. L., ed. *The Penguin Book of English Folk Songs*. Harmondsworth, Middx: Penguin Books, 1959.

Williams, Raymond. *Culture and Society 1780–1950*. Harmondsworth, Middx: Penguin Books Ltd, 1961.

Williams, Raymond. *The Country and the City*. St Albans, Herts: Granada Publishing Ltd, 1975.

W[inter], E[ric]. 'Discussion: Topic Folk Song Label.' *Sing*, V:4 (Oct.-Nov. 1956), 51.

Winter, Eric. 'Achievement: The Story of Twenty One Years.' *Sing*, III:6 (Feb.-Mar. 1957), 82–3.

Winter, Eric. 'Ewan, a Bonnie Fechter.' *7 Days*, 4 Nov. 1989, p. 11.

Winter, Eric. 'The Big Ewan.' *Folk Roots*, nos. 79–80 (Jan.-Feb. 1990), 31–2.

Withington, Robert. *English Pageantry: An Historical Outline*. 2 vols. Cambridge, Mass.: Harvard University Press, 1918.

Woods, Fred. *Folk Revival: The Rediscovery of a National Music*. Poole, Dorset: Blandford Press Ltd, 1979.

Woods, Fred. *The Observer's Book of Folk Song in Britain*. London: Frederick Warne (Publishers) Ltd, 1980.

Yates, Mike. "The Best Bar in the Capstan': William Bolton Sailor and

Chantyman.' *Traditional Music*, VII (mid-1977), 10–11.
Young, Percy M. *Vaughan Williams*. London: Dennis Dobson Ltd, 1953.

Index